George Berkeley

EIGHTEENTH-CENTURY RESPONSES

Volume II

Edited by
DAVID BERMAN

GARLAND PUBLISHING, INC.
NEW YORK & LONDON 1989

For a complete list of the titles in this series, see the final pages of this volume.

These facsimiles are reproduced from copies in Yale University Library. "An Essay on the Existence of Matter," from a copy formerly in the library of Sir G. Keynes. Material from *An Essay on the nature and immutability of truth,* from a copy in Trinity College, Dublin, Library. *A Catalogue of the valuable library of the late Right Reverend Dr Berkeley,* from a copy in the British Museum.

Library of Congress Cataloging-in-Publication Data

George Berkeley: eighteenth-century responses/ edited by David Berman.
p. cm.—(The Philosophy of George Berkeley)
ISBN 0-8240-2444-3
1. Berkeley, George, 1685-1753. I. Berman, David. II. Series.
B1348.G46 1989 192—dc19 88-30832

Printed on acid-free, 250-year-life paper.
Printed in the United States of America

CONTENTS

Volume I

SECT. II.

Dean Berkeley's *ſcheme againſt the exiſtence of matter, and a material world examined, and ſhewn inconcluſive.*

SOME men deny all *immaterial*, and others all *material* ſubſtance; ſo that between them they leave *nothing at all* exiſting in nature. Theſe two oppoſite *parties* help to expoſe each other; and it is hard to ſay, every thing conſidered, whoſe ſhare is greateſt in the abſurdity of *expunging all Being out of exiſtence.* Yet thus much we may obſerve, that the exiſtence of *both ſubſtances* muſt be very plain, ſince each ſide maintains that the exiſtence of the ſubſtance which they themſelves aſſert muſt be ſelf-evident: for it would be abſurd in either of the parties to ſuppoſe arguments *neceſſary* to prove that any thing at all exiſts. Our dreams having no real external objects, and ſome of the *ancient Writers* having ſuggeſted that *this* might be made a ground for doubting whether there were really any ſuch objects; a late ingenious and learned *Author* hath taken the

the hint, not only to doubt of the reality of matter and a material world, but to pretend to demonstrate *the existence of any such thing impossible and contradictory* (*a*). The attempt certainly

(*a*) Whatever way our dreams may be accounted for, whether by thin membranes rising from the surfaces of bodies, as *Democritus* thought; or motions continued in the sensory after the objects cease to act, as *Aristotle* and *Hobbes* maintained; or by *new impressions* made upon it in the time of sleep, as I have endeavoured to shew in the last Section: all these ways still suppose the real existence of matter, in supposing both a *sensory* and *objects* acting upon it. Hence it seems inconsistent in *Plato*, to think the existence of matter might be called in question from this appearance of our dreams; since on any *hypothesis* for solving it, the *existence* of matter must be allowed: or *if it be not allowed*, all indeed is but a dream, even while we are awake, and the *very distinction* between dreaming and not dreaming is taken quite away. For what reason can we have to argue that objects are imaginary and *unreal*, while we are awake, because they are imaginary and *unreal* while we sleep; if we allow no previous difference? Waking itself is made but the most deceitful dream, and we then determine the question, without referring to dreams, and take away all difference between the two states, as to the reality of external objects. And if we previously allow a difference, how can we infer from allowing a difference, that there is no difference? We thus cut off the conclusion a contrary way.

certainly is ſurpriſing. If his books had been written with a deſign to excite men to try what

way. Therefore we can never draw the deſigned inference, let us make which of the ſuppoſitions we pleaſe. This is generally the fate of ſcepticizing; *the deſign fruſtrates itſelf.*

To make this a little plainer. If matter be ſuppoſed *neceſſary in the repreſentation of this phænomenon* of dreaming, it muſt be contradictory to infer from the phænomenon *itſelf* that matter does not exiſt. And if matter be ſuppoſed not to exiſt in the repreſentation of the phænomenon; it muſt be equally abſurd from ſuppoſing it *not to exiſt*, to infer that therefore *it does not actually exiſt*. There is no difference made on that ſuppoſition between the appearances of objects in ſleep, and their appearance at other times; *i. e.* the difference on which the argument proceeds, *is taken away* by the very ſuppoſition of the argument; and it is made to contradict itſelf, as before.

If it ſhould be ſaid, that it is not neceſſary *to make any ſuppoſition at all* concerning the exiſtence of matter in this appearance, but to take the appearance itſelf as we find it: I anſwer, *firſt*, That is impoſſible; the *queſtion* is concerning the exiſtence of matter, and it is to be proved dubious from a certain appearance; therefore it muſt be ſuppoſed either *dubious*, or not *dubious*, before-hand. And, *ſecondly*, not to conſider with exactneſs and care every circumſtance of an appearance, from which we would infer ſuch a weighty inference, as

what they could say, in case *such a kind* of Scepticism should begin to prevail; or as an *exercise* in an university, to shew how far wit and invention might go to maintain a paradox, there had been little in it: but when a

as the existence of a material world, shews a *willingness* to mistake, or misrepresent things in this momentous affair. And, *thirdly*, to say it is not necessary at all to make any supposition concerning the existence of matter in this case, is to suppose that the *appearance* may be produced indifferently, whether matter exist, or not; and that again is to contradict all the evidence we have for the existence of matter in a waking state, before we come to the doubt of it from the appearance of dreaming; or it is to confound the distinction of the two states, from which nevertheless we pretend to raise our doubt and suspicion. Wherefore at any rate it is inconsistent to think this appearance can afford us a ground of doubting.

Whether our Author could have any other ground to call the existence of matter in question, shall be considered afterward; though it seems evident in itself, that the reality of external objects could never have been questioned, unless we had some time or other been deceived in this point, either while asleep, or while awake. Had not this happened, all suspicion would have been prevented, and doubting thought a piece of extravagance.

person

person of great capacity and learning seems serious, and writes pieces, one after another, to support this kind of Scepticism, and continues in these sentiments for such a number of years; if it be not carrying an ungenteel sort of a *banter* a great deal too far, one cannot tell what to think of it. For it seems impossible that a man should be seriously persuaded that he has neither *country* nor *parents*, nor any *material body*, nor *eats*, nor *drinks*, nor lyes in a *house*; but that all these things are mere *illusions*, and have no existence but in the fancy.

That which makes it necessary here to examine this scheme, which denies the possibility of matter, is because all the arguments I have offered for the *Being* of a *God* in Sect. I. and II. Vol. I. are drawn from the consideration of this *impossible thing*; *viz*, from the *inertia* of matter, the *motion* of matter, the *cohesion* of matter, &c. and every one sees what impropriety, or rather what repugnance there must be, to speak of the *vis inertiæ* of ideas, the *motion* or *gravity* of ideas, the *elasticity* or *cohesion* of ideas. Whence these arguments must amount to nothing, if there be nothing but ideas instead of the objects

jects

jects of our ideas, as being drawn from *properties* which can belong to no ſubject, and which therefore muſt be *impoſſible.* Thus there muſt either be no truth in what I have ſaid, or in what this *Author* advances; for *two ſuch oppoſite accounts of nature* cannot both be true: and if the concluſions in theſe two Sections be ſolid, this itſelf will be a weighty argument againſt his ſcheme. However, I ſhall here endeavour to ſhew the inconcluſiveneſs of it from reaſons particularly applied; and try at leaſt to remove ſo weighty an objection, if I cannot add more light to what hath already been ſaid.

II. In conſidering this new ſcheme, the following particulars are to be remarked. The *nature* or *eſſence* of things is altogether different from their *exiſtence*; the former being the ideas of the Divine Intellect, eternally conſiſtent ſo as to be made to ſubſiſt together in the ſame ſubject, by his power, whenever it ſhould ſo ſeem good to his wiſdom: the latter, *viz.* their exiſtence, then commences, when his power is exerted to this effect; or when this *co-ſubſiſtence* of properties is firſt actually effected, with reſpect to a deter-

determined time and place (*b*). And from thence it follows, that there are eternal properties in the natures of all things, as being

(*b*) In the *Univerſal dictionary*, or *Cyclopædia*, under the word *Exiſtence*, it is obſerved, that the exiſtence of created beings hath relation to *time*, *place*, and a *cauſe*: That *eſſence* is explained by the chief and radical property of a thing, or all the properties and *exiſtence* by ſpecifying the time, place or cauſe; and then it is added—— " The foundation and occaſion of this diſtinction, is this; " that *eſſence* belongs to the queſtion, *What is it? Quid* " *eſt?* But *exiſtence* to the queſtion, *Is it? An eſt?* 3tio, " *Exiſtence* neceſſarily preſuppoſes *eſſence*, and cannot be " conceived without it; but *eſſence* may be conceived " without *exiſtence*; in that *eſſence* belongs equally to " things that are *in potentiâ*, and *in actu*; but exiſtence " only to thoſe *in actu*. Note however, that this does " not obtain in *God*, about whoſe *nature* and *eſſence*, the " mind cannot think, without conceiving his *exiſtence*." By being *in potentia* here, muſt be underſtood, being producible by the power of God, according to his ideas. Farther, *nature* and *eſſence* are here ſynonymous, and, I think, rightly. *Laſtly*, It is well obſerved here that as *eſſence*, *nature*, eternal properties, or eternal truth, have no relation to a *particular time*; ſo neither have they to *place*, or *cauſe*; or, they are as little circumſcribed in *place* as *time*; and to have a *cauſe* is incompetent to them, being eternal. This is one way of coming at a view of the eternity and immenſity of the *neceſſary mind*, where theſe were eternally known.

VOL. II. R originally,

jects of our ideas, as being drawn from *properties* which can belong to no ſubject, and which therefore muſt be *impoſſible*. Thus there muſt either be no truth in what I have ſaid, or in what this *Author* advances; for *two ſuch oppoſite accounts of nature* cannot both be true: and if the concluſions in theſe two Sections be ſolid, this itſelf will be a weighty argument againſt his ſcheme. However, I ſhall here endeavour to ſhew the inconcluſiveneſs of it from reaſons particularly applied; and try at leaſt to remove ſo weighty an objection, if I cannot add more light to what hath already been ſaid.

II. In conſidering this new ſcheme, the following particulars are to be remarked. The *nature* or *eſſence* of things is altogether different from their *exiſtence*; the former being the ideas of the Divine Intellect, eternally conſiſtent ſo as to be made to ſubſiſt together in the ſame ſubject, by his power, whenever it ſhould ſo ſeem good to his wiſdom: the latter, *viz.* their exiſtence, then commences, when his power is exerted to this effect; or when this *co-ſubſiſtence* of properties is firſt actually effected, with reſpect to a deter-

determined time and place (*b*). And from thence it follows, that there are eternal properties in the natures of all things, as being

(*b*) In the *Universal dictionary*, or *Cyclopædia*, under the word *Existence*, it is observed, that the existence of created beings hath relation to *time*, *place*, and a *cause*: That *essence* is explained by the chief and radical property of a thing, or all the properties and *existence* by specifying the time, place or cause; and then it is added—— "The foundation and occasion of this distinction, is this; "that *essence* belongs to the question, *What is it? Quid* "*est?* But *existence* to the question, *Is it? An est?* 3*tio*, "*Existence* necessarily presupposes *essence*, and cannot be "conceived without it; but *essence* may be conceived "without *existence*; in that *essence* belongs equally to "things that are *in potentiâ*, and *in actu*; but existence "only to those *in actu*. Note however, that this does "not obtain in *God*, about whose *nature* and *essence*, the "mind cannot think, without conceiving his *existence*." By being *in potentia* here, must be understood, being producible by the power of God, according to his ideas. Farther, *nature* and *essence* are here synonymous, and, I think, rightly. *Lastly*, It is well observed here that as *essence*, *nature*, eternal properties, or eternal truth, have no relation to a *particular time*; so neither have they to *place*, or *cause*; or, they are as little circumscribed in *place* as *time*; and to have a *cause* is incompetent to them, being eternal. This is one way of coming at a view of the eternity and immensity of the *necessary mind*, where these were eternally known.

 originally,

originally, eternally consistent ideas; for the eternal consistency and agreement of these ideas, makes these eternal properties. And from hence again it follows, that we can demonstrate several eternal truths concerning the *natures* or *essences* of things: for to shew the necessity, or necessary consistence, of these eternal properties, is to demonstrate eternal truths concerning their natures. To exemplify this. *Solidity* and *extension* were eternally consistent in the divine ideas, so as to be made to subsist in the same subject, (of which subject indeed we have no idea; but God hath, and had it before the subject itself was:) this eternal consistency makes the nature of this *thing* eternal. There was farther, a necessary connexion between the ideas of *solidity* and *resistance*; if it did not resist it would be unsolid: or the idea of *not-resisting* is inconsistent with the idea of *solidity*. Moreover there was an inconsistency between the idea of *resisting* and the idea of *effecting* what it resisted, [*viz.* a change of its present state.] And therefore from this respect, or habitude, of these ideas to each other, this property, That it is impossible this *thing* should ever effect a change of its present state, *eternally* and

and *neceſſarily* belongs to the nature of it. And therefore, when we ſhew the neceſſity of this property, we demonſtrate an eternal truth concerning the nature of this *thing*. Therefore, as before, I infer that we can demonſtrate ſeveral eternal truths concerning the *natures* or *eſſences* of things (*c*.)

III. On the other hand, the *exiſtence of things* hath no eternal properties; that is, eternally conſiſtent, or neceſſarily related ideas, belonging to it. Theſe were all in the Divine Mind, long before any thing but himſelf actually exiſted; and belong to their *natures*, not their *actual exiſtence*, which was arbitrary and depended upon his good pleaſure to affect. The property juſt now mentioned, *v. g.* is no way predicable concerning the exiſtence of matter, nor true only when it exiſts; but concerning its nature, and true whether it exiſts, or not. Therefore there is no eternal truth demonſtrable concerning the exiſtence of Beings, (the *ne-*

(*c*) The natures of things with reſpect to us, are the conſiſtent ideas in our minds, which are copies (though but imperfect, and in part) of the eternally conſiſtent ideas in the Divine Mind.

R 2 *ceſſarily*

cessarily existing Being excepted, who is out of the present controversy) unless it be this, That their existence was eternally possible, as depending upon his pleasure, and being performable by his power; for such truth would have supposed such eternal necessary properties predicable concerning their existence; or that it had been necessary (*d*.) Therefore, since the existence of *matter*, the *soul* of man, or other finite immaterial *Beings*, is only possible, or contingent, the only question concerning their existence is, *Whether it be actually effected, or not?* It is not demonstrable as the existence of God is; for his existence is a part of his nature, and inseparable from it: but there is no necessary connexion between *their nature*, which was eternal in the Divine Mind, and *their existence* which is only possible. Nor can there be a connexion between any thing that is necessary, and a thing that is but barely possible.

(*d*) The existence of a thing, which is but barely possible, implies no contradiction (absolutely speaking) never to be; otherwise its existence would become some time or other necessary; and that eternal properties should belong to a thing that may never be, is absurd.

IV. Thus

IV. Thus it appears that to require an *absolute demonstration* of the existence of matter, of the soul of man, (of man in general I mean, for no man wants a demonstration of the existence of his own soul) or of other finite immaterial Beings, is to mistake the nature of such a demonstration, and of the subject it is conversant about. It is to require a demonstration of the necessary existence of those Beings, whose existence, *ex concessis*, is contingent: for such an *absolute demonstration* must have been always true; just as any demonstration of the property of a *geometrical figure* was always true. That is, it must have been always true that matter existed. Supposing a possible being really existed, there is no other way to shew the existence of it to another, but by the *effects* it produces, or the *perceptions* it raises in some percipient Being; or by shewing it would be an absurdity for such *effects*, or *perceptions*, to have any other cause.

V. Yet because this contradiction, *viz. That a contingent Being exists necessarily*, cannot be demonstrated; some men have un-

R 3 skilfully

ſkilfully reſolved to make a doubt of it, Whether matter actually exiſted. This is a wilful determined kind of Scepticiſm: becauſe a contradiction cannot be ſhewn true, therefore they *reſolve* (nay I may ſay *force* themſelves) to doubt; and if it could be ſhewn true, there would be no need of forcing themſelves to become Scepticks; for it would be unavoidable. All truth, as has often been ſaid, ſtands or falls together. The exiſtence of *neceſſary* and *contingent* Being would be upon the ſame level: either all Being would be but barely poſſible, and once nothing at all might have exiſted; or all Being ſhould be equally neceſſary, and nothing that exiſts could ever have not exiſted.

VI. *Matter* therefore, the *human ſoul*, and other *finite ſpirits*, are contingent Beings; the idea of matter, *v. g.* was eternally conſiſtent in the Divine Mind, and is conſiſtent in our minds: but the idea of any thing impoſſible to exiſt, or of an impoſſible effect, can never be conſiſtent. The reaſon is, an inconſiſtency in the idea and conception. And this ſhews the poſſibility of matter's exiſting, whenever it ſhould pleaſe Infinite Wiſ-

dom.

dom. Since therefore the existence of it is possible, nor implies any contradiction; it is impossible for any man to demonstrate the non-existence of it. For that would be to undertake to demonstrate a possibility *impossible*. This, in few words, might be an answer to, and shews us the absurdity of, Dean *Berkeley*'s undertaking, who (as I said) pretends to prove, that the existence of matter, or bodies, out of a mind, is a contradiction in terms (*e*). He all along allows the consistency of the idea of it; and yet contends, by a new kind of reasoning, that the object of this consistent idea implies a contradiction in terms to be made exist: for by the same argument, whatever it be, he might prove that any thing, besides the Deity, implies a contradiction in Terms to be made exist; or deny entirely a creating power to him: since the consistency of the ideas in the Divine Intellect is that which constitutes the possibility

(*e*) Under the word Body, in the *Cyclopædia*, a part of the long citation from Dean *Berkeley* is——" On " the whole it appears, that the existence of bodies out " of a mind perceiving them, is not only *impossible* and " a *contradiction in terms*; but were it possible, nay real, " it were impossible we should ever know it."——

R 4 of

of the exiſtence of all other things. If we add to this, that the exiſtence of body without the mind; or of a *real, ſolid, figured, diviſible, reſiſting ſubſtance*; for the idea of it in the mind is no more ſuch a ſubſtance, than the idea of a Centaur is a *real Centaur*; if, I ſay, we add to this, that the exiſtence of matter hath all the evidence for it, as will ſoon appear, that the nature of the thing can admit of, without requiring the contradiction above to be proved; it is not eaſy to gueſs what juſtifiable deſign a man could propoſe to himſelf in ſuch an extraordinary attempt, as to demonſtrate that the beautiful ſyſtem of material nature; heaven and earth; the ſun, moon, and ſtars; the bodies of men and beaſts; all the wonders in the vegetable and animal œconomy; their uſefulneſs to mankind; and the kindneſs of God in beſtowing them, *are nothing but a dream within the mind.*

VII. But to be more particular as to the nature of this undertaking: A man who believes there is no ſuch thing as a *ſolid, reſiſting, figured ſubſtance*; *no material world*; *no ſuch Beings as men*, compounded of *body* and *ſpirit*;

3

ſpirit; in fine, *no books*, *writing*, *printing*, *ſpeaking*, *&c.* but that all theſe are ideas in the mind only, having no exiſtence without it; can never propoſe conſiſtently with his own belief, to diſpute *with men*, or propagate his doubting among them. He knows not *what things* they are which he would convince, or if there be *any Beings* differing from him in opinion: for all theſe ideas that are excited in him, as of beings maintaining the contrary of what he maintains, may be only ideas raiſed in him, by ſome ſpirit that hath a deſign to make a fool of, and impoſe upon him; as he thinks all the world beſides are cheated with other deluſory ideas: What greater evidence hath he for the exiſtence of other men's *ſouls*, than of their *bodies*; though he may have more for that of his own? We only collect concerning the ſouls of other men from the *ſpontaneous motions*, and *actions* of their *bodies*: *theſe*, according to him, *belong* to nothing. Beſides, he hath nothing but ideas, or dreams, when he ſpeaks, writes, publiſhes books. How doth he pretend that theſe dreams of his ſhould be communicated to other Beings, granting that they exiſted? In ſhort, his whole enterpriſe proceeds

proceeds upon the ſuppoſition of the reality of what he is going to confute. And thus, I think, he puts it in his adverſary's power, to prove from the very nature of his attempt, that he doth not believe himſelf, and ſo to confute him without uſing any other arguments. This is the fate of the generality of Sceptics: their very deſign oppoſes and defeats itſelf, as may be obſerved in other caſes (*f*).

A man

(*f*) This is obſervable in the *ancient Sceptics*, the followers of *Pyrrho*, thoſe who firſt affected to be diſtinguiſhed by that name, and to be reckoned a *ſeparate Sect*: They pretended to *give a demonſtration*, to prove that no demonſtration could be given, which was very extraordinary; for if their demonſtration *were true*, the deſign of it was defeated, and if it were *not true*, the deſign of it would ſtill be defeated: and at any rate they could not believe themſelves. *Diogenes Laertius* ſays, (in the life of *Pyrrho*) "They took away *all demonſtration, judgment,* "*ſign, cauſe, motion, learning, generation*, and that any "thing was *good* or *evil* by nature;" and then gives their general Demonſtration for all this——Ἀνῄρουν δ' οὗτοι ϗ πᾶσαν ἀπόδειξιν, ϗ κριτήριον, ϗ σημεῖον, ϗ αἴτιον, ϗ κίνησιν, ϗ μάθησιν, ϗ γένεσιν, ϗ τὸ φύσει, τὶ εἶναι ἀγαθὸν ἢ κακόν. [Their demonſtration of this follows.] Πᾶσα γὰρ ἀπόδειξις (φασὶν) ἢ ἐξ ἀποδεδειγμένων σύγκειται χρημάτων, ἢ ἐξ ἀναποδείκτων· εἰ μὲν οὖν ἐξ ἀποδεδειγμένων,

A man of this belief, not to contradict himself, should never open his mouth, (the *idea* of

δεδειγμένων, κἀκεῖνα δεήσεται τινὸς ἀποδείξεως, καὶ οὕτω εἰς ἄπειρον· εἰ δ' ἐξ ἀναποδείκτων, ἤτοι πάντων, ἢ τινῶν, ἢ καὶ ἑνὸς μόνου διστάζομένου, καὶ τὸ ὅλον εἶναι ἀναπόδεικτον. Here is a Demonstration in *rigorous form*. And, as if one general demonstration was not enough, they proceed to give particular demonstrations concerning *all the points* mentioned. Here, by the by, we may observe, that even *denying* supposes some certain principle; otherwise there could be no reason for denying any thing (as was observed before) more than for affirming; and that the *Sceptic* or *Pyrrhonist*, while he blames other men for the presumption of affirming and maintaining, *affirms* and *maintains* out of opposition, and that with great vehemence; in which case he acts quite out of character; for to be consistent with himself, he should observe a profound silence. [See Sect. V. N° 2. Vol. I. and the Note (*b*) N° 3.]

But how do they support the character of *doubting* in all this fury and heat of *maintaining* and *affirming*?—— Why, nothing is more easy. They *affirm* and *maintain* that their arguments, after they have overthrown all other arguments, at length overthrow themselves, like a dose of physick, which last of all purges itself off.—— Καὶ αὐτῷ δὲ τούτῳ τῷ λόγῳ λόγος ἀντίκειται· ὃς καὶ οὗτος μετὰ τὸ ἀνελεῖν τοὺς ἄλλους, αὐτὸς ὑφ' ἑαυτοῦ περιτραπεὶς ἀπόλλυται· κατ' ἴσον τοῖς καθαρτικοῖς, ἃ τὴν ὕλην προεκκρίναντα,

of his mouth, perhaps I ſhould ſay) but lament in *ſilence* the miſery of his condition, his

lonely

ἀκυρώσαντα, καὶ αὐτὰ ὑπεκκρίνεται καὶ ἐξαπόλλυται. Ibid. Thus they are ſatisfied, provided their reaſon had the honour of being overthrown by nothing *but its own forces* They *affirmed,* That we muſt not affirm *that there are four elements, becauſe there are four elements.*—Οὐδὲ γὰρ τὸ τέτταρα εἶναι τὰ στοιχεῖα, ἐκ τοῦ τέτταρα εἶναι τὰ στοιχεῖα, βεβαιωτέον. That we muſt either ſay, *every thing is true, or every thing is falſe.*—Ἤτοι γοῦν πάντα ἀληθῆ ῥητέον, ἢ πάντα ψευδῆ. They ſaid things were *hot* or *cold,* not from any natural quality, but by *law* and *cuſtom*—Δημόκριτος δὲ τὰς ποιότητας ἐκβαλών· ἵνα φησί. Νόμῳ ψυχρὸν, νόμῳ θερμόν. Accordingly, *Demophon* was *cold* in the *ſun,* and *warm* in the *ſhade.*——Ἐν σκιᾷ ἐθάλπετο, ἐν ἡλίῳ δὲ ἐρρίγου. They did not all agree whether they ſhould be called *Pyrrhoniſts,* or not; becauſe allowing that they knew *Pyrrho*'s ſentiments, was allowing that they *knew ſomething,* contrary to their great *principle*——Εἰ γὰρ τὸ καθ' ἑκάτερον κίνημα τῆς διανοίας ἄληπτόν ἐστιν, οὐκ εἰσόμεθα τὴν Πύῤῥωνος διάθεσιν· μὴ εἰδότες δὲ, οὐ Πυῤῥώνειοι καλοίμεθα ἄν. This was the *accuracy* of doubting!

But none of *Pyrrho*'s followers came up to his own pitch; for having taken away the diſtinction between *honeſt* and *diſhoneſt, juſt* and *unjuſt;* having found out that *nothing was according to truth;* that men acted by *cuſtom* or *law,* not according to *nature,* becauſe any thing was

not

lonely ſtate, and the miſt and darkneſs he is inextricably bewildered in.

And

not *that very thing* more than *another thing*: he ſet about making his life agreeable to his *principles*; (if we could ſay that a Sceptick had principles againſt *their own principle*;) he avoided no danger, would not ſtir out of the way, though a *chariot* or *waggon* was to go over him; would not go about, if a *precipice* was before him, nor beat off a *dog*, if he came upon him; and in this rigid obſervation of his principles, his friends were obliged to follow him to prevent accidents. I ſhall ſtill give my authority.——Οὐδὲν γὰρ ἔφασκεν οὔτε καλὸν, οὔτε αἰσχρὸν (ſays his Hiſtorian) οὔτε δίκαιον, οὔτε ἄδικον: καὶ ὁμοίως ἐπὶ πάντων, μηδὲν εἶναι τῇ ἀληθείᾳ, νόμῳ δὲ καὶ ἔθει πάντα τοὺς ἀνθρώπους πράττειν· οὐ γὰρ μᾶλλον τόδε ἢ τόδε εἶναι ἕκαστον· ἀκόλουθος δ' ἦν τῷ βίῳ, μηδὲν ἐκτρεπόμενος, μηδὲ φυλαττόμενος, ἅπαντα ὑφιστάμενος, ἁμάξας, εἰ τύχοι, καὶ κρημνοὺς, καὶ κυνὰς, καὶ ὅσα τοιαῦτα, μηδὲν ταῖς αἰσθήσεσιν ἐπιβλέπων· σώζεσθαι μέντοι (καθά φασιν οἱ περὶ τὸν Καρύστιον Ἀντίγονον) ὑπὸ τῶν γνωρίμων παρακολουθούντων. If he would yield nothing to his ſenſes (as here 'tis ſaid) he ſhould not (agreeably to his *own principles* it ſeems) have at all made uſe of them, nor walked upon his legs, nor done as other men do; but lain in one place, without motion or action. He was once greatly aſhamed for having driven away a dog that would have torn him, and made a ſcrupulous apology for acting againſt his principles. But of this enough.

Now

And this argument from the *inconsistency of the method* is applicable to him who but barely

Now where can we expect to get free from *bigotry*, if it runs to such heights in *Scepticism itself?* It is impossible those men could understand or believe themselves; and yet we see to what absurdity their zeal for *maintaining* [one cannot tell what] carried them. How little reason therefore have men of this way of thinking to object *credulity* and *bigotry?* The man who refuses his assent to plain truths is every way worse, and commits a greater violence on his faculties, than he who believes things without sufficient proof, and certainly more *sophistry*, *cunning* and *disingenuous shifting* is required to maintain that *Truth cannot be found out*, than there would honest application and industry to find it out: and farther, since this is the great principle of *Academism* and *Scepticism*, *That Truth cannot be perceived*, on maintaining of which their honour is staked; the men under these denominations cannot be said so much to have a *disposition* to find out the truth, as a *fixt resolution* to oppose it. *Cicero* does all he can to make good *Pyrrho*'s ἰσοσθένεια τῶν λόγων, or equality of arguments on both sides; he *labours* to keep a due balance between *truth* and *falshood*. It is mean and unworthy to see him, upon this account, endeavouring to undermine the truths in geometry, by little impotent cavils. Mr. *Bayle*, in his Controversy concerning the preferableness of *Atheism* to *Superstition*, doth not so much as endeavour to keep the balance; but leans with all his force to the wrong

barely doubts, if he offers to dispute with the *Beings themselves*, in order to be satisfied *himself* whether *they are*; or to convince *them* that *they are not*: for this disputing supposes the *reality* of the thing he pretends to doubt of (*g*). But when one undertakes to demonstrate

wrong side. And a certain great Author is sometimes a *Dogmatist*, and gives us a scheme of virtue independent of any Deity; and sometimes a regular and precise *Academist*. "There is nothing so foolish and deluding (says "he) as a partial Scepticism. For while the doubt is "cast only on one side, the certainty grows so much "stronger on the other." Can any thing be more absurd than to cast the doubt upon two *opposite* and *contrary propositions*, as if both might be false, or both true! I do not mean that objections should not be put with all their force: but there are some truths so glaring that a man cannot *cast doubt upon them*, without committing much violence on his reason. The art of writing is made to consist in keeping an æquilibrium between the arguments on opposite sides. This may catch a little vain applause; but it is against the interests of truth, and against the rational nature.

(*g*) Mr. *Woollaston* says, [Sect. 3. Prop. 4. pag. 43. in the Note (*a*).] "The question in *Plato*, Τί ἂν τις "ἔχοι τεκμήριον ἀποδεῖξαι, εἴ τις ἔροιτο, νῦν οὕτως ἐν τῷ "παρόντι, πότερον καθεύδομεν, καὶ πάντα ἃ διανοούμεθα "ὀνειρόττομεν, κ. τ. λ. may have place among the *velitations*

3

ſtrate to us, *that we have nothing whereby another could know that we exiſt*; ſince he cannot do this, but by ſuppoſing the *truth* of what he pretends to demonſtrate *falſe*, one is at a loſs what notion to form of ſuch a procedure. He may be juſtified, I think, in ſaying, "The ſtrangeneſs of the attempt is "not to be parallel'd." And how our Au-

"*litations* of *Philoſophers*; but a man can ſcarcely pro-"poſe it to himſelf ſeriouſly. If he doth, the anſwer "will attend it." But, with ſubmiſſion, I think it can have no place even *diſputandi gratiâ*, without this *contradiction* in the method. For the ſuppoſing *every thing which we think* to be but a dream (though we are certain that we ourſelves, who thus dream exiſt) is ſuppoſing *all other things* unreal, or only phantaſtical illuſions: and then we muſt ſuppoſe ourſelves left alone, ſurrounded only with our own *viſions* and *fancies*; and how a man can *velitate* with others in this ſolitary condition is hard to imagine, unleſs he make a contrary ſuppoſition, *deſtructive of the firſt*, *viz.* That other Beings *are not* unreal. And if men cannot find a handle to ſcepticize from, without making contradictory ſuppoſitions, they ſhould be ſatisfied of the abſurdity of the attempt. We cannot conceive how *truth* and *certainty* could have been more guarded than it is. Men muſt previouſly ſuppoſe a contradiction, before they can attack it. And if this be conſidered, we may juſtly wonder why the reputation of Scepticiſm ſhould be ſo great.

thor

thor can be vindicated from this contradictory procedure, I do not see: for he pretends to demonstrate the impossibility of the existence of mens *bodies*, and thereby denies all evidence that other men can have for the existence of their *souls*; which indeed amounts to denying their existence altogether, and demonstrating the impossibility of it to *those very beings* at the same time.

VIII. The great reason why this Author pretends to doubt of the existence of material substance, or to demonstrate it impossible, is because *we are percipient of nothing but our own perceptions* and ideas; and because *figure, colour, resistance, &c.* is not this substance (*b*).

(*b*) In the *Cyclopaedia*, the citation above begins thus; ——(Against the existence of *Bodies*, or any external *world*, Mr. *Berkeley* argues very strenuously.)——That neither our *thoughts*, *passions*, nor *ideas* formed by the imagination, exist without the mind, he observes is allowed; and that the various sensations impressed on the mind, *whatever objects they may compose*, cannot exist otherwise than in a mind perceiving them, is not less evident. This appears from the meaning of the term exist, *&c.*——Here, that sensations *compose* their objects, wants a little proof, and is at best a very equivocal expression.

Now (to observe here the extent of this kind of doubting) this argument will equally shew spiritual substance to be a *contradiction in terms*, as well as matter: for we are percipient of nothing but our own perceptions and ideas, with respect to the *soul* of another man, as well as with respect to his *body*; or if this be true in either, it is true in both. *Activity* and *perceptivity*, the only properties whereby we infer the existence of spiritual substance, are not that substance, but qualities belonging to it, any more than *figure*, *motion*, &c. are corporeal substance. If then this argument is good for any thing in the first case, it is as good in the second; and if it demonstrate matter out of existence, it equally demonstrates all substance out of existence, save the mind thus percipient, without excepting the Deity himself. So that, brought to its genuine and undissembled issue, it ends in that kind of knowledge mentioned once or twice above, called *Egomism* (*i*). Dean Berkeley,

(*i*) *Quelques Spinosistes sentant que l'evidence leur échappe a tout moment, dans les pretendues démonstrations de leur Maître, sont tombés dans une espece de Pyrrhonisme insensé, nomme l'Egomisme, où chacun se croit le seul etre existent.* Mr. *Ramsay's* Discourse upon Mythology, Part. I. near the end.

I think,

I think, is not far from owning this. In Sect. 138. of what he calls his *Principles*, he hath these words;——" If therefore 'tis " impossible that any degree of these powers " [willing, thinking, and perception of ideas, " to wit] should be represented in an idea or " notion, 'tis evident *there can be no idea or* " *notion of a spirit*,"—Here we may observe that, if we neither have any idea or notion of spiritual substance itself, nor of these properties whereby we could only come to the knowledge of such a substance, (*activity* and *perceptivity*, the examples of which he assigns) it seems impossible that such a thing could ever have entered into the thoughts of men. These particulars ought to be well considered by those who run so greedily into this scheme. It is true, *thinking*, *willing*, &c. cannot be painted in the imagination, as objects having figure and magnitude may: but might not this *Author* thus prove, that we can have no idea or notion of *virtue*, *justice*, *truth*? And if this consequence be fair, as it seems to be; this scheme is a complication *of all the species of Scepticism* that have ever yet been broached. *Notion* extends not only to the images of corporeal objects

S 2 in

in the fancy, but to whatever is the object of the understanding (*k*). It is not enough that an *Author* is not explicit in owning all the absurdities which arise from his scheme; or that he denies them: others will assign

(*k*) *Des Cartes* and Mr. *Locke*, take the word idea itself in the same sense. Mr. *Locke* says, (*Introduction, sect.* 8.) "It being that Term, which, I think, serves "best to stand for whatsoever is the object of the under-"standing, when a man thinks, I have used it to ex-"press whatever is meant by *Phantasm, Notion, Species,* "or whatever it is, which the mind can be employed "about in thinking." *Des Cartes* says in his geometrical method of proving the existence of God, and the Soul, Defin. 2. *Ideæ nomine intelligo cujuslibet cogitationis formam illam, per cujus immediatam perceptionem ipsius ejusdem cogitationis conscius sum; adeò ut nibil possim verbis exprimere intelligendo id quod dico, quin ex boc ipso certum sit in me esse ideam ejus quod verbis illis significatur. Atque ita non solas* imagines *in phantasia depictas ideas voco*: *imo* ipsas *hic* nullo modo voco ideas, *quatenus sunt in phantasia corporea, boc est in parte aliqua cerebri depictæ, sed tantum quatenus mentem ipsam in illam cerebri partem conversam informant.* This is very distinct and full. Dean *Berkeley*, who will not allow us to have any notion or idea of thinking, willing, &c. should give us his acceptation of the word; or shew us what is amiss in Mr. *Locke* or *Des Cartes*'s acceptation. Whatever he may say about *abstract ideas*, it is certain all true demonstration is in abstract ideas.

his

his authority to juſtify their maintaining them. *Epicurus* ſaid many things well——*Cùm bene præſertim multa, ac divinitus ipſis Immortalibus de Divis dare dicta ſuërit*——and hath left many fine things in writing: and yet when this was obſerved to *Cicero*, who condemned his *philoſophy*, he anſwers, *Non quæro quid dicat, ſed quid convenienter rationi poſſit, & ſententiæ ſuæ dicere.*

IX. But to return. If Dean *Berkeley*, to evade the inconſiſtency mentioned in N° 7. of diſputing with, and endeavouring to convince no body at all for ought he knows, ſhould ſay that God excites the ideas of mens ſouls in him, (provided he will allow that there can be any idea, or notion, of ſouls) then all his certainty for the exiſtence of mens ſouls, is becauſe God would not excite the ideas of theſe Beings in us, to make us believe they were, unleſs they really were. And this would be founding his belief of immaterial ſubſtance, preciſely upon *the reaſon* which Dr. *Clarke* hath brought, to ſhew that we cannot poſſibly be deceived, in concluding that material ſubſtance really exiſts without the mind. That is, he cannot avoid

S 3 proceed-

proceeding in contradiction to himself; and his own tenets, without having recourse to the force of the Doctor's demonstration (*l*): and that demonstration overthrows his tenets. This I take to be a hard *Dilemma* upon the scheme.

X. Here we may farther observe, since Dean *Berkeley*'s argument demonstrates all substance out of existence, equally with material substance; what small reason he had to proclaim (Sect. 93. of his Book) his victory over the *Atheists* and *Sceptics*. His words are——" Without which [unthinking mat-" ter, to wit] your *Epicureans*, *Hobbists*, " and the like, have not even the shadow " of a pretence, but become the most cheap " and easy triumph in the world."—And again, Sect 96. " Matter being once *ex-* " *pelled out of nature*, drags with it so many " sceptical and impious notions, *&c.*" This is, I think, as if one should advance, that the best way for a woman to silence those, who may attack her reputation, is to turn a

(*l*) See this Demonstration in the *Cyclopædia*, under the word Body, immediately after Dean *Berkely*'s arguments against the existence of matter.

common

common prostitute. He puts us into a way of denying all things, that we may get rid of the absurdity of those who deny some things.

XI. If we will talk soberly, though the evidence of sense is not the greatest we are capable of; yet since it is the most universal and constant, fitted to all the concerns of life, and the capacities of all men; since (except in a few cases, the causes of which we know, and can rectify the judgment) there is a satisfactory agreement between the informations of it, through all different ages, and in all countries; and since it is in effect, the first foundation of all our knowledge, in our present state of union with matter; the man who endeavours to overturn *the evidence of sense universally*, endeavours to introduce the *wildest* and most *unbounded Scepticism*, let his pretences be what they will. And Dean *Berkeley*, by teaching men to distrust their senses, teaches them to distrust his *Book* in the first place; it is but an idea like other things, every word and line in it: all his actions and great undertakings are but *mere dream and chimæra*; and his designs disap-

S 4 point

point themſelves in every reſpect. If once we refuſe that reaſon which Dr. *Clarke* has aſſigned for believing the exiſtence of *external objects*, and a *material world*; there is in truth no ſtopping till a man has denied every thing that exiſts without his own mind, except it be perhaps the exiſtence of ſome *deluſory Being* who conſtantly cheats and impoſes upon him. How this can be ſuch an *antidote* againſt *Scepticiſm* and *Atheiſm* is not eaſy to be imagined. We might with equal reaſon affirm, I think, that putting out the eyes is *the beſt cure* for dimneſs of ſight (*m*).

XII. It may not perhaps be foreign to the purpoſe, to take notice here of the contradiction in terms, which is pretended to be in aſſerting the exiſtence of matter. It is (if any where) in Sect. 4. of Dean *Berkeley*'s *Principles*; for in Sect. 7. he ſpeaks of having *demonſtrated his concluſion*; and in Sect. 21. he ſays, *Arguments, à poſteriori, are unneceſſary for confirming what, if he miſtakes not, has been*

(*m*) It is true, *Des Cartes* doubts of the evidence of ſenſe; but it was only to ſhew it more certain afterwards; it was rather calling his knowledge to an examen; yet I humbly conceive his method was wrong; of which more immediately.

been ſufficiently demonſtrated, à priori; therefore in Sect. 22. he apologizes for dilating on that, which may with the utmoſt evidence, be *demonſtrated in a line or two*, to any one that is capable of the leaſt reflection. In ſhort, all that I could find for it is in that fourth Section, and contained in the following queſtions.—" For what are the forementioned objects [*houſes, mountains, rivers,*] " but the things we perceive by ſenſe? And " what, I pray you, do we perceive, beſides " our own ideas or ſenſations? And is it not " plainly repugnant, that any of theſe, or " any combination of them, ſhould exiſt unperceived?" — This is but a ſorry affair to be the ſubject of three new pieces. We ſhall conſider it query by query, as it is propoſed. And firſt, *What are the forementioned objects, but the things we perceive by ſenſe?* This query ſeems not to agree well with the next. Here it is allowed that *we perceive things* by ſenſe, or by the mediation of ſenſe (for theſe things ſeem at a diſtance from the ſenſe) which are ſuppoſed, and called *objects* (of ſenſe it would ſeem); and in the next it is taken for granted, that we *perceive nothing* but our own ſenſations; that is, nothing by means

means of the ſenſes. This is what one may call ſleight-of-hand reaſoning. Let us join both queſtions in one. *What are the objects of our ſenſations, but thoſe very ſenſations themſelves?* This queſtion propoſed thus ſomewhat leſs juglingly, implies or ſuppoſes the truth of this propoſition, *Our ſenſations have no objects exiſting without the mind:* which is really the whole point in controverſy. And to take this for granted, is to beg the thing to be proved; or to ſuppoſe the debate at an end. Thoſe *mountains, rivers, houſes,* we all ſuppoſe to exiſt without the mind; and although we ſhould be wrong, it remains to prove that we are wrong, that being the whole of the diſpute. To *affirm* this, or *aſk* if it be not ſo, will never do any thing, We may farther add, ſince he allows objects perceived by ſenſe in this query, that *ſenſations* cannot be objects to themſelves: a ſenſation may become the *object* of a reflex act of the mind upon it; and it can become an object to the mind in no other manner. But when a ſenſation thus becomes the object of a poſterior perception, it is not the object to itſelf (*n*). When a man beholds the *circulation* of

(*n*) At this rate we muſt ſay, that brutes have no objects

of the blood, by the help of a microscope, he doth not admire his own simple *perception*, more than when he beholds a pebble; but something which he thinks at least, the *cause* and *object* of it. We might as well say, when a man laughs at some ridiculous thing, he laughs at his own laughter only. However, we may answer the question categorically: That these *forementioned objects*, [rivers, houses, mountains,] are *the very things* we perceive by sense. This is a proper answer enough to such a question; and we may add, that these *objects* excite sensations in the mind, by motion, or acting on the organs; whether by reflecting the rays of light, by raising an undulation in the air, by immediate contact, &c. and this motion is propagated by the nerves to the brain, where the soul (there present) is apprized of them thus acting. Now, it is no matter whether what we say be true or not; though it be only a *conjecture formed at random*, if it assigns to sensations their

jects of their sensations, since sensations cannot be objects to themselves; for they make no reflex acts of the mind, and there are no material objects from without, according to this scheme.

distinct

distinct objects, without a *contradiction in terms*: this puts D. *B.* to the trouble of another demonstration, as much as if it were the real case that obtains.

XIII. His second question is, *And what I pray you do we perceive, besides our own ideas and sensations?* A consistent answer to this follows from what was said just now. We perceive, besides our sensations themselves, the *objects* of them; or we perceive objects existing from without, by the mediation of sensation, or motion produced; since we are conscious not only of sensation excited, but that it is excited by some cause besides ourselves; for we suffer it, often against our will. This cause we call matter: and D. *B.* says it is *God Almighty*. Hitherto there is no contradiction. He says it is *one thing*, and we say it is *another*: and so far he hath no reason to say we contradict ourselves, more than we have to say the same of him: nay nor so much. It is pleasant to observe D. *B.*'s address: he would have us to allow that *matter is a sensation*; or that our *sensations* are the same thing with their *objects*, which being the thing in debate, is still begging the argument,

gument, by an equivocal question. So he might prove that, if a man in a dark night were groping out his way, with a long pole in his hand, and felt something resist it, which made him turn another way, lest he should run his head against the wall; so he might prove, I say, that it were *a contradiction* for the man to say, there was any thing there, besides the pole itself, by *this same query*——For what, I pray you, says he, do you perceive, besides the pole in your own hand?

XIV. We may here again observe, as in N° 8. that this query of D. *B.*'s easily turns against himself. We say, that which excites sensations in us is generally the objects of those sensations, existing from without: unless in the instances of dreams and phrensies, in which there is still a manifest difference from ordinary sensation. He says, God, who is not the object of our sensations, is the immediate cause of them. How doth he disprove what we assert? Thus. You perceive *nothing* but your perceptions. The *cause* of your perceptions, which you assign, is not your perceptions themselves.

There-

5

Therefore you do not perceive this cause of your perceptions. Therefore *this cause of your perceptions is not at all*; or is but the same thing with those very perceptions. Here the fundamental reason of this inference is, because we perceive nothing but our own perceptions. But D. B. doth not perceive any thing but his own perceptions, more than other men: and if his not perceiving the *cause* of his perception, is a sufficient ground of *denying* such cause, or of making it the same thing with the very perceptions themselves; then God, not being perceived, either is not; or is but a very perception in the mind of man: *Absit blasphemia!* And thus his own argument will exterminate out of nature, any other cause of perception he pleases to pitch upon. He says, matter being once expelled out of nature, drags with it, *&c.* It is true, matter is but a contingent substance in nature; but being once expelled out of nature, it drags more along with it, in his method of reasoning, than he is aware of: and it drags least of all our sceptical and impious notions with it, as he pretends. To suppose it absent multiplies these notions without end.

XV. The

XV. The laſt queſtion in this demonſtration, and which he deſigned ſhould carry home the conviction of the whole, is, *And is it not plainly repugnant, that any of theſe* [ideas] *or any combination of them, ſhould exiſt unperceived?* Here you ſee, he preſumes you have allowed him, according to his laſt query, that *ſenſations* and their *objects* are the ſame thing; and on this preſumption, his argument indeed is concluſive: but if you are not thus far complaiſant, he is at a loſs. And I anſwer, Our *ideas* ſurely cannot exiſt without the mind: but their *objects* may; and do. And they are ſtill ſenſible objects, though they fall not under the ſenſes, at all times and in all places: *i. e.* though they are not *objected to the ſenſe*, in places where they are not; and at times when our ſenſes are not directed to the places where they are. With reſpect to this it is obſervable, that he hath another very ſhort way of demonſtrating his main point. He *ſuppoſes* that the term [to *exiſt*] hath the ſame import, when applied to corporeal things, as to be *perceived* (o): aſſerting (ſtrongly indeed) that it

(o) In the *Cyclopædia, loc. citat.*——This appears from

it is otherwise unintelligible. Whence it clearly follows; Matter which is *not perceived*,

from the meaning of the term *exist*, when applied to sensible things. Thus, the table I write on exists: *i. e.* I see and feel it.——But the existence of unthinking Beings, without any relation to their being perceived, is unintelligible: their *esse* is *percipi*.

One cannot well pass by the argument here, without enquiring a little into the reasonableness of it. This proposition [their *esse* is *percipi*] is delivered with the air of an *axiom*; but if it be, it is incumbent on the *Author*, I think (who seems to be the first that discovered it) to shew the necessary connexion between the terms *esse* and *percipi*, in it. It cannot be said to be *self-evident*, on which account certain propositions were first called axioms; since others cannot find out the *self-evidence*, or even the *truth* of it. We say indeed with respect to the *Deity*, his *esse* is *existere*, because *necessary existence* belongs to his *nature*; but no body allows that *to be perceived* belongs to the *esse* or *nature* of matter; so that this axiom appears to me, after the exactest enquiry I am able to make, to be such an *axiom* as begs the question.

He argues from the meaning of the word [*exist*] that, when spoken of material things, it is the same as *to be perceived*; but who besides the *Author* himself, hath affixed this meaning to that *term*? Is it the common acceptation of the word, when applied to material things? Hath he the *Philosophers*, or even the *vulgar* on his side in this, as he seems to insinuate elsewhere? *Pythagoras* afferted

ed doth *not exist!* But the *Artificer* seems to understand that his *tools* exist all the intermediate

asserted that the earth was *spherical*, and *habitable quite round* [——γῦν, ϗ αὐτὴν σφαιροειδῆ, ϗ περιοικουμένην· εἶναι ᾗ ϗ ἀντίποδας· ϗ τὰ ἡμῖν κάτω, ἐκείνοις ἄνω. Diog. Laert.] But he did not mean that the *Antipodes* did not *exist* because he did not *perceive*, *i. e. hear* and *see* them; as he must have done according to our Author's acceptation of the word. Again, *Virgil* says,

Est *in secessu longo locus: insula portum*——

He doth not mean that the place he describes did not *exist*, because he was not there at the time to *look upon*, or *perceive* it. If it should be said, that *Pythagoras*, or *Virgil*, did not speak *philosophically*; we may be sure at least that they spoke *common sense*; and as all men have spoke both since, and before. Which shews his sense of the *term* to be quite new.

Moreover, what reason can be assigned why the existence of matter should be confined to *the being perceived*, more than the existence of other substance? If the reason of the *Author*'s assertion be, That what is not perceived, neither *by itself*, nor *any other thing*, doth not exist, then any other substance (*the human soul*, v. g.) if it doth not always perceive itself, must have *intervals* of non-existence, as it ceases to perceive itself, or otherwise: at least the Author should have proved that it *always thinks*, to shew it has no *pauses* or *blanks* of existence. It is true, it must always think upon his scheme, having no restraint or interruption from matter; but

termediate time, after he lays them by at night, till he takes them up again next morning. And after this, it is unaccountable how this Author could pretend (Sect. 82.) that he doth not deny even corporeal substance, in the *vulgar sense*; but only inert senseless matter; as if the Artificer thought his tools were *artful*, *sensible* matter; or disappeared when he had them not in his hands; or even then, were nothing but the *ideas* of instruments in the *ideas* of his hands,

then he will have a difficulty to explain, how it could be so affected without matter, as to make this appear doubtful. I might take notice of the *variation* and *proportion* of existence, (so to speak) the *rising* and *falling* of it, upon his scheme: for instance, The *Table* I write on, when I do not perceive it, *doth not* exist; but when I sit down to write on it, *it comes again into* existence. If another person perceives it along with me, must it have a *double existence?* And if three of us sit at it, must its existence be three times greater, than if I looked at it alone? And, lastly, if it were true that *being perceived* constituted the existence of *matter*, and *all created substance*, the *Infinite Mind* perceives them without intermission; and this will constitute the continued existence of matter upon his own principles, I think; unless he would say that matter *exists continually*, as the Deity perceives it, and *doth not exist continually*, as other Beings do not perceive it.

All

All this then ends in the following *childish sophism*: *sensible things* are but the *objects of sense*. Whenever they are not the objects of sense, *they are no longer sensible things*. Therefore, when they are not the objects of sense, or not perceived, they *are not*. But would not *D. B.* allow his house to be a *combustible thing*, unless it were actually on fire? He might, with equal force of reason prove, that unless it were in flame, it were *no house* at all.

XVI. This is his demonstration. We may farther observe that it doth no great honour to this new scheme, nor those who pretend to admire it, that it forces the Author to suspect, that even Mathematicks may not be very sound knowledge at the bottom. In Sect. 118. he says, "To be plain, we suspect the Mathematicians are no less deeply concerned, than other men in the errors arising from abstract general ideas, and the existence of objects without the mind." And in Sect. 119. he says, the theorems in Arithmetick are *difficiles nugæ*. A man ought to have a vast deal of merit, and to have obliged the world with surprising discoveries, to

T 2 justify

justify his attacking these sciences at this rate; or rather no merit possible can warrant it. And it must give us but a bad opinion of the notions that necessitate a man to declare himself thus. What necessity they lay him under, we shall see instantly. In Sect. 22. he expresses himself after the following manner.——" It is but looking into your " own thoughts, and so trying whether you " can conceive it possible for a *sound*, or a " figure, or a motion, or a *colour* (*p*), to " exist without the mind, or unperceived. " This easy trial may perhaps make you see " that what you contend for is a *downright* " *contra-*

(*p*) D. *B.* hath perplexed himself about the *sensible qualities* of bodies; and insists much upon it as a demonstration of the non-existence of matter, because these qualities cannot exist without the mind. But he might have observed *that heat*, for instance, is an *equivocal word*; and may either stand for the *sensation* excited in the mind, or the quality in external bodies, raising that sensation. It is very trifling, because the *first* cannot exist without the mind, to infer that the *last* cannot; to conclude, that because *sensation* is not in the fire, there is no *quality* in it to raise sensation in a sensitive Being. Here *figure* and *motion* are nicely shuffled in with *colour* and *sound*; though they are qualities of a different kind.

contradiction. Insomuch that I am content to put the whole upon this issue; If you can but conceive it possible for any one extended, moveable substance, or in general for any one *idea*, [here *extended moveable substance*, and idea, are supposed *species* and *genus*; in which case he is very safe] or any thing like an idea, to exist any other ways, than in a mind perceiving it, I shall readily give up the cause. And as for all the *compages* of external bodies you contend for, I shall grant you its existence; though you can neither give me any reason why you believe it exists, nor assign any use for it, when it is supposed to exist. I say the *bare possibility* of your opinion's being true, shall pass for an argument that it is so."——This is very solemn! A man that is so generous had need be wonderfully secure of his conclusion.

XVII. But we take him at his word. Having shewn that his demonstration doth not conclude; and conceiving it very possible that the whole *compages* of external bodies may exist without the mind, and no ways in it;

T 3 the

the argument is at end with him (*q*). No man can ever be seriously persuaded, that this Author's scheme is true in fact, let him use the utmost violence possible to his reason. The thing itself is of such a nature, that it will not admit of belief: so far is the contrary from being a *downright contradiction*, as he says. And it is wonderful that he should be so peremptory in direct opposition to the sense of mankind. However we shall go on to shew, in consequence of what was said in N° 6. how possible matter is; and that there is all the evidence for the real existence of it, that the nature of things can admit of, unless we will require the contradiction there named to be proved. And first, if matter had not been possible at least, no man would ever have had any idea of it at all. To omit the reason of this before given, (N° 6.) let us consider that whatever part of an idea is not perceived, is *no part* of it; its *esse* is really

(*q*) It is to no purpose to insist longer on any thing contained in his Book. It will all be found to be a repetition of this supposed demonstration. He carps very much in his Introduction at abstract ideas; but the usefulness and necessity of them is never a whit the less; a remarkable enough instance of which will appear immediately.

percipi,

percipi. (See D. *B.*'s *Principles*, Sect. 132. as also his *Opticks.*) A part of a perception not perceived, is a contradiction indeed, being a part of it that is *no part* of it. Consequently a part less than the *minimum sensibile* (see again Sect. 127.) is no part of it, or nothing. Therefore *in the idea* of a solid inch of matter, *v. g.* there is no part that might be expressed by this number 1,000,000,000,000 in the denominator, having unit for its numerator, (or we may make the number greater, for those who have very good eyes) such a part being less than the *minimum sensibile*: or such a part is nothing at all. But if there be no such part; or if the million-millionth part is precisely nothing; the *whole idea* is made up of a million of million of *no ideas*: or the whole idea is no idea. For undoubtedly, a million or any number of nothings, will never make something: nor will any number *of negations* of an idea, ever make a *real idea*. Two, ten, a hundred, *&c. negations* of a thing, will never amount to the *thing itself*. Thus unless a *real*, *solid*, *figured substance*, were at least possible to exist without the mind, such a part of which would be a real part, of the same nature with the whole; our idea of the whole would be *impossible*, and *no idea*. This follows from asserting such a scheme, as makes it necessary to maintain, that *whatever we perceive not of matter is not*, which this Author doth very explicitly (*r*). A little *abstraction of ideas*, to which he is such an enemy, would have been of use to him here. The same may be shewn concerning the ideas of *motion*, resistance, weight, &c. We do not perceive the resistance of an atom; therefore we could not perceive that of a cannon-ball: for the last is but so many times the first. And if the first be nothing, so many times *no perception* will never make perception. Again, we have no sense of a motion extremely slow, or extremely swift: therefore such motions are not. We have no perception of the motion of the index or hour-hand of a clock: and yet this *no perception*, so many times repeated, becomes real perception,

(*r*) Here we might ask a reason from the Abettors of this scheme, why our ideas do not reach the very intimate essence of other things, as well as body! Our ideas come not up to those in the Divine Mind, with respect to body, more than other things.

2

ception, with respect to the minute-hand (*s*).

XVIII. Again,

(*s*) We may draw it as a corollary from the argument in this paragraph, That our perceptions in general *have no parts*, or are indivisible; and *particularly* that our ideas or perceptions of divisible, extended substance, are themselves *indivisible*, without *parts* or *extension*. If they were not, then the million-millionth part of the perception of an inch long, would be *some part* of it, or *perceived* by the terms. And from this again it will follow, that the percipient Being in us *is not matter*; because if our perceptions of length, breadth, figure, were in a material substance, they *should* necessarily have dimensions. For such ideas of figures would be then affections, or modifications of matter; but all affections or modifications of matter, must be inherent in the matter whose modifications they are. And if the perception or idea of a figure, be an *inherent modification*, or *affection of matter*; it is clear *it must inhere in all the matter percipient of it*, and therefore have equal superficial dimensions at least. And, secondly, our perceptions of extension being without parts illustrates and confirms what was said in Sect. 3. *viz.* That the soul hath no parts, or is a *simple, indivisible substance*. We must say, I think, that *all the soul is percipient*: if any part of it were impercipient that would not have the nature of *soul* (or of percipient Being.) And if all the soul be percipient, and yet its perceptions *be without parts*, we must say that *it hath no parts*. If the soul were extended as matter is, certainly our perceptions would be extended,

XVIII. Again, *solidity*, *figure*, *divisibility*, &c. are either properties inhering in some extended, or have parts; *infinite divisibility of extension* would not only be conceived by abstract reason, but the actual infinite little parts would be *pictured down*, if I may so express it; or they would be *as much perceived*, as any parts, and that by the terms being *parts of the perception*. And lastly, from this corollary I ask the following question; If the faculty of imagination requires a *picture extended in length and breadth*, but no idea or perception, *as it is in the mind*, is extended, Does not the power of imagination as much infer a material sensory or organ, as a pure or simple perception requires an unextended or immaterial percipient? In imagination, or in sensation of visible objects, the perception *is not itself a picture*; but undoubtedly *it is the perception* of a picture somewhere lodged. And if this be so; imagination, as it is the perception of a picture, shews not only that the soul is immaterial, *but that it is united to a material sensory*, where the picture is impressed, and to which it applies for the perception of it; or that matter exists. How far this argument is applicable to overturn D. *B.*'s scheme the Intelligent will determine; but *Cartes* himself, who, it may be presumed, shewed D. *B.* the way of calling material substance in question, says—*Nam attentiùs consideranti quidnam sit imaginatio, nihil aliud esse apparet quàm quædam applicatio facultatis cognoscitivæ ad corpus ipsi intimè præsens* [the sensory] *ac proinde existens*. Meditat. 6.

substance;

substance, or substance itself (*that thing*, to wit, in which properties inhere, which we call, and must call substance:) if they are substance, *solidity* and *figure* will prove a *solid, figured* substance upon us. If they are only properties, they are either properties of our ideas, or not; if they are, then our ideas *are substance*, with respect to these *properties* or the thing in which they inhere; and therefore solid, figured substances. A thing that hath solidity, figure, *&c.* as properties belonging to it, or predicable concerning it, must be *a solid, figured thing*. But that our ideas should be such, as upon this scheme they must be, is monstrous. At least therefore, a substance must be possible, of which these are properties: for they are certainly properties of something. And if it be allowed that such properties exist now; or that the thing exists to which they belong; they will infer not only the *possibility*, but the *actual existence* of matter.

XIX. Again, all geometry is conversant about *quantity*. If there be nothing that can be called *quantum* in nature, or without the mind; nothing to which *quantity is applicable*;

cable; then we have a large body of fine demonstration, and men have discovered vast numbers of *eternal* and *undeniable properties* (as of a *triangle, circle, cylinder, sphere*) precisely of nothing; *immutable truths* conversant about an *impossible object:* which is strangely contradictory. It hath been always allowed that *nothing* can have no properties predicable of it, nor truths demonstrable concerning it. Our ideas are not *quantity:* to say that would be to deny again the principal hypothesis maintained in this scheme *of an utter want of extension* in rerum natura. And if we allow *extension,* why not *an extended substance?* They are only ideas of quantity; and those truths are purely demonstrable of the *objects* of our ideas. No man ever spake of a *circular thought;* a *spherical,* or *triangular perception:* the *sine* or *tangent* of a *sensation* would be a new monster in science. Where will these absurdities end? Nothing ever exposed men so much as this late species of Scepticism. It is a wonder it should find admirers; and among Mathematicians! For upon this scheme the object of their whole science is unphilosophically universal and abstract.

XX. More-

XX. Moreover, What a fine branch of knowledge have we concerning *extended* and *resisting quantity*, or body? The *shock* of bodies against each other, particularly of *elastic bodies*; their perpendicular and inclined *descents*; their *motion*, circular, or in other curves; their *centrifugal forces*; their *centers* of gravity, oscillation or percussion? What fine and surprising theorems, concerning bodies moving in, or supported by *fluids*? These truths have still nothing for their object. Our ideas are not *heavy*, *resisting*, *projectile*, *fluid*; capable of being *compressed*, or *dilated*; have no properties of *inflexion*, *refraction*, *&c.* To allow that our ideas had any of these properties, would be to allow them to be solid, resisting, figured, divisible *things*. And to say it is impossible there can be any *substance* of which these are properties; or to doubt only of this; is to doubt if several useful truths may not be found out, and demonstrations given, about *nothing*. Let me ask, what kind of philosophy would such propositions as these make; the *centrifugal forces* of two *equal ideas*, revolving in the same time, in in unequal ideas, are as their distances from the *centers* of these *ideas?* Or, the *volumes* of *compressed* ideas, are reciprocally as the *weights* of the *superincumbent* ideas? Or, the spaces run over by an *idea*, falling by its own *gravity*, are as the squares of the times? This would still run more oddly if dressed entirely in the language of this hypothesis, thus: The *ideas* of the spaces *run over* by an *idea*, falling by the *idea* of its own gravity, are as the *ideas* of the squares of the *ideas* of the times: for here all must be expressed by *idea*, their objects being impossible. These are shocking to the last degree. It is no wonder that the men who broach this scheme, should bear a grudge to Mathematicks. They are diametrically opposite to each other: and if there be any truth in that science, this must fall. Or rather we may ask universally, the particulars in N° 8. and 14. being also taken into consideration, what philosophy these men would retain; or what kind of knowledge would they leave to be pursued? Indeed what throws us into general and unbounded Scepticism, must strike at the roots of all science.

2 XXI. But

XXI. But it will be ſaid could not *God Almighty* have excited all theſe ideas in ſeparate ſpirits, and made them capable to inveſtigate theſe properties of a ſolid, extended ſubſtance, which never actually exiſted? To this it is anſwered, that indeed *theſe truths* concerning a *ſolid extended ſubſtance*, were eternally in the *Divine Intellect*, before ſuch ſubſtance exiſted: but then ſurely they were truths only, with regard to that *ſubſtance* itſelf, and not with reſpect to *immaterial ſubſtance*; unleſs we ſhould ſay that the real properties of matter, were applicable to, and true concerning a ſubſtance *not matter*. Thus, even Infinite Power could not prompt us with theſe ideas in reſpect of any thing but what we believe to be the *objects* of them, not of our ideas themſelves. *Which, by the way, realizes our knowledge and philoſophy about material things more than it is of late faſhionable to follow* (*t*.)

XXII. This

(*t*) I beg that the following axiom of *Des Cartes* may be conſidered in this view, and it ſeems to me nothing needs be more evident. Axiom. 5. *Unde etiam ſequitur realitatem objectivam idearum noſtrarum requirere cauſam, in quâ eadem ipſa realitas non tantum objectivé, ſed formaliter*

XXII. This being so; the next question is, Whether God Almighty (*a Being of infinite veracity*) would have made it necessary for all those separate spirits (whom we call *men*) to pursue and attain a knowledge, less or more, or at least an experience, of the nature of a *substance* which no way existed, as fancying that a great part of their ease and comfort depended upon *this*; and have so constituted them, that all of this species of Beings in the world, not excepting one, are verily persuaded, that they are continually conversant with this substance, and that it enters into the composition: the *question* is, I say, Whether this Being could have performed such a constant and universal *piece of juggling* (*u*)? If it could answer a good and wise

maliter vel eminenter contineatur. Notandúmque hoc axioma tam necessariò esse admittendum, ut ab ipso uno omnium rerum tam sensibilium, quàm insensibilium cognitio dependeat.

(*u*) It is extremely absurd to suppose that God Almighty should have given us so costly an *apparatus* of senses, as *Anatomy* discovers ours to be, especially of *seeing* and *hearing*; made us capable of investigating the nature and method of sensation; of seeing the contrivance

wise end, that this substance should exist; *why doth it not exist?* If otherwise; *why make us believe a thing exists*, whose real existence could have answered no good and wise end? Can any supposition lay God under a necessity of constantly deceiving his creatures? and his rational creatures too? Will not such a supposition contradict his reason and his truth? This will have all the force of a just

vance and wisdom, and the relation between the *object* and the *faculty*; and all designed only to misguide and deceive us, as if these were to be the organs for communicating the action of external objects, when in truth there is no such thing. This in the language of the present scepticism is, That God *excites* in us (or rather leaves us to *investigate)* certain wonderful ideas [of *eyes* and *ears*] for the reception of other ideas, [*men*, *houses*, *animals*, *&c.*] which we are incapable of receiving by the ordinary manner, if these first ideas are any way disordered. And all the art and experience men have acquired, to procure themselves ease and relief from such disorders, is only at the bottom helping an *idea* that is *distempered*; a mere juggle (as I said) played upon us by the Author of our nature. Let me suppose that the Deity himself possessed us with a notion, that our bodies were made of *China-ware* or *Glass*, (*vel caput habere fictile*, *vel totos esse cucurbitas*, *vel ex vitro conflatos*, as *Cartes* says) and then ask, If that would be a greater imposture, than the present, on our Author's scheme?

 demon-

demonstration to sober men. Besides, since no man can be certain of the existence of other men, upon this scheme; and since it is said that God excites in us all the ideas, which we fancy are excited by bodies; we must say that, when we think we are tempted by other men, to commit an *unjust* or *immoral* action, God immediately tempts us: and this, not only by exciting the ideas of the persuasives in the temptation (of the words and actions, to wit, which are nothing external;) but in formally *contriving*, and *suggesting* the *obliquity* of the sin we are tempted to; for, as hath been said, taking away the existence of their bodies, there is no kind of evidence left for the existence of the souls of men, who by the *abuse* of their *freedom* might tempt us. They who allow God to be a *Deceiver* as to the first, can make no scruple of supposing him to impose on us in the last. I might mention the influence of this *new refinement* on the lives and practices of men. Though the obliquity of actions rises from the will; he who thinks *theft*, *murder*, or *adultery*, nothing real beyond bare idea, and that for ought he knows, he injures *no body*, will be surely under less restraint to satisfy

tisfy his inclinations of any kind. I might also mention the direct tendency of this improvement to *Atheism*. Men will hardly allow the exciting illusory ideas in our minds, of *beauty* and *order*, which no where really exist, such a proof of the power and wisdom of God, as an actually existing frame of material nature, where the *grandeur*, *harmony*, and *proportion* is permanent and real, existing from without, as well when we turn our thoughts *from*, as *to it*. And indeed it is not; for take away the existence of the material Universe, and all the surprising scene of Providence discovered above, Sect. II. Vol. I. where the God of nature by *real power exerted*, constantly preserves the world, and influences every *particle* and *atom* of this substance, by incessant various, wonderful *impulse*, ends in a dream and chimera. In that case no power could be exerted but to delude us: How could we believe the abilities of a Being, who was forced to have recourse to a deceit, to raise in us a notion of them? Or what opinion must we have of his wisdom and address, when we ourselves can detect the imposture? How much better is it as otherwise ordered! We cannot *convince*

U 2 *God*

God of a lie; nor shall we be able *in an after-state* to say, he deceived us *in this*. What a noble school is the frame of nature, where we see the Creator's mighty power put forth, in constantly moving and regularly directing, the vast, unweildy bulks of dead matter; where all the works are real, nothing phantastical! How would it grieve a rational mind to think that all this was performed in shew only; and our ignorance laid hold on to raise our amazement! Doth it not appear that the good and wise end designed, and in some measure attained by the real existence of the material world, is to train us *rational Beings* up to the knowledge of the perfections of the Deity, in a way adapted to our nature and capacities?

XXIII. Now to return to where we began. Matter is *possible*, as hath been shewn just before; but not *necessary*, as hath been also shewn: What kind of evidence, or demonstration then, would we have for the existence of such a substance, which we have not? In reason and philosophy, its existence should be known from the *effects* it produces, or the *perceptions* it excites in us, and the

3 *perfections*

perfections of that Being, who conſtituted it and our nature ſuch, that it ſhould act, and we perceive it acting. To expect we ſhould know it *without ſenſation*, is to demand a proof of its exiſtence, inconſiſtent with the very idea we have of it. To inſiſt that its exiſtence ſhould be inveſtigable by abſtract notions, though we get our ideas originally from ſenſe, by which matter muſt firſt enter, is to ſhew a great *unſkilfulneſs* (*v*), or a *fixed reſolution* to doubt; it is to ſuppoſe it a *neceſſary*, and not a *contingent* Being. Its exiſtence hath no eternal neceſſary properties belonging to it; nor the exiſtence of any thing ſave the Deity. Therefore I conclude, that the knowledge of the exiſtence of external material objects, by ſenſe, is *certain knowledge*, and the evidence as great, as poſſibility, and the nature of things can admit

(*v*) Mr. *Ramſay* obſerves well, *La ſource du Pyrrboniſme vient de ce que l'on ne diſtingue pas entre une demonſtration, une preuve, & une probabilite. Une demonſtration ſuppoſe l'idee contradictoire impoſſible; une preuve de fait eſt, ou toutes les raiſons portent à croire, ſans qu'il y ait aucun pretexte de douter; une probabilite eſt, ou les raiſons de croire, ſont plus fortes, que celles de douter,* Travels of *Cyrus*, Book 6. in the Diſpute between *Pythagoras* and *Anaximander*.

U 3 of;

of; and therefore, as great as the reasonable soul (as such) can desire (*x*.)

XXIV. Before

(*x*) Mr. *Locke* says, (Book 4. chap. 2. sect. 14) "So "that, I think, we may add to the two former sorts of "knowledge, this also, of the existence of particular ex-"ternal objects, by that *perception* and *consciousness* we "have of the actual entrance of ideas from them; and "allow these three degrees of knowledge, *viz. Intui-"tive*, *Demonstrative*, and *Sensitive*; in each of which "there are different degrees and ways of evidence and "certainty." See also chap. xi. of the same Book. Mr. *Ramsay* in the place just now cited, says,——*Je crois qu'il y a des corps, non sur le temoignage d'un seul, ni de plusieurs sens, mais sur le consentement unanime de tous les sens, dans tous les hommes, dans tous les temps, & dans tous les lieux. Or comme les idees universelles & immuables nous tiennent lieu de demonstrations dans les sciences, de meme l'uniformite continuelle, la liaison constante de nos sentiments, nous tiennent lieu de preuves, lorsqu'il s'agit de faits.*——After this let me observe, since this scheme denies the existence of matter, *contrary to the testimony of sense*; and since the Epicurean scheme allows of nothing but matter, *from the testimony of sense*, setting the certainty of sense above that of reason, (see *Lucr.* lib. 1. ver. 420 & *seq.*) let me observe, I say, that it is not easy to conceive, how these two should agree in this particular of the testimony of sense; though it is observed in the *Cyclopædia*, under the word [*fallacy*] they do,——Lastly, (says the Author) "*Reason* cannot shew "our

XXIV. Before we put an end to this Section, it will not be amiſs, in conſequence of what has been ſaid N° 1. to take ſome farther notice of the ridiculous cauſe that hath raiſed all this doubting concerning the *exiſtence of the material world*, and carried ſome to deny directly the poſſibility of any ſuch thing; *viz. That we have no certain mark to know whether we are awake or aſleep.* This is what a man of plain, common ſenſe would laugh at: only *Philoſophers* think it enough to prove the world may be *nothing* rather than *ſomething*. In an objection made to *Des Cartes* concerning his doubting, the *Objector* readily grants, There is no mark to know which of

"our *ſenſes* miſtaken, ſince all reaſoning depends on previous ſenſations; and the ſenſes muſt firſt be true, "before any reaſoning founded thereon, be ſo. Thus "the Epicureans, whoſe ſyſtem is ſtrongly confirmed by "what we have already laid down from D. *B.* concerning the external world." Theſe two ſeem to me to agree in nothing unleſs in perverting all true philoſophy. ——Yet (ſays the ſame Author, under the word Abſtraction) has a *late eminent* and *ingenious Author* D. *B.* conteſted the reality of any ſuch ideas [*viz.* abſtract] and gone a good way towards overturning the whole ſyſtem, and conſequently towards ſetting our philoſophy on a new footing.

U 4 the

the ſtates we are in, and only finds fault with *Cartes* for publiſhing, as a new method of doubting, that which *Plato* and *others* had broached long before him (*y*): which, by the way, is a ſtrange ſort of an objection. The inconſiſtency of this *doubt*, or this queſtion, is plain, I think, in that no man has a right to make it, but he who hath experience of both the different ſtates. If he has only been in one of them, he can know *no difference*, and therefore be in *no doubt*: and if he has been in both, and remembers a difference, he muſt know it; and therefore is obliged to anſwer himſelf, as having a conſcious experience of the thing he deſires to be informed in. Since ſleep is a ſtate in which the faculties of the ſoul are obſtructed, or impeded, by the indiſpoſition of the matter of the body, eſpecially memory; ſince this is ſo, I ſay, for a waking man to deſire a *mark* or *ſign*, whereby to know if he be awake, is as if he ſhould deſire another man to tell him,

(*y*) *Satis conſtat ex iis quæ dicta ſunt in hac Meditatione* [*prima ſcil.*] *nullum eſſe* κριτήριον, *quo ſomnia noſtra a vigilia, & ſenſione verâ dignoſcantur*; ——— *veritatem hujus meditationis agnoſcimus. Sed quoniam de eâdem incertitudine ſenſibilium diſputavit* Plato, *&c.*

him, *Whether he hath the powers of his ſoul at liberty or not?* which he himſelf can know beſt. The ſoul hath not ſome powers to be impeded, and *other powers* of the ſame kind to remain ſtill free; it ſhould then have *two conſciouſneſſes*; therefore it is improper to aſk, if a ſleeping man can have a mark to know whether he ſleeps? nor is it leſs improper for a waking man to aſk a mark to know if he be awake. In the *firſt caſe*, there is a want of conſciouſneſs of the ſtate we are in; and in the *ſecond*, a conſciouſneſs that we are not in the *firſt ſtate:* what doubt can there then remain here? If the powers of the ſoul were not impeded in ſleep, that ſtate would not differ from being awake, except in the indiſpoſition of the body: but ſince it differs ſo widely otherwiſe, who can be excuſable in pretending not to know the difference? At this rate, men might aſk a ſign to know, whether they are blind, or not, or how they can be certain that they are in their ſober ſenſes rather than mad (z); and whether, when

(z) *Pyrrho* indeed, and the *Sceptics*, ſeem to deny a difference between *theſe two*——ὐδὲ γὰρ οἱ μαινόμενοι παρὰ φύσιν ἔχουσι. Τί γὰρ μᾶλλον ἐκεῖνοι ἢ ἡμεῖς: but

when they are confcious of a thing, they can be fure that they are confcious of it (*a*.)

XXV. Thus

but to defend this, was, I think, *to own themfelves mad* in effect.

(*a*) The argument in this paragraph, which is faid not to be intelligible enough, would perhaps become plainer, if we fhould afk the queftion, Whether it is a *waking man,* or a *fleeping man,* who propofes the doubt? And to this we may reafonably expect an anfwer, fince the *doubt* fuppofes a *Difference* of the two ftates, and that this difference *hath been obferved*; for otherwife the *ground* of doubting vanifhes. It may, I think, be probably fuppofed that *Plato,* and *Cartes* were awake, when they propofed this *nice* and *philofophical* manner of doubting; and that they ftarted it from fome experience of the two different ftates, otherwife they would ftill have doubted without reafon; and yet that *very experience* anfwers the doubt. The *doubt* could never be greater than the *experience* on which it was founded: If this experience is fuppofed *nothing*, the doubt becomes *nothing* at the fame time; and the *greater* the experience is fuppofed to be, the doubt becomes the *lefs*; fince much experience of the *difference* could beft teach them that *difference.* This, I prefume, makes the argument intelligible; and fhews the *inconfiftency* of fuch doubting, if a man allows himfelf to be awake. And if he fays *he dreams when he doubts thus*, what he owns here alfo anfwers itfelf; when he awakes, he will find it but a dream. Befides, he owns the *difference* between dreaming

XXV. Thus much of the different *state* of the mind itself in these two conditions, of sleeping and not dreaming, and the former argument will still be applicable.

But allowing the *Scepticism* to be pushed as far as may be. If one should say, " I never dreamed in my life." (Since some of *these men* affirm this of themselves) what reason would he have for asking a *κριτήριον*, whereby to distinguish *dreaming* from *not dreaming*, when he owns he never dreamt in all his life? And if he should say, " I had such a dream last night, and was verily per-" suaded of the *real existence* of the things seen; and " why may not the things I see and hear now be as " phantastical as these were?" I answer, first, he is incapable of being satisfied; because on his own principles, he will still have equal reason to think any answer as phantastical as the *person* [or rather *φάντασμα*, according to him] who gives him the answer: and therefore, as I said in the beginning of the Section, he should for ever hold his tongue, and doubt on in silence. When he desires satisfaction, he supposes the *reality* of the thing he pretends to *doubt of*. This is always the fate of *Scepticism*. And, secondly, when he says, "He dreamed last night, &c." He owns he is awakened out of *that dream* now, otherwise he could not perceive that it was but a dream: Or else he must allow he is still dreaming on; and, as I said, whatever answer is made to him must still appear a dream. If he should say, " I am not certain whether I ever dream-" ed

ſleeping and waking, which brings the τεκ-μήριον ſought to *ſelf-conſciouſneſs*. But the great

" ed in my life, or not." It is as if he ſhould ſay, " I am " not certain, that ever I was in a different ſtate of con-" ſciouſneſs from what I am in at preſent." And then why ſhould he demand a κριτήριον or mark to know which of the two ſtates he is in, who never obſerved any dif-ference? He can have no doubt of the *reality* of exter-nal objects, who was never impoſed on, by being made to think *phantaſtical* objects real. And how could any anſwer give ſatisfaction to ſuch a man? If he thinks all things real, he will need no ſatisfaction; and if he thinks them *phantaſtical*, the anſwer muſt appear to be *ſuch*, as much as all other things. In a word, he hath either per-ceived a difference, of the ſtate of conſciouſneſs he hath been in; or he hath not: if he hath not, he can have no doubt; and if he hath obſerved a *difference*, he ſhould conſider that difference, and is obliged to anſwer himſelf, as having a *conſcious experience* of the thing he deſires to be informed of. For it is *mere humour*, and in effect *ab-ſurdity*, for a man to ſay, " Inform me of a particular, " of which I have experience in my own conſciouſneſs " from your experience of it in *yours*;" ſince *ſelf-con-ſciouſneſs* of what paſſes in one's own mind, is the *laſt appeal* in all controverſy.

From all this, it appears ſtill more plain, I think, that *Scepticiſm*, in any ſhape that may be given it, is incon-ſiſtent with itſelf, in ſuppoſing the thing concerning which it pretends to doubt; and therefore it defeats its own de-ſign

great difficulty pretended, is, *How can we be sure that any thing exists?* All from N° 1 to 24. is an answer to this; to which let me add, that if we never dreamed in sleep, we should not at all doubt of the *existence* of the frame of nature. But have we less evidence now, than if all were a *blank* then? Or can the existence of the world depend upon the indisposition of our bodies, or the different state of consciousness of our minds? Suppose a *whole nation* of men should never dream, (see N° 33. Note (*c*) of the last) and *another nation* never sleep, while *we* both sleep and have visions in our sleep; can the *standing* or *falling* of the fabrick of the universe *depend* upon *this diversity?* We see the heavens represented in a *pool* of standing water, and images reflected from a *mirrour:* is that *hea-*

sign every way. Whence it must appear a very *extraordinary attempt* to endeavour to raise doubts, in spite of the *absurdities* that attend doubting, and to render *truth* suspected without any ground. Though I were able to perplex *plain* and *well-meaning* men, by this subtile kind of doubting; I must be conscious to myself of a disingenuity and perverseness in the *undertaking*; unless I also shewed them a way how to get free of such *puzzling sophistry.*

ven,

ven, or the objects of these images less real because the stars are made appear *below* the ground; or men, trees, houses, represented as hanging *above us*? What if some idle Philosopher had made this a handle to become a learned Doubter? Though perhaps we might have had another Denomination of Sceptics from this man, that would not however have made the existence of heaven and earth less certain. This may be thought a strange supposition; and yet the *Sceptics* pretended to doubt of the *existence of material objects* on this very account; *viz.* from the *different appearances* they made by mirrours.——καὶ ἡ αὐτὴ δὲ μορφὴ παρὰ τὰς διαφορὰς τῶν κατόπτρων ἀλλοία θεωρεῖται· ἀκολουθεῖ οὖν μὴ μᾶλλον εἶναι τοῖον τὸ φαινόμενον, ἢ ἀλλοῖον. Diog. Laert. Pyrrho. And as this very phænomenon of exhibiting the appearances of things by the *pool*, or the *glass*, supposes and proceeds from the *reality* of external objects existing: so even our dreams, though they have no external real objects, yet *suppose such*, and are exhibited in imitation of them; and upon this account deceive us. Therefore rightly considered, they bring no argument against

againſt the real exiſtence of material things, but rather one for it. Thus *Cartes* himſelf ſays (though againſt his own purpoſe) in the ſame place where he propoſes his *univerſal doubting*,——*Tamen profectò fatendum eſt viſa per quietem eſſe veluti pictas quaſdam imagines, quæ non niſi ad ſimilitudinem rerum verarum fingi potuerunt*——This is remarkable in itſelf; but ſtill more ſo as ſaid by *him* and on ſuch an occaſion too. He continues —*Ideoque ſaltem generalia hæc, oculos, caput, manus, totumque corpus res quaſdam non imaginarias, ſed veras exiſtere: nam ſane pictores ipſi, ne tum quidem cùm ſirenas & ſatiriſcos maxime inuſitatis formis fingere ſtudent, naturas omni ex parte novas iis poſſunt aſſignare ſed tantummodo diverſorum animalium membra permiſcent; vel forte*——In our dreams we have repreſentations of ſome things that cannot be imaginary, as *figure, magnitude, number*; and of ſome that are neceſſary, as *time, place:* every viſion muſt have *duration*, and a *ſcene* of exiſtence. So *Cartes* in the ſame place——*cujus generis eſſe videntur natura corporea in communi, ejuſque extenſio; item figura rerum extenſarum, item quantitas, ſive earundem magni-*

I *tudo,*

tudo, & numerus: item locus in quo exiſtant, tempuſque per quod durent——(*Meditatio* 1.) From this the *Intelligent* will ſee that dreams are but ſuperficially conſidered, when they are made a *pretence for doubting*; and that *Cartes* himſelf cuts off the chief pretence he had for calling in queſtion his former knowledge; though with the deſign of becoming more certain, and placing it on a ſurer foundation than it formerly was.

XXVI. Let me here obſerve to young people who have not perhaps conſidered it before, that this *great Man* was not able with his utmoſt effort ſeriouſly to *doubt of every thing*. Having alledged all the reaſons for doubting in his *firſt Meditation*, that he could think of; he is forced at length to come to this, *That if he could not doubt on other terms, he would deſignedly deceive himſelf by doubting.* His words are, *Quapropter, ut opinor, non male agam, ſi voluntate plane in contrarium verſâ,* meipſum fallam *illaſque omnino falſas imaginariaſque* fingam, *donec tandem velut æquatis utrimque præjudiciorum ponderibus, nulla amplius prava conſuetudo judicium meum um a recta rerum perceptione detorqueat.* As if he had said, "If I cannot doubt with "my eyes open, let me shut them: if I "cannot believe things false, let me sup- "pose them false against my belief." Is it not plain here, he only said he doubted, without being able to do so? Those things could not be called prejudices, with which he was forced to take this method. A man should not doubt where he is forced to feign causes of doubting (*b*). And in the *Synopsis* of his *Meditations*, he says, (speaking of the external world the bodies of men, and other things of that nature) *De quibus nemo unquam sanæ mentis serio dubitavit.* The other great reason he assigns for *universal doubting*, is the very worst, I think, that could be given; the supposition, to wit, *that God may be malicious and a deceiver. Quid autem nunc ubi suppono deceptorem aliquem potentissimum, &, si fas est ita dicere, malignum, datâ operâ*

(*b*) If any one *doubts* that he may *become more certain*, and is forced to feign causes (nay to deceive himself) that he may *doubt*; I ask if he can *become more certain*, by this method than he was before? Or if being reduced to the necessity of such a method before he can doubt, be not itself the greatest mark of certainty.

VOL. II. X *in*

in omnibus quantum potuit, me deluſiſſe—— May we not here ſay, that this is a coſtly way of doubting, which forces *Des Cartes* to make an *almighty devil* of the Deity before he can make his doubting feaſible? They who have the lameſt notions of the Deity, conceive him as ſomething perfect: he ſays elſewhere, *Ex quibus ſatis patet illum* [*Deum*] *fallacem eſſe non poſſe: omnem enim fraudem, & deceptionem, à defectu aliquo pendere, lumine naturali manifeſtum eſt.* If this is plain from the light of nature, eſpecially to ſuch men as *Cartes*, and I believe no body will deny it; was it philoſophical in him to ſuppoſe God a deceiver, merely that he might doubt of truths, which otherwiſe forced his aſſent? Pray obſerve whether I do him injuſtice. He ſays, *Nam ſive vigilem, ſive dormiam, duo & tria ſimul juncta ſunt quinque, quadratumque non plura habet latera quàm quatuor; nec fieri poſſe videtur ut tàm perſpicuæ veritatis in ſuſpicionem falſitatis incurrant:* and yet in the very next ſentence the reaſon why he doubts of theſe ſelf-evident truths, is no better than becauſe God may be a deceiver. Is it not mighty inconſiſtent to ſuppoſe an *evidently* *falſe*

falſe thing true, that he may be at liberty to ſuppoſe *evidently true things* falſe? But leaving this, I ſhall only obſerve, that the manner in which he ends his meditations is very remarkable——*Sed hyperbolicæ ſuperiorum dierum dubitationes, ut riſu dignæ ſunt explodendæ, præſertim* ſumma illa de ſomno, quem à vigiliâ non diſtinguebam; nunc *enim adverto permagnum inter utrumque eſſe diſcrimen*——By ſpeaking thus [*nunc enim adverto*] *Des Cartes* would have it thought, that he had got *a new light* from this manner of univerſal doubting: though one muſt be at a loſs to conceive whence the light could come. Could he not perceive the difference between *dreaming* and *not dreaming*, till he had firſt called in queſtion the truth of ſelf-evident propoſitions? Muſt every individual man follow this method, before he can tell whether he be awake, or aſleep? Or can the forcing ourſelves to ſuppoſe God an *Almighty Deceiver*, be the only way to diſcover that he is a Being of infinite veracity! Whatever *vertue* ſuch a method of doubting may have, to open a *Philoſopher*'s eyes; I am ſure it will never open any body's elſe. The only thing I can find worth

X 2 our

our imitation through the whole method, is *the exploding this hyperbolical doubting, as deserving our laughter*; though it was inconsistent in him to speak thus of it, if it had served him for such great purposes (*c*.)

(*c*) I shall here take notice of some exceptions made to the reasoning in some of the preceding paragraphs, and endeavour to remove them. It is observed, that D. *B*.'s scheme takes away the existence of *other minds*, and perhaps of *our own*, and of all sorts of *substrata*, as they are called; and therefore that most of what I have said seems right. But then it is added, "It is true, one "*Sovereign Mind* may be sufficient to produce all these "ideas; and many Philosophers affirm, that *He* actually produces them in us, though they allow *the objects* "*to exist*. The question is, Whether he produces them "according to a certain order, and certain laws established by himself; or whether he produces them agreeably to the real state of a *certain third object*, "which we call the *sensory*. D. *B*. will say, that the "*order* and *laws* which rule their connexions and appearances in our minds, are in every respect the same "to us, as the real existence of the material Universe. "From *this order*, he will answer your query, How "he can *communicate* his thoughts to others, on which "you seem to lay much stress? And this order will "serve him to answer your queries about the beauty of "nature, and of natural philosophy.—If he had contented himself with denying the actual existence of "matter, he would have avoided many absurdities."

In

In anſwer to this, I own, firſt, I do not ſee that D. *B.*'s reaſoning takes away the exiſtence of *our own minds*, or invalidates *Des Cartes*'s principle, *Cogito ergo ſum.* Thoſe *Philoſophers*, who allow the *objects* of our ideas to exiſt, affirm, I think, without neceſſity, That the Sovereign Mind *produces* the ideas of them in us; in ſo far I mean, as the objects themſelves may do this; or otherwiſe than by *co-operation.* Matter, I know, cannot act of itſelf; or it acts only by reſiſtance; but if the reſiſtance between the matter of our bodies and other matter, be enough to excite the idea of that reſiſtance in our minds, it would be unneceſſary to ſuppoſe *God* to excite the idea, and the reſiſtance itſelf to have no effect. And if we do not allow that the matter of our bodies affects our minds directly, and by itſelf; the union between them will ſeem in a great meaſure to no purpoſe. The reaſon, I believe, why thoſe *Philoſophers* affirmed that God excited the ideas of matter, and material action in our minds, was, becauſe we cannot formally conceive the manner how *matter* affects *ſpirit*, or how ſpirit acts on *matter*; but we are certain this is matter of fact in many inſtances, whether we conceive it or not. The Deity himſelf moves matter, in almoſt all the phænomena of nature; and the ſoul of man perhaps moves ſome matter of the body, though in an infinitely leſs degree.

And as to the manner in which our ideas are produced; *though they are produced agreeably to the real ſtate of a certain third object, which we call the ſenſory,* they are nevertheleſs produced according to a certain order and laws eſtabliſhed by this *Sovereign Mind*; the one of theſe doth not exclude the other. To allow this *third*

X 3 *object,*

object, the *Senſory* namely, is all that is deſired. To allow this, and conteſt the exiſtence of *material objects* would be inconſiſtent.

D. *B.* cannot anſwer my *firſt Query* concerning *communicating his thoughts to others.* For if *any Being* excites the ideas of *other men's bodies* in us; if, as he maintains, it is *impoſſible* and *contradictory* there ſhould be any ſuch bodies; and if it be from theſe deluſory ideas which *this Being* excites in us, that we infer the exiſtence of other men's minds: how can he be certain of the exiſtence of their minds, which he collects from falſe appearances? 'Tis he himſelf who has made the foundation of all a *cheat* and *impoſture.* But ſuppoſing the *ſame Being* excited in us directly the ideas of other men's minds; how could we have a greater certainty in the one caſe than in the other? The veracity of *this Being* becomes now ſuſpected. And why ſhould we truſt him again after a *former illuſion? Cartes* only ſuppoſed, but this *Author* endeavours to prove him a *Deceiver.* He ſhould by all means have given a Demonſtration of the exiſtence of men's minds, when he aſſerts the exiſtence of their bodies impoſſible, by which only we inferred the exiſtence of their minds. And if the argument which I have taken notice of in N° 9. be good; he can offer no proof for the exiſtence of their minds, which will not equally prove the exiſtence of their bodies. So difficult is it, I conceive, to anſwer this Query. Beſides, how can it be ſaid that D. *B.* may anſwer this Query; and yet at the ſame time be owned, that his reaſoning takes away the exiſtence of *other minds,* nay and perhaps of our own too?

Nor

Nor do I think he can anſwer the *other Queries* concerning the *beauty* and *order* of the Univerſe. Can a thing impoſſible and contradictory have any beauty, or order, or, in general, *any property?* I have ſhewn in No 21. that even *Infinite Power* could not prompt us with the ideas of this beauty, order, or properties, any farther than as they relate to theſe very objects, which are controverted. And if theſe objects be impoſſible to exiſt, it is farther evident, *that the Infinite Mind itſelf could have no ideas of them*; for an impoſſible thing there can be no conception. We muſt *neceſſarily* therefore, in explaining the *phænomena of nature*, ſuppoſe the exiſtence of the objects of our ideas; ſince *theſe phænomena* are true only of the objects of our ideas, not of our ideas themſelves. What I mean is, though we conceive the beauty, order and proportion in the Univerſe *by our ideas*, we do not conceive theſe to be beauty, order, or proportion exhibited *in our ideas*, but in the things we ſuppoſe the *objects of them*. I have ſhewn in a place or two above, what *ridiculous* philoſophy it would make, to ſubſtitute our *ideas* inſtead of the *objects* of them. Therefore, I think, D. *B*. could have no reaſon to ſay, *That the order and laws which rule the connexions of our ideas, and appearances in our minds, are in every reſpect the ſame to us as the real exiſtence of the material Univerſe.* This, I conceive, is a great miſtake; and the generality of men allow too haſtily, that it is conſiſtent enough with philoſophy to ſuppoſe nothing but ideas, inſtead of the objects of ideas; and that demonſtrations may be given, and the *phænomena* explained, as well upon the one ſuppoſition as the other. This is that which hath

X 4 made

made D. *B.*'s scheme appear *so impregnable*, and in effect not altogether absurd; whereas in truth, *no one appearance in nature* can be explained, nor *any one proposition* in abstract geometry demonstrated without supposing the objects of our ideas, instead of our ideas themselves.

As this is the main difficulty, I shall endeavour to make it plain by an instance or two. It hath been shewn in N° 17. that our ideas, as they are in the mind, have no parts nor magnitude; and our Author's scheme supposes, or rather asserts this. A want of extension *in rerum naturâ* is the great principle. Let us then take this proposition, *In a right angled triangle, the square of the hypotenuse is bigger than either of the squares of the other sides* (as being really equal to them both.) Now this proposition is directly false, if you substitute the *idea* of this square instead of the *square itself*, which is the object of the idea; for this idea hath no parts nor magnitude whereby to exceed the other ideas; and it is absurd to say it is either *greater* or *less* than another idea, or equal to two or more, or to institute any *proportion* between them; for all such proportion is in respect of *dimensions* or *magnitude*, which can never be applicable to ideas, either in reality, or on the Author's Scheme. And the argument is the same in respect of all *lines*, *surfaces*, *solids*, *angles*; every thing about which geometry is conversant. And as to *philosophy*, I need not give an instance in it, after what hath been said in N° 20. If we apply this proposition [*The spaces run over by a body, falling by its own gravity, are as the squares of the times*] to our ideas, instead of their objects, it is downright *nonsense* and *contradiction*. In short, it is as trifling and sophistical, because all demonstration

stration *is in ideas*, to say it is conversant about no *object but ideas*; as it would be to say, because all demonstration must be pronounced in *words*, or written on *paper*, it can relate to nothing but the *words* it is pronounced in, or the *paper* it is written upon. Omitting therefore other instances, I shall give one, which seems to prove directly the existence of objects without the mind, and that from the *perceptions* of the mind itself.

If our ideas have no parts, and yet if we *perceive parts*; it is plain *we perceive something* more than *our own perceptions*. But both these are certain; we are *conscious* that we perceive parts, when we look upon a *house*, a *tree*, a *river*, the *dial-plate* of a clock or watch. This is a short and easy way of being certain that something exists without the mind. We are certain of this from *consciousness itself*; since we are as conscious that we perceive parts, as that we have perceptions at all. And this argument proves at once, *and from the same perceptions*, the existence of *both the parts* of our composition; (see the Note (*s*) N° 27. above) and therefore makes the existence of both equally certain. Our ideas as they are in the mind, are without parts; and as they make us *conscious* of perceiving parts, *we are conscious* that an extended object exists without the mind, where the extended image is exhibited, *viz.* an extended *sensory*. Our *very sensations*, and the faculty of *imagination*, as much prove the existence of this sensory, as they prove the existence of the *sensitive Being*; and this whether it be in a *dream*, *fever*, or *any way* a Sceptic pleases to suppose, provided only *parts* be perceived. The wildest *chimeras* in sleep prove the certainty of the thing they were brought

to

to render suspected. If these sensories were not, there would be no such illusions: and if *some other cause* than matter, did not make these impressions, there would be still no such illusions. Our sleeping sensations infer the existence of *one cause more*, than our waking sensations shew us.

I am persuaded, if *Des Cartes* had observed this property of our ideas as they are in the mind, *viz.* that they are without parts or extension, (and the definition he gives of an idea which I have quoted above, leads him directly to it) he would have owned that *the same perception of parts* proved to us the existence of both substances. He does indeed in some places point full at this truth. *Præterea* (says he) *ex imaginandi facultate, quâ me uti experior, dum circa res materiales versor, sequi videtur illas existere.* He saw here there was no other way of accounting for the faculty of *imagination*, but by the existence of a material sensory. It were to be wished, he had gone a little farther. But he comes still nearer below. —*Ad, hæc considero* istam vim imaginandi *quæ in me est, prout differt* a vi intelligendi, *ad mei ipsius, hoc est, ad* mentis meæ essentiam, *non requiri; nam, &c.* Meditat. 6. How near is this to proving the existence of *both substances* from the *same perception* of parts or extended images!

One who considers this argument, can make no objection to it from the *images* formed by *specula*. For these are *extended*, and *prove* what I advance, as much as any appearance. In this instance, *magnifying* the *image*, i. e. *enlarging the extension of it*, is the great end proposed, and every one knows that such images are

are formed by *rays* of *light*, which are corporeal things. Neither can there be any objection from the power of an *omnipotent Being*, who may exhibit *extended, figured images*, without any extended, figured subject, in which they may inhere. To bring in Omnipotence to help out an objection, by performing a contradiction, such as to make *properties* exist by themselves without a *subject*, is ridiculous to the last degree.

Others will determine how far this realizes our knowledge concerning matter and material objects, Mr. *Locke* speaks of *sensitive knowledge* with much fairness and candor, giving it the third place, or making the degrees of our knowledge to be *intuitive*, *demonstrative*, and *sensitive*; (see Note (*x*) N° 23.) but with much submission, the existence of matter in general, or at least of material sensories to which the soul is united, seems to me, from what has been said, to be nearer *intuitive* than *demonstrative* knowledge, if the same *perception* of *parts* proves to us both the *spirit* and a *material sensory*. Be it as it will there is but one step in the Demonstration, *viz.* to shew that perceptions, as in the mind, have no parts. But D. *B.* confounds *perception* as in the mind itself, with the *image* perceived in the sensory; and thus endeavours to make our own perceptions of no use to us in shewing us the existence of matter. We had the *conviction* in our own *consciousness* and *perception*; but he made us believe we had it not; and then we were at a loss to find it any where else. A certain great *Author* seems to follow the same tract.——" But thought (says he) we own pre-" eminent, and confess the realleſt of Beings, *the only ex-*" *istence* of which we are made sure by being conscious.

2 " *All*

"*All these may be only dream and shadow.* All which even "*sense* suggests may be deceitful; the sense itself remains "still; reason subsists; and thought maintains its elder-"ship of Being, &c." This is carrying things too far. From what has been said just above it appears, that we are *sure* of the existence of matter by being conscious, or having perceptions of some kind; that as long as sense or sensations remain, this is certain; and that our very dreams shew that *all else* is not a dream. This Author elsewhere makes matter as necessary as *thought itself*; and here he says, all that sense suggests may be but a dream. It is hard to reconcile this. If matter be as necessary as thought, and yet but a dream, nothing at all will be left real.

From what is here said it will follow, that separate Spirits have a superior power or faculty of conceiving extended substance, and not our formal manner of *imagination*; but this, I think, is as it should be; agreeable to reason and philosophy. We are under a necessity, as hath been said before, of applying to impressions on the sensory; being by our union kept at a distance from the objects of sensation: in such a state the sensory must be a *necessary artifice* to supply that defect. Hence our present *imagination* and *reminiscence*, are but a kind of *vicarious faculties*, in which separate Spirits must exceed us. These inferior *helps* seem in *them* to be swallowed up *in intellect*, or the best way of conceiving. That wonderful appearance taken notice of in the end of the last Section, makes this in some measure conceivable. That there is a superior way in this case is certain. The Deity is not confined to our narrow faculty of imagination; every thing is *intellect* in him. It may be so in a lower degree in

2 created

created separate spirits. All this is more intelligible and reasonable than to run into the contradiction of asserting that living Beings can know, or perceive nothing, when not confined to dead matter. But to return.

As to what is said, *that if D. B. had contented himself with denying the actual existence of matter, he had avoided many absurdities*; I must observe that this is a common mistake, and too readily allowed by us. It should be considered, that if he had granted the existence of matter a possibility, he could not have had one argument for denying it to exist actually. Why deny a thing which is allowed possible enough to be, and which hath all the reasons that the nature of things can admit of, to shew that it actually is? To have written Books then *against the actual existence of the Universe*, would have appeared, if possible, a more extraordinary attempt, than the present. Let any one, to satisfy himself, try if he can find out a reason, on this supposition——"It "is very possible the world may exist, yet it is certain "that it doth not really exist, because——." Or thus: "There is no impossibility in supposing myself to have "hands, feet, and a body; and yet nothing is more true "than that I have *neither hands*, *feet*, *eyes*, nor *ears*, for "——." It is not conceivable what plausible reason a man could assign to fill up these arguments. But let us suppose that one should recur to the *great topick* and *pretence* for doubting, *viz.* our dreams, and say, "I find "that I am often imposed upon and deceived in dreams; "therefore, *&c.*" I reply; "Those things which you "dream of, and see in your sleep, really exist; and it is "very possible for the same *individual Being* to become "a *man*,

" a *man*, a *brute animal*, a *monster*, &c. successively, as " you see it *represented*. How can you disprove this apparent existence; or shew it not to be real, and that " you are imposed upon in sleep?——By the testimony " of your senses perhaps; since you neither hear nor see " these things when you awake?——I answer, This " is ridiculous in you: you are inconsistent with yourself; you make opposite reasons conclude the same " thing; you have quite thrown aside the testimony of " your senses, when you conclude against that testimony, *that the material world doth not really exist*. If " sense can prove any thing, your whole scheme is an " absurdity." Thus these men cannot prove a dream *to be a dream* on their own principles: The reason is, they suppose all a dream antecedent to any proof, and make use of *that supposition* as a proof; as was argued in the beginning of the Section. This comes from casting off the testimony of sense. There is no laying aside the methods of certainty which God hath appointed, and finding any consistent *succedaneum* in the place of them. We stumble from one absurdity to another, till at length we are lost amidst the inextricable mazes of *error* and *contradiction*. And from all this it appears, that to allow the existence of the material world possible, and yet deny its actual existence, is at least as difficult as the method D. *B.* has taken to deny it; he had not another possible method to answer his purpose, but to pretend it could not exist.

Some other objections have been made, but not urged with that candor, strength and accuracy as the former; however, I shall mention them. One is, " That the " *existence* of material objects may be called in question, " from

"from the different appearances they make, when "placed at different distances from the eye; for why "should they have one *magnitude*, or *figure*, rather "than another." This, which our *Author* and his *Followers* insist much on, is taken from *Pyrrho*, and his *Disciples*——Κατὰ τοῦτον τὸν τρόπον τὰ δοκοῦντα εἶναι μεγάλα, μικρὰ φαίνεται· τὰ τετράγωνα, στρογγύλα· τὰ ὁμαλὰ, ἐξοχὰς ἔχοντα· τὰ ὀρθὰ, κεκλασμένα.—— It is against the first *Elements* of *Geometry*, that any object, this *Book* for instance, should subtend the same angle by rays proceeding from it to the eye, at all the various distances at which it may be placed. Thus upon the supposition that objects really exist, there is a demonstrable necessity that they should appear of different magnitudes and figures, placed at different distances from the beholder. Hence it seems very unskilful to make such an *appearance* an objection against the real existence of extended objects, which must necessarily obtain, supposing them to exist. If such an objection prove any thing, it proves extended objects impossible, because another *impossibility* cannot become *fact*; *viz.* That the *same line* should always subtend the same angle, by lines drawn from it to any point.

It is said, "I have pretended to ridicule this scheme, "by endeavouring to put some propositions, according "to it, in ridiculous language." This I directly deny. The language into which I have put these propositions, is very proper according to this scheme. This was designed as an argument against the scheme, not as ridicule; and I still think it is one. When it is said in the objection, "That an *object* (this *Book*, v. g.) placed "within

" within a foot of the eye, appears of one magnitude; " and removed to the diſtance of ten feet from it, appears " to be of another; and at the diſtance of a hundred " yards, ſtill of another, *&c.*" I aſſert that this is no language for this ſcheme; or it is captious and ſophiſtical language. It ſhould be " The *idea* of a Book, placed " within the *idea* of a foot of the *idea* of the eye, *&c.*" To expreſs this in common language, and yet ſuppoſe the expreſſion proper, is firſt to ſuppoſe the Book *placed*, and *really exiſting*; and then to infer from this ſuppoſition *that it is only an idea.* To apply common language to a quite contrary ſenſe, and then to ſuppoſe this *arbitrary application* an argument to overturn common ſenſe, or to contend for the *propriety* of ſuch application, is as inconſiſtent as any thing in the ſcheme. It is plain *figure*, *diſtance*, *magnitude*, *motion*, are no language on this hypotheſis. Theſe are ſuppoſed real in the *language*, and it is thence concluded there are no ſuch things. This is an open fallacy. It is certain, arguments for a *true hypotheſis*, may be expreſſed in words agreeable to that hypotheſis; and not in ſuch a language as *contradicts* and *ſuppoſes it falſe*. And ſince it is impoſſible for any man living, to do this on our *Author*'s principles; this itſelf is an invincible argument againſt them. Common language is adapted to the *objects* of our ideas, and *theſe principles*, to the *ideas* of objects: this muſt occaſion a conſtant oppoſition between any language and theſe principles, and ſhews that they contradict common language, as much as common ſenſe.

SECT.

A N

E S S A Y

O N T H E

EXISTENCE of MATTER,

WHEREIN

The extraordinary Philoſophy of the celebrated Dr *Berkeley*, Biſhop of *Cloyne*, is impartially conſidered, and fully confuted, and the Manner of the Exiſtence of external Bodies clearly explained.

In God we live, move, and have our Being.
Acts of the Apoſtles, xvii. 28.

——————*Jovis omnia plena.* VIRGIL.

L O N D O N:

Printed for E. CAVE, at St *John's Gate*. M,DCC,LI.
(Price Six-Pence.)

AN

ESSAY

ON THE

EXISTENCE of MATTER.

TO enumerate the various opinions of the antient philoſophers concerning matter, and to enter into an hiſtorical detail of all the diſputes about it, would afford a fine opportunity of making a ſhow of learning, and of ſwelling the bulk of a pamphlet; but as their opinions have been for the moſt part wild and extravagant, and as my ſole deſign is the advancement of knowledge, and the diſcovery of truth, I ſhall decline ſo tedious and ſo uſeleſs a taſk.

It may not, however, be amiſs juſt to obſerve, That the queſtion chiefly agitated amongſt the antients was, Whether matter was or was not eternal? And this ſeems to have been generally determined in the affirmative, by the moſt eminent philoſophers. Some of them were ſo thoughtleſs as to maintain that the world itſelf was eternal;

B but

but others, more penetrating and judicious, endeavour'd to qualify and moderate the glaring absurdity of this position, by asserting, That the original atoms, or particles of matter, the materials whereof the world was form'd, were indeed eternal; but that the world itself, the formation and disposition of these materials, must have been the work of an infinite intelligence. What inclined them still to maintain the eternal existence of the original atoms was, That they could not conceive how it was possible for matter to be created: as if what they could not conceive, could not be or as if the eternal existence of a matter, void of activity, were more easy to conceive than the creation of it.

But several learned moderns, and particularly the celebrated Dr *Samuel Clarke*, have demonstrated, by irrefragable arguments, that matter must have been created; and this they have done, even supposing matter to exist in a manner peculiar to itself, distinct from spirit, and in a sort of independency thereon, according to the vulgar notions of its existence; but that this supposition is erroneous will be fully shewn hereafter.

Nor have the moderns been altogether free from disputes and diversity of opinion, upon the manner of the existence of matter. There have appeared amongst them two systems, equally singular, but diametrically opposite. One of them has for its author *Benedict Spinoza*, a *Jew* born at *Amsterdam*.

This

This man not being able to conceive that matter could be created out of nothing, nor that a ſubſtance void of activity, could exiſt neceſſarily and from eternity, to avoid theſe difficulties fell into the groſſeſt abſurdities. He maintained, That there was but one ſubſtance in nature, which is God; That this ſubſtance has an infinitude of attributes, amongſt which are cogitation and extenſion; and that all the beings in the univerſe, whether material or ſpiritual, are nothing but modifications of this ſubſtance form'd in it, and by it, by an immanent act, and a certain natural power and virtue inherent therein: Poſitions ſo repugnant to all ſenſe and reaſon, that barely to mention them is to confute them. This chaos of a doctrine would probably have by this time ſunk into oblivion, had not numbers of learned men, inſtead of diſregarding it and truſting it to its own abſurdity and extravagance for an antidote; had not they, I ſay, over zealouſly confuted it over and over again, and by that means kept the remembrance of it alive. But ſuch is the veneration paid by mankind to learned language, and elegance, and perſpicuity of expreſſion, that the ſame ſentiments, which, in an illiterate man, would have been at once, and without heſitation, pronounced to be the effect of ſtupidity, folly, or madneſs, when eſpous'd and deliver'd by a *Spinoza*, are aſcribed to an extraordinary ſtrength of genius, and an uncommon ſagacity and penetration, and

and thought worthy of a ſerious regard and confutation.—Whoever is not at firſt ſight convinced of the abſurdity of this doctrine, may ſee it effectually confuted in *Chambers*'s Dictionary under the article *Spinoziſm.*

The other ſyſtem is that of Dr *Berkeley*, the preſent Lord Biſhop of *Cloyne*, which, as it is not attended with the impious, horrid, and abſurd conſequences, which flow from *Spinoziſm*, ſo it is much more ingenious and plauſible, and has never yet been effectually confuted, and therefore deſerves to be more particularly conſidered. *Spinoza* would have matter to be the only ſubſtance in nature, His Lordſhip on the contrary is ſuppoſed to contend, That matter has no external exiſtence at all, but is a mere *ens rationis*, and exiſts no where but in the percipient mind.

This ſyſtem was probably at firſt regarded more on account of the high reputation of its author, and its novelty, and paradoxical ſingularity, than from any the leaſt likelihood of its proving true. It was doubtleſs not expected that an opinion, ſo contrary to the ſeeming evidence of our ſenſes, our natural notions of things, and the univerſal conſent of mankind in all ages, could be proved. People, however, were curious to know by what ſubtilties and refinements ſo ſtartling a paradox could be maintained; and upon reading His Lordſhip's book his reaſoning appeared ſo plauſible and ſpecious, that many who read only to laugh, began to doubt, and they

they who ſought only amuſement, found, or thought they found, concluſive arguments, and irrefragable proofs.

In effect, Mr *Chambers*, in the *Cyclopædia*, ſpeaks very favourably of this opinion; and, by what has been publiſhed in the *Gentleman*'s *Magazine*, it appears that many gentlemen of good underſtanding, and unqueſtionable abilities, have been converted and perſuaded of its truth. Previouſly therefore to what I have to offer myſelf upon the ſubject, I ſhall impartially conſider the moſt material arguments by which this doctrine is ſupported.

To prevent the perplexity ariſing from ambiguities and confuſion of terms, and the better to enable us to diſcern the ſtrength or weakneſs of the arguments we are about to examine, I think it neceſſary to premiſe the following obſervations.

1. That uſing the terms Idea and Senſation as ſynonymous, has occaſion'd ſome confuſion in this ſubject. The actual perception of the ſun, and the idea of the ſun are very different things, and ought to be carefully diſtinguiſh'd. By Senſation then is always to be underſtood, an impreſſion made upon the mind, whereof the mind itſelf is not the cauſe: And by Idea is meant an image or perception form'd by and in the mind by the power of imagination. — Our ſenſations are not in our power, nor dependent upon us, as our ideas are.

2. That

2. That secondary qualities of external bodies, as they are improperly called, are not qualities of the bodies themselves, and do not exist therein, but are sensations or affections of the mind impressed upon, or excited in it, by those things which we call external bodies. They are perceptions of the effect of something external upon the mind, and exist only therein, but are no more qualities of that something, than the agitation of the surface of the water by a stone thrown into it, is a quality of that stone, or than the impression of a seal in wax is the quality of the seal. Thus the secondary qualities, as they are called, of heat, cold, colours, tastes, smells, are not any qualities existing in the bodies by which they are occasion'd, but mere sensations and affections of our minds, or the effects of such bodies upon the mind.

3. That some of our sensations are simple, others complex: some are attended and inseparably connected with certain qualities, circumstances, or modifications, which enable us to perceive something beyond the bare sensation itself; whilst others are quite pure, simple, and unattended by any circumstances at all. Thus, heat, cold, tastes, smells are simple sensations, but colour is a complex one. Colour is always figured and extended, at rest, or in motion, *&c.* Whence we conclude, that extension, figure, rest, motion, *&c.* are qualities or cir-

circumſtances which exiſt in the immediate cauſe of the ſenſation of colour; extenſion, figure, &c. are manifeſtly not ſenſations themſelves, but only circumſtances or modifications wherewith certain ſenſations are always attended. Figure, &c. cannot be ſaid to make an impreſſion, or have any effect at all upon the mind: 'tis colour conſidered abſtractedly in itſelf, which is the affection or impreſſion made upon the mind; and figure muſt be a quality exiſting in that thing which is the immediate cauſe of this impreſſion.

4. The evidence which our ſenſes afford of the exiſtence of external bodies, is preciſely this and no more. We perceive a colour, it is figured and extended, we know we are not the cauſe of this perception, and it ſeems to proceed from ſomething external. To be more fully ſatisfied of the exiſtence of this ſomething, we apply to it ſome of the other organs of ſenſe, and find that we feel, taſte, ſmell it, &c. and hence conclude that this ſomething, from whence all theſe different ſenſations ſeem to proceed, has a real external exiſtence; the manner of which exiſtence will be conſidered and explained hereafter.

Theſe things being premiſed, will ſerve inſtead of a clue to conduct us through the mazes of the *Berkleian Labyrinth*. In the firſt argument which we think proper to take notice of, His Lordſhip begins with ob-

obſerving, That when we ſay any thing exiſts we mean no more than that we perceive it. " Thus, ſays he, the table I write on ex- " iſts, *i. e.* I ſee and feel it, *&c.* What " are light, colours, heat, cold, extenſion " and figure, in a word the things we ſee " and feel, but ſo many impreſſions on the " ſenſe? And is it poſſible to ſeparate, even " in thought, any of theſe from perception? " —— The things we perceive are colour " figure, motion, *&c. i. e.* the ideas (or " *ſenſations*) of thoſe things; but has an " idea (or *ſenſation*) any exiſtence out of " the mind? To have an idea (or *ſenſa-* " *tion*) is the ſame thing as to perceive; " that therefore wherein colour, figure, *&c.* " exiſt, muſt perceive them. —— But you " may argue, if the ideas (or *ſenſations*) " themſelves do not exiſt without the mind, " there may be things like them, whereof " they are copies or reſemblances, which " exiſt out of the mind: It is anſwer'd, " an idea (or *ſenſation*) can be like nothing " but an idea (or *ſenſation*); a colour, or " figure, can be like nothing but another " colour, or figure.——It may be further " aſk'd, Whether thoſe ſuppos'd originals, " or external things whereof our ideas (or " *ſenſations*) are the pictures, be them- " ſelves perceivable or not? If they be, " they are ideas (or *ſenſations*); if they be " not, I appeal to any one, whether it be " ſenſe to ſay a colour is like ſomething " which is inviſible, *&c.*" Up-

Upon this paſſage I would obſerve firſt, That his Lordſhip makes uſe of the term *idea* throughout, whereas he is manifeſtly ſpeaking of our ſenſations; wherefore, wherever the term *idea* occurs, I have added the words " or ſenſations" (the definition whereof is premiſed) in order to render the paſſage more intelligible. I would further obſerve, That his Lordſhip conſiders our ſenſations as pictures, copies, or reſemblances of thoſe external things which his opponents ſuppoſe to exiſt; which is wrong. Our ideas indeed are pictures or copies of our ſenſations, but our ſenſations in general cannot be ſaid to be pictures of external bodies. Is it ſenſe to ſay, that taſte or ſmell are pictures of the external bodies which excite them? I thought theſe obſervations neceſſary to diſembarraſs the paſſage a little, and when it is thus clear'd up, it will appear, that the arguments made uſe of prove nothing more than that our ſenſations have no exiſtence but in our own minds: a point wherein we entirely agree with his Lordſhip; but then we deny that extenſion and figure can be properly called ſenſations (*See the third obſervation premiſed*) and inſiſt they are qualities of the immediate cauſe of our ſenſations, and only perceived by means of a ſenſation wherewith they have a neceſſary and inſeparable connection; but this will be further explain'd as we go on.

C The

The next paſſage which merits conſideration is this; " Some diſtinguiſh between " primary and ſecondary qualities, and maintain, that the former, as extenſion, figure, " ſolidity, motion, reſt and number have " a real exiſtence out of the mind; but that " the latter, *viz.* ſounds, taſtes, ſmells, *&c.* " exiſt only in the mind. Now can any " one conceive the extenſion and motion of " a body without all the other ſenſible " qualities? For my part I find it impoſſible " to frame an idea of a body extended and " moving, without giving it ſome colour, " *&c.* In effect extenſion, figure, motion, " abſtracted from all other qualities, are inconceivable. Where the other are, therefore, theſe muſt be too, that is, in the " mind, and no where elſe".

The truth is, that ſecondary qualities alone (as they are improperly called) are the things by which the mind is affected, and which indeed are ſenſations exiſting only therein. And ſome of theſe ſenſations, colour for inſtance, we can neither conceive nor perceive without its neceſſary concomitants, figure and extenſion. But whether it be more reaſonable to conclude from this, that figure, extenſion and the other primary qualities exiſt only in the mind, or that they are qualities which exiſt (without us) in the immediate cauſe of our ſenſations, and which occaſion certain ſenſations (as colour) to be modified in a particular

cular manner, I leave to every impartial reader to determine. (*See the observations premised.*)

"Again, continues His Lordship, great "and small, swift and slow, are allowed to "exist no where without the mind, being "merely relative, or changing as the frame "or position of the organ changes. The "extension therefore that exists without "the mind is neither great nor small, the "motion neither swift nor slow, *i. e.* they "are nothing". With submission to His Lordship, I think this way of reasoning very strange. Who allows that great and small, *&c.* exist no where without the mind? For my part, I allow no such thing. Because an object appears great or small as its distance from us is either greater or less, is therefore that object neither great nor small? And is it therefore a mere non-entity? Is it not much more reasonable to conclude that, because we find the magnitude of objects changes as the position of the organ changes, therefore extension must be something which exists without us? For if it existed only in the mind, changing the position of the organ could not alter it all, because, with respect to the mind, the organ is always in the same position.

"That number, says the Bishop, is a "creature of the mind is plain (even though "the other qualities were allowed to exist) "from this; that the same thing bears a "dif-

" different denomination of numbers as the " mind views it with different respect: " thus the same extension is 1, 3, or 36, " as the mind considers it with reference to " a yard, a foot, or an inch."

This way of reasoning, I must own, is much too refined for my comprehension. What! because we can divide a thing into 3 or 36 equal parts just as we please, does it therefore follow that number does not exist without us? Is the number of the stars the creature of my mind? and can I make them either more or fewer? One can hardly forbear lifting up one's hands and eyes at such a demonstration.

His Lordship endeavours to prove, by some other observations, that number, extension, and motion have no existence without the mind: but as the arguments he uses are much of the same nature with those already produced, and have still less force in them, we shall not weary the reader with confuting the same things over and over again, but proceed to his chief and *Herculean* argument, which is this: "Again, were it possible for " solid, figured bodies to exist out of the " mind, yet it were impossible for us ever " to know it; our senses indeed give us sen- " sations, but do not tell us that any things " exist out of the mind, or unperceived, " like those which are perceived: This " the Materialists allow. No other way " therefore remains but that we know them

" by

"by reasons inferring their existence from "what is immediately perceived by sense. "But how should reason do this, when it is "confessed there is not any necessary con-"nection between our sensations and these "bodies? It is evident from the phænome-"na of dreams, phrenzies, &c. that we "may be affected with the ideas we now "have, though there were no bodies ex-"isting without us. Nor does the suppo-"sition of external bodies at all forward us "in conceiving how our ideas should come "to be produced. The Materialists own "themselves unable to conceive in what "manner body can act on spirit, or how it "should imprint any idea upon the mind. "To suppose therefore bodies existing with-"out the mind, is to suppose God has crea-"ted innumerable beings entirely useless, "and serving no purpose at all. On the "whole, it appears, that the existence of "bodies out of a mind perceiving them, is "not only impossible, but a contradiction "in terms. But were it possible, nay real, "it were impossible we should ever know "it. And again, supposing there were no "such things, yet we should have the very "same reason to believe there were, that we "now have. Suppose, *v. g.* an intelli-"gence affected with the same train of sen-"sations, impressed in the same order, and "with the same vividness; would it not have "all the reason to believe the existence of "bo-

" bodies, reprefented by its ideas, that we
" have?

Now in anfwer to this, I beg leave to obferve, that I have already partly fhewn, that from what is perceived by fenfe, we may fairly infer the exiftence of fomething external. It is true indeed that, fuppofing external bodies to exift, we cannot conceive perfectly how, by their means, fenfations are excited in the mind; but it does not follow from thence, that it is impoffible external bodies fhould have fuch an effect upon our minds. We fhould make fine work of it, were we to conclude, that every thing we don't know, or cannot conceive, is impoffible. Befides, we cannot conceive *how* our fenfations are produced either way; this difficulty is the fame, whether external bodies be fuppofed to exift, or not to exift: if therefore this argument proves any thing, it proves that it is impoffible we fhould have any fenfations at all; which is falfe and abfurd. As to what we perceive in dreams, or phrenzies, they are the ideas formed by our own minds, which, in thefe circumftances, are more ftrong and vivid, becaufe, in the former cafe, the works of our imagination are not contrafted nor interrupted by fenfations from without; and, in the latter cafe, the body and the organs of fenfe are difordered in fo particular a manner, as to ftrengthen and invigorate the effects of the imagination. But we are not to conclude
from

from thence, that any other power or being whatever could excite ideas in our minds, in the ſame manner, without the mediation of external objects. His Lordſhip owns we are not the cauſes of our ſenſations (as will preſently appear); the cauſe of them then is ſomething external, and it will be ſhewn that this cauſe does not excite them any other way than by rendering external objects perceptible to us. With reſpect to the ſuppoſition which cloſes the paſſage cited, I beg leave to ſay, That it is nothing at all to the purpoſe; it is perhaps ſuppoſing an impoſſibility. Intelligences affected with the ſame ſenſations we are affected with, would conclude as we do, with good reaſon, that external bodies exiſted; and they would alſo ſee that it was impoſſible they ſhould have any ſuch ſenſations, if external objects did not exiſt. In ſhort, His Lordſhip's ſuppoſition amounts to no more than this; *Suppoſing the matter in diſpute to be as I repreſent it to be, will it not follow that I am in the right?*

From the nature and tendency of the foregoing arguments, ſome perſons, and one very learned man amongſt the reſt, have imagined, that it was His Lordſhip's opinion that external bodies are *entes rationis*, mere creatures of our own minds, formed only in them, and by them: but this is a miſtake, His Lordſhip was incapable of ſo abſurd an opinion. He maintains indeed, that what we call external bodies are only ſenſations or ideas,

ideas, which exiſt no where but in the mind perceiving them, and have no external exiſtence at all: but he does not aſſert that we ourſelves are the cauſes of theſe ſenſations; on the contrary, he declares, that they are excited in our minds by the ſupreme being. For thus he afterwards explains himſelf: "It "has been proved our ſenſations do not de-"pend on any external body, as their "cauſe: it remains therefore that their cauſe "be an incorporeal, active ſubſtance or ſpirit. "For that I am not the cauſe of my own "ſenſations, is plain from this, that, when "I open my eyes in broad day-light, I can-"not help ſeeing various objects. Now the "fixed rules or methods wherein the mind "we depend on excites ſenſations in us, are "called *laws of nature*, theſe we learn by "experience.—Ideas (or *ſenſations*) are not "any how or at random produced; there "is a certain order and connexion eſtabliſhed "amongſt them, like that of cauſe and effect; "and there are ſeveral combinations of "them, made in a very regular and artful "manner, which we call bodies; and the "ſyſtem of thoſe, the world, *&c.*"—Now from this doctrine, thus explained by himſelf, it will inevitably follow, that bodies have an exiſtence external to our minds. For the originals of our ſenſations muſt pre-exiſt in that mind by which our ſenſations are excited: it is utterly inconceivable that one mind ſhould excite ſenſations in another,

without

without firſt, preconceiving ideas, or originals of ſuch ſenſations in itſelf. Thoſe things therefore which we call external bodies, do exiſt externally, for they really exiſt in the univerſal mind, and are indeed no other than its ideas; and our ſenſations ariſe from theſe ideas being rendered in a certain degree perceptible to us. It looks therefore very like a contradiction; and is ſeemingly an inconſiſtency, for His Lordſhip to contend in one part of his book, that bodies have no exiſtence but in *the mind* perceiving them, and in another part to own (as indeed he could not avoid owning) that our ſenſations are excited by the univerſal mind. For if they be (as undoubtedly they are) the originals of our ſenſations, or thoſe things we call external bodies, they muſt really exiſt in the univerſal mind, and in that alone, and our ſenſations muſt be only the effects of them upon our minds, by which they are rendered perceptible to us. To evince this yet further, Let us ſuppoſe a million of men gathered together in the ſame place, viewing the heavens, and all the hoſt of them, in a clear night. I would aſk His Lordſhip, whether it be more probable to ſuppoſe, that a million of different perceptions of the heavens are at the ſame inſtant excited by the ſupreme being, in all thoſe different minds (which amounts to much the ſame thing, as inſtantaneouſly creating a million of univerſes) or that there is an heaven really exiſting in

D the

the universal mind, and consequently external to our minds, which, being one and the same object, is rendered perceptible to this million of spectators, by their being respectively endowed with the proper organs of perception? Again, the universal mind either perceives some of the things which we perceive, or it does not: To assert the negative is to assert, that the supreme being has no perception of the visible world; which His Lordship, I dare say, does not believe. The supreme being then has some perceptions in common with us; and what are they? They cannot be colours, tastes, heat, or cold, or any other of our sensations, which are purely relative to our minds, and which all agree exist only in them: and, with respect to them, to say this, would be little better than blasphemy. The things therefore which remain for the universal mind to perceive, in common with us, are extension, figure, rest, motion, number, *&c.* which do not exist in our minds, but are indeed qualities of the ideas of the divine mind, and have their existence in it alone. The primary qualities of bodies (as they are called by philosophers) are therefore the qualities of the divine ideas; and secondary qualities, as sounds, colours, *&c.* are no other than sensations excited in our minds in consequence of the divine ideas being rendered perceptible to us. The truth therefore is, not that bodies or matter have no existence without the mind perceiving them,

them; as the Biſhop contends; but that they have a real exiſtence external to our minds, and are indeed the ideas of the univerſal mind, formed in it, and by it, and perfectly perceived and comprehended by it, but imperfectly by us: A truth, which will be fully and ſatisfactorily eſtabliſhed, by conſidering the nature of ideas formed in a mind or ſpirit, ſo far as is diſcoverable by reflecting upon what paſſes in our minds.

We are told by an inſpir'd writer, That we were created in the image of God; and perhaps this reſemblance to our Creator is nothing more plainly manifeſted than in the power of imagination we are endued with. It may perhaps to ſome appear derogatory to the perfections of the ſupreme being to attribute any thing like this to him, becauſe of the irregular excurſions and wanton extravagancies, whereof this faculty of the human mind is frequently guilty. But if we conſider it ſimply, as a power of forming ideas, it will appear to be one of the prime and moſt excellent faculties of the mind. It is even much to be queſtioned whether without this power we ſhould be capable of remembring, meditating, or reflecting at all. Nor are even the light and ſportive exertions of this faculty, when regular and rational, the leaſt valuable, or leaſt delightful operations of the ſoul. We can retire within ourſelves, and form at pleaſure a little world of our own. We can preſently, by by this power, bring into being an elyſium bleſs'd with unclouded ſuns, enliven'd with all the verdure, and adorn'd with all the flowery tribes of ſpring, or enrich'd with all the plenty of autumn; a world wherein we rule with deſpotic ſway, admit or reject what we pleaſe, and give or take away being as we think proper. Now what is this but a ſort of creation in miniature? And could we form in our minds percipient beings, or ideas, to which this ideal elyſium ſhould be perceptible as well as to us, we ſhould exactly imitate the great Creator: but here we are ſtopp'd. This is a privilege which the univerſal mind has reſerved to itſelf, a power of forming percipient beings belongs to it alone. From the whole we may conclude, That to attribute the power of imagination to the univerſal mind, is ſo far from being derogatory to its perfections, that it is probably a power eſſential to all mind or ſpirit whatever, and that very power by which the viſible world was created and ſubſiſts.

But when we conſider this power as exiſting in the divine mind, we muſt carefully keep in view the vaſt diſparity there is between finite and infinite; and remember that it muſt be, as well in nature as degree, infinitely ſuperior to the ſimilar power in our minds. The manner of exertion may probably be the ſame, but its operations and effects muſt be infinitely more per-

fect

fect and excellent. The divine ideas must be more perfect, more permanent, and have a far different, and much more real existence than ours. The properties of our ideas are only these, to be perceivable by the mind wherein they are form'd, and to be similar to, or compounded of the sensations which such mind had before perceived. The divine ideas may have properties which we can neither know nor conceive; this extraordinary property they certainly have, to be capable of being perceived by all created minds, so far as their properly-adapted perceptive powers permit. The universal mind has probably establish'd a certain order amongst certain classes of its own ideas, governs them by various rules and laws, compounds and connects them in a certain regular and determinate manner. The supreme being may also permit created minds, by means of the powers he has furnish'd them with, to make slight alterations in some of his ideas to a certain degree, and to adapt and apply them to certain ends and purposes, which he has enabled them to discern, and inclined them to aim at. And is not this the same thing as to create a world? Is not the creation better conceived in this view, than by supposing matter to be a substance distinct from spirit, and existing in a sort of independency?—In fine, the more I consider, the more I am convinced, that all mat-

matter, and all its various compoſitions, or (to uſe the Biſhop of *Cloyne*'s expreſſion) All the choir of heaven, and all the furniture of earth, are but a part, and that a very ſmall part too, of the divine ideas rendered perceptible to created minds, in a certain meaſure, proportion, and degree, by means of different and properly-adapted inſtruments or organs of ſenſe.

And here let us pauſe a little, to contemplate the grandeur and immenſity of the new ſcene of things, which this manner of conception opens to our view.—If the power of forming ideas be ſo unlimited in created minds, if our thoughts have ſuch an unmeaſured ſcope, how infinitely numerous, how inconceivably extenſive, muſt be the thoughts and ideas of an univerſal infinite mind! Vaſt and immenſe beyond our reach, grand and magnificent beyond conception, does this little ſyſtem of ideas appear, which we call the univerſe, and whereof we have but a very partial and ſuperficial view. But when we conceive things in the manner juſt now explained, when we take them in this light, how little and inconſiderable does all this comparatively appear! What a very ſmall proportion muſt that part of the divine ideas, which is rendered perceptible to our narrow minds, bear to the infinitude of ideas which muſt exiſt in an infinite mind!——When we conſider the nature of ſpirit, is it not

not probable, that this universe, vast as it is, is no more than a single thought or idea of the universal mind, and bears no greater proportion to the infinite number of ideas, and systems of ideas, existent therein, than a grain of sand does to the sphere of the fixed stars? There are probably immense numbers of classes and degrees of created intelligences, to each of which classes the supreme being has render'd a certain portion of his ideas perceptible, by means of proper organs, suited and adapted to the nature of each system of ideas, and to the nature of each class of percipients, in some such like manner as this universe, or system of ideas, is by our organs rendered perceptible to us. In short, each class of created intelligences has probably its universe, to the perception whereof its perceptive powers are adapted and confined. Nay, for ought we know, there may be, and probably are, classes of spirits, whose perceptive powers may be so general and extensive, as to give them a view and insight into several universes, or spheres of perception of subordinate classes of spirits; not only one but many systems of the divine ideas may be perceptible to them, they may have views and superintendencies more or less general. Hence perhaps the distinctions of thrones, dominions, principalities and powers, into which revelation divides the hierarchies of spirits.—We may push our conjectures one step

ſtep farther, and with great probability ſuppoſe that there are ſyſtems of ideas in the univerſal mind, which have never yet been communicated to any created minds or intelligences whatever.—But to reſume our reaſoning.

The Schoolmen and Platoniſts have indeed diſtinguiſhed between the ideas of things in the divine mind, and the things themſelves conſidered as actually created, and brought into exiſtence: A diſtinction, for which there is not the leaſt ground or foundation. As ſoon as an idea is formed in the divine mind, it muſt have all the perfection and real exiſtence it can poſſibly have. To ſuppoſe it has any further degree or reality of exiſtence, is utterly abſurd and inconceivable; for, in the univerſal mind, to conceive a thing, and to bring it into being, muſt be one and the ſame act. We ourſelves indeed firſt form ideas in our minds, and then carry them into execution, and give them a real external exiſtence, by impreſſing the likeneſs of our preconceived ideas upon matter, which is an idea of the univerſal mind, and by that means render our ideas univerſally perceptible. And hence the diſtinction of the idea of a thing, and the real exiſtence of that thing, with reſpect to the acts and operations of our minds. But it is plain no ſuch diſtinction can ſubſiſt with reſpect to the univerſal mind, becauſe an idea exiſting

therein

therein is univerſally perceptible, and actually perceived, by created minds, ſo far as their circumſtances and perceptive powers permit; and therefore any further realization of ſuch idea, is neither neceſſary nor conceivable. Add to this, that it is agreed on all hands, that this material world is immediately preſent to, and perceived, and pervaded by the univerſal mind: and if ſo, it can be nothing elſe but a ſyſtem of ideas formed in, and by that mind; for it is ſcarce conceivable how ſuch an intimate connexion ſhould ſubſiſt between a ſpirit and any thing elſe but its own ideas. The divine ideas may indeed be conſidered in two different reſpects, either as exiſting in the divine mind, unperceived by any other mind whatever, or as they are perceived by created minds: but their being rendered perceptible to us, does not give them an exiſtence different from, and more perfect than the exiſtence they had before. Creating therefore, or bringing a thing into being, with reſpect to us, is only furniſhing our minds with proper powers to perceive that thing: but, with reſpect to the univerſal mind, when an idea exiſts therein, it is both perceived by that mind, and capable of being perceived by all other minds; ſo that there can be no reaſon nor foundation for diſtinguiſhing between the ideas of things, and the things themſelves, with regard to the univerſal mind.

Nor is the doctrine we have been inculcat-

E ing

ing altogether unſupported by authorities. That external bodies are nothing elſe but the divine ideas, ſeems to have been the ſentiment of the great *Newton*, tho' he never fully explained and inſiſted upon it. It was an applauded notion of his, that infinite ſpace is the *ſenſorium* of the deity, and that as the ſpecies of things are preſent to our *ſenſoriola*, ſo in like manner to the *ſenſorium* of the deity the things themſelves are preſent: A ſentiment, which, if it be explained, examined and purſued, will be found to approach very near to, if it does not perfectly coincide with, the opinion we have endeavoured to eſtabliſh.

This ſyſtem, as it is not a mere hypotheſis, but is founded upon our knowledge of our own minds, and the analogy ſubſiſting between a finite and infinite mind, ſo it furniſhes us with ſuch clear conceptions as enable us to overcome difficulties which have perplexed the philoſophers of all ages, and upon that account acquires the greater probability.

Many are the difficulties which have been raiſed concerning the creation and annihilation of matter, which upon our ſyſtem entirely vaniſh. For if, as we think, we have ſufficiently proved, the univerſe be nothing but a ſyſtem of the divine ideas, it is plain and eaſy to be conceived, that theſe ideas muſt be formed by the divine mind with as great, perhaps much greater, facility than our ideas

ideas are formed in and by our minds; and that with the fame eafe they may be expunged and annihilated. How indeed this is effected, is impoffible for us to know: we don't know how we form our own ideas (but we know we do and can form them) much lefs can we expect to know how the divine ideas are formed. It is manifeft, therefore, that to create an univerfe, or to annihilate it, nothing more is neceffary than a refolution or volition of the univerfal mind. And how confonant and agreeable is all this to the language of revelation!—"Let there be light, and there "was light."——"He fpake, and they were "made: He commanded, and they were "created."

Various have been the opinions of philofophers concerning the age of the world, and by many ftrange arguments have they attempted to inveftigate it. *Ocellus Lucanus*, *Plato*, and *Ariftotle* were of opinion that the world flow'd from God as rays from the fun, and that it muft be eternal, becaufe it was impoffible an eternal agent, having an eternal paffive fubject (for they fuppofed the original particles of matter to be eternal) could continue long without action. An argument, which fhews they had very imperfect and erroneous notions both of matter and fpirit. An infinite mind could always find employment in the pure contemplation of its own ideas. But fuch ridiculous reafoning will always be the confequence of attempting to deter-

determine things by reafon which are not determinable by it. It is not improbable indeed but that the feveral fyftems of ideas in the divine mind may have their refpective durations, or times of exiftence allotted them, at the expiration whereof they may ceafe to be, and be fucceeded by new fyftems. But when any particular fyftem of ideas began to exift, or when it will ceafe to exift, are circumftances which can be known only to that mind wherein they exift, which depend entirely upon the divine will, and can be known to no other minds any further than it pleafes the univerfal mind to reveal them.

Queftions have been agitated concerning the locality of heaven or hell, which are equally vain and indeterminable. The heaven or hell of a rational and percipient mind, confifts in its being affected with perceptions infinitely pleafant and agreeable, or exceffively painful and tormenting; but thefe perceptions have no neceffary relation to place at all, and may very probably not be caufed by, nor have any relation to, any of the bodies whereof the univerfe we at prefent perceive confifts, but may arife from quite different fyftems of the divine ideas, whereof we can at prefent form no notion or conception at all. Certain it feems to be, that when our minds are deprived of their prefent organs of fenfe, by which the communication between them and

and the present external world is kept open, they will not be able to perceive any of the things which they now perceive, and probably an entirely new system of perceptions will break in upon them, either in consequence of their disembodied state, or by means of some new perceptive powers they may be furnished with.

Men have been very bold and presumptuous in their disputes concerning free-will, and some have even gone so far as to pronounce it irreconcileable with the goodness of the supreme being to create free-agents. Such rash judgments, in things whereof we have a very imperfect knowledge, are inexcusable. We have seen that impercipient bodies are ideas of the divine mind, inactive in themselves, and entirely dependent thereon. Their existence is easily conceivable: To form beings with perceptive powers, and perceptions, distinct from those of the universal mind, is a far higher exertion of omnipotence; an operation whereof we can form no analogous conceptions at all. Only thus much we may discern, that the very nature of a distinct perception seems necessarily to require a good measure of freedom and independence in the percipient; and it is therefore probable, and I strongly suspect, that free-will is the necessary result, an inevitable consequence of endowing a being with reason and perception: and to say that free-agents ought not to have been created, is in ef-

being, That they exiſt only in our minds, and have no external originals, or ſecondary cauſes at all. The opinion maintained in this pamphlet is, That our ſenſations (properly ſo called) exiſt indeed in our own minds alone, but that the immediate cauſes of them are external, and are indeed no other than the divine ideas, which make theſe impreſſions upon our minds by means of the organs of ſenſe.

Of theſe three opinions, the firſt, which maintains external bodies to be a ſort of diſtinct and independent ſubſtances, is utterly inconceivable. The ſecond we have ſhewn to be partly falſe, and partly imperfect, contradictory and indigeſted. To prove the third, which aſſerts that thoſe things which we call external bodies, and which are the immediate cauſes of our ſenſations, are no other than the divine ideas; to prove this, I ſay, to be the moſt probable opinion of the three, nothing more ſeems to be neceſſary, than to ſhew that the divine ideas may be rendered perceptible to us, without the intervention of any diſtinct ſubſtance. To evince this, it may ſuffice to obſerve, that tho' our minds have no direct and immediate communication at all with each other, but are kept apart, and as it were ſhut up ſeparately and impriſoned, yet by means of certain ſounds and characters we can communicate, and impreſs our ideas upon each other. And ſurely the univerſal mind which per-

effect to ſay that no rational percipient beings at all ought to have been created. And to aſſert that man ought to have been placed in better circumſtances than he is placed in, is perhaps to aſſert; that different ſyſtems of ideas ought not to have been formed in, nor different claſſes of intelligences created by, the univerſal mind; and for men to talk in this manner; is to ſet themſelves above their creator.

Thus much may ſuffice to ſhew, that difficulties are more eaſily ſolved upon this ſyſtem than upon any other. The ſingularity of it however ſeems to require, that, by way of concluſion, we ſhould briefly recapitulate the arguments made uſe of, that being collected together and abridged, they may have a greater force and effect, and leave a deeper impreſſion upon the mind of the reader.

That our ſenſations are excited in our minds by ſome external cauſe, is evident, and acknowledged by all: That the firſt and original cauſe of them is the ſupreme being, is no leſs certain: The only point in diſpute is, What is the ſecondary or immediate cauſe of them. The common opinion is, That they are the impreſſions of external bodies, or ſubſtances which are diſtinct from ſpirit, and in ſome degree independent thereon. The opinion of the Biſhop of *Cloyne* is, That they are immediately excited in our minds by the ſupreme be-

pervades all things, to which all created minds are immediately preſent, open, and acceſſible, muſt have a power of communicating its ideas to, and impreſſing them upon our minds, by properly-adapted means, in a manner much more ſtrong and lively. Nor will it avail any thing to object, that ideas are mere forms and phantoms, fugitive and ſhadowy beings, which are not real and ſubſtantial enough to produce the effects we would aſcribe to them: for this is only true of the ideas we form in our own minds. They are indeed ſuch, for they are only ſlight, imperfect, imitations of the effects which the divine ideas have upon our minds. We cannot form any real or original ideas, we can only copy, combine, or compound the ſenſations or impreſſions made upon our mind. But it is manifeſt that a power of forming ideas of ſome ſort is eſſential to all minds, and conſequently the univerſal mind, which has nothing to copy after, muſt have a power of forming real and perfect ideas. All its ideas muſt be originals, and endued with qualities and properties which our ideas have not. The divine ideas muſt be as much more perfect than ours, as a living man is a more perfect being than his picture, or in the ſame degree as the creating mind is more perfect than the created; and conſequently muſt have all the qualities and properties aſcribed to external bodies, and all the requiſites to

excite

excite perception. Upon the whole it ſeems very clear, that matter and all its various compoſitions, which we call external bodies, are nothing but the divine ideas exiſting in the divine mind, in much the ſame manner as our ideas exiſt in our minds; and that real, poſitive, and abſolute exiſtence can be predicated of nothing but ſpirit, *i. e.* the univerſal and created minds, all other things having only an exiſtence relative thereto, and dependent thereon. So that if by a figure of ſpeech we ſubſtitute the effect for the cauſe, that of *Cato* in the *Pharſalia* would be true,

Jupiter *eſt quodcunque vides, quocunque moveris.*

FINIS.

THE FIRST PRINCIPLES OF METAPHYSICS and LOGIC.

Together with

The Progress of the Human Mind towards its Perfection.

CHAP. I.

Of the Mind in general, its Objects and Operations.

The Design.

1. IT is my Design in the following Essay, to trace out, in as short a Compass as I can, the several Steps of the Mind of Man, from the first Impressions of Sense, through the several Improvements it gradually makes, till it arrives to that Perfection and Enjoyment of itself, which is the great End of its Being.——In order to which, it will first be expedient to define what we mean by the *Human Mind*, and to give some Account of its various Objects, Powers and Operations, and the Principles and Rules by which they

they are to be conducted in attaining to the Knowlege of Truth, which is the Business of that Science which is called *LOGIC*, or *The Art of Thinking* and *Reasoning*; the Foundation of which is the *Philosophia prima*, which is also called *Metaphysics* and *Ontology*, or *the Doctrine of the general Notion of Being, with its various Properties and Affections*, and *those applied in general both to Body and Spirit*. And as *Truth* and *Good* are nearly allied, being in effect but the same Thing under different Considerations, this will pave the Way towards the Attainment of that supreme Good, in the Choice and Enjoyment of which consists our highest Happiness; the particular Consideration of which is the Business of *Ethics*, or *Moral Philosophy*, which teach *the Art of pursuing our highest Happiness by the universal Practice of Virtue*.

The Definition of Mind.

2. THE Word *Mind* or *Spirit*, in general, signifies any *intelligent active Being*; which Notion we take from what we are conscious of in ourselves, who know that we have within us a Principle of conscious Perception, Intelligence, Activity and Self-exertion; or rather, that each of us is a conscious, perceptive, intelligent, active and self-exerting Being: And by Reasoning and Analogy from ourselves we apply it to all other Minds or Intelligences besides, or superior to us; and (removing all Limitations and Imperfections) we apply it even to that *Great Supreme Intelligence*, who is the universal Parent of all created Spirits, and (as far as our Words and Conceptions can go) may be defined, *an infinite Mind* or *Spirit*, or *a Being infinitely intelligent and active*. But by the *Human Mind*, we mean that Principle of Sense, Intel-

Intelligence and free Activity, which we feel within ourselves, or rather feel ourselves to be, furnished with those Objects and Powers, and under those Confinements and Limitations, under which it hath pleased our great Creator to place us in this present State.

3. WE are, at present, *Spirits* or *Minds* connected with gross *tangible Bodies* in such a Manner, that as our Bodies can perceive and act nothing but by our Minds, so, on the other Hand, our Minds perceive and act by Means of our bodily Organs. Such is the present Law of our Nature, which I conceive to be no other than a meer arbitrary Constitution or Establishment of Him that hath made us to be what we are.—And accordingly I apprehend that the Union between our Souls and Bodies, during our present State, consists in nothing else but this Law of our Nature, which is the Will and perpetual *Fiat* of that infinite Parent Mind, who made, and *holds our Souls in Life*, and *in whom we live, and move, and have our Being*, viz. That our Bodies should be thus acted by our Minds, and that our Minds should thus perceive and act by the Organs of our Bodies, and under such Limitations as in fact we find ourselves to be attended with.

Of the Union of Body and Mind.

4. THE immediate Object of these our Perceptions and Actions we call *Ideas*; as this Word has been commonly defined and used by the Moderns, with whom it signifies any immediate Object of the Mind in Thinking, whether sensible or intellectual, and so is, in Effect, synonymous with the Word *Thought*, which comprehends both.-----*Plato*, indeed, by the Word *Idea*,

Definition of Idea, Notion, &c.

Idea, underſtood the original Exemplar of Things, whether ſenſible or intellectual, in the eternal Mind, conformable to which all Things exiſt; or the abſtract Eſſences of Things, as being Originals or *Archetypes* in that infinite Intellect, of which our Ideas or Conceptions are a Kind of Copies.----But perhaps, for the more diſtinct underſtanding ourſelves upon this Subject, it may be beſt to confine the Word *Idea* to the immediate Objects of Senſe and Imagination, which was the original Meaning of it; and to uſe the Word *Notion* or *Conception*, to ſignify the Objects of Conſciouſneſs and pure Intellect, tho' both of them may be expreſſed by the general Term *Thought*; for theſe are ſo entirely, and *toto Cœlo* different and diſtinct one from the other, that it may be apt to breed Confuſion in our Thoughts and Language, to uſe the ſame Word promiſcuouſly for them both; tho' we are indeed generally obliged to ſubſtitute ſenſible Images and the Words annexed to them, to repreſent Things purely intellectual; ſuch, for Inſtance, are the Words, *Spirit*, *Reflect*, *Conceive*, *Diſcourſe*, and the like.

The Original of our Ideas.

5. Our Minds may be ſaid to be created meer *Tabulæ raſæ*; i. e. They have no Notices of any Objects of any Kind properly created in them, or concreated with them: Yet I apprehend, that in all the Notices they have of any Kind of Objects, they have an immediate Dependance upon the Deity, as really as they depend upon Him for their Exiſtence; *i. e.* They are no more Authors to themſelves of the Objects of their Perceptions, or the Light by which they perceive them, than of the Power of Perceiving itſelf; but

but that they perceive them by a perpetual Intercourse with that great Parent Mind, to whose incessant Agency they are entirely passive, both in all the Perceptions of Sense, and in all that intellectual Light by which they perceive the Objects of the pure Intellect.-------Notwithstanding which, it is plain from Experience, that in Consequence of these Perceptions they are entirely at Liberty to act, or not to act, and all their Actions flow from a Principle of Self-exertion. But in order the better to understand these Things, I must more particularly define these Terms. And, as all the Notices we have in our Minds derive to them originally from (or rather by Means of) these two Fountains, *Sense* and *Consciousness*, it it necessary to begin with them.

Of the Senses;

6. By *Sense*, we mean, those Perceptions we have of Objects *ab extra*, or by Means of the several Organs of our Bodies.—Thus, by *Feeling* or Touch, we perceive an endless Variety of *tangible Objects*, *Resistance*, *Extension*, *Figure*, *Motion*, *Hard*, *Soft*, *Heat*, *Cold*, &c. By *Sight* we perceive *Light* and *Colors*, with all their endlesly various Modifications, *Red*, *Blue*, *Green*, &c. By *Hearing*, we perceive *Sounds*: By *Tasting*, *Sapors*: By *Smelling*, *Odors*, &c.---These are called *Simple Ideas*. And of these, sorted out into a vast Variety of fixed Combinations, or *Compound Ideas*, distinct from each other, and in which they are always found to co-exist, consists every Sort and individual *Body* in Nature, such as we call *Man*, *Horse*, *Tree*, *Stone*, *Apple*, *Cherry*, *&c.*-----And of all these various distinct Combinations or Compounds, connected together in such a Manner as to constitute one most beautiful, useful and harmonious

monious Whole, consists what we call *Universal Nature*, or the intire *sensible* or *natural World*.

In which we are passive.

7. In the Perception of these Ideas or Objects of Sense, we find our Minds are meerly passive, it not being in our Power (supposing our Organs rightly disposed and situated) whether we will see Light and Colours, hear Sounds, *&c.* We are not Causes to ourselves of these Perceptions, nor can they be produced in our Minds without a Cause; or (which is the same Thing) by any imagined unintelligent, inert, or unactive Cause, (which indeed is a Contradiction in Terms). From hence it is a Demonstration that they must derive to us from an Almighty, intelligent active Cause, exhibiting them to us, impressing our Minds with them, or producing them in us; and consequently (as I intimated) it must be by a perpetual Intercourse of our Minds with the DEITY, the great Author of our Being, or by His perpetual Influence or Activity upon them, that they are possessed of all these Objects of Sense, and the Light by which we perceive them.

Ideas of Sense not Pictures, but the real Things.

8. These Ideas or Objects of Sense are commonly supposed to be Pictures or Representations of Things without us, and indeed external to any Mind, even that of the Deity himself, and the Truth or Reality of them is conceived to consist in their being exact Pictures of Things or Objects without us, which are supposed to be the real Things.---But as it is impossible for us to conceive what is without our Minds, and consequently, what those supposed Originals are, and whether these Ideas of ours are just Resemblances of them or not; I am afraid this

this Notion of them will lead us into an inextricable Scepticism. I am therefore apt to think that these Ideas, or immediate Objects of Sense, are the real Things, at least all that we are concerned with, I mean, of the sensible Kind; and that the Reality of them consists in their Stability and Consistence, or their being, in a stable Manner, exhibited to our Minds, or produced in them, and in a steady Connection with each other, conformable to certain fixed Laws of Nature, which the great *Father of Spirits* hath established to Himself, according to which He constantly operates and affects our Minds, and from which He will not vary, unless upon extraordinary Occasions, as in the Case of Miracles.

Instanced in Things visible and tangible.

9. THUS, for Instance, there is a fixed stable Connection between *Things tangible* and *Things visible*, or the immediate Objects of *Touch* and *Sight*, depending, as I conceive, immediately upon the permanent, most wise Almighty Will and *Fiat* of the great Creator and Preserver of the World. By this, however, it is not meant, that visible Objects are Pictures of tangible Objects (which yet is all the Sense that can be made of our Ideas of Sense being Images of real Things without us) for they are entirely different and distinct Things; as different as the sound *Triangle*, and the Figure signified by it; so different, that a Man born blind, and made to see, could have no more Notion that a visible Globe hath any Connection with a tangible Globe, by meer Sight, without being taught, than a *Frenchman* that should come into *England*, and hear the Word *Man*, could imagine, without being taught, that it signified the same Thing with the Word

C *Homme*,

Homme, in his Language.—All that can be meant by it, therefore, is, That, as *tangible Things* are the Things immediately capable of producing (or rather, being attended with) ſenſible Pleaſure or Pain in us, according to the preſent Laws of our Nature, on Account of which they are conceived of as being properly the *real Things*; ſo the immediate *Objects of Sight* or *viſible Things*, are always, by the ſame ſtable Law of our Nature, connected with them, as Signs of them, and ever correſpondent and proportioned to them; *Viſible Extenſion*, *Figure*, *Motion*, &c. with thoſe of the *tangible Kind*, which go by the ſame Names: and ſo in the Compounds or Combinations of them; the viſible *Man*, *Horſe*, *Tree*, *Stone*, &c. with thoſe of the tangible Kind, ſignified by the ſame Names *.

Of Archetypes.

10. NOT that it is to be doubted but that there are *Archetypes* of theſe ſenſible Ideas exiſting, external to our Minds; but then they muſt exiſt in ſome other Mind, and be Ideas alſo as well as ours; becauſe an Idea can reſemble nothing but an Idea; and an Idea ever implies in the very Nature of it, Relation to a Mind perceiving it, or in which it exiſts. But then thoſe Archetypes or Originals, and the Manner of their Exiſtence in that eternal Mind, muſt be intirely different from that of their Exiſtence in our Minds; as different, as the Manner of His Exiſtence is from that of ours. In Him they muſt exiſt, as in original Intellect; in us, only by Way of Senſe and Imagination; in Him, as Originals; in us, only as faint Copies; ſuch as he thinks fit to communicate to us, ac-

* See Bp. *Berkeley's Theories of Viſion*, *Principles of Human Knowlege*, and *Three Dialogues*.

cording

cording to ſuch Laws and Limitations as he hath eſtabliſhed, and ſuch as are ſufficient to all the Purpoſes relating to our Well-being, in which only we are concerned. Our Ideas, therefore, can no otherwiſe be ſaid to be Images or Copies of the Archetypes in the *eternal Mind*, than as our Souls are ſaid to be Images of Him, or as we are ſaid to be *made after his Image* *.

Of Conſciouſneſs, Imagination and Memory.

11. THUS much for *Senſe.*—By *Conſciouſneſs* is meant, our Perception of Objects *ab intra*, or from reflecting or turning the Eye of our Mind inward, and obſerving what paſſes within itſelf; whereby we know that we perceive all thoſe ſenſible Objects and their Connections, all the Pleaſures and Pains attending them, and all the Powers or Faculties of our Minds employed about them. Thus I am conſcious that I perceive *Light* and *Colors*, *Sounds*, *Odors*, *Sapors*, and *tangible Qualities*, with all the various Combinations of them; and that of theſe, ſome give me, or rather are attended with, *Pain* or Uneaſineſs, others with *Pleaſure* or Eaſe, and the comfortable Enjoyment of myſelf. I find, moreover, that when I have had any Perception or Impreſſion of Senſe, I retain a faint *Image* of it in my Mind afterwards, or have a Kind of internal Senſe or Remembrance of it; as having ſeen the *Sun*, a *Flower*, a *Horſe*, or a *Man*, I retain the Image of their Figure, Shape, Color, &c. afterwards. Thus I have now a faint Idea of the *Sun* at Midnight, and of a *Roſe* in Winter: I know how ſuch a *Tree*, ſuch a *Horſe*, or ſuch a *Man* looks, tho' I have neither of them before my

* See on this Head, *Norris's Ideal World.* Part 1.

C 2 Eyes.

Eyes. This Power of the Mind is called *Imagination* and *Memory*, which implies a Conſciouſneſs of the original Impreſſion (tho' indeed the Word *Memory* may imply the Recollection of intellectual as well as ſenſible Objects, but chiefly *thoſe* by Means of *theſe*, which is alſo called *Reminiſcence*) and theſe Ideas of the Imagination may be truly ſaid to be Images or Pictures of the Ideas or immediate Objects of Senſe. We are moreover conſcious of a Power whereby we can not only imagine Things as being what they really are in Nature, but can alſo join ſuch Parts and Properties of Things together, as never coexiſted in Nature, but are meer Creatures of our Minds, or Chimeras; as the Head of a Man with the Body of an Horſe, *&c.* which muſt alſo be referred to the Imagination, but as influenced by the Will.

Of the pure Intellect and its Acts.

12. But beſides theſe Powers of *Senſe* and *Imagination*, we are conſcious of what is called the *pure Intellect*, or the Power of conceiving abſtracted or *ſpiritual Objects*, and the *Relations* between our ſeveral Ideas and Conceptions, with the various Diſpoſitions, Exertions and Actions of our Minds, and the complex Notions reſulting from all theſe; of all which we cannot be properly ſaid to have *Ideas*, they being intirely of a different Kind from the Objects of Senſe and Imagination: and therefore I would rather call them *Notions* or *Conceptions*; which again are either *ſimple*, ſuch as *Perception*, *Conſciouſneſs*, *Volition*, *Affection*, *Action*, &c. or *complex*, as *Spirit*, *Soul*, *God*, *Cauſe*, *Effect*, *Proportion*, *Juſtice*, *Charity*, &c. Now of all theſe, and what relates to them, conſiſts the intire *ſpiritual*

of

or *moral World*. But in order the better to underſtand or conceive of theſe, it is neceſſary more particularly to purſue and explain theſe intellectual and active Powers whereof we are conſcious within ourſelves; ſuch as, 1 The *ſimple Apprehenſion* of Objects, and their ſeveral Relations, Connections and Dependencies, ariſing from our comparing our Ideas and Conceptions one with another. 2. *Judging* of *true* or *falſe*, according as Things appear to agree or diſagree, to be connected or not connected one with another. 3. *Reaſoning* or inferring one Thing from another, and methodizing Things according to their Connections and Order. All this is the Subject of *Logics*; to which ſucceeds, 1. Affecting, or diſaffecting Things, according as they appear *good* or *bad*, agreeable or diſagreeable to us, *i. e.* attended with Pleaſure or Uneaſineſs. 2. *Willing* or *Nilling*, *Chuſing* or *Refuſing*, according as we affect or diſaffect them. 3. *Liberty* of *Acting*, or forbearing to act in Conſequence of the Judgment and Choice we have made of them. All this is the Subject of *Ethics*. But it is neceſſary to define theſe Terms, and give ſome Account of theſe ſeveral Acts and Exertions of our Minds (which, as well as thoſe of Senſe, Conſciouſneſs, Imagination and Memory above-mentioned, are only ſo many Modifications of them) in order to what is next to follow.

Of intellectual Light or intuitive Evidence.

13. BUT before I proceed, I would, in order thereunto, firſt obſerve, That no ſooner does any Object ſtrike the Senſes, or is received in our Imagination, or apprehended by our Underſtanding, but we are immediately conſcious of a Kind of *intellectual Light* within

within us (if I may ſo call it) whereby we not only know that we perceive the Object, but directly apply ourſelves to the Conſideration of it, both in itſelf, its Properties and Powers, and as it ſtands related to all other Things. And we find that, as we are enabled by this *intellectual Light* to perceive theſe Objects and their various Relations, in like Manner as by *ſenſible Light* we are enabled to perceive the Objects of Senſe and their various Situations *; ſo our Minds are as paſſive to this *intellectual Light*, as they are to *ſenſible Light*, and can no more withſtand the Evidence of it, than they can withſtand the Evidence of Senſe. Thus I am under the ſame Neceſſity to aſſent to this,—That *I am* or have a Being, and that I *perceive* and *freely exert myſelf*, as I am of aſſenting to this,—That I *ſee Colors* or *hear Sounds*. I am as perfectly ſure that 2+2=4, or that the *Whole is equal to all its Parts*, as that I *feel Heat* or *Cold*, or that I *ſee the Sun* when I look full on it in the Meridian in a clear Day. I am intuitively certain of both. This intellectual Light I conceive of, as if it were a *Medium* of Knowlege, juſt as ſenſible Light is of Sight. In both there is the *Power* of perceiving, and the *Object* perceived; and this is the *Medium* by which I am enabled to know it. This *Light* is alſo one, and common to all intelligent Beings, and *enlightens* alike, *every Man that cometh into the World*, a *Chineſe*, or *Japoneſe*, as well as an *European* or *American*; an *Angel* as well as a *Man*. By it they all at once ſee the ſame Thing to be true or right in all Places at the

* This is *Plato*'s Doctrine, in his Rep. 6. &c.

ſame

ſame Time, and alike invariably in all Times, paſt, preſent, and to come.

14. Now if it be aſked, Whence does this Light derive, whereby all created Minds at once perceive, as by a common Standard, the ſame Things alike to be true and right?——I anſwer, I have no other Way to conceive how I come to be affected with this intuitive intellectual Light, whereof I am conſcious, than by deriving it from the univerſal Preſence and Action of the DEITY, or a perpetual Communication with the great *Father of Lights* *, or rather his eternal *Word* and *Spirit*, exhibiting and impreſſing. For I know I am not the Author of it to myſelf, being paſſive and not active with regard to it, tho' I am active in Conſequence of it.----Therefore, tho' I cannot explain the Manner how I am impreſſed with it (as neither can I how I am impreſſed with Objects of Senſe) I humbly conceive that God does as truly and immediately enlighten my Mind internally to know theſe intellectual Objects, as he does by the Light of the *Sun* (his ſenſible Repreſentative) enable me to perceive ſenſible Objects. So that thoſe Expreſſions are indeed no leſs Philoſophical than Devout, that GOD *is Light, and in his Light we ſee Light.*----And this intuitive Knowlege, as far as it goes, muſt be the *firſt Principles*, from which the Mind takes its Riſe, and upon which it proceeds in all its ſubſequent Improvements in Reaſoning, and diſcovering both

Whence it is derived.

* See the *Archbiſhop* of *Cambray*, on this Subject, in his Demonſtration of the Exiſtence of God. And *Norris* or *Malbranch*. Alſo *Cudworth*'s Int. Syſt. p. 736. Ed. 1743.

C 4 Truth

Truth in Speculation, and Right in Action; so that this intellectual Light must be primarily and carefully attended to, if we would avoid and be secure from either Error or Vice.

Nor must this Manner of Thinking be suspected to favour of *Enthusiasm*, it being the settled Course or Law of Nature, according to which the great Parent Mind enlightens us; and that in Things, in their own Nature capable of clear Evidence: Whereas *Enthusiasm* implies an *imaginary*, as *Revelation* is a real and well-attested adventitious Light, above and beyond the settled Law or Course of Nature, discovering Truths not otherwise knowable, and giving Directions, or enjoining Rules of Action in Things arbitrary, or Matters of meer Institution. Lastly, from this intuitive intellectual Light it is (as I conceive) that we derive what we call *Taste* and *Judgment*, and, with respect to Morals, what some call the *moral Sense* or the *Conscience*, which are only a Sort of quick intuitive Sense or Apprehension of the *Decent* and *Amiable*, of *Beauty* and *Deformity*, of *True* and *False*, and of *Right* and *Wrong*, or *Duty* and *Sin*: And it is the chief Business of Culture, Art and Instruction, to awaken and turn our Attention to it, and assist us in making Deductions from it.

CHAP.

An Authentick

NARRATIVE

Of the SUCCESS of

TAR-WATER,

In curing a great NUMBER and

VARIETY of DISTEMPERS,

WITH

REMARKS,

AND

OCCASIONAL PAPERS

Relative to the Subject.

To which are ſubjoined,

Two LETTERS from the Author of *SIRIS*.

Shewing the Medicinal Properties of TAR-WATER, and the beſt Manner of making it.

By *THOMAS PRIOR*, Eſq;

To do good, and to communicate, forget not. HEB. xiii. 16.

DUBLIN Printed,

LONDON Re-printed,

For W. INNYS, C. HITCH, and M. COOPER, in *Pater-noſter-row*; and C. DAVIS, in *Holbourn*. MDCCXLVI.

[Price Two Shillings.]

To His Excellency

PHILIP,

Earl of CHESTERFIELD,

Lord Lieutenant General, and General Governor of *IRELAND*.

HIGH Stations furniſh great Opportunities of doing Good, where there is a Head to diſcern, and a Heart to apply. Your Excellency is eminent for both. Since your Arrival in this Kingdom, you have acquired a thorough Knowledge of its Intereſts, which you apply to the Service of his Majeſty, and the Public; in ſuch a Manner, that your Adminiſtration will be always remembered with Gratitude and Honour. Your Management, ſo generous of your own, and ſo frugal of the public Treaſure, joined with a Conduct ſo ſo open and ſincere, without the leaſt Tincture or Suſpicion of private Views, leave us at a Loſs to determine, which to admire moſt, the true Policy, or the Probity of our Governor.

THAT benevolent and diſintereſted Spirit, which diſtinguiſhes your Character, hath emboldened me to Addreſs this ſmall Treatiſe to your Excellency; which, as it is calculated to promote the public Good, coincides ſo far with your own Views, as to ſeem entitled to ſome Share of your Protection and Patronage.

I am,

With the greateſt Reſpect,

Your Excellency's moſt Obedient,

and moſt humble Servant,

THOMAS PRIOR.

An AUTHENTICK

ACCOUNT

OF THE

EFFECTS

OF

TAR-WATER.

1. HAVING publiſhed, in the *Dublin Journal* of the Third of *July*, 1744, Remarks on an Advertiſement, and upon certain Affidavits mentioned therein, concerning the Effects of Tar-water in *Stephens*'s Hoſpital, and having promiſed to communicate to the Public, an Account of ſeveral Perſons, who have been entirely cured, or greatly relieved by the Uſe of Tar-water only, together with their Names, Places of Abode, and Nature of their Ailments; I now addreſs myſelf to the Performance of my Promiſe, which hitherto has been delayed by many intervening Affairs, and by the Length of Time that was requiſite to obtain full Information in a Multitude of Caſes that daily occurred; but this Delay hath given me an Opportunity of procuring a more par-

B ticular

ticular and exact Account of the Cases of many Patients, and the Progress of their Relief, which must give more Satisfaction, than a short imperfect Detail of the Effects of Tar-water on the first Tryals could possibly afford. And finding that new Tryals and Discoveries were made of the Virtues of Tar-water in many different Distempers, and that some Patients, who drank it for one Ailment only, yet found surprising and unexpected Relief in other Ailments they laboured under; I thought it proper to wait for the full Effect of those Tryals, and to find out if others, in the like Cases, had not also received the same Benefit; which would be a farther Confirmation of the Efficacy of Tar-water in such Distempers.

2. Many on the general Invitation given in the Journal above-mentioned, several others, on particular Application, very freely communicated their Ailments and Reliefs for the Good of Mankind. Some who had received Benefit by Tar-water on the first drinking of it, chose to postpone sending their Accounts, till they had received the full Benefit they expected by a longer Use of it. Some, especially of the Female Sex, communicated their Cases, and the Benefit they received, yet were unwilling to have their Names mentioned in Public. Some Cases required a long Use of Tar-water, before any Judgment could be formed of the Efficacy of it, and before a Cure could be effected. It was also suggested by some, who decried the Use of Tar-water, that whatever seeming Benefit some might have received on their first drinking of it, yet that towards the Fall of the Leaf, or the Winter following, they would feel fatal Consequences from it, insinuating, at the same time, that it was dangerous to drink it in the Dog-days, or in cold Weather, by which Means several were prevailed upon to lay aside the drinking of it for some Months; but finding

ing no ſuch Conſequences, they have ſince reſumed the drinking of it with great Advantage.

3. For theſe, and many other Reaſons, the Publication of the Effects of Tar-water has been ſo long deferred; but now that we find many Thouſands have drank Tar-water, and great Numbers have received Benefit thereby; ſince Time, Experience, and many Tryals (the ſureſt Guides in Caſes of this Nature) have eſtabliſhed the Credit and Uſe of this Medicine, it would be a Prejudice to the Public, and an Injury to Mankind, to defer any longer the Publication of the many unexpected and ſurpriſing Cures effected by Tar-water. And as particular Inſtances and Facts, within the Knowledge and Obſervation of every one, make ſtronger Impreſſions than general Aſſertions and Reaſonings can do; it is with great Satisfaction I can inform the Public, that I am furniſhed with a great Number of authentic Accounts of the Effects of Tar-water, (more perhaps than ever happened in the Caſe of any other Medicine in ſo ſhort a Time) and that chiefly from the Patients themſelves, moſt of them Men of Character and Integrity, who, beſides the Pleaſure of recounting the Benefits they received, had no other View in communicating their Caſes, but to promote the Good of others, and particularly of thoſe, who might have the Misfortune of labouring under the ſame Diſorders.

4. Having no other View in publiſhing this Narrative, but to promote the ſame good Intentions, I can aſſure the Public, that I have, with the greateſt Candor and Impartiality, laid before them the Facts and Caſes, as they were communicated to me; for which Purpoſe I beg Leave to publiſh the Letters of particular Gentlemen, who have been ſo good as to give a Detail of their own Diſorders, or of thoſe of their Neighbours and Acquaintance, and of the Benefit they received; the Originals of which may

B 2 be

be viewed in my Hands, and I hope thoſe Gentlemen will excuſe the Liberty I have taken in publiſhing their Letters, which, as they were deſigned for the Good of Mankind, ſo I do not, in the leaſt, doubt, but that they were communicated with the ſame beneficent Intentions; and as they come from Gentlemen of Character and Worth, they will not fail to be much regarded, make the following Narrative more Authentick, and be the Means of procuring the Good of Thouſands.

5. From ſome, I had the Accounts of their Caſes from their own Mouths; and any one, who will give himſelf the Trouble of enquiring, may be ſatisfied of the Truth thereof from the Perſons themſelves, whoſe Names are herein mentioned. Some Gentlemen in the Country hearing of the Succeſs of Tar-water among their Neighbours, made a ſtrict Enquiry, and were pleaſed to ſend me Accounts of ſeveral relieved thereby. I have alſo taken Notice of the Caſes of ſeveral Perſons, without mentioning their Names, in Compliance with their Deſires not to have their Names publiſhed; but if any ſhould be deſirous to know who the Perſons are, whoſe Names are omitted, I ſhall be ready, for their private Satisfaction, to let them know ſo much.

6. At firſt many Caſes occurred, of Perſons troubled with Colds, Coughs, Difficulty of Breathing, want of Reſt and Appetite, which were ſoon removed by the Uſe of Tar-water; but as it may be thought, that theſe Ailments might be removed by Exerciſe, Air, proper Diet, or other Medicines, without being beholden to Tar-water, I have omitted moſt of thoſe Caſes, though the Quickneſs and Eaſe with which they were relieved, and the Number of the Cures muſt greatly recommend the Uſe of this Medicine. Thoſe Caſes were thought too ſlight to lay any Streſs upon: But the Inſtances produced in this Narrative, are, for the moſt part, Caſes

Cases of the most grievous and dangerous Distempers, Acute and Chronicle; such as the Gout, King's-Evil, inveterate Scurvies, and Ulcers, confirmed Asthmas, and Coughs, Fevers, Pleurisies, Rheumatisms, and Colics, *&c.* which rarely give Way to any Medicines; those in common Use having generally failed in the Instances herein mentioned; but they all, in a great measure, yielded to the Power and Efficacy of Tar-water, as will appear by the subsequent Narrative.

7. But, in order to lay the Whole in a fair Light before the Reader, I shall beg Leave, by Way of Introduction, to republish the *Affidavit*, and my *Remarks* thereon, which gave the first Occasion of writing on this Subject, together with some Observations, published in *England*, relating to that *Affidavit*, and shall then proceed to give an ample Account of the Effects of Tar-water, according to Promise.

8. The said *Remarks* were as follow:

Remarks *on a late* Advertisement, *and upon certain* Affidavits *mentioned therein, concerning the Effects of Tar-water in* Stephens's *Hospital.*

9. The *Advertisement* was published in the *Dublin Journal* of the Second of *June*, 1744, in the following Words, *viz.* "We are very well informed, that many voluntary *Affidavits* have been made before Alderman *Walker*, of the unsuccessful Use of Tar-water in Dr. *Stephens*'s Hospital, by Numbers of Patients in that House, setting forth, that, after a long Series of using Tar-water in the most strict and regular manner, none found themselves in any wise better, but many of them much worse; and that these *Affidavits* are in the Hands of the Visitors of the Hospital, and may, at any Time, be viewed by the Curious in this Matter."

10. Being surprized to hear, that in *Stephens*'s Hospital alone, none found themselves any Way better,

better, and many of them worſe, by the Uſe of Tar-water, when, at the ſame Time, great Numbers both in Town and Country had received great Benefit thereby; and being fully perſuaded, by the ſurprizing Benefits which many of my Acquaintance have received, and daily do receive by Tar-water, that it is a uſeful and moſt ſafe Medicine; my regard to Truth and the good of Mankind induced me to make an Enquiry into the Contents of thoſe Affidavits, on which ſo much Streſs had been laid in the Advertiſement.

11. I accordingly addreſſed myſelf to the viſiting Phyſician of the Hoſpital, who ſhewed me the original Affidavits, and gave me leave to take Copies of them, and at the ſame time declared, that the ſaid Advertiſement was publiſhed without his Knowledge.

12. That the Public may be better able to judge of the Force of thoſe Affidavits, and the Truth of the Advertiſement, I ſhall here publiſh one of them, which may ſerve for the reſt, all of them being written in the ſame Form and Words, except an Addition to three of them, which I ſhall alſo take notice of. The Affidavit I ſhall mention, is in the following Words;

County of the City of *Dublin.* } *Sylveſter Dowdal*, one of the Patients in *Stephens's* Hoſpital, came this Day before me, and made Oath, that he conſtantly drank the Tar-water by the Directions of Dr. *Lehunte*, for about nine Weeks, and depoſed that he hath not found any Benefit thereby.

Sworn before me the 25th of *May*, 1744.
William Walker.

His
Syl O Dowdal
Mark.

13. The

13. The Doctor informed me, that the ſaid *Dowdal* had an Impoſthume in his Stomach, and mentioned the Diſeaſes which the others laboured under, and ſaid the Patients began to drink the Water on the 26th of *March*, and that ſome, who were ordered to drink the Water, neglected ſo to do.

14. There were but ſix Affidavits in all, the Depoſitions of the remaining Five, which were taken at the ſame Time, are to the following Purpoſe.

15. "*James Martin* in a high Degree of Leproſy ſwears he drank Tar-water near ſix Week without any Benefit.

16. "*Bartholomew Hughs*, in an Aſthma and Conſumption of the Lungs, drank Tar-water ſeven Weeks without any Benefit as to his Shortneſs of Breath, which was his principal Diſorder.

17. "*Mary Malone*, for the Itch drank the Tar-water five Weeks without any Benefit; but being put into another Courſe for three Weeks, finds herſelf much better.

18. "*Patrick Shaghnuſſy* for an inveterate Itch, drank Tar-water ſix Weeks, found no Benefit, but found himſelf much worſe; but being put into another Courſe finds himſelf much better.

19. "MA.—— in the foul Diſeaſe, drank Tar-water ſix Weeks, without any Benefit, but found herſelf much worſe; but being put into another Courſe, finds herſelf much better."

20. This is the Subſtance of the Affidavits, whereof four were made by Perſons that could not write their Names.

21. When Tar-Water firſt began to obtain ſome Vogue, it was expected, that the learned would have left it to its own Fate, as was done in the Caſe of Quick-ſilver, and *Ward*'s Pill; and indeed one would have thought, that an Oppoſition to a Me-

dicine of this Nature, muſt have been either needleſs or criminal: If the Medicine be bad, it will die away of itſelf; if good, it is plainly unwarrantable to oppoſe it. How far this Oppoſition, coming from a Quarter that may poſſibly be ſuſpected of having ſome Intereſt in the Matter, can be reconciled with the Rules of Prudence, is ſubmitted to the publick Conſideration: The Doctor, who is known to be a Man of Worth and Skill in his Profeſſion, acted very properly, and with good Intention, in preſcribing this Water, to be taken, even in the worſt Caſes, in the Hoſpital; and I hear he has preſcribed it to others, out of the Hoſpital, with Succeſs; but the Uſe that others have made of what he had done, without his Knowledge, gives room for making the following *Remarks.*

22. It is ſaid in the *Advertiſement*, that many voluntary *Affidavits* have been made by Numbers of Patients in the Hoſpital, ſetting forth, that "after a "long Series of uſing Tar-water, in the moſt ſtrict "and regular manner, none found themſelves in any "wiſe better, but many of them much worſe;" now upon comparing the *Advertiſement* with the *Affidavits*, we can find no Words in the latter to ſupport thoſe Aſſertions; not a Word of a *long Series*, or *the moſt ſtrict and regular Manner*, or that *none received Benefit*; and it was impoſſible that any one Patient could ſafely ſwear, that none in the Houſe received the leaſt Benefit, whatever he might have ſaid of his own Caſe: And by the Words mentioned in the *Advertiſement*, that many voluntary *Affidavits* have been made by *Numbers of Patients* in that Houſe, one might have expected to have met with a numerous Train of ſuch *Affidavits*; but behold, they are dwindled to Six only, by which it appears, that the *Advertiſement* doth no way tally with the *Affidavits*, nor can be ſupported or warranted by them. Six of the moſt deſperate Caſes in the whole Hoſpital, were

were culled out for the Affidavits, and theſe made the only Teſts of the Virtues of Tar-water, upon ſo ſhort a Trial as five or ſix Weeks; altho' the Diſtempers were inveterate, and chronical, and plainly required a Length of Time, to effect a Cure. Did ever any prudent Man try the Force of a Medicine at firſt, in deſperate Caſes only? What Medicine in the World could ſtand, if a few Inſtances of its Unſucceſsfulneſs were ſufficient to deſtroy its Credit? or what would become of the Practice, or Credit of Phyſicians, if Inſtances of their failing to cure, by the Medicines they preſcribe, ſhould be urged againſt their Medicines or Practice? were not ſeveral of the ſaid Patients in the Hoſpital without Relief many Months before they drank Tar-water?

23. It does not appear by the Affidavits, that Juſtice was done to Tar-water in Quantity, in Time, in accompanying it with any outward Waſh of Tar-water, as was proper in the Caſe of outward Sores, or in acknowledging that it concurred in the Cure of the Itch; in which laſt Caſe Tar-water, by driving the Venom from the Blood to the Surface, will increaſe the Sores for a time, and make ignorant Patients think themſelves worſe. And probably this very Thing facilitated and proved the main Part of the Cure; for as ſoon as they were anointed with Brimſtone, they found themſelves better; and it is not propable they would have been kept in the Hoſpital, ſo long before they drank Tar-water, if a bare outward anointing, could have cured them. The Conduct of the Advertiſers doth not appear to be very fair; in order to diſcourage the Uſe of Tar-water, they ſay that none of the Patients in the Hoſpital received any Benefit by Tar-water, though they produce Affidavits of but ſix of them, and thoſe in deſparate Caſes; but they take not the leaſt Notice at the ſame time of any Perſons, who received any Benefit by it: In this Point they are intirely ſilent; I ap-

I appeal to the Publick, if this be fair and equal Dealing, but we ſhall take Care to ſupply that Defect: They themſelves know, and the whole City can teſtify, the many Inſtances of Perſons of all Ranks, who have received the greateſt Benefit by Tar-water, and this in a great Variety of Caſes.

24. In Proof whereof, for the Good of Mankind, and for the Sake of Truth, we ſhall publiſh a Liſt of thoſe within our Knowledge, who have been either intirely cured, or greatly relieved by the Uſe of Tar-water alone, with the Places of their Abode, and in what Ailments they received Benefit; that every other Perſon, who may have the ſame Sort of Ailment, may know what Perſons to apply to, and be informed of the Particulars of their Cure, and thereby may have an Opportunity of obtaining the like Relief themſelves; and in order to make the Liſt as complete as poſſible, it is earneſtly deſired, that they who have received Benefit by Tar-water, would be ſo good, and humane, as to ſend their Names and Places of Abode, to *Thomas Prior*, Eſq; at his Houſe in *Bolton-Street*; and at the ſame Time it is alſo deſired, that they who have received any Harm by Tar-water, (if any ſuch there be) would be ſo good to ſend their Names, and Places of Abode, in like manner; and we have the greateſt Hopes of being gratified in this Particular, as we have no other View or Intention in this Affair, but, on the one hand, to do all the Good in our Power, and on the other, to guard againſt all the Evils that may poſſibly happen, and ſo do equal Juſtice to the Publick.

25. By what we have already experienced, and daily do experience, of the good Effects of Tar-water, we have great Reaſon to be perſuaded, and greater ſtill to rejoice, that the World is bleſt with a Medicine, ſo efficacious as ſeldom to fail of Succeſs, ſo general as to relieve in moſt Diſeaſes, ſo ſafe as never to be attended with Danger, and yet ſo cheap, as to be

be in the Power of the pooreſt Perſon to purchaſe, and we hope in God, that every Day's Experience will, more and more, confirm us in this Perſuaſion.

26. The aforeſaid Advertiſement from *Stephens*'s Hoſpital, being publiſh'd in the *Engliſh* News-papers, moved a Gentleman, in the *North* of *England*, to ſend a Letter to the Publiſhers of the *Newcaſtle Journal*, which they printed in their Journal, with a Preface, and was after re-printed in the *Dublin Journal* on the 21ſt of *Auguſt*, in the Words following:

27. " There appears ſo benevolent a Deſign in the following Letter, that ſhould we delay the Publication of it, we might be accuſed, not only of Ingratitude to the ingenious Author, but of Injuſtice to the Public."

To the Publiſhers of the Newcaſtle Journal.

Gentlemen,

28. I was moved with no little Indignation and Concern, at reading a ſly inveterate Paragraph againſt Tar-water, in a late *Newcaſtle Courant*, publiſhed, it ſeems, originally for an Article of News in the Papers of *Dublin:* But what Quarter it ſhould come from there, together with the Purpoſes intended it ſhould anſwer, are plain enough to be gueſſed at: To obviate, therefore, as much as in me lies, the ill Effects of ſo malevolent a Deſign, I think myſelf indiſpenſibly obliged, as well by the Ties of Juſtice and Gratitude, to the excellent Writer upon the extenſive Virtues of Tar-water, and Diſcoverer of its powerful Effects, as by thoſe of Charity and Benevolence to my Fellow-Creatures and Sufferers, to make known to the Public, through the Means of your Paper, the ineſtimable Benefits that have accrued to me, and mine, from the Uſe of it.

29. I had long laboured under theſe following complicated Diſtempers, *viz.* Palſy, Colic, Rheumatiſm,

matiſm, Gravel and Piles; in all which Caſes I found ſurpriſing Relief from Tar-water, and that in conſiderably leſs time than a Month from beginning to drink it. And it has worked ſtill greater Effects upon my Wife, who was infeſted to the higheſt Degree, with that *Engliſh* Plague, the Scurvy, together with a large Train of Diſorders, naturally incident to ſuch a Height of it; from which, by the ſame Means, and in the ſame Compaſs of Time, ſhe is recovered in ſuch a manner, as amazes all who were acquainted with her Condition; and for the Time it has been effected in, both ſhe and myſelf are reſtored to Health, in a degree infinitely beyond our moſt ſanguine Expectations; the Truth whereof I am ready to atteſt to any one who ſhall require it of me; moreover, I have been a Witneſs of its extraordinary ſalutary Effects in ſome of my Acquaintance, to a Degree little ſhort of our own: So happy an Experience, therefore, both in myſelf and others of its wonderful Operation and Force, leaves me not the leaſt room to doubt that Tar-water is the moſt ſovereign, and extenſive Remedy, and Cure for Diſeaſes in general; ſafeſt to be taken, as well as the eaſieſt in the Operation, that ever was found out in the whole *Materia Medica*; and as ſuch, may be recommended to the World, notwithſtanding the ſiniſter Paragraph above mentioned. And, if it is not an Abſurdity to ſuppoſe ſuch a Thing in Nature as a Panacea, nothing ſurely, ever bid ſo fair as this for that Character before. In my thus praiſing Tar-water, I think I cannot be ſuſpected of being actuated by any other Intereſt than the general Welfare and Happineſs of the human Species, willing them to ſhare and enjoy the precious Effects of it equally with myſelf. I purpoſely forbore, Gentlemen, troubling you with this ſooner, becauſe I would firſt be well warranted in my own Mind for whatever I had to ſay upon the Subject,

Subject, that I might not, in the leaſt invade the bounds of Truth, which in all Caſes, and eſpecially in ſo delicate an Affair as this, every one ought to be very cautious of.

30. I ſhall conclude with the good Biſhop's own Words, (ſelected from his admirable Treatiſe of *Siris*, for the generous diſintereſted Preſent whereof, together, with the invaluable Services likely to reſult therefrom, the World will for every remain the Debtor;) *viz.* " Men may cenſure and object as they " pleaſe, but I appeal to Time and Experiment. " Effects miſimputed, Caſes wrong told, Circum- " ſtances overlooked, perhaps too, Prejudices and " Partialities againſt Truth, may for a Time prevail " and keep her at the Bottom of her Well: From " whence, nevertheleſs, ſhe emergeth ſooner or la- " ter, and ſtrikes the Eyes of all, who do not keep " them ſhut." I am, Gentlemen, yours, *&c.*

N. B. If the Genuineſs of the above Letter ſhould be doubted, or any one deſire further Information concerning it, the Author, who lives in the County of *Durham*, has authorized us to ſatisfy any Perſon, upon Application to the Printer of this Paper.

31. This Inſtance ſhews that many different Ailments in the ſame Perſon, and a Complication of Diſtempers, may be all cured at the ſame Time by the ſame Medicine.

32. *William Ward* of *Cockerton* near *Darlington* in the County of *Durham*, Eſq; having ſeen the aforeſaid Advertiſement and Remarks in the *New-caſtle Journal*, was pleaſed to communicate his Caſe and Relief in ſeveral Letters, according to the Progreſs of his Cure. And his Caſe being very ſingular and worth taking Notice of, I take this Opportunity of publiſhing Extracts of his Letters in his own Words, which are as follow.

From

From his Letter, dated *June* 8, 1744.

33. " I began to drink Tar-water for an Afthma this Day fortnight, and take it Night and Morning a Glafs, whereof three make a Pint. I find it opens my Body gently, about two Stools a Day; but I have had my Fits, as often and violently as before. I am not fo weak as to think I was to have found a perceptible Benefit in fo fhort a Space, but fhall ftill continue it; I have had my Afthma upwards of twelve Years, but not fo violent as at prefent, and for feven Years laft; in which Time I have not been in Bed, or at moft, not above three or four Hours, once in a Year, when I have flattered myfelf with being tolerably well; and then, as foon as I awaked, I found by the Head of the Bed, I was quite loaden, as I thought, with Phlegm, though a dry Afthma; fo that I was obliged to get up and have Recourfe to a Pipe of Tobacco, which I ufe all the Time I am ill, for I have no Eafe when I do not fmoak. I am feldom without a Fit above three or four Days, and continue as long in it, and as foon as Rain comes I am eafy; I have it alfo againft the leaft Change of Weather.

My Father has it, and my Grand-mother died of it; fo that I have lefs Hopes of a Cure, as it feems to be hereditary. I have tried many of the moft eminent Phyficians in *England*, but never found Benefit. I have had Iffues in my Shoulders, and at prefent one under each Breaft, but cannot fay I reap any Advantage. The Medicines I have taken are innumerable."

From his Letter, dated *July* 27, 1744.

34. " I now relate to you the Succefs I have met with from the Tar-water. The firft Month I took it, my Fits were as violent and frequent as ufual. The fecond Month I had not one Fit, but one Night,

Night, which was very eaſy; and I believe I might have continued to have found a daily Benefit, if I had not been obliged to attend at the Aſſizes; where I have received a moſt violent Cold, which has brought on both my Aſthma and a Cough: So that at preſent I am very ill, but am taking all the Care I can now to recover myſelf; for I found ſo much Pleaſure in that Month's Eaſe, that no Temptation can induce me to ſwerve from Rules. I can't ſo much as lye back in an eaſy Chair; for I have a Table ſet by the Side of my Chair, with Pillows on it, ſo I lay my Arm on them, and my Head on my Arm; and if I am very ill, can't even reſt that Way, ſo that no Bed can be contrived for me to reſt on yet; and though I ſay above, that I had not a Fit for a Month, yet if I lay back in my Chair then, it made me uneaſy in two Minutes: I drank Tar-water frequently in the Day, but not a Quarter of a Pint at a time, for I find it agrees better with my Stomach, than drinking a larger Quantity; and in the Day, I may take ſuch a Quantity five or ſix times, as agrees with me. I muſt beg to take Notice of one very great Effect it has had on me (which I hope is a good Symptom:)

35. Before I drank the Tar-water, my Feet were always as cold as Ice, ſo that I had not the leaſt Perſpiration in them; for if I had not waſhed them for a Year, they were as clean and dry as the back of my Hand: But now, in the laſt Month, I was ſo eaſy, I found my Feet ſweat very copiouſly, and found, in wearing a Pair of new Stockings only a Week, that all the Soals were worn, and mouldered away; and what was left was very red, as if I had burnt them.

36. I beg Pardon for dwelling ſo long upon this Particular, as it was ſo ſurpriſing; and my Apothecary telling me, when I related it to him, that he was ſure I ſhould be cured by drinking the Tar-

Tar-water, as it had this Effect; for it was what he and all my Phyſicians had drove at, to make me have a Perſpiration in my Feet, which was never in their Power to get, not even by ſitting with my Feet in warm Water."

Extract from his Letter of *September* 18, 1744.

37. " As to my preſent State of Health, I have the Pleaſure to tell you, I was in Bed the 10th, 11th, 12th, and 15th Inſtant at Night; I went to Bed about eight a Clock, and lay until ſeven the next Morning, as well as ever I was in my Life; and found when I awaked, I was lying on my Back; and am quite another Man."

Extract from his Letter of *January* 16, 1744.

38. " I find the leaſt Cold does me Harm, and therefore keep cloſe to my Houſe, which is no Inconveniency to me, ſince I am all Air and Vivacity, which before was a meer State of Hebetude. I was obliged to go on the 4th of *November* laſt into *Northumberland*, when it was very cold with Snow; and as the Roads would not admit of Wheels, I was compelled to go on Horſe-back; and when I had rode a Mile eaſily (for it is only ſince I took Tar-water I could ride above a Mile on Horſeback) I found I was able to go faſter, and put on ſo faſt, that I obſerved by my Watch, that I rode at the Rate of ſix Miles an Hour. My Journey was thirty-ſix Miles, which I completed between the Hours of Ten in the Morning, and Four in the Afternoon, without drawing Bridle; I reſted one Day, and came home on the 6th of *November* in the ſame Time.

This I declare upon my Honour to be Fact, and which was as great a Surprize to myſelf as others."

39. So extraordinary a Caſe as this, and ſo well vouched by the Patient himſelf, gives us Reaſon to believe,

believe, that any Aſthma whatſoever may be cured by a Courſe of Tar-water, and at the ſame Time ſhews, that People ought to wait for the Effect of this Medicine, and not lay it aſide on a ſhort Tryal; though it is very probable, as will appear by other Inſtances, that if Mr. *Ward* had drank a greater Quantity of Tar-water at firſt, and avoided catching cold, he would have been much ſooner relieved.

As I had a few more Caſes, and printed Accounts from *England*, which ſhew the Power and Efficacy of Tar-water in a high Degree, I ſhall beg Leave to introduce them in this Part of the Narrative, before I mention *Iriſh* Caſes. The Singularity of the Caſes will, I doubt not, juſtify my exceeding the firſt Intentions, of publiſhing only ſuch Accounts, as occurred to me in this Kingdom.

Extract of a Letter from *John Hardcaſtle*, Eſq; of *Houghton*, near *Darlington*, in the County of *Durham*, a Civilian.

40. " My Diſorder began with violent Pains in my Breaſt, which, being removed by Fomentation, were ſucceeded by a great Cough. I was, in ſome Time, almoſt freed from it; but within two or three Days after it was ſtopped, I was ſuddenly ſeized with a Palpitation of the Heart, in a very high Degree, which laſted, with very little Intermiſſion, for two Days. That Diſorder being partly calmed by bleeding, my Cough returned again with as much Force as ever. I became much emaciated, loſt my Appetite, grew very weak, and had frequent Sweats; my Urine was loaded, during this Illneſs, with a large Quantity of red Matter, which, when evaporated to Drineſs, did not ſeem, to the Touch, to be of the Nature of Sand or Gravel, but rather like Loam or fine Clay. The Phyſician declared my Caſe ſcorbutic, and treated it accordingly. As I had been

C long

long following the Prefcriptions of the Phyfician I confulted, I cannot impute my Recovery, with any Certainty, wholly to Tar-water. But, I think, the fenfible, and almoft immediate Alteration I perceived in myfelf after taking it, leaves me no room to doubt, that Alteration was caufed by the Tar. It refrefhed my Stomach with a kindly and agreeable Warmth, reftored my Appetite, and, in all Probability, caufed a good Digeftion: As thefe gradually increafed, my Cough declined, my Sweats abated, and my Strength returned.

41. Having received feveral Letters from *Liverpool*, giving an Account of the extraordinary Virtues of Tar-water, in the Cure of a great Number of Negroes in the Small-pox, on board the little *Fofter* of *Liverpool*, Captain *Drape*, Commander, on the Coaft of *Guinea*, I fhall here mention the Particulars of my Information. The Reverend Mr. *Thomas Hayward*, of *Warrington* in *Lancafhire*, in a Letter dated the 18th of *October*, 1744, writes, that having received from a Friend an Account of this furprifing Cure of the Negroes, he made a Journey, on purpofe, to *Liverpool*, to be fully informed of the Particulars of the Fact; and there was thoroughly fatisfied of the Truth thereof, by Mr. *Conliff*, Mr. *Armitage*, Mr. *Reed*, and Mr. *John Atherton*, Perfons of the beft Credit, and the moft confiderable Merchants of the Place, the three firft Owners of the faid Ship; and they all affured him, that they received the Account from Captain *Drape* himfelf, who was ready and willing to make an *Affidavit* of the Truth thereof, at any Time when defired. And as fo new and extraordinary a Cure, in a diftant Country, required the beft Proof and Evidence, which the Nature of the Cafe could afford, to fupport the Credit thereof, Mr. *Atherton* was afterwards pleafed to tranfmit to me, at my Requeft, Captain *Drape*'s Narrative, and his *Affidavit* fworn before

before the Mayor of *Liverpool*, at the public Seſſions, where Mr. *Conliff*, and the other Gentlemen were preſent, and who were ſatisfied of the Truth of the Particulars, before it was confirmed by Oath; which *Narrative* and *Affidavit* I here publiſh, for the Satisfaction of the Public, in the Words of the Original, now in my Poſſeſſion, which are as follow.

42. "The *Little Foſter*, of *Liverpool*, Captain *Drape*, Maſter, in the Year 1742, made a Voyage to *Guinea*, and having taken in 216 Negroes, before he left the Coaſt, he had the Misfortune to ſee the Small-pox break out amongſt them: In a very ſhort Time there were no leſs than one hundred and ſeventy ill of that Diſtemper all at once.

43. The Captain was under great Concern, and fully expected, that, for want of Room, and other Neceſſaries, he muſt infallibly loſe the greateſt Part of them. A Perſon on board adviſed the Maſter to infuſe a Quantity of Tar in Water, and give it the Slaves to drink, ſaying, it was practiſed in the ſame Caſe with good Succeſs: The Tar-water was prepared, but the firſt, to whom it was offered, obſtinately refuſed it, and ſo did many more; that Man died in two or three Days, which the reſt ſeeing, were more eaſily brought to Compliance, ſo that, partly by Perſuaſion, partly by Force, the reſt were all brought to drink. The good Effects followed ſoon after, and were ſo plainly perceived, by the poor Creatures themſelves, that they came upon Deck, and crouding about a Tub of Tar-water, that was ſet there for them, drank plentifully of it, from time to time, of their own Accord.

44. This had an Effect that could hardly be expected under the moſt commodious Circumſtances; for of thoſe one hundred and ſeventy (moſt of them grown Perſons) not one died, except that one Man, that could not be brought to drink the Tar-water.

C 2 Captain

Captain *Drape* says farther, that the Negroes continued drinking Tar-water after their Recovery, which they found so much Relief from, that they could hardly be brought to drink any other; and that, from the Time of their Departure from *Guinea*, to their Arrival in *Jamaica*, he verily believes they did not drink above a Hogshead of Water, that was not impregnated with Tar, though the ordinary Consumption of Water, for so many Slaves, could not be less than a Hogshead a Day.

I do hereby certify, upon Oath, that the Contents of the above Narrative are actually and *bona fide* true.

Liverpool the 14th of *January*, 1744.

Joseph Drape.

Taken and sworn before me,
Owen Prichard, Mayor of *Liverpool*."

45. The said Mr. *Atherton*, in a Letter dated the Fourth of *February*, 1744, writes in the following Words:

" We have a very high Opinion of the Virtues of Tar-water in my Family; my Wife having drank a Pint a Day of it for eight Months last past, and by which she received surprising Benefit in an inflammatory Disorder, in which Physick and Bleeding had brought her very low; neither of which she has made use of since: Doctor *Dickins*, one of the most eminent Physicians in this Part of the Kingdom, had her under his Care, and advised her to Tar-water, as an Alterative. So you see Doctors differ about it! Some asserting it to be inflammatory, the contrary of which, I have the strongest Instances of in my own Family, and for which Mrs. *Atherton*, and myself, think ourselves under the greatest Obligations to the Bishop of *Cloyne*. These Instances of the Virtues of Tar-water, so well authenticated, together with many others, which will

will be mentioned hereafter, put it out of all Doubt, that Tar-water is ſo far from being of an inflammatory Nature, or dangerous in inflammatory Diſorders, as has been ſuggeſted by ſome, that it is a moſt ſafe and ſovereign Medicine in ſuch Caſes. And I am very well informed, that it is now become a conſtant Rule and Practice at *Liverpool*, and other Places, which fit out Ships for the *Guinea* Trade, to provide a ſufficient Quantity of Tar, to make Tar-water, in order to be adminiſtered in Plenty, to ſuch Seamen, as may happen to be ſeized, in their Voyages, with the Small-pox, Scurvies, and other Diſtempers, which Seamen are ſubject to.

46. Mr. *Hayward* writes, in the ſaid Letter, that he had laboured under an Ague of four Months Continuance, which had reduced him to a very low State, but that he very happily recovered his Health by the uſe of Tar-water only; and in his Letter of the 29th of *June*, 1744, he adds, that he was in no manner of Pain about the Return of his Ague; that he had ſpent the Winter, thus far, in the moſt comfortable Manner, and enjoys a more lively and comfortable Flow of Spirits, than ever he did in his Life; which, upon all Occaſions, are apt to exert themſelves in extolling the Source from whence they are drawn, and giving others as high an Opinion of Tar-water, as he had himſelf; he alſo makes this Obſervation, that the Virtues aſcribed, and that very juſtly, to Tar-water, particularly that of removing the Load, which, at times, hang heavily on the Spirits, and infuſing into the Soul, thoſe lucid gladſome Senſations, which many unhappily ſeek for in Drams and Cordials, would almoſt incline one to think, the *Egyptians* were not ignorant of Tar-water. If that ſovereign Cordial of theirs, deſcribed by *Homer* under the Name of *Nepenthes*, was not Tar-water, he is ſure it was ſomething very like it, as, he ſays, will appear from theſe and

C 3 the

like it, as, he ſays, will appear from theſe and the following Lines in *Homer*'s *Odyſſes*, 4th Book.

Ἑλένη Διὸς ἐκγεγαῦα
Αὐτίκ' ἄρ' εἰς οἶνον βάλε φάρμακον, ἔνθεν ἔπινον,
Νηπενθές τ' ἄχολόν τε, κακῶν ἐπίληθον ἁπάντων.
Ὃς τὸ καταβρώξειεν. Hom. Odyſſ. Δ.

Thus Tranſlated by Mr. *Pope.*

Mean Time with genial Joy to warm the Soul,
Bright *Helen* mix'd a Mirth-inſpiring Bowl;
Temper'd with Drugs of Sov'reign Uſe, t'aſſuage
The boiling Boſom of tumultuous Rage;
To clear the cloudy Front of wrinkled Care,
And dry the tearful Sluices of Deſpair;
Charm'd with that virtuous Draught, th' exalted Mind
All Senſe of Woe delivers to the Wind:
Theſe Drugs ſo friendly to the Joys of Life,
Bright *Helen* learn'd from *Thone*'s imperial Wife,
Who ſway'd the Scepter, where prolific *Nile*
With various Simples cloaths the faten'd Soil.

Milton *mentions this* Nepenthes *in his Maſk of* COMUS.

Behold this Cordial Julep here,
That flames and dances in his cryſtal Bounds;
Not that *Nepenthes*, which the Wife of *Thone*
In *Ægypt* gave to *Jove*-born *Helena*,
Is of ſuch Pow'r as this, to ſtir up Joy
To Life ſo friendly, or ſo cool to Thirſt.

A Letter from the Reverend Mr. *James Menteath*, from *Adderbury* in *Oxfordſhire*, dated the 12th of *February*, 1744.

47. "As ſoon as I heard of the Treatiſe on Tar-water, and of the Directions therein mentioned, I made the Water with different Proportions of Tar, and drank between two and three Gallons of it; but felt

felt no other Effect, but that it increased a good Appetite to a stronger, from which Time I gave it over; having, I thank GOD, no Need of that, or any other Medicine. As to myself, I was by no Means a fair Subject to make an Experiment of its Virtues upon, being young, of a robust Constitution, which I have kept so, by drinking only common Water and Tea, and eating little animal Food; and I only drank the Tar-water to convince others, that it could do them do Harm. On the Second of *May* last, being Curate of this Place, I was sent for to pray by a young Woman, who, I was told, lay at the Point of Death: When I came, I found her no better than was represented; speechless, so weak, that she could scarcely open her Eyes; her Parents told me, that a Physician of this Country, a Man of much Knowledge, and great Integrity, had just been with her, and said, there was no Hopes of a Recovery, for that she could not live above three Days. The young Woman was about Twenty, born of poor Parents; she had, for some Months, been troubled with a Cough, and a Swelling in her Legs and Arms, which was now become a Dropsy, and was seemingly in the last Stage of a Consumption. After performing my Duty, as a Clergyman, I told the Mother, that as the Doctor said her Case was so desperate, if she would give Leave, I would try a Medicine, which I believed might possibly do her Service; she readily consented, and I gave her two Quarts of the Water, and gave Directions, that she should drink Half a Pint of it at a time, twice, or, if she could bear it, three times a Day, and that warm; as the Case was desperate, the greater Quantity I thought necessary. After two Days, she was able to sit up, in four or five was brought down Stairs, had some Appetite, her Cough abated, and the Swellings of her Legs and Arms much sunk; in six Weeks she ſeemed ſo well, that I adviſed her to let alone the Tar-water for ſome Time. I did not ſee her again till the beginning of *Auguſt*; when her Mother came and told me that her Daughter was again out of Order. I went to ſee her, and found her a little ſwelled, with a Cough, her Appetite in ſome Meaſure loſt, and a pale Look; upon this I ſent her more of the Water, made according to the printed Directions, which ſhe drank for a Month, and which intirely recovered her; inſomuch, that ſhe went out to Service at *Michaelmas* Term, and, I underſtand, has been well ever ſince. As ſhe was going to ſome Diſtance from this, I gave her Directions how to make the Water, and adviſed her to drink it, whenever ſhe felt the leaſt Complaint.

48. This is the moſt extraordinary Cure that has come to my Knowledge, though I had many Patients, who have found great Benefit from it. But I had particular Succeſs with young Girls, who have been troubled with that deſtructive Diſorder, the Green Sickneſs; though I could not inquire into ſuch Complaints, I can eaſily diſcover them from the Complexion; indeed of the almoſt innumerable Experiments that have been made of it, many of which were by my Recommendation, I am fully ſatisfied, that there is no Proof of its ever doing hurt, ſo far from it, that,when properly taken, I have never found that it failed of Succeſs."

49. Thus far Mr. *Menteath*, on which I ſhall make the following Obſervation. That ſince it is always allowed, in Caſes where all Hopes of Recovery are loſt, to make Tryals of any Kind which may give the leaſt Hopes of preſerving Life, it is humbly ſubmitted, whether it is not adviſeable in ſuch deſperate Caſes, when every Thing elſe has failed, to make Uſe of Tar-water, which may poſſibly recover the Patient from the Brink of Death: As it has done in this and many other Inſtances mentioned

tioned in the Courſe of this Narrative, to the great Surprize of all, Phyſicians and others, who knew the Diſorders of thoſe Patients.

An Extract of a Letter from Mr. *John Berry* of *Mancheſter* in *Lancaſhire*, dated the 30th of *May* 1744.

50. "I have taken Tar-water twenty-four Mornings, and ſometimes in the Afternoon, for a Dizzineſs in my Head, which I have had at Times for twelve Months paſt, and ſince I began taking it, am as well (bleſſed be God) as ever I was in my Life."

Part of a Letter from a Phyſician in *York*, to one at *Bath*, dated *Auguſt* 25, 1744.

51. "The Biſhop of *Cloyne* is no better treated here than at other Places; but for your Satisfaction, I can inform you, that a Lady, tho' reduced to nigh a Skeleton by a bleeding Cancer, and thought only fit for *Guy*'s Hoſpital of Incurables, by the Uſe of Tar-water is ſo much better, as to be thought in a fair Way of enjoying a comfortable State of Health. She has recovered her Appetite and Fleſh, and all bad Symptoms are almoſt overcome, and her Breaſt is become ſoft and eaſy. This I think will ſtand as a Sort of Ballance to the Hoſpital Account from *Dublin*."

Part of a Letter from one in *Liſbon*, to his Correſpondent at *Bath*, dated the 21ſt of *January*, 1744.

52. "In reſpect to Tar-water, I am ſure it has been of great Service here in many Caſes. It is in Vogue in the *Portugal* Hoſpital, and they gave it the Princeſs *De Bocra* in the Small-pox, and ſhe has done very well. I am not a Friend to Quack Medicines,

dicines, but there is nothing to be ſaid againſt Proof."

53. I ſhall here add ſome Pieces printed in the *Engliſh* News-papers on the Subject of Tar-water.

A Letter to the Author of the *General Evening Poſt*, *June* the 4th, 1744.

SIR,

54. While Thouſands daily experience the Benefit of the Biſhop of *Cloyne*'s Tar-water, give me Leave to teſtify my Thanks for the Pleaſure I have received from his Diſcourſe upon it. I little expected on ſo low a Subject, to have met with ſuch Variety of Matter, ſuch Penetration of Thought, or that it was poſſible to have expreſſed either in Language ſo clear, and eaſy. Where ſhall we ſee a more accurate Theory of various Diſtempers, or of the Operations of the moſt prevailing Medicines upon them? How beautiful his Anatomy of Trees and Plants? How rational his Principles of Vegetation? How refined his Doctrine of Metals, and of their being tranſformed into each other? How learned his Hiſtory of the Opinions and Syſtems of the Antients? While he gradually leads me on from the ſimpleſt Operations of Nature, through the animal and vegetable World, up to the great Author of both, I am charmed with my Progreſs, and think I ſee in this *Chain* of his, that golden one, which hung down to Earth from Heaven, as this by ſeveral Links carries us up thither. Whether he teaches, reaſons, preſcribes, or analyzes, he does all with the Knowledge of a Profeſſor, the Humanity of a Gentleman, and, to crown all, with a good Biſhop's Piety; and leaves us uncertain whether to admire in him moſt, the Chemiſt, Phyſician, Philoſopher, or Divine. Somewhat like that fine ſubtile Spirit, which, he tells us, operates through the Univerſe, diſtinguiſhes his Writings; a Principle of pure Light, which

which you feel in him, as in other Syſtems nothing but Gravitation. I am, Sir, *&c.*

A Pindarique by the Right Honourable, *L. C. J. M.* inſcribed to the Author of *Siris.*

55. Majeſtick thus great *Nilus* ſhrowds
His ſacred Head in Darkneſs and the Clouds,
His Birth divine from vulgar Eyes conceals,
But to the Wiſe by Miracles reveals.
Homage to him ten thouſand Torrents pay
Replete with æther's vital Flame,
While thro' the burning Zone he wings his Way,
While *Siris* is his myſtick Name.
Parch'd *Africk* courts him to the *Libyan* Plain,
And ſtrives to intercept his Courſe;
But marble Mountains are oppos'd in vain,
Reſiſtleſs his as Ocean's Force.
From the ſteep Cataracts impetuous as he bounds,
Earth trembles at his Voice, each diſtant Rock reſounds:
Then ſmooth o're *Egypt*'s Plain his welcome Deluge flows,
And ſmiling Plenty brings, and chearful Health beſtows:
Hail *Egypt*, happy Realm, thy Monarchs were the Gods,
There Arts, and Wiſdom there firſt fix'd their bleſt Abodes.

On the Diſputes about Tar-water.

56. To drink, or not to drink, that is the Doubt,
With *Pro* and *Con*, the Learn'd would make it out.
Britons, drink on, the jolly Prelate cries:
What the Prelate perſuades the Doctor denies.
But why need the Parties ſo learnedly fight,
Or Choleric **I—r—n* ſo fiercely indite?
Sure the Senſes can tell, if the Liquor be right.

* A Phyſician, and Writer againſt Tar-water.

What

What agrees with his Stomach, and what with his Head,
The Drinker may feel, tho' he can't write or read.
Then Authority's nothing, the Doctors are Men;
And who drinks Tar-water will drink it again.

57. On the Enemies of *Siris*, by a Drinker of Tar-water.

How can devoted *Siris* ſtand
Such dire Attacks? The licens'd Band
With up-caſt Eyes and Viſage ſad
Proclaim, alas! " The World's run mad.
" The Prelate's Book hath turn'd their Brains,
" To ſet them right will coſt us Pains.
" His Drug too makes our Patients ſick,
" And this doth vex us to the Quick.
And vex'd they muſt be, to be ſure,
To find Tar-water cannot cure,
But makes Men ſicker ſtill and ſicker,
And Fees come thicker ſtill and thicker.
Burſting with Pity for Mankind,
But to his own Advantage blind,
Full many a Wight with Face of Funeral,
From Mortar, Still, and Urinal,
Haſtes to throw in his ſcurvy Mite
Of Spleen, of Dulneſs, and of Spight.
To furniſh the revolving Moons
With Pamphlets, Epigrams, Lampoons
Againſt this *Siris*, you'd know why?
Think who they are; you'll ſoon deſcry,
What means each angry doleful Ditty,
Whether themſelves, or us they pity?

From the *Daily Gazeteer*, publiſhed in *London*, *April* 5, 1745.

To the Right Reverend the Biſhop of *Cloyne*.

My Lord,

58. Upon the Foundation of ſome Hints I took from the 29th and 49th Sections of your *Siris*, I reſolved

resolved to attempt a Solution of Myrrh, by a low, aqueous Menstruum; and considering the Affinity, and similar Properties that are in Tar, and in Myrrh, I was led to think, that as all homogeneous Bodies attract more strongly than those of different Classes; so possibly, the native Vegetable, or acid Spirit of Tar, when gently fermented, might invite the like Principle from Myrrh. Accordingly I put a Drachm of coarse Myrrh, without any Delicacy of Choice, into half a Pint of Tar-water, and set it in a Pint Bottle, in a Degree of Heat of my Fire, equal to that of a hot Sun: In two or three Days I obtained so per ect a Solution, that, upon filtring, I found no other Residuum, than such as is apt to stick to gummy Bodies.

Of this Infusion, I mix about half an Ounce in each Half pint of Tar-water, which I daily drink; and take them so mixed, with good Success. It makes the Tar-water much more pleasant, giving it an agreeable sub-acid bitter Taste.

59. The second Process I used, after having spent my first Preparation, was very inaccurate; for I threw in an indeterminate Quantity (but as near as I can guess) four Drachms of fine pick'd Myrrh to a Pint of Tar-water. Upon filtring off this Infusion, I had Cause to think the Tar-water was more than saturated with Myrrh, because, among the Residuum, I found a kind of Stacte, or fine, transparent, liquid Myrrh, of the Consistency of the best Turpentine; which, however, might perhaps have yielded to a longer Infusion.

60. To you, my Lord, we owe the Tar-water; and to you, how nearly had we owed the Solution of Myrrh? since you furnished the only aqueous Menstruum that will dissolve, and render it fit for internal Use: As you Lordship suggested the first Hint, so I know no Person so capable of improving, and so willing to apply this Discovery (if it be one) to

to the Good of Mankind as your Lordſhip. To you, therefore, I addreſs it, with all its Virtues, all its Honours. For my Part, I have not Skill enough in any Branch of medical Knowledge, to aſſure whether there be any thing new or valuable in this Experiment of mine, only I conjecture, that at leaſt, it muſt be a good vulnerary Water; but, were the Secret as rich as the Treaſures of *Loretto*, both my Fortune and my Love to Mankind, forbid me to make any private Advantage of it; therefore I freely give it to the Publick under your Lordſhip's Patronage. I am, with great Duty and Eſteem,

Your Lordſhip's moſt obedient humble Servant,

Philanthropus.

61. I ſhall now proceed to give a Narrative of ſuch Caſes, which happened in *Ireland*, as they were communicated to me by Letters from Gentlemen of known Character and Integrity, in this Kingdom, giving a particular Detail of their own Diſorders, or of thoſe of their Neighbours and Acquaintance, and of the Relief they received, together with ſuch farther Accounts as I had from ſeveral Patients from their own Mouths, in and near *Dublin*, with their Names and Places of Abode.

A Letter from the Reverend Mr. *Nat. France* of *Yoaghall* in the County of *Cork*, dated *July* 6 1744, to *Thomas Prior*, Eſq;

SIR,

62. Reading an Advertiſement in the *Dublin Courant*, dated *July* the 3d, I thought myſelf bound by the ſtrongeſt Obligation, Gratitude for an ineſtimable Benefit received; as well as for the good of Mankind, which every Man ought to have at Heart, to give Teſtimony to the Truth. Upwards of 20 Years I have laboured under a very dreadful Diſorder, occaſioned, as I am fully perſuaded, by a prevailing

prevailing Acid in my Stomach. Frequently, for many Weeks together, I never rose from sleep, without violent vomiting, and a continual Sickness in my Stomach; rarely free from a Heart-burn, and that commonly ending in a violent Colick; nervous Disorders, frightful Spasms, a frequent Palpitation of the Heart in Bed, were the sure unhappy Consequences; my Disorder baffled the Art of Physick, the whole Power of Medicine. The *Pyrmont* and *German* Spaw-water, with the constant Use of Gum-pills for the nervous Complaint, gave some little Relief, but were very far from rooting out the Cause of my Disorder. I industriously shun'd every Acid; my Drink for many Years was Wine and Water, not daring to touch Malt-liquor or Cyder. I have drank Tar-water these three Years past, and, I bless God for it, have no Complaint to make; no Heart-burn; no vomitting in the Morning, which almost deprived me of my Sight; no return of any nervous Disorder, unless occasioned by a violent Cold, from which I am quickly relieved, by taking a plentiful Draught of Tar-water. Last Summer I laid a-side Tar-water for three Months, believing, I did not any longer stand in need of it; and that the Medicine would cease to be efficacious by the constant Use of it; my Colick, Heartburn, and nervous Spasms return'd upon me as violent as ever. I again had recourse to Tar-water; its happy Effect was beyond Expectation, in a few Days it perfectly relieved me. I do now, and shall for the Remainder of my Life, make it my Morning Draught; having no other Complaint against it, but this one; that by creating an Appetite, which it never fails to do; by strengthning the Stomach, and causing a good Digestion, it renders me more corpulent, than I could wish to be.

I am, Sir, your very humble Servant,

Nat. France.

36. A

63. A Letter from the Corporation of *Augher* in the County of *Tyronne*, dated *July* 7, 1744.

S I R,

Agreeably to your Inſtructions in the laſt News-paper, we the Under-written, Inhabitants of *Augher*, take this Opportunity of informing the Public, that moſt of us, having for many Years been greatly afflicted with chronical Diſeaſes, ſuch as the Gout, inveterate Scurvy and rheumatick Pains, *&c.* were induced from the high Character given to the Tar-water, to make Trial thereof.

That thoſe of us, who had any out-breaking, found, after a Fortnight's Trial, the Spots rather more inflamed and painful, but afterwards daily growing eaſier and better. That ſome of us who were ſeized with the Rheumatiſm found after the like Time a ſenſible Remiſſion of the Pains; how far it may anſwer in the Gout we cannot yet pretend to ſay, but, from the ſurprizing Recovery of moſt of us, we in the Gout reſolve to continue the regular and conſtant Uſe of that moſt excellent Remedy, and all of us do, in the moſt affectionate Manner, return our public Thanks to the Author of the Tar-water.

Edmund Mac Girr. *Robert Thompſon.*
Revd. Mac Quigan. *Adam Smyth.*
Dudly Harvey. *Uri. Mac Dowall.*

64. A Letter from the Reverend Mr. *Thomas Squire* from *Tallow* in the County of *Waterford*, dated *July* 11, 1744.

S I R,

The Enemies of Tar-water, I find, are greatly provoked, ſeeing they endeavour to have it ſworn out of Credit and Practice; however, I make no doubt, but that for the ſix Affidavits againſt it, you will ſoon have many Hundreds of creditable Vouchers for

for it; I send you some Cases: first my own. Turned of sixty, my Stomach began to fail me, and what little I did eat, lay heavy there for two or three Hours after Dinner; my Flesh wasted so that my Cloaths were much too big for me, the Calves of my Legs became soft, and hung from the Bones, and the Red in my Cheeks grew dark and livid; I look'd on these, and some other bad Symptoms, as Warnings from my Creator to prepare for my appearing before him in another State.

I had the Honour of being known to the Bishop of *Cloyne*, who advised me to drink Tar-water; which I did for fifteen Months, in which Time I found my Appetite restored, my Food sat easy on my Stomach, I grew up to my former Dimensions, my Flesh became firm, as it had been twenty Years before, and the Blood in my Cheeks of a good Red, so that I reckoned myself in as fair a Way of living as any Man of my Age, in the Neighbourhood.

65. A Gentlewoman in my House far advanced in Years, of a tender Constitution, and in a bad State of Health, has for near two Years taken a small Glass of Tar-water every Morning, and often another about Noon; the Physician who has attended her for eight Years, and consented to the Tar-water, has frequently for this last Year expressed his great Surprize at her being so much better, than at any Time since she was first under his Care. I must observe to you, that she takes several other kinds of Physick by the Doctor's Directions; it may not be amiss likewise to observe, that her Apothecary's Bill was last Year reduced to less than half of what it has formerly been, and I am sure, when it comes in next, will fall very short of that.

66. A Servant of mine was so ill of a Cold and violent Cough, that he was going to take to his Bed. I ordered him to drink about half a Pint of Tar-water warm'd; he then set about his Business, and I

D have

have not heard him complain ſince, tho' I forgot to make him repeat the Medicine. I could give Inſtances of many in this Neighbourhood, who have received great Benefit by Tar-water; this Morning a Gentleman, who, by a Cold taken in *February* laſt, was apprehenſive of a Decay, told me that his Fears were over by drinking Tar-water for three Weeks; and Yeſterday a Phyſician, who ſtudied under the great *Boerhaave*, told me that he had preſcribed the Courſe of Tar-water to five of his Patients lately; of thoſe it is probable I may give you an Account hereafter, as well as of two more, whoſe Caſes were very deſperate, and recovered, but I am not fully informed in the Particulars as yet.

I am your moſt humble Servant,

T. S.

67. A Letter from the ſaid Mr. *Squire* from *Curryglaſs* in the County of *Cork*, dated *November* 30, 1744.

SIR,

When I wrote to you formerly, I propoſed to ſend you ſome farther Accounts of the Cures effected by Tar-water; one of which was on a Gentlewoman near *Limerick*, (whom I have not leave to name.) Her Huſband was in this Village laſt *Chriſtmas*, who deſcribed his Wife's Diſtemper in ſuch a manner, that ſhe ſeemed to have ſuffered more by the Scurvy, than Mr. *Connor* of *Bandon*; ſhe was, as the Expreſſion was, juſt ſlayed alive, and had almoſt loſt the Uſe of her Limbs. I adviſed Tar-water, which a Phyſician approving, ſhe drank for ſome Time; ſo that the Scurvy-ſplotches are perfectly healed, and ſhe is recovering daily the Uſe of her Limbs. This I had from her Huſband's Brother.

68. The following Account I had from Mr. *Robert Atkins* near *Mallow*. A young Gentlewoman related to him had been long ill; ſhe had a great hard Swelling

ling in her Side, loſt her Stomach, was extremely thin and pale; ſome Phyſicians, who had attended for a conſiderable Time, at length gave her up. She earneſtly entreated one of them, Doctor *Connell*, for Advice, who recommended Tar-water; ſhe drank it for ſome Months and perfectly recovered.

69. In *Curryglaſs*, fourteen, as I find, have drank Tar-water, every one of them have received Benefit thereby, but the moſt remarkable, after thoſe in my former Letter, were *Hanna Evans*, Wife to *Henry Evans*, Maſon, cured of an hereditary Aſthma, under which ſhe laboured for two Years, and could not lie down in Bed; but now goes to Bed as formerly, and adds to her nightly Devotion, GOD *bleſs the good Biſhop*.

70. *Henry Evans* in the great Froſt took a violent Cold, and every Winter ſince, has kept his Head and Jaws tied up in Handkerchiefs; he drank Tar-water, the Pain in his Jaws is gone, and he bears Cold as well as ever he did. *Lawrence Linehan*, a Paper-maker, had taken ſo great Cold at his Work, that he waſted away, had a moſt deadly Cough, and was thought by all to be in a Decay; he drank Tar-water, and is now as well as ever.

71. Mr. *Crips* drinks Tar-water for an hereditary Aſthma; when he is regular in it, ſome Splotches break out in ſeveral Parts of his Body, and the Aſthma quite gone; but when he is careleſs the Splotches diſappear, and the Difficulty of breathing returns.

72. Mrs. *Rolleſton*, who nurſes her Child, had ſome Occaſion to drink Tar-water, which ſucceeded well with her; ſhe had a vaſt Flow of Milk, when ſhe drank it, and her Child was extremely well; our Phyſicians here preſcribe Tar-water frequently, and all own that no Medicine has ever made ſo great a Progreſs in ſo ſhort a Time.

I am your moſt obedient humble Servant,

Thom. Squire.

D 2 73. A

73. A Letter from Mr. *Henry Parſons*, Attorney, dated from *William-ſtreet*, *Dublin*, *July* 26, 1744.

SIR,

I lately read an Advertiſement in Mr. *Faulkener*'s *Weekly Journal*, deſiring, that Perſons who had received Benefit from drinking Tar-water, would ſend you an Account thereof, with the Nature of their ſeveral Diſorders; as that Advertiſement was chiefly intended for the Benefit of Mankind, I think every one ought readily to comply therewith. I therefore ſend you the following Account:

I have been theſe twenty Years paſt, and upwards, grievouſly afflicted with violent Pains and Swellings in my Limbs; and for want of my natural Reſt, which they frequently prevented, I was reduced to a very great Weakneſs; and I had loſt my Stomach to that Degree, that I may ſay, *My Soul abhorred all manner of Meat, and I was even hard at Death's Door.* I was reduced to that unhappy State, which the Biſhop of *Cloyne*, in his Treatiſe on Tar-water, calls *Tædium Vitæ:* a wearineſs of Life, that I could have bleſt the Means that would have finiſh'd my Days; and if any one was to have bought an Annuity on my Life, I am ſure no one would have given ſix Months Purchaſe for it. I am certain that every one, who has known me theſe twenty Years paſt, can and will readily vouch the Truth hereof; and not above five Months ago, a Gentleman falling into a groundleſs Paſſion with me, for no other Reaſon, but becauſe he was loſing a Game at Backgammon, declared to ſome Gentlemen, who afterwards informed me thereof, that he would certainly have been the Death of me, but that he was well ſatisfied I would ſoon dye by the Courſe of Nature.

74. I was alſo afflicted with a violent ſcorbutic Humour, which broke out to a great Degree in my Face; and about the Beginning of *May* laſt, on my firſt

first hearing the Virtue of Tar-water so greatly recommended, and on reading the Magazine for the Month of *March*, wherein it is set forth, I resolved on drinking it, and tho' I have only drank about five Gallons thereof, it has not only perfectly cured me of the Scurvy, but has also intirely eased me from all my Pains; restored me to my former Strength, a good Stomach, and a great Flow of Spirits; that now (I thank GOD) I may justly say, I am a Man again.

I am, Sir, your humble Servant,

Henry Parsons.

Mr. *Parsons*, who may be seen every Day in the Streets of *Dublin*, continues in a perfect State of Health, and Flow of Spirits, and constantly drinks Tar-water.

75. A Letter from the Reverend Mr. *Bernard Ward*, dated from *Belfast*, *July* 23, 1744.

SIR,

Inclosed I send you, the Cases of three Persons, who have received Benefit by the Use of Tar-water. In the first I prescribed it myself; the 2d, I had from the Mother of the young Lady, and her Permission to send it to you; the 3d, I had from the Father of the Child, who perused and approved of the Account which I send you. I think it the Duty of every Person, as far as he can, to make the World acquainted with the Cases of such as receive benefit from the Use of new Medicines; especially if they be such as are safe in the Application, and cheap, so as to render them of Use to the Poor: Tar-water, I am persuaded, is of this Kind, and I dare say it will give the good and most ingenious Author of *Siris*, a very sensible Pleasure, to find that his Medicine is likely to answer the End, which he had in publishing it, that is, to become of universal Use, and to

D 3 remove

remove moſt of the Diſorders to which Men are ſubject.

I venture to ſend you the incloſed without any Apology, the Truth of theſe Facts you may depend upon. I am, Sir,

Your moſt obedient humble Servant,

Bernard Ward.

The Honourable *Arthur Hill*, Eſq; adds by way of Poſtſcript, that though theſe Inſtances are but three, yet Tar-water is in great and univerſal Repute here, and I have no Doubt, but, in a little time, abundance more may be given.

76. N° 1. *William Gawdy* of the Pariſh of *Kirdonnell*, and County of *Down*, Farmer, aged about forty Years, had been many Years afflicted with the Rheumatiſm. About two Years ago he applied to me, when by the Uſe of *Ætherial* Oil of Turpentine, his Complaint was removed for that Time: In *May* laſt I met him near his own Houſe, moſt grievouſly tormented with the ſame Diſorder, which had then fixed itſelf in his Loins, and had for ſome Weeks entirely diſabled him from doing any Work; he told me he had uſed the Turpentine, but without Succeſs; that for ſome Weeks he had ſcarce been able to walk. I recommended the Uſe of Tar-water, four Quarts of which did ſo effectually remove his Diſorder, that, to uſe his own Words, he was able to lift a Hogſhead Sack full of Corn, and to put it upon his Horſe, and, in ſhort, was as well as he ever had been.

77. N° 2. Miſs *Small*, of the Pariſh of *Knockbreda*, in the County of *Down*, a young Lady of about ſixteen Years of Age, had for ſome Time been troubled with a Pain in her Side, Shortneſs of Breath, a Palpitation of the Heart upon the leaſt Motion, and an entire Loſs of Appetite; her Mother was apprehenſive of a Conſumption; yet by drinking Tar-

water

water about a Fortnight, all the above Symptoms were removed, and ſhe can now walk a Mile or two without giving her the leaſt Uneaſineſs, and is in perfect Health.

78. N° 3. *John*, the Son of the Reverend *Anneſly Baile*, Curate of *Comber* in the County of *Down*, at the Age of two Years, was active and ſprightly, and could walk as well as any Child of his Age; he was then ſeized with a Fever, which deprived him of the Uſe of his Limbs; his Joints grew large, and his Belly hard, like a ricketty Child; he continued in this Condition about two Years, till, upon the Publication of *Siris*, his Father made him drink Tar-water, a Wine Glaſs full three Times a Day, and in three Weeks time, he recovered the Uſe of his Limbs, and has been ever ſince in the higheſt Spirits, and very good Health.

79. A Letter from the Reverend Mr. *Uſher*, of *Maryborough*, dated *Auguſt* 23, 1744.

Margaret Large of the Pariſh of *Coolbanagher* near *Mountmelick* in the *Queen*'s County, being about forty-three Years old, laboured under a violent Cough and Oppreſſion on her Stomach for ten Years, which afflicted her without Intermiſſion, to that Degree, that ſhe loſt her Appetite, her Body was emaciated, and her Spirits low and depreſſed; but that by drinking Tar-water conſtantly every Morning ſince the Beginning of *June* laſt, the Cough and Oppreſſion on her Stomach were intirely removed, her loſt Appetite reſtored, her Spirits became briſk and lively, and her whole Conſtitution and Habit of Body wonderfully improved, and this Change evidently appeared in about ſix Weeks after ſhe began to drink the Tar-water. This Account, he ſays, he had from the Patient herſelf.

80. A Letter from Mr. *Henry Garvais* of *Lismore* in the County of *Waterford*, dated the 15th of *September*, 1744, to *Thomas Prior*, Esq;

Pursuant to your Desire signified in the public Prints, I take the Liberty of communicating to you the Case of Mr. *William Bryen*, which may not be unworthy of Notice. Mr. *Bryen*, who is an Attorney in Lord *Burlington*'s Manor-courts, after riding five Miles about two Years since, without a great Coat, in a Winter's Night of very heavy Rain, and so fuddled, that, when he came home, he could not put off his Cloaths, threw himself on his Bed, where he slept about six Hours, and when he awoke, was in an high Inflammation, and not able to speak. A Physician, of no small Repute in this Country came to his Aid, and by the common Process in such Cases, by bleeding, blistering, *&c.* brought some present Relief; but in a little Time a violent Cough ensued, attended with a grievous Pain in his Side, spitting of Blood, and large Sweats; so that having suffered much, and gone through the Apothecary's Shop for a Course of six Months, and exhausted his little Substance, the Physicians in a Consultation pronounced that he would dye tabid. The Patient not being able to purchase costly Medicines, in Despair had recourse to Tar-water, which he has ever since continued the Use of, with the greatest Benefit; insomuch, that when I talk'd with him, some little Time ago, he told me that he had recovered his Appetite and Rest, and was free from the Pain in his Side, and as well in Health as he could wish, saving a light Cough which remained, but was, in his Opinion, gradually wearing off.

81. Mr. *Gervais* mentions his own Case in the following Words. "I was under great Apprehensions from the Reliques of the Influenza, which in its Course seized me in a most heavy Manner, and left an acute Pain in my Head, violent Palpitation in the Heart,

Heart, a conſtant Pulſation in the Brain, and Spaſms through my whole Body. *Flagherty cum Sociis* had me in hand for Months; Gum pills and Spirits of Vitriol I almoſt lived upon, and to no Purpoſe; but now, by the Uſe of Tar-water, I am (GOD be praiſed) reſtored to good Spirits and Health."

82. He alſo mentions the Caſe of Mrs. *C*——— of *Limerick*, who was, many Years, afflicted with a Scurvy in the higheſt Degree; that he had been informed, by a near Relation of hers, that ſhe had been quite flay'd from Head to Foot, ſo that, for many Months, ſhe lay in Cere-cloths, and could not turn in her Bed, but as ſhe was helped by the Sheets: When all Remedies prov'd ineffectual, Tar-water was the dernier Reſort, by the Uſe whereof, for ten Weeks, ſhe has got a new Skin, her Sores have ceaſed to run, and her Health is throughly retrieved.

83. Mr. *Gervais*, ſoon after, ſent me the following Caſe, drawn up by Doctor *William C*——, of *Mallow*, in the Words following:

Carrol Daly, of *Ardprior* in the County of *Cork*, aged about 28, on exerciſing ſeverely in the Year 1742, was ſeized with a violent Cough, ſtreightneſs in his Cheſt, difficulty of Reſpiration, and had large Quantities of Blood diſcharged from his Lungs; in which State he remained near ſix Months, without other Aſſiſtance than what his poor Neighbours could adminiſter; till at length (quite emaciated, and in a hectick State, with fluſhings in his Face, ſucceeded by Rigors, and conſtant Night-ſweats) he applied to the neighbouring Phyſicians, who recommended a Courſe of pectoral and balſamic Medicines, with Tincture of Jeſuits Bark, and a Milk-diet, which Regimen he ſtrictly obſerved ten Months and better, when finding little Amendment, and no Hopes of Recovery, he applied to me; I recommended his continuing the ſame Method for ſome time longer, which he ſubmitted to, without further Benefit, than that

that his Sweats somewhat abated; he was now set down as incurable, and, at most, not likely to survive the following Spring; when hearing so much of the Virtues of Tar-water, published by the Bishop of *Cloyne*, and willing to try the Success, as every Thing else failed; I recommended earnestly the constant Use of it to him, and prepared it for him according to the Bishop's Directions. At first it disagreed prodigiously, inducing frequent Nausea's, Sickness in the Stomach, and a Lax, which, in his Condition, I was very apprehensive of; notwithstanding, I made some lighter, which, in a few Days, was so reconcileable to his Stomach, that he took it in large Quantities after, and is now perfectly recovered from all his Symptoms, only a small Cough, which he is subject to, on taking Cold, or any Irregularity.

84. *A Letter from Mr.* William Peacocke, *Merchant, in* Abbey-street, Dublin, *dated* Sept. 22, 1744.

SIR,

My Brother, *Marmaduke Peacocke*, Merchant, in *Abbey-street*, was, for several Months, very unwell, he had a great Cough, little or no Appetite, and a great Lowness of Spirits; he could not walk the Length of a Street, without being in a violent Sweat, and was very much emaciated; he applied to some Physicians here, and to no Purpose. He, by Accident, heard of the Virtues of Tar-water; he made some, drank of it Morning and Evening, and in less than three Weeks, he was as heal as ever, in great Spirits, and as well as he could wish; this I aver for Truth.

85. Last Spring I had a Fit of the Gout coming on me; the Reason I say so, is, because I was seized with the Cramp in my Legs, most violently, for several Nights. I had a great Loss of Appetite, and my Stomach faint and weak, with great Tenderness in my Feet; this is always a Foreruner of a Fit of the Gout with me. I was prevailed upon, by my Brother,

Brother, *Marmaduke Peacocke*, to drink Tar-water, which I did Morning and Evening: The doing ſo occaſioned great Perſpiration in my Feet, and in three Nights after, I had no Cramps, no Tenderneſs in my Feet, I had a good Appetite and Digeſtion, and was every other Way very well. I continued drinking this Water for two Months, afterwards I left it off for a Week, and drank of it only every Morning. I ſtill do the ſame, and am now (thank God) as well as any one. Given under my Hand this 22d of *September* 1744.

William Peacocke.

Mr. *Peacocke*, who may be ſeen every Day at *Lucas*'s Coffee-houſe informs me now in *June* 1745, that he has all along, and now continues to drink Tar-water every Day, and that with Pleaſure; that he has by Means thereof a great Perſpiration in his Feet, and Strength in his Limbs, and is free from all Symptoms and Apprehenſions of the Gout which ſo long troubled him.

86. *A Letter from* Stephen Bernard, *Eſq*; *Member of Parliament from* Youghall, October 2, 1744.

SIR,

As ſoon as I could completely, and with certainty, I was determined to communicate and acknowledge the Services I had received from the Uſe of Tar-water; which I have taken for three Months, Morning, Noon, and Night, half a Pint each time warm; and which I can now with certainty ſay, has relieved me from a Sickneſs in my Stomach, that ever attended me, but more ſevere for ſix Years laſt paſt, and ſo much more for the two laſt, that it was very rare to have a Day paſs without being troubled with violent Heavings, at leaſt twice, and a Loathing of all Suſtenance; which reduced me to ſo low a Condition, as utterly diſabled me from uſing any Exerciſe. I was alſo ſubject to a frequent Giddineſs, which

which remained, and was encreasing, notwithstanding a long Course of Vomits; in less than a Week after I drank the Tar-water, I not only found my Stomach relieved, but I had really an Appetite, which, I thank God, still continues, and I think strengthens, and the Giddiness is almost gone; these are the Particulars I can with Truth and Certainty aver. As to my other Complaints which are a flatulent Colick, a Numbness in my Hands, and Obstructions, the Relief not being very sensible, I would not presume troubling you with an Account of it; tho' with God's Permission, I have the utmost Confidence, I shall be able to give you an Account of a complete Cure; and make all the Acknowledgments in my Power for the Good received from the most ingenious learned Labour of the excellent Author of *Siris*. I am, Sir, your most obedient humble Servant,

Ste. Barnard.

P. S. A Servant of mine, for Years was troubled with a consumptive Cough, and is quite recovered by Tar-water.

87. *An Extract of a Letter from* Charles Coote, *Esq; Member of Parliament from* Cootehill, October 6, 1744.

SIR,

I am to inform you, that I drink Tar-water constantly; besides the Disorders, I have always been subject to, which are called nervous, I have the Gravel to a great Degree, but without Pain. I discharge great Quantities, by Urine, and my Stomach, Digestion, and whole Frame, used to be greatly disordered when I was loaded with it; the Use of this Water, not only discharges it, but I believe alters that Disposition in my Constitution, and I have always found myself better in Spirits, Digestion, and the Enjoyment of myself since I drank it.

88. By

88. By the Teſtimonies of *Samuel Moore*, and *John Maxwell*, Eſqs. the Reverend Mr. *Handcock*, Curate of *Cavan*, and many others of this County, Mr. *Donaldſon*, of *Cavan*, late Sub-Sheriff of this County, has been long afflicted with the Gout in an extreme Degree: He has drank the Tar-water ſome Months, and from a cloſe Confinement to his Bed and Chair, to his great Loſs while he was Sub-Sheriff, he is now walking about the Streets, and does not remember when he was able to do ſo for many Years paſt, and refers it wholly to that ſingle Medicine.

89. Mr. *Waren*, within two Miles of me, is Agent to Alderman *Dawſon*; he was aſthmatic, and ſeemed to be conſumptive to the laſt Degree. I have not ſeen him lately, but Mr. *Richardſon*, our Rector, aſſures me, that he is recovered of all his Complaints to a wonderful Degree, ſolely by the Tar-water, and that he confeſſes he never knew tolerable Comfort, ſince his Illneſs, till he took it.

90. A poor Fellow, in ſome Under-Office about the Church of this Town, was alſo aſthmatick, and almoſt incapable of any Action, and is now reſtored by it, as our Rector aſſures me. I am, dear Sir,

Your moſt affectionate Servant,

Charles Coote.

91. *P. S.* My Brother-in-law, Mr. *Pratt*, who has been extremely ill, many Years, of ſcorbutick Diſorders, and has, in vain, drank all the Waters in *Europe*, drank the Tar-water a good while, and I believe continues to do ſo; he is now active in Spirits, and able to do Buſineſs, and, indeed, appeared to me, not long ago, to be quite recovered; he made it but of half the Strength, the full Strength diſagreeing with him, and he declared, he thought his Amendment was entirely owing to it.

92. *A*

92. *A Letter from* William Ryves, *Esq*; *from* Castlejane *near* Tipperary, *dated* October 11, 1744.

SIR,

I shall always take Pleasure in any Thing for the publick Good, therefore with Pleasure sit down to answer your's, and to give you the Account you desire, of the Benefit my Tenant, *John Cornick*, received from the Use of Tar-water.

This Man has been, for many Years past, a Mower and a Plowman, in the Occupation of which, by Heats and Colds, he acquired a Cough, which continued on him for several Months, and which sometimes (especially in the Spring) disabled him from following the Plow; but about *March* last, he was obliged to keep his Bed, notwithstanding he had the Advice and Directions of two Physicians, at different times; and being worn away to perfect Skin and Bone, the Physicians pronounced him very near his End. About *July* last, I got, and read *Siris*, and immediately directed this poor Fellow to drink Tar-water, which he did constantly, twice or three times a Day: For the first Week, or ten Days, he coughed prodigiously, and brought up great Quantities of fetid Corruption; every Day after, his Cough abated, and his Stomach increased, and at the End of three Weeks drinking, he was able to walk half a Mile with Pleasure, which he did, every Morning, between his first Draught and Breakfast; and, in five Week's time, had gathered a good deal of Strength; his Tar being then out, and he thinking himself pretty well, he omitted drinking since; but I have now ordered him a fresh Parcel of Tar, and do not doubt but he will be as well able to hold his Plow, next Spring, as ever, and mow the following Summer: In short, his Cough is gone, and he finds himself hearty; I this Day examined him.

93. *Edward*

93. *Edward Moore*, Esq; of *Moore's Fort* in the County of *Tipperary*, a Gentleman of Fortune, was extremely out of Order, and, by all the Physicians that attended him, was judged to have an Ulcer in his Bladder, and was preparing to go to some Waters proper for him; he had quite lost his Stomach and Complexion, but by the Use of Tar-water, for five or six Weeks, is not only quite well of his Disorder, but has recovered his Stomach and Complexion; and, I do believe, still continues to drink it. I can also assure you, my Wife has drank it, for some time, for a little barking Cough, which she has had these three Years past, which afflicts her most, just as she gets up in the Morning; and she has found such an Abatement of it, that I do not doubt, but, in a little time, she will be quite free from it. If these Accounts be of any Use to the Publick, and a satisfactory Answer to your Letter, it will fully answer the Design of, Sir,

Your very humble Servant,

William Ryves.

94. *A Letter from* William Connor, *Esq; from* Bandon *in the County of* Cork, *dated* October 23, 1744.

SIR,

I am favoured with your's of the Sixth Instant, and have since communicated the same to my Brother *George Connor*, who is the Person, you heard, had been relieved, in a scorbutick Disorder, by the Use of Tar-water; for which he is full of Acknowledgments to the Author of *Siris*; and (had not the Badness of the Weather, and some other Accidents, in his Family, hitherto prevented) he designed, ere now, to have paid his Compliments personally to the Bishop of *Cloyne*, and have acquainted him with the whole Progress of his Disorder, and almost incredible Benefit he had received in less lefs than a Month, by the Ufe of that moft fovereign and univerfal Remedy; for which Purpofe, he defired me to let you know, that he intends waiting on his Lordfhip as foon as he can conveniently leave Home; there are feveral other Inftances in this Neighbourhood, of Perfons benefited by the fame Means, but none more fo (that I have heard of) than one of my Daughters, who had laboured under a kind of hyfterick and nervous Diforder for fome Months, which afflicted her with a Palpitation and Difficulty of Breathing, infomuch, that fhe frequently imagined fhe was expiring; of which Complaint, fhe is now (God be praifed) quite free, and attributes her Cure folely to that moft excellent Remedy, Tar-water, having received little or no Benefit from any Thing elfe; tho' fhe had been under a Courfe of Medicines, for fome Months, before fhe took to the drinking Tar-water, for the Difcovery of which fhe is infinitely obliged to the good Bifhop, and fo is, Sir,

Your moft obedient Servant,

William Connor.

95. Mr. *George Connor*, whofe Name is mentioned in the precedent Letter, having been pleafed himfelf to communicate his own Cafe, and Relief, in *November*, 1744, I fhall here infert the Particulars thereof, which fhew the wonderful Powers of Tar-water.

Mr. *Connor* had been, feveral Years, afflicted with a fcorbutick Diforder, and finding no Relief here, from the Prefcriptions of Phyficians, he went to *England*, where he made ufe of the *Bath*, and other Waters, without receiving any Benefit; upon his Return to *Ireland*, his Diftemper became fo violent, and increafed to fuch a Degree, that his Phyficians, not knowing what to do elfe, were for fending him to *Bath* again, when, by Chance, he met with *Siris*, which

which put him upon the making and drinking Tar-water, which quite recovered him in a Month or ſix Weeks Time; his Caſe was wonderful, his Body was all over one continued Sore, he was obliged to ſhift himſelf four times a Day, and his Shirts ſtood on End, ſtiffened by Corruption; his Limbs and Body were wrapped up in Linen ſpread with Suet, to keep any Thing from touching him.

The ſharp Humours uſed to run through his Cloaths on the Ground. He could neither digeſt, ſleep, nor reſt. The firſt Effect of the Tar-water was that an incredible Number of blind Boils appeared in the Skin over his whole Body, and very ſore, by which the morbifick Humour was driven to the outward Parts, and by conſtant drinking Tar-water, theſe Boils grew milder, and by Degrees healed and dried away, ſo that in leſs than ſix Weeks, he was quite eaſy, and he attributes his Cure ſolely to Tar-water. Upon firſt taking the Water, he was very coſtive for ſeveral Days, which frightened him, and made him take ſome gentle opening Purge. But this rather retarded his Cure, for where the Tar-water throws out the Venom into the Skin, it ſhould not be diſturbed by the Revulſion of a Purgative, howſoever ſuch caſting out may naturally produce a Coſtiveneſs. Such Coſtiveneſs is not to be reckoned a bad Effect, but a good Symptom; it ſhews that Nature is throwing out the bad Humours through the Skin, and not by Stool, and when it has ſufficiently done that Service, in which it ought not to be diſturbed, the Body will naturally return to its uſual Diſcharges; as many have experienced.

96. A

96. *A Letter from* Cornelius Townſend *of* Betſborough *near* Mallow *in the County of* Cork, *Eſq*; *dated the 30th of* October, 1744.

S I R,

I received the Favour of yours, but a Hurry of Buſineſs prevented my anſwering it ſooner; I aſſure you, I never had it in my Inclination to conceal any Thing that I thought may be of general Uſe to Mankind. Before I enter on the Particulars of my complicated Diſorders, I muſt beg leave to obſerve to you, that I am thoroughly convinced, from my own Experience, and my Obſervations on others, that nothing yet diſcovered ſtands fairer for being conſidered as an univerſal Medicine for all Diſorders, than Tar-water, taken as lately directed by that great good Man, the Biſhop of *Cloyne*, in his Treatiſe on the Virtues thereof. As to my own Experience, about fifteen Years ago, and about the 32d of my Age, after a moſt remarkable good Stock of Health from my Infancy, I was firſt ſeized with a violent Heartburn, and ſoon after had ſlight Fits of the Rheumatiſm, which in a few Years became very violent, and then getting the better of my often envied good Conſtitution, a moſt inveterate Scurvy appeared, particularly on my Temples, and Forehead; my Fits of the Rheumatiſm were in the Beginning irregular, and did not hold above a Month or ſix Weeks at a Time; but about eight Years ago, they became regular, and uſed to confine me to my Bed during the whole Winter and Spring, and always began with a light Fever and terrible Head-ach, which generally held for the firſt nine or ten Days. I have been likewiſe ſubject to a Scurvy in my Gums, and in ſpight of all my Care, apt to get cold, which frequently afflicted my Lungs and Glands, and occaſioned a Deafneſs; till about three Years ago by the Advice of the preſent Biſhop of *Killaloe*, I began the Uſe of Tar-water, which

which within a Month carryed off the Heart-burn; and soon after the Scurvy in my Gums, Temples, &c. began to lessen, and about that time twelve Month, was quite gone; it has also carryed off the Inflammation of my Glands, and I am not so apt to get cold, or be very deaf as formerly; and when, through Carelessnes of myself, it happens I get either, I am under no Apprehension about any ill Consequences, finding that honest Tar-water does the Business. My Fits of the Rheumatism, since the Use of Tar-water, have indeed been as tedious, with as great a Weakness in my Knees and Ancles as ever, so that I am not able to stand, but not near so painful and almost free from the Fever and Head-ach I have mentioned. I am now under a Course of bathing my Legs in warm Tar-water, by Direction of the Bishop of *Cloyne*, and hope in some Time to be able to give you an Account of its Success. I fear I have tired your Patience, but as you desired I should be particular in the Account of my Ailments, I must farther let you know, that from the Beginning of my Disorders, I have had such a costive Constitution, that I seldom had the Benefit of Nature, without the Help of Electuaries, or some other Openers; my Fundament was so inflamed with Piles, that I was very apprehensive of a Fistula, my Flesh was bloated and very tender every where; I was subject to a Palpitation of the Heart, Cramps, Meagrims, &c. from all which (I thank God) I am quite free by the constant Use of Tar-water only.

The famous Doctor *Barry* several Years ago, put me under a Course of Rhubarb and Sulphur, to which I regularly stuck for upwards of two Years; and other Physicians since put me under different Courses of Physick for my Rheumatick and other Disorders, but all to no manner of Purpose.

E 2 97. As

97. As to my Obſervations on others, a Gentlewoman in my Family, who had a paralytick Diſorder, and the Scurvy to a great Degree, with many Diſorders in her Stomach, for which ſhe ſtuck to the *Mallow* Waters for ſeveral Seaſons, and was only for the Preſent relieved thereby, and my Wife, who has been tormented with the Scurvy, Hiſtericks, *&c.* are both recovered, and very well by the Uſe of Tar-water.

98. One Mrs. *Buſtid*, who lives near *Killmallock*, having had a Heart-burn for ſome Years to ſuch a Degree, that in her Strainings, ſhe would frequently diſcharge Blood out of her Stomach; ſhe was ſubject to a racking Pain in her Bowels, had a Ganger in her Mouth, and her Teeth were all looſe; ſhe was given over by all the ſkilful Perſons in her Neighbourhood; but, hearing of the great Benefits I received by the Uſe of Tar-water, began to drink it, and ſoon found herſelf much better. Of which an Apothecary in *Killmallock* having had an Account, ſent her word, that ſhe was ill adviſed to take it that way, and ordered her by all Means to mix her Tar with hot Water, and then drink it; which ſhe accordingly did; but it operated ſo violently by purging up and down, that ſhe was at Death's Door; however, ſhe afterwards found, that taking it even that way, did her vaſt Service; ſhe is now perfectly recovered, and firmly reſolved never to take the Advice of an Apothecary again. I could mention ſeveral more, who, by my Advice, in various Diſorders, received very great Benefit, or were perfectly cured by drinking Tar-water; in ſhort, I make it my Buſineſs to recommend it to all my Acquaintance, and whatever your Diſorders are, you may ſafely take it; if you do, I don't at all doubt but you will ſoon join in the Praiſe of Tar-water, with, Sir,

Your moſt obedient humble Servant,

Corn. Townſend.

99. *An*

99. *An Extract of a Letter from a Physician, whose Name I am not at Liberty to mention; communicated to me in* November, 1744.

" A Man of about thirty-five Years of Age consulted me, who from a pleuritic Disorder imperfectly cured, fell into an hectic Fever, attended with a desperate Cough, with this dreadful Symptom, an Ulcer in the left Lobe of his Lungs; which plainly appeared, first from his being at first attacked by the Pleurisy in the left Side. Secondly, from almost an impossibility of lying on the right Side. Thirdly, from a vast Heaviness and suffocating Burthen he complained of in the left Part of his Thorax; till relieved in some Measure by throwing up a vast Quantity of fetid purulent Matter, intermixed with pure Blood, and (I may say) *sanguine spumoso*, so justly called by the great *Hippocrates*; which Excretion generally happened to him once a Month or thereabouts, and which, as he informed me, had always like to have suffocated him. This evacuated Pus must have been gathered in its proper Vesicula, which being external in the Lobe was usually broke by a strong Fit of Coughing, or some other violent Shock of Nature. Upon further Examination, I found he had cold nocturnal Sweats, and almost all the Signs of the *Facies Hippocratica*. You may easily judge, that the Prognostic I formed, was very doubtful, as his Case was both dangerous and difficult. However, I ordered him immediately to drink Tar-water, and, as the Indication required, I prescribed some balsamic and detergent Pills, besides some Stomachic Medicines, as he almost entirely lost his Appetite; I have also ordered him to take a Ride, Morning and Evening constantly. I can now with great Truth and Pleasure assure you, that he is quite recovered; which I must in Justice attribute to the Tar-water, as the last Medi-

E 3 cines,

cines, though prescribed before Tar-water, had little or no Effect. I have tried this Medicine of Tar-water in two Cases of the asthmatic Kind, and in three acute ones, in all which it has had wonderful Success."

100. *An Extract of a Letter from* Henry Edgworth *of* Lizard *in the County of* Longford, *Esq; Member of Parliament, dated the* 10*th of* November, 1744.

" I shall soon be able to send you some very remarkable good Effects of Tar-water, which has been taken both by myself and two others of my particular Friends, and those of Judgment and good Sense, who have given this innocent, useful, and cheap Medicine, fair Play. I can't have their Leave to mention their Names; but as to myself, I must do it the Justice as to say, that few Men of my Age and temperate Way of Life, I believe, have been more afflicted with the Rheumatism; more especially in the Winter Season, and in changeable Weather: and after the Violence of the Fits abated, it frequently and almost these fourteen Years past, (about which Period of Time I was first attacked by that inveterate Enemy) left me in a worse Condition, even Pain cannot in my Apprehensions in any Sort be compared to the excessive Lowness and Dejection of Spirits, I laboured under for certain Times, more or less, till I took Tar-water; and though my Affairs would not permit me to have Recourse to it as regularly as I ought, yet even as I took it, it has pleased God, not only in a great Measure to mitigate the Violence of the Fits of the Rheumatism, but I have in no Sort had the least Return of any Dejection of Spirits this whole Winter. I am no Bigot of any Sort, I assure you; but I am fully persuaded this most excellent Remedy, if properly prepared and taken, would work more miraculous Cures, than

than ever were pretended to have been wrought at the Tomb of *Thomas a Becket*; and has more real Virtue in it, than the Touch or Blood of any of the Line of the *Stuarts* whatever; and this Account you may publish whenever you think fit, as Truth and Matter of Fact."

101. *A Letter from* Charles Tottenham *of* Tottenham Green *in the County of* Wexford, *Esq*; *Member of Parliament*, November 18, 1744.

"For the good of the Publick, and in Honour of the Bishop of *Cloyne*, I inform you, that *William Cooper*, my Servant, on *Tuesday* the 9th of last *October*, fell ill of a violent Fever, Stich and Pleurisy; on *Wednesday* and *Thursday* was bled, his Blood very bad each Time, on *Wednesday* Evening he began to drink warm Tar-water, and by *Thursday* at Noon, had drank above two Quarts; at which Time his Stich and Fever left him; he sweated greatly; a blistering Plaister was sent for on *Thursday* Morning, which was brought to the Patient that Evening, but finding himself easy would not suffer it to be applyed; he continued free from Pain till *Saturday* Morning, at which Time his Stich returned, his Lungs so greatly oppressed, that he could scarce breath, his Inside very sore, and his Head very painful. On *Saturday* Evening a blistering Plaister was put on between his Shoulders; he continued very ill till *Sunday* Evening, at which Time his Blister began to run, on which he had immediate Ease, and continuing to drink Tar-water, by eleven o'Clock that Night his Head was free from Pain, his Stich and Cough gone, slept well that Night, and on the 20th of the same Month, was, as hearty and as heal as ever. Said *William Cooper* is between fifty and sixty Years old, has had a violent Cough and bad Lungs these thirty Years past, until now, not having any Cough, Pain withinside,

ſide, or Oppreſſion on his Lungs: This ſhould have been ſooner ſent, but that I thought it proper to wait, and know whether any of his old Diſorders returned; they did not, he never was better nor ſo full of Spirits.

P. S. It is to be obſerved that the Patient drank Tar-water the whole Time."

102. *A Letter from Mr.* George Johnſon, *a young Officer in the Army, to* Thomas Prior, *Eſq; dated the 25th of* November, 1744.

" I was greatly afflicted with the Bloody-flux from *February* 1742-3. to the Beginning of *May*, 1744, the greateſt Part of which Time, I was ſo ill, that I was not expected to live, nor could I eat or drink any Thing that would ſtay upon my Stomach; nor had I any Eaſe during the whole Time, but when I uſed to ride, which I did three or four Weeks ſucceſſively, three or four Times during my Illneſs, on Buſineſs; a Week or ſix Days after which, I was tolerably eaſy, and could eat pretty hearty, after which tho' I took ſeveral Things, and by the beſt Advice, I ſtill grew worſe. I was adviſed to take Tar-water, which I did once a Day for near a Week in the Beginning of *April*, 1744, but it would not ſtay on my Stomach, and made me ſick, ſo I left it off for about three Weeks; but continuing to grow worſe, I was adviſed to take it *May* following, which I did (I thank God) with Succeſs, for by taking regularly twice a Day, with a Doſe or two of Rhubarb during the Time which was about three Weeks, (I thank God) I was perfectly well.

N. B. I ſeveral Times before took Rhubarb during my Illneſs in all Shapes, without any Benefit."

103. *An*

103. *An Extract of a Letter from the Revered Mr.* Thomas Collier *of* Aunfield *near* Rofs *in the County of* Wexford, *to* Thomas Prior, *Efq*; *dated* January 24, 1744.

SIR,

I have had it often in my Thoughts to communicate to you a particular Account of the Cafe of the Woman mentioned in your Letter, and of fome others, in regard to the Effects of Tar-water. The poor Woman had for three Years before fhe drank the Tar-water, been troubled every Summer with very ugly Blotches and Ulcers, efpecially on her Face; and as the poor People about me generally apply for fome Cure or other for their Diforders, I advifed her to a Courfe of Marfh, or wild Celery-Tea. This gave fome Relief for the Prefent, but fhe grew worfe in the main, that is, every Summer the Ulcers increafed in Number and Size, fo that I advifed to the Hofpital in *Waterford*. Juft as I had read *Siris*, fhe came to my Door, her Face fwelled to a monftrous Size, hardly any Eyes to be feen, and in as loathfome a Way as ever I faw one in the worft and moft difmal Stage of the Small-pox. She told me fhe was dying, and begged a little Charity from me: I had fome Tar-water juft made for myfelf, and I made her take along with her two Quarts, and defired her to drink them off, and come to me again; I did not fee her for a Week, and then fhe told me, fhe had tried to take the Water, and it was fo cold on her Stomach, that it almoft killed her; that inftead of comforting her, it threw her into a cold Sweat, all mortal Symptoms. I then advifed her to go home and take it as warm as fhe could poffibly bear it; fhe did fo, and in a Week came to me for more Water. By that Time, the Swelling had much fubfided, and fhe could fee with both her Eyes. I then gave her a Gallon of Water more,

more, and in about a Month after ſhe came to me quite well, no Swelling in any Part of her Body, and only a Redneſs in her Face juſt as after the Small-pox. I forgot to mention, that, when ſhe firſt came to me, her whole Body was greatly ſwelled; ſhe continued well till laſt Summer, when ſhe had a ſmall Return of the Diſorder, which was cured the ſame Way, and is at this Time ſeemingly well. In this Caſe the Cure was prodigious, and what I eſteemed almoſt miraculous, becauſe I had known the Woman's Ailment a long Time before ſhe took the Tar-water, and as it was inveterate and of a long ſtanding, I thought it would take up a good deal of Time and Water, if ſhe could be cured at all. As far as I am able to judge, her Diſorder was a Scurvy occaſioned by poor Living in every Senſe, and this in its laſt Stage attended by a Dropſy. Her Name is *Catherine Dobbin.*

104. The next Caſe I tried was for a violent Pain in the Stomach, which had greatly troubled a young Gentlewoman of my Acquintance for about a Twelve-month, and for removing which, ſhe had taken ſeveral Things, but to no Purpoſe; one Gallon of Water cured her, and ſhe has had no Complaint of the Kind theſe fourteen Months paſt.

105. A third Patient who received Benefit by drinking Tar-water, was an old labouring Man, who was ſo weakened by a long dry Cough, that when I ſaw him I took him to be on the extreme Verge of Life. He was ſo weak, that he was aſſiſted in coming a Quarter of a Mile to my Houſe, and was obliged to ſtop at every third or fourth Step: I gave this Man a Pitcher of Tar-water, and in about a Month he came to me to know if I had any Work for him, his Cough quite removed, and with a ruddy healthy Countenance; he has been ſince labouring conſtantly, and is in a better State of Health this Moment, than he was for any time during

during three Years before he took the Water. His Name is *Edmund Dunfy*.

106. Within this Month paſt a very extraordinary Cure has been owing to Tar-water: A Servant-Maid in this Pariſh, was ſeized about a Month paſt with a violent Itching all over her Body, which in three or four Days broke out all over her in watery Puſtules, which as they broke, threw out a ſcalding ſharp corroding Liquor, which burnt the Skin wherever it touched it; ſo that the poor Creature was almoſt diſtracted: But prepoſſeſſed violently againſt Tar-water. At laſt, with great Perſuaſion, ſhe was prevailed on to take it, and by the time ſhe had finiſhed two Bottles the Puſtules diſappeared, and ſhe is now free from all the Symptons, and in very good Health: The common People called it the St. *Anthony*'s Fire, but I can't pretend to ſay what the true Name of the Diſorder was. If any thing elſe remarkable ſhould occur, I ſhall make bold to let you know it, and am,

Sir, Your moſt obedient humble Servant,

Tho. Collier.

107. *A Letter from Col.* Nicholas Loftus, *of* Loftus-hall *in the County of* Wexford, *Eſq*; *Member of Parliament, to* Thomas Prior, *Eſq*; *dated* Feb. *the 1ſt*, 1744.

I have your Favour of the 29th of laſt Month: I have drank Tar-water theſe three Months paſt, half a Pint Morning and Evening, with great Succeſs: My Diſorder was ſevere Pains in all my Bones, and particularly in my Joints, which I believe were Rheumatick, and was very apprehenſive of a Return of the 'Sciatica, having had a ſevere Fit of it laſt Spring. I had a Stiffneſs in my Limbs, which made walking very uneaſy to me: Which Exerciſe I uſed a great deal of before. My Pains are now all

all vaniſhed, and I can walk ſome Miles in a Morning as well as I ever did. Some in my Neighbourhood have taken it, for a Year paſt, in the Gout, and the Fits of it have been much lighter than they had been many Years before.

108. I have a Servant who had a very violent Aſthma, who I made drink it, and he hath been ſince ſurprizingly relieved: I am convinced that it is very good for many Diſorders; I have found it very diuretick. I am told, that you are about publiſhing ſomething about it, for the Good of the Publick: As you deſerve their Thanks in many Inſtances, pray accept of theſe, particularly from, Dear Sir,

Your moſt obedient humble Servant,

Nicholas Loftus.

109. *A Letter from* Peyton Fox, *Eſq*; *of* Weſtmeath, *to* Thomas Prior, *Eſq*; *dated* Feb. *the* 15*th*, 1744.

Dear SIR,

I had Yeſterday the Favour of your's of the 29th of laſt Month; and according to your Deſire acquaint you, that for theſe ſeveral Years paſt, I have been ſubject to great Colds; but laſt Winter I had ſuch a violent Cold and Cough, as confined me within Doors for five Months, and found not the leaſt Benefit from Remedies, of which I took a vaſt Quantity: But when I got the good Biſhop's *Siris*, I took the Tar-water, which perfectly recovered me, and do not find I am ſo apt to get cold as I was. My Stomach is not extraordinary good, but much better than it was. Within theſe three Months I got, by venturing too much in my Garden in cold Weather, two Colds; but the Tar-water, in a few Days, carried them off without ſevere coughing. Since I firſt took the Tar-water, I have not had the leaſt Touch of the Gout, and my Spirits are more lively: I look on my Cure to be the more extraordinary, conſidering my great Age, being ſeventy-four.

I hear

I hear of many who have received Benefit by the Tar-water, but can't be particular: If I hear of any worth acquainting you with, I will; and aſſure yourſelf, I am,

Dear Sir, Your moſt humble Servant,

Pey. Fox.

110. *A Letter from the Rev. Mr.* Roger Lyndon, *of* Ballyſax *in the County of* Kildare, March 26, 1744.

Dear SIR,

I had the Favour of your Letter by laſt Poſt, deſiring I would inform you concerning my drinking Tar-water, and the good Effect it hath had on me.

Laſt Summer, and ſometimes before, I found myſelf under ſeveral Diſorders, as Gravel, Pains in my Back, confining me ſome ſhort Times to my Bed; great want of Appetite, frequent Dizzineſs in my Head, unſeaſonable Sleepineſs, Soreneſs in my Gums, and the looſening and falling of ſome of my Teeth, inſomuch that I could ſcarcely chew my Meat; and by ſuch great Uneaſineſs in my Mouth, I was often reduced to Broths, and other ſoft Aliments. All theſe Diſorders, I was informed, proceeded from the Scurvy; and therefore I was reſolved to try the Benefit of the ſo much talk'd-of Tar-water. I began to drink it, purſuant to all the Rules, laſt *Michaelmas*; and have continued it to the middle of this Month, without Intermiſſion: I was from the beginning very exact in keeping up to Diſcipline, and therefore ſoon found the Benefit; and, I bleſs God, have not, in the leaſt Degree, felt any of the Diſorders before-mentioned: I can walk great lengths; have a conſtant and good Appetite; can eat my Meat, with Teeth as well-faſtened and eaſy in my Mouth, as I could for ſome Years paſt. This, Sir, is in Fact all I have to acquaint you with, the Arguings I leave to better Judgments; and if you think this Account may be of any Service to others, you may

may (as you have desired) communicate it, in what manner you please, to so good an End. I am, Sir,

Your affectionate humble Servant,

Roger Lyndon.

111. *A Letter from* John Usher, *of* Lismore *in the County of* Waterford, *Esq*; *dated from* Lismore, Feb. *the* 4*th*, 1744, *to* Thomas Prior, *Esq*;

In Performance of my Promise, I send you the two following Cases, which happened lately, and may be relied upon. A Soldier in Capt. *Burston*'s Company, in General *Frampton*'s Regiment, whose Name I cannot learn, tho' he was some time in this Town, being afflicted with a spitting of Blood and purulent Matter, for a considerable Time (which Disorder was occasioned by a Peripneumony or Pleurisy, tho' he could not tell which, having had it before he came to Quarters to *Dungarvan*, about two Years ago) and having also a violent Cough and strong Night-sweats, Symptoms of a deep Decay, which quite emaciated him, Mr. *Charles Smith*, Apothecary in that Town, ordered him to drink Tar-water, which was made with Lime-water, instead of common Water, knowing Lime-water to be a great Dryer of Ulcers: He had not used it long, when he found his Cough and other Symptoms left him entirely, and in a short time he grew surprizingly fat and healthy.

112. *Richard Kearney*, Servant to Mr. *Thomas Barbon* in *Dungarvan*, was for many Years afflicted with a Cough and Difficulty of Breathing, which arrived at length to a confirmed and violent Asthma, so that upon the least Pressure of the Atmosphere he was constantly visited with his Disorder, and disabled from rendering his Master any Service: About four Months since, by the Persuasion of his Master, he began to drink Tar-water; and had not used it above a Fortnight, when, to his Surprize, he found a great

a great Heat and Scalding in his Urine, and a *Gonorrhœa* of a moſt virulent Colour enſued, which ſo frighted him, that he left off drinking the Tar-water, attributing theſe Symptoms to the Uſe of it; but upon his Maſter's urging him to it, he again took to the Uſe of it, when, in about a Month, not only theſe Symptoms left him entirely, but, in a great meaſure, his Cough and Aſthma. He ſtill uſes the Tar-water, and is much recruited in both his Strength and Fleſh, inſomuch that laſt Week he walked up a ſteep Hill at the Back of the Caſtle here, nimbly and in a few Minutes, which, he aſſured me, before he took the Tar-water, he could not crawl up in an Hour. The above *Charles Smith* enquired of him, whether formerly he had not ſome venereal Taint, which he did not deny, and he attributes the above Symptoms to ſome Remains of that Diſtemper, which the Tar-water carried off; it wrought him and ſtill doth much by Urine. Theſe two ſhall ſuffice for this time; in my next you ſhall have more on the ſame Subject, from

Your moſt humble Servant,

John Uſher.

113. The ſaid Mr. *Uſher* having alſo communicated the Effects and Virtues of Spruce-beer, which he juſtly reckons to be a Kind of Tar-water, both proceeding from the Juices of the Fir Kind: I ſhall beg Leave to inſert, in this Place, the Particulars thereof: He writes " that having an Eſtate on the Coaſt in the County of *Waterford*, from whence many of his Tenants go yearly to the Fiſhery of *Newfoundland*, he frequently obſerved, that ſuch of them as went out meagre and pale, like Skeletons, and troubled with Itch and Scurvy, always returned fat, with ruddy Complexions and great Health, notwithſtanding their great Fatigues there; and on Enquiry into the Cauſe thereof, he found that they all attributed their Recovery to their conſtant drinking

ing of Spruce-beer while they are there; that as soon as they arrive there, they cut the Branches of the black Spruce Fir, which is the only Fir made use of there for Spruce-beer, and therewith make their Beer in the manner mentioned hereafter; and this Practice of making and drinking Spruce-beer, they continue during the Time they stay there, and in their Return, and bring great Quantities of the Branches with them to make Spruce-beer after their Arrival, which they are very fond of; and notwithstanding they live on salt Provisions many Months, and have frequently thick Fogs on the Banks, yet they are no way troubled with Scurvy, Itch, or any Eruptions whatsoever, owing, as they say, to the constant drinking Spruce-beer. They say farther, that the People are very prolific, and that no Part of the World has so many Children as St. *John*'s in *Newfoundland*, considering the Number of the Inhabitants; probably this may be owing to the constant Use of Spruce-beer, or their living so much on Fish, or both."

114. *The Way of making Spruce-beer in* Newfoundland, *as communicated from the Fishermen to Mr.* Usher.

Let sixteen Gallons of Water be well boiled in a Pot, along with a good Quantity of the Branches of the black spruce Fir cut into short Pieces, as much as will fill the Pot; it will take three or four Hours boiling, and the Method to know when it is boiled enough, is when the Bark of the Spruce slips readily off the Sticks between your Fingers. The Spruce is then taken out, and a Gallon of Molasses put to the Water, which is sufficient to make a sixty Gallon Cask, and proportionably a greater Quantity of Molasses for a larger Cask. The Water is then to be well stirred and well boiled once after the Molasses is put to it; it must then be put into a Cask, which is is to be filled up with cold Water, and to be very well ſtirred with a Stick at the Bung, and, by the Help of the Grounds remaining in the Caſk from a former Brewing, will immediately ferment, and the next Day the Bung is to be cloſed up, and the Day following it will be fit for Uſe. But if you have no Grounds of a former Brewing, then put a ſmall Quantity of Barm to it, which will in one Night's Time ſufficiently ferment it; next Morning cloſe it up, and it will be fit for Uſe the Day following, and will hold good a Fortnight. But if you would make Spruce-beer to laſt ſeveral Months, then you muſt add a greater Quantity of Molaſſes two or three, or more Gallons, and more Spruce to give it a ſtronger Body.

115. *A Letter from* John Uſher *of* Liſmore, *in the County of* Waterford, *Eſq*; *dated* April *the* 6*th* 1745, *to* Thomas Prior, *Eſq*;

The conſtant Employment, I have here, has hindred me from collecting Caſes relating to Tar-water; however, you ſhall have ſome in a Poſt or two: My own is worth taking Notice of, and is as follows. I have been, for twelve or fourteen Years, troubled with a Diſorder in my Nerves; it came on gradually, but at laſt to ſuch a Pitch, that there was ſeldom a Night that I have not been obliged to get out of my Bed, and walk about the Room for ſome Minutes, before I could compoſe myſelf to Reſt; eſpecially on the leaſt Exceſs in Drinking, or the leaſt Cold. As I was ready to drop aſleep, my Mind uſed to be extremely agitated, in a manner not to be deſcribed: I uſed to feel at the ſame time a Thrilling down my Thighs, and a Deſire to ſtretch, as in an Ague Fit, which relieved me for that Moment: The Bed was then intolerable to me, nor could I find any Relief but by getting up and walking about tho' I have bore it with the utmoſt Pain for

F above

above an Hour. I was at *Spa*, and took all the nervous Medicines from divers Phycifians to no Purpofe. Doctor *Lacky*'s Advice concurred with my own Inclinations, to induce me to drink Tar-water; and I folemnly affirm, that in a Fortnight's drinking it, I never had a fingle Return of it from that Day to this, which has made my Life comfortable, as I ufed before to dread the Approach of Night. This I the rather infift on, as I am very fure I never drank a Drop of good Tar-water: For a Cafk of Tar I had from *Cork*, I am now confident, had been all ufed before; and I am now, to my great Concern, obliged to difcontinue it for want of good Tar; for there is not a Drop to be had in *Cork* that is good; and I have had Complaints from the good Bifhop on that Head: However, I have had no Return of my Diforder.

116. *P. S.* I am not at Liberty to mention the Names to you of two Women that have been cured of an inveterate *Fluor albus*, even by bad Tar-water, and in a fhort Time; in fuch Diforders Names are not to be mentioned, but I am thoroughly convinced of the Facts, and have as much Evidence as the Nature of them will admit. I fhall for the prefent conclude this long Letter with affuring you, that I am yours, &c.

117. *A Letter from Mr.* Lewis Lloyd *of* Kinfale, *dated* March *the 8th*, 1744.

A poor Labourer of this Town, rendered incapable to get his Bread, by a moft violent Itch that feized both Legs; after the Advice of Doctors, Surgeons and Apothecaries, and the laft Expedient, Salivation, proved ineffectual, being advifed to rub the Sores with Tar-water, was in three or four Days perfectly cured, to the great Surprize of thofe who had before adminiftred to him.

111. *A*

118. *A Letter from the Reverend Dean* Isaac Gervais *of* Lismore *in the County of* Waterford, *dated* May *the 8th*, 1745.

I have, for a considerable Time, been prevented by many incidental Avocations, from communicating a Case, as much to the Honour of Tar-water, as perhaps any yet publickly known, and the more so, in that it is the only Instance of that Nature I have heard of.

Being in *Waterford*, some time in *July* last, I advised a Sister of mine, now in Years, who had been long afflicted with an inveterate Rheumatism, to the Use of Tar-water, which she readily complied with; so that, having a Call there about seven Weeks since, I had the Pleasure of seeing her strong enough to meet me on the Stairs without Stick, without which, for a long time, she was not able to walk across her Room.

119. That is not all, but an usual Effect of it; for besides, she had, for near two Years before, been grievously tormented with a cruel and unquenchable Thirst, to which the other Disorder was nothing, in Comparison. It was become the Plague of her Life. She had by scrupulous Care, and Choice of Diet, the Advice of Neighbours and Acquaintance, and others, pretending to more Skill, done all that could possibly be devised to get the better of it; but all in vain, till, by the Blessing of God on the Use of Tar-water, her Thirst gradually lessened; so that at present, she is perfectly easy, and so effectually cured, as she seems almost to have lost her Appetite to drink itself; though not yet quite relieved from the other Disorder, yet she bears it patiently, it being easy in Comparison of the Torment she has got rid of. I am yours,

Is. Gervais.

 SIR,

June 18, 1745.

SIR,

In Compliance with your Request, I send you the following Account of certain Persons in my Neighbourhood, who have received Benefit by drinking Tar-water. Many others, about me, have taken it to good Effect; but I mention none but such whose Maladies and Cures fell within my own Knowledge. I am,

Sir, your very affectionate humble Servant,

Benj. Everard.

An Account of certain Persons, near Blessington *in the County of* Wicklow, *who have received Benefit by drinking Tar-water, to wit.*

120. *Catherine Cardy*, forty-one Years of Age; troubled with a Cough, Stuffing in her Chest, and Shortness of Breath, all the Winter of 1742, not free from these Complaints in the Summer of 1743, and feeling them all more severely in the following Winter; but in the Spring of 1744, affected with them all in the highest Degree, labouring under a Difficulty of Breathing, without Appetite, not being able to work or walk, or lie down at Night, getting little or no Sleep, her Body emaciated, her Breast, Neck and Face, swelled; and her Lips black, and scarce able to speak. She began with Tar-water the 4th of *April* 1744, and thought herself recovered with drinking six Bottles; but finding a Streightness in her Breast, after leaving it off four Days, she took two Bottles more, and became quite well.

The first Morning after taking it, she spit a Quart of tough Phlegm and ropy Matter, after much Coughing. She coughed for ten Mornings after with less and less spitting: In this time her Complaints wore off; in three Days she could lye down in her Bed, and sleep all Night; her Stomach

mach came to her, and ſhe recovered her Strength and Freedom of Breathing; ſo that, on the eighth Day, ſhe walked a Mile up Hill, and back again, without being diſordered, and towards the latter End of *May*, was able to bear the Fatigue of nurſing a Foundling Child, left at her Door, and walked with it ſeven times in that Month, to and from *Bleſſington*, which is a Journey of more than three Miles. She paſſed the laſt Winter and Spring without any other Diſorder than a Cough, at odd times, upon catching Cold; which was always removed by a Bottle or two of Tar-water.

121. *James Dooling*, Labourer, aged about thirty-five Years, taken with a Fever in the Spring of 1744, which increaſed with threatening Symptoms, particularly a Looſeneſs, ſo that his Life was deſpaired of: On the 9th Day Tar-water was given him, and on the 13th the Fever turned; in a Week after he got out of Bed, and walked about his Cabbin; in about another Week he went abroad, and ſoon after fell to his Work, looking clear and ruddy, and of a healthful Countenance.

122. *Anne Oſborn*, about fifty Years old, troubled with Stitches at times, for four or five Years, kept her Bed for three Months in the Winter of 1743, labouring under Stitches, a Cough, and Shortneſs of Breath, without Appetite or Sleep, and worn away to Skin and Bone, drank Tar-water, Night and Morning, the Beginning of *April* 1744, and with eight Bottles was perfectly recovered. At firſt, ſhe threw up a great deal of foul Stuff from her Stomach: In three takings her Stitches left her; ſhe ſoon recovered her Appetite and Reſt, and was able to lye down in Bed; her Cough ceaſed, ſhe gained Fleſh and Strength, and walked abroad in three Weeks Time.

123. *Eleanor Dowling*, aged about thirty-five Years, troubled with a hard dry Cough for ten

F 3 Years

Years together, worn away by it greatly, and troubled with a Wheezing and Shortneſs of Breath, by drinking Tar-water in the Summer of 1744, all the above Complaints wore off equally to her Surprize and Joy; which ſhe expreſſed by ſaying, "That "if ſhe had twenty Cows, inſtead of two, ſhe "would have parted with them all, to have become "as well as a few Gallons of Tar-water had made "her.

124. *Joan Ardle*, a Gatherer of Ruſhes for Candles, ſtuffed up and choaked with a Cough, without Stomach or Sleep, and her Huſband affected much the ſame way, both cured by two Bottles of Tar-water: They are aged Perſons.

125. *Lawrence Kane*, Pedlar, about fifty Years old, laboured under an Ague, about *Hollandtide*, 1743, which was followed by a ſevere Cough, that held him for ſix Months; he drank but two Bottles of Tar-water in *May* 1744, and found himſelf perfectly recovered.

126. *Bryan Mee* troubled with a Pain in his Stomach, and Loſs of Appetite, cured with one Bottle of Tar-water.

127. Three Children, in one Family, between ſix and eight Years old, took the Small-pox in the Summer of 1744, and came very ſafe and well through the Diſtemper, without any other Preparation or Medicine than Tar-water, which they had drank conſtantly from *April* foregoing, and continued to drink it during the whole Time of their Illneſs, except about two Days, when the Pock in their Mouths and Throats became ſore, and broke, and ſmarted by the Tar-water; they have gone on drinking Tar-water ever ſince without any Reluctance to, or Miſchief from it; on the contrary, they fall a crying, if by any Accident, they do not get it at the uſual Times; and by the conſtant Uſe thereof, one of them hath been kept from the Re-

turns

turns of a threatening Fever, to which he was subject, and had been seized by it three Times in the space of six Months. Another was troubled with Lumps under his Jaw, and other glandular Swellings, which have abated since his drinking Tar-water, and are now almost gone; and all the three, since their drinking Tar-water, have better Stomachs and more Spirits, and are much freer from Coughs and Colds than formerly.

128. *A Letter from a Gentleman of Character and Integrity, who desires his Name might not be mentioned, dated* June *the* 18*th*, 1745, *to* Thomas Prior, *Esq*;

What Mr. *Arthur Hill* told you, of the Benefit I have received by Tar-water, is so much Fact, that I now enjoy a very good State of Health, compared with what I had for several Years past, owing entirely, under God, to that easy, useful Medicine, as I have Reason to believe.

As you desire a particular Account of my Disorder and the Relief I have had from it, I think it is but imitating the Benevolence of the Author, to give you that as distinctly as I can, in hopes the same may prove useful to others in the like Circumstances.

129. You must know then, that about twenty-five Years ago, I had the first regular Fit of the Gout, which used to lay me up frequently after, in Autumn and Spring especially; but never affected me higher than my Feet or Ancles, until 1738, when I was seized with a most violent Fever, which occasioned my being severely blister'd on my Legs, which gave the Humours a Course that Way, and being mixed with gouty Matter, prevented the Sores, made by the Blisters, from healing, though all Care was taken by the Physicians for that End:

F 4 After

After I recovered from my Fever, it was thought that this prevented the regular Fits of the Gout, which I uſed to have, and made it fly about my Body and Head, from whence Indigeſtion, Lowneſs of Spirits and Sweatings followed; and at length I uſed to be freqnently ſeized with a Giddineſs or Swimming in my Head, eſpecially after eating, which would continue until I had lighten'd my Stomach by puking: In hopes to get better Relief for theſe Diſorders from the Phyſicians in Town, I went to *Dublin* in 1742, and by the Directions of two there, juſtly eſteemed for their Knowledge, I went through a continued Courſe of gentle Phyſick, and was forbid every Thing of Nouriſhment, but light, white Meats, and a little Port-wine, until Summer 1743, when they ordered me a Courſe of *Spa* Water with Exerciſe. Theſe Rules I obſerved pretty carefully, and found myſelf a good deal relievd from my Lowneſs of Spirits, and the Giddineſs in my Head, until the Autumn following, when I had a ſevere Return of both, to which, I believe, my great Hurry and Fatigue contributed not a little. This put me under a Neceſſity of returning to my Courſe of Phyſick during the Winter 1743, and until *May* 1744, when I read the worthy Biſhop's elaborate Treatiſe on Tar-water, of which (tho' in many Parts too refined for my Knowledge) I underſtood ſo much, as convinced me of its Uſefulneſs, and the kind Deſign of the Author; whereupon I altered my Intention from *Spa*, to Tar-water, and drank about Half a Pint in the Morning, and as much in the Evening, with due Regard to the Rules preſcribed, as to not eating before or after for two Hours; which produced a regular and pretty ſharp Fit of the Gout in my Feet and Ancles, ſoon after I began the Courſe, and ſeem'd to warm me and increaſe my Sweatings. In about two Months after I had a Return of the Gout, but much gentler

gentler, and my Sweatings abated. Then I had a violent Itchineſs over all my Body and Limbs, which was followed by Blotches and Eruptions on the Skin. In Autumn I got ſome Cold, and I believe had lived too freely for an Invalid, which was attended with a little of the Swimming in my Head, and Diſorder in my Stomach; but I had ſo much Faith in Tar-water, that I made uſe of it air'd, inſtead of Sack-whey, or Tanzey and Sack, which I formerly uſed to take, with Intention to repel the Gout; and through this laſt ſevere Winter, I have continued in very good Spirits, freed from the Diſorder of my Head and Stomach, tho' I have not confined myſelf to any regular Diet; and notwithſtanding I am much thinner of Fleſh, I find myſelf much ſtronger and abler to undergo Fatigue than at any Time ſince my Fever. The Benefit I have received, makes me recommend and prepare it for ſeveral of my poor Neighbours, who generally receive Benefit by it, if they will continue to uſe it.

130. A Collier, that was forced to quit his Labour by an aſthmatic Diſorder, is wonderfully recovered, tho' he uſed it but about a Fortnight.

131. And my Maſter *Salter* was often ſeized with a violent Palpitation in his Heart, and had taken ſeveral Medicines for it, but it was rather increaſing; when he made uſe of Tar-water about three Weeks he recovered from a violent Fit, and was ſo well that he quitted the Water, and then had a Return; upon which he was again relieved by the ſame Means, which he now continues to uſe, and enjoys better Health than for ſome Years paſt.

132. We have many Inſtances in this Neighbourhood of Perſons being relieved by Tar-water, under very different Diſorders, tho' I am ſurprized they ſhould, for if the common People do not immediately receive all the Relief they wiſh and promiſe to themſelves upon once or twice drinking of it, like a Charm,

Charm, they give it up, not confidering what the Bifhop has fo plainly urged; that in all chronical Cafes it is an alterative, that requires Time to change the Mafs of Blood. I find I am going out of my Depth, and I am fure I have trefpaffed too long upon your Time, if any Enthufiaft in Praife of Tar-water can do fo; therefore I will now releafe you with only this Obfervation, that if thefe Hints can afford you any Matter, to be reduced into more ufeful Form for the Benefit of others, I fhall be highly pleafed.

133. *The Cafe of Mr.* John Brooks *Engraver, living at the Sign of Sir* Ifaac Newton'*s Head, on* Cork-Hill, Dublin; *communicated by him to* Thomas Prior, *Efq*; *on the* 22*d of* June, 1745.

The faid Mr. *Brooks* was, in *November* 1744, feized with Stiches, and a pleuritic Fever, which continued eight or ten Days; he was blooded once and became better, but going abroad too foon, caught Cold and relapfed, and was much worfe than before, being feized with more violent Stiches, Oppreffion on his Cheft, Difficulty of Breathing, with moft profufe Sweatings fo as to wet his Bedcloaths twice a Night, which fo weakened him in fome Time, that he was reduced to Skin and Bone, without any Appetite or Reft, fo that it was thought he could not live an Hour, as he could hardly draw his Breath; he was advifed to go out of Town to the Park, and drink Tar-water, which he did at the Rate of three Pints a Day for ten Days warm, going to Bed, and getting up, and cold at other Times, at eight different Times a Day; along with which he only took thin Gruel, or Chicken-broth; at the End of Ten Days he was able to go abroad, mending every Day, the Tar-water having removed his Stiches, Sweatings, and made him breathe as free as ever. He was advifed

vifed to ride, which he did, and on the firft Day of riding an Impofthume broke, which lay upon his Lungs; the firft thing thrown up was a Bag which contained the impoftumated Matter, which was followed by a great Difcharge of corrupted Stuff mixed with Blood: He was immediately feized with a violent Spitting of Blood, which continued feveral Days, and was blooded, but ftill continued to drink the Tar-water as before, which he found to heal his Lungs, and ftop his Spitting of Blood, and in a Fortnight's Time got into fo good a State of Health as to be able to purfue his Bufinefs; he is now as well as ever he was, his Spirits and Appetite rather better than at any Time before, and he ftill continues to drink Half a Pint every Morning.

134. Mr. *Benjamin Prince*, of *Great Britain-Street*, an Officer in the Excife, came to me, on the 7th of *Auguft* 1745, out of a ftrong Senfe of the Benefit he received by the Ufe of Tar-water, and communicated his Cafe, which I took from his own Mouth, as follows: He faid, that for four Years he had been troubled with violent Pains in his Back and Kidneys, and frequent Colics; that he ufed to have two or three fharp Fits of the Gout every Year, and, after a Fever, had a fixed Pain in one of his Arms, fo that he was not able to lift it up; he had loft his Appetite, Spirits, and Reft: But being advifed to drink Tar-water to get him a Stomach, he began to drink it in *June* 1744, at the Rate of half a Pint every Morning, and no more. In a Fortnight's time the Pain in his Arm abated, and foon after went off; fo that he got the full Ufe of it; in lefs than a Month's drinking he voided, by Urine, a great deal of flimy Matter, and in two or three Months, after frequent Stoppages of Urine, he had great Pains in his Reins, and at laft difcharged a Stone as large as an Olive-ftone, which was nine

nine Days paſſing; after which he voided, from time to time, twenty-five Gravel-ſtones, of different Sizes, nine at once, and frequently diſcharges ſmall Gravel or Sand all jagged and pointed, which ſeem to be broken off from a larger Body of Stone: He is now at eaſe as to his Gravel, and but ſeldom troubled with Colics, and what Pain he has that way, he imputes to the Remainder of the Gravel, not yet diſcharged; he had no Apprehenſion or Suſpicion, before he drank Tar-water, and diſcharged Gravel, that his Pains aroſe from the Stone or Gravel; he thought his Diſorder was nothing but a Colic, for which he took many things to no Purpoſe. He alſo ſays, that he has not had the leaſt Fit or Symptom of the Gout ſince he drank Tar-water, which is near fifteen Months ago; and he never fails to drink it conſtantly every Day, finding that he has thereby got a good Stomach, high Spirits, and good Sleep, and imputes all his Relief to Tar-water only.

Auguſt the 15th, 1745.

135. This Day Mr. *John Powell*, living at the Glaſs-ware-houſe in *Crow-ſtreet*, Merchant, was pleaſed to come to me, and gave the following Account of his Caſe and Relief, which I took down in Writing, from his own Mouth, as follows: Mr. *Powell* had the Gout for near twenty Years, off and on, but in the Winter 1743, he had a violent Fit which laſted twelve Weeks. He was alſo troubled with violent Pains in his Bowels, for two Years before that time, which he thought was a Colic, had no Appetite, a bad Digeſtion, and little Sleep; he had thoſe Fits of the Colic twice or thrice a Week, each Fit laſting twenty four Hours, with racking Pains, ſo that it was thought that his Life was in great Danger. In the beginning of the Year 1744, on

on reading the Treatiſe on Tar-water, he was adviſed by his Phyſician to drink the Water, which he did regularly for ſix Weeks at the Rate of a Pint a Day, taken in the Morning and Evening; and in three Weeks time his Pains began to abate, and in ſix Weeks all his Colic-pains went off, and he has not had the leaſt Fit ever ſince: He ſeldom fails to drink the Water every Morning, and reſolves to continue the conſtant Uſe of it, having got a very good Stomach and Digeſtion, and ſleeps very well; nor has he had the leaſt Fit of the Gout ever ſince he began to drink Tar-water, being perfectly free from all Symptoms of it; he has the full Uſe of his Limbs, and walks as well as ever he did, and he imputes all his Cures to Tar-water only.

136. *James Brown*, about ten Years old, to whom the late Earl of *Kildare* left an Annuity of twenty Pounds a Year, for his Father's long and faithful Services under him, was miſerably afflicted with the King's Evil for four Years, and being long under the Care of Surgeons in *Dublin*, was ſent in *Auguſt* 1744, to his Relations in the County of *Cork* to take care of him, as there were no Hopes of his Recovery in *Dublin*. When he came there, he had many running Sores in his Arms, Hands and Feet, and Swellings on each ſide of his Throat without Appetite or Digeſtion. In this Condition he was immediately put into a Courſe of Tar-water; he drank about a Quart a Day, a Naggin at a time, and after ſome Days drinking the Water, they waſhed his Sores with ſtrong Tar-water, and for a Plaiſter uſed the Oil of Tar, which was ſkimmed off the Water, ſpread on Lint or Linen: The Effect was, that in a Fortnight's Time moſt of his Sores were healed up, and Swellings gone, and in leſs than ſix Weeks Time he was perfectly recovered, and now continues very well, with good Appetite and Spirits. This Account the Author had from the young

young Man himſelf, and from his Relations; and though he is very well, yet he continues to drink Tar-water, by which he received ſo much Benefit, but in ſmaller Quantities.

137. *Another Inſtance of the Efficacy of Tar-water in the Cure of the King's Evil, is as follows.*

Michael Carney of *Proteſtant Row in Cavan-ſtreet*, about ſixteen Years old, was troubled with the King's Evil ſix Years, having running Sores in his Arms, Neck, Legs and Body, and had been in *Mercer's* Hoſpital a Year without Benefit, and had almoſt loſt one of his Eyes by the Evil; the Author being informed that this Boy was in Danger of having his Eye rotted out of his Head by the Evil, directed the Wriſt Plaiſter to be applied to him, which was attended with ſuch Succeſs, that in a Fortnight's Time, in the latter End of the Year 1743, the Evil was quite driven from his Eye; but the Boy continuing full of running Sores, and great Pain in one of his Arms, of which he had little Uſe, in *April* 1744, I gave him Tar-water to drink, a Pint a Day; in a little Time he diſcharged two Splinters of Bone, black and carious, from his Arm, whereby he had immediate Eaſe there, and continuing to drink Tar-water, and waſhing his Sores with it alſo, in two Months Time all his Sores healed up, his Appetite and Strength returned, and he was perfectly recovered, and continues very well, and now lives with Mr. *Barry Colles*, Attorney, at *Stephen*'s *Green*. Theſe Inſtances, and many more come to my Knowledge, convinces me, that the King's Evil, hitherto reckoned incurable, may, in a ſhort Time, by the Method before mentioned, be perfectly cured.

The

The Rev. Dean Madden, *of* Molesworth-street, Dublin, *was pleased to give me, in* July 1745, *the following Instances of Cures by Tar-water, which came to his Knowledge.*

138. The Rev. Mr. *George Philips*, of *Anne-street, Dublin*, was seized last Summer, with a violent Pleuritick Stitch: He was then in the Country, three Miles from *Dublin*. He sent for a Surgeon to bleed him; as he was long a coming, his Pain increased. He drank freely of Tar-water warm, and in a few Hours his Pain so far abated, and the Heighth of his Pulse lessened, that, when the Surgeon came, it was resolved not to bleed him. He continued to drink Tar-water; the Disorder abated, and in a few Days went entirely off.

139. *John Waller*, of the Parish of St. *Anne, Dublin*, aged sixty seven Years, had in Spring 1745, a violent Cough, and a general Failure of Nature. He was reduced so low, that all who saw him gave him over. He was persuaded to drink Tar-water in his extream low Condition, and in five Weeks, he was able to go about his Business, and continues hearty and well.

140. Mrs. *Stear* of *Ginnets* in the County of *Meath* near *Trim*, had the worst Symptoms of the most violent Scurvy, her Hands and Arms black in some Parts, so that a Mortification was sometime apprehended. She drank Tar-water for several Months; it struck the most virulent Humour out on her Face and Arms, so that no one could know her: She was not discouraged, but continued to drink Tar-water, and in a few Months her Skin was entirely clean. Before she drank Tar-water, she was often sick and low spirited; while she drank it, she was hearty and well every way, and has continued well many Months.

141. Mrs.

141. Mrs. *Woodrof*, who lives near *Cork*, was troubled with a Rheumatiſm in her Head, Dropſy in her Legs, and an Aſthma, from which ſhe was relieved in two Months Time by drinking Tar-water. Her Son Mr. *Woodrof*, a Clergyman who gave this Account, ſays, that above two Years are paſſed ſince ſhe was relieved.

142. The Reverend Mr. *Thomas Goodwin*, of *Dawſon-ſtreet*, *Dublin*, was relieved of a Megrim and a Sleepineſs by the Uſe of Tar-water, and continues well, *June* 29, 1745.

143. Mr. *Palma* the Muſician, was troubled with a Rheumatiſm, his Limbs ſwollen ſo, that he could not walk, but was cured in a Month's Time by drinking Tar-water, and continues well.

144. The Reverend Mr. *Edmond White* of the County of *Wexford*, was in like manner relieved of violent Pains in his Limbs, and a Colic of a long ſtanding.

145. Mr. *Jones* of *Grafton-ſtreet*, between ſixty and ſeventy Years old, had for ſeveral Years a violent Aſthma, attended with a great Cough and frequent ſpitting of Blood and Corruption in great Quantities, finds himſelf greatly relieved in every Reſpect, by the Uſe of Tar-water; and he neither ſpit Corruption, nor Blood laſt Winter.

146. Mr. *Wollaſton* of *Trim*, Clerk to Mr. Juſtice *York*, was aſthmatick for a long Time, and not able to live in *Dublin*, was relieved by Tar-water in ſix Weeks Time, and is an altered Man, and continues well, *June* 29, 1745. Thus far Dean *Madden*.

147. Mrs. *Ann Fitzgerald*, Wife of Mr. *Will. Fitzgerald* of *Ballyrone* in the *Queen*'s County, was for ſeven Years afflicted with violent Hyſtericks, Pain and Wind in her Bowels, which threw her frequently into ſuch Diſtractions as deprived her of the Uſe of her Underſtanding, ſo that ſhe was utterly uncapable

I

uncapable of minding the Affairs of her Family, and a Servant was conſtantly employed to take care of her, and ſometimes to prevent her laying violent Hands on herſelf. Many Phyſicians in *Dublin* and the Country, had her under their Care, and preſcribed many Medicines, which had no Effect; at laſt ſhe was prevailed upon to drink Tar-water, and in a few Days, found ſome benefit, and by continuing to drink it for a conſiderable Time, ſhe is now perfectly recovered, and free from all her Ailments; and the only Inconvenience ſhe had from Tar-water is, that as it gave her a good Appetite, ſhe is grown much fatter and more corpulent than ſhe was before, or deſires, and ſhe ſtill continues to drink the Water in ſmall Quantities by way of Prevention. This Account I had from herſelf and her Huſband.

148. The ſaid Mrs. *Fitzgerald* alſo informed me, that ſome Years ago, one of her Sons was grievouſly troubled with a running Sore in one of his Arms, that the Humour which iſſued out was ſo corroſive, that it eat into the Fleſh, and ſpread all over his Arm, notwithſtanding all the Pains taken, and Plaiſters applied to ſtop the Progreſs of it, whether it was a Tettar or Cancer, or what elſe ſhe could not tell; ſhe then recollected what ſhe had formerly been told, that a Plaiſter of Tar had been uſed with Succeſs on ſuch Occaſions; accordingly, ſhe put ſome Tar into a Pot over the Fire, and added ſome Mutton Suet to it, and having gently boiled and mixed them well together, ſhe made a Plaiſter and ſpread it thin on Linen, and applied it to the running Sore as hot as the Child could bear; the Effect was, that in ten Days Time, all the Sores were healed up, and the Arm entirely cured, and continued ſo ever after.

149. *A Letter from the Reverend Mr.* Robert Brereton, *of* Burton *in the County of* Cork, *dated* November 9, 1745.

I here ſend you an Account of the Benefit receiv-ed by me from drinking Tar-water.

I had been greatly afflicted with a Jaundice for two or three Years, which returned on me ſeveral Times in that Period, and was always attended with exceding lowneſs and dejection of Spirits. I was adviſed by my Phyſicians to enter on a Courſe of Steel Preparations; but unwilling to undergo a tedious Courſe of Phyſick, I had Recourſe to Tar-water, from which in five or ſix Weeks I found great Relief, and at length a perfect State of Health, and good Spirits, which I now enjoy.

150. I am farther to inform you that Mr. *Ralph Crofts* of *Liſcarrol* in the County of *Cork*, my Neighbour, above ſeventy Years old, was greatly emaciated, and worn out with lowneſs of Spirits and want of Appetite, and, did not expect to live out the Winter 1744. He was adviſed to drink Tar-water, from which in leſs than a Month, he was much better, and in two or three Months perfectly recovered to as good a State of Health and Spirits as he had in any Part of his Life.

I am, Sir, your moſt humble Servant,

Robert Brereton.

151. Mr. *Jocelyne Daviſon*, of the Town of *Carlow*, came to me on the 19th of *November* 1745, and gave me the following Account of his Diſorder and Relief, which I took down in writing from his own Mouth, and is as follows:

In Winter 1744, he got a great Cold, which cauſed a violent Cough, and an Inflammation in his Lungs, attended with very great Spitting and Diſ-charges;

charges; he continued in this miserable State for near four Months, without receiving any benefit by the Medicines he took, so that it was thought he could not live; his Father advised him to drink Tar-water, which he neglected to do for some Time, but finding his Disorder increase, he took to Tar-water, and drank about half a Pint warm every Day in the Morning as soon as he got up, and in six Days Time, he found himself much easier; he then observed, that the Tar-water had thrown out a great Rash, like an Itch or Scurf on the Surface of his Body, which alarmed him at first, and inclined him to lay aside the Water, but finding himself still better, and that the Venom of the Distemper was cast off that Way, he continued the Use of it, and in six Weeks perfectly recovered from all his Ailments, and now continues very well.

152. He also informed me, that Mr. *David Simms* the Presbyterian Minister at *Carlow*, was long troubled with an Asthma and Difficulty of breathing and speaking, so that it was thought by all who saw him that he could not live long; but by drinking Tar-water a considerable Time, he is quite recovered from all those Disorders, and as well as can be expected of one of his Age.

The Reverend Doctor *Bacon* of *Lemavaddy* in the County of *Derry*, communicated to me in *November* 1745, the three following Cases.

153. *James Crowders*, Postillion to Colonel *Forward* of the County of *Donnegal*, Member of Parliament, was seized with a violent asthmatick Cough, swelled all over his Body, and no Appetite, so that it was thought it was impossible he could live: He drank Tar-water about a Month, Morning and Evening, a large Glass, which purged him violently, and perfectly cured him: This happened about a Year

Year and half ago, and he continues perfectly well ever ſince. This was confirmed to me by Mr. *Forward* himſelf.

154. Mrs. *Ann G——e*, a Widow Lady of the County of *Derry*, had been troubled with an aſthmatick Diſorder for about ſeven Years; her Caſe was, that ſhe breathed freely in a ſmoaky or foggy Air, but was ready to expire in thin ſharp Air. After trying many Medicines, and eſpecially Goat-whey in vain, ſhe drank Tar-water, of which ſhe took only a Wine Glaſs full at Night, when a-bed, and in the Morning before ſhe got up, (for it made her very ſick, when ſhe took it in the Day, and was obliged to go to Bed immediately.) The Effect was, that ſhe grew better upon her taking the Tar-water, and was quite cured upon drinking it three Months; ſhe has continued well ever ſince, which is ſix Months, and has begun to drink a little lately by way of Precaution.

155. The Reverend Mr. *S——t* of the Dioceſe of *Derry*, was troubled with an Aſthma of the oppoſite Kind, could not live in foggy Air, and was obliged to remove from his own Houſe, which was in a low Situation, to a Friend's Houſe ſituated upon a Hill, where he found himſelf better; at length he drank Tar-water, which recovered him ſo much that he returned to his Dwelling quite well, and has continued ſo for a Twelve-month paſt.

156. Mr. *Cunningham*, Collector of *Portpatrick* in *Scotland*, arrived in *Dublin* in *June* 1744, and then declared to me and ſeveral others his Caſe and Relief, which I had from his own Mouth, and is as follows. He had been troubled with the Gout for many Years, but the laſt two Years he was ſo miſerably afflicted with it, that he was confined to his Bed and Chamber for many Months, not being able to go abroad or walk at home, having ſuch a Stiffneſs

Stiffneſs in his Knees after the Fits were over, that he had not the Uſe of his Limbs; but in *May* 1743, he was adviſed by Mr. *Makenny* a Surgeon, to drink Tar-water, which he did for four or five Months, the firſt Effect was, that in a little Time he was freed from a Difficulty of breathing he laboured under, and finding his Limbs grew eaſier and ſtronger by Degrees, he drank the Water till Winter following, by means whereof he recovered the Strength of his Limbs ſo much, that in the Spring following he had the full Uſe of them. Whereas for ſeveral Years before, he never failed to have a Fit in the Beginning of Winter, and another in Spring; ſince that Time he has had no Symptom of the Gout; and he told me that he could then mount the higheſt Horſe in *Ireland* with Eaſe, and could walk as well as ever he did, and was reſolved to drink Tar-water three Months in every Year of his Life.

157. Mr. *John Milton*, Confectioner in *Caple-ſtreet*, *Dublin*, gave me in *November* 1745, the following Account of the Benefit he received by Tar-water. He was afflicted with the Gout ever ſince he was ſixteen Years old, frequently attended with very violent Pains, ſometimes he was laid up three or four times in a Year, and laſt Spring was laid up for eight Weeks; and it left ſuch a Weakneſs after it, that he was hardly able to crawl for a long Time, till he had recourſe to Tar-water, to which he was adviſed by one who received Benefit by it. He began to drink it in *July* 1745, and continued the Uſe of it to the middle of *November* following, taking a Pint each Day, half a Pint in the Morning, and the ſame at Night; which has fully reſtored him to the Uſe and Strength of his Limbs, and removed all his other Complaints: He has got a good Appetite and Digeſtion, which he had not for many Years before, and tho' he uſed to be

G 3 laid

laid up at this Seafon of the Year, yet he has not the leaft Symptom of the Gout, and is as ftrong, and can walk as well as ever he did. He had alfo great Pains and Swellings in his Bowels, and Hardnefs in his Belly, which were quite carried off in a Week or ten Days Time by drinking Tar-water only.

158. Mr. *Cavanaugh*, Hatter, at the Raven in *Skinner-row*, *Dublin*, was long afflicted with Rheumatick Pain, great Swellings and Stiffnefs in his Loyns, Thighs and Knees, infomuch that he could not walk abroad, or ftir at home without Difficulty and Pain; to remove which Ailments, he tryed every Thing that was prefcribed by Phyficians and Surgeons, but to no Effect. In Summer 1744, when Tar-water began to be in Vogue, he drank near a Pint a Day for fix Week, without any fenfible Benefit as to the Weaknefs and Pains in his Limbs, but got much better Appetite and Spirits. However he ftill perfifted in drinking the Water, and in three Months Time he found his Swellings abate, his Limbs grow ftronger every Day, and in a few Months after all the Swellings, Stiffnefs, Hardnefs and Pains in his Limbs went off, and he recovered the Ufe of them; and continuing ftill to drink Tar-water, he can walk without Difficulty or Pain, and is in great Spirits. This Account I had from himfelf in *July* 1745, and now in *December* 1745, he continues perfectly well.

159. Mrs. *Duggan*, Midwife, living at the Cradle in *Great Britain-ftreet*, *Dublin*, gave me the following Account of her Cafe, That fhe had been long troubled with a violent inveterate Scurvy, attended with a great Oppreffion in her Cheft and Heart, and Difficulty of breathing, that fhe had loft all Appetite, and was in a miferable Way, that fhe took many Things for her Relief to no manner of Advantage, that at laft fhe had Recourfe to Tar-water,

water, which ſhe took at the Rate of half a Pint a Day every Morning, and before ſhe drank three Gallons, all the ſcorbutick Heat and groſs Humours were driven out on the Surface of her Body, and continuing ſtill to drink it, all the aforeſaid Symptoms went off, ſhe breaths freely without the leaſt Oppreſſion, recovered her Appetite, and ſhe never knew herſelf in better Health or Spirits, and reſolves never to be without Tar-water, finding it always relieves her when ſhe catches Cold, or is out of Order.

160. *A Letter from Mr.* James Hanning, *of* Cloyne *in the County of* Cork, *to* Thomas Prior, *Eſq*;

My Daughter, *Mary Hanning*, about eleven Years old, was laſt *May* taken ill of a Fever, after which, ſhe came by Degrees to be entirely deprived of the Uſe of her Tongue and Limbs, being unable to ſpeak, ſtand, or put her Hand to her Mouth, and all her Joints ſhaking with the Palſy. She took Medicines preſcribed by a Phyſician, and was often exerciſed in open Air, while the Weather permitted, but all to no Purpoſe. Whereupon we put her into a Courſe of Tar-water about the beginning of *November* laſt, and ſhe has ever ſince drank a Quart a Day, which in five Weeks has ſo far recovered her, that ſhe can ſpeak and read plain, feed herſelf, ſtand and walk without Help, and even go up and down Stairs, to the Amazement of all thoſe, who had ſeen her lately carried about dumb and helpleſs like an Infant. She has taken no other Medicine ſince ſhe began to drink Tar-water, nor had ſhe the Benefit of Air and Exerciſe from that Time, the Weather not permitting. One of her Arms continues ſomewhat weak, and ſhe has a Weakneſs too in one of her Legs, but as ſhe daily grows better, I hope Tar-water, with God's

G 4 Bleſſing,

Bleffing, will perfect her Cure. *December* 17, 1745.
James Hanning.

161. *A Letter from a Gentleman of Character and Credit, giving a particular Detail of an extraordinary Fever cured by Tar-water, dated* December 20, 1745.

A Youth about fifteen Years of Age, being feized with a Fever in *April* 1745, an old *French* Woman of the Family, who was appointed to attend him, with Directions to give him Tar-water (the only Medicine prefcribed) about a Pint every Hour, gave him a much fmaller Quantity, and indulging his Appetite, fed him fecretly, five Days together, with Roaft Beef, feafoned Pye, Cheefe, Ale, and fuch like Diet inftead of Water-gruel, which alone had been ordered.

162. This unnatural Diet terribly inflamed his Fever, and produced fuch an entire Proftration of Appetite, that for thirteen Days together, he took no Nourifhment of any Kind but Tar-water, whereof he drank about a Gallon every Day, which made him fleep at Night and kept up his Spirits by Day in a furprizing Manner. Having fo long fafted, he at length took a little *Naples*-Bifcuit, with two or three Spoonfuls of Sack and Water, which increafed his Fever and difordered his Head, but he was foon quieted by Tar-water. While he regularly took this wholefome Draught he flept found every Night. But one Day being difgufted at the Tar-water, it was judged proper to change it for Sage and Baulm Tea, which he drank plentifully though not with equal Succefs. For his Spirits funk, he loft his Colour and Look, he paffed the Night reftlefs and anxious: All which Symptoms were removed next Day by Tar-water.

163. After this, his Diftemper took feveral ftrange and violent Turns, being fometimes attended with the

the worſt Symptoms. He was at Times ſpeechleſs, convulſed, delirious, and his Bliſters would not riſe. In the Delirium Tar-water could not be given, he was then bliſtered, and the Bliſters not riſing, he was brought with ſome Difficulty to drink his Tar-water again, which had a ſpeedy good Effect, when nothing elſe gave him Relief. And in general, it was obſerved, that upon neglecting to give him Tar-water, the feveriſh Symptons of Heat, Anxiety and difficult Reſpiration became very troubleſome, being conſtantly heightened by omitting, and as conſtantly allayed by returning to drink it.

164. It were tedious to relate all the ſurprizing Changes in the Courſe of this Illneſs, which laſted ten Weeks. Probably ſuch a Caſe was never known before, as it is probable, that no Fever ever happened to be inflamed and heightened by the ſame Cauſe. For I believe no Patient was ever known to have been dieted in the firſt Days of a Fever on ſuch extraordinary Food, which Nature is accuſtomed to loath at thoſe Seaſons. But Tar-water gives an Appetite even in Fevers.

165. Tar-water, during its long and obſtinate Conflict with the Venom of the Diſeaſe, operated in divers Manners, as a cardiac, diaphoretic, ſudorific, emetic, carminative and paregoric, ſeeming to adapt itſelf to the ſeveral Symptoms and Stages of his Malady, and for the moſt Part gave him a great Flow of Spirits, a florid lively Look, a clean well-coloured Tongue, with ſuch Vigour in his Voice and Eyes, as aſtoniſhed all who ſaw him, and knew how long he had been ill, and how little Nouriſhment he had taken. It is to be obſerved, that on ſome Days he drank greedily, even ſo far as ten or twelve Quarts of Tar-water, calling for it with great Impatience, even though it wrought him as an Emetic; whereas both before and after his Illneſs, he ſhewed the greateſt diſlike and loathing of it.

166. In

166. In the laſt Stage of the Fever, his Face and Body ſwelled, and a general Eruption appeared all over both, ſomewhat like an Eriſipelas or cohæring Small-pox, which laſted a Week. For two or three Days of this Period, he drank ſparingly of Tar-water, perhaps not more than a Quart a Day. But during all that Time, he conſtantly by his own Choice, held his Mouth to the Spout of a Tea-pot, half filled with hot Tar-water, ſucking the Vapour, which, he ſaid, he found very chearing and comfortable.

167. At the Cloſe of this tenth Week, he fell into a moſt copious Sweat, and the next Day his Puſtules were quite gone, and his Fever left him, not ſpiritleſs, puny and pale, but as lively and hail, in appearance, as ever he had been known, though after an Illneſs, that for Length of Time, and Variety of deſperate Symptoms, ſurpaſſed any I remember to have heard of, or met with in the Hiſtory of Fevers.

168. But he did not continue in this healthy State; for the very ſame Day, he expreſſed ſuch an earneſt longing Deſire to change his Bed and ſhift his Linen, that it was thought proper to indulge him, and although this Step was made with the utmoſt Caution, yet it gave him a freſh Cold, which ſeized upon his Head, and produced a new Fever with a Raving or Frenzy, that continued many Weeks, in all which time, he could not be prevailed on to take one Glaſs of Tar-water. But at length by a proper Uſe of Aſſes-milk, and Ground-ivy, with a careful Regimen, he was recovered ſo far, as that he might be perſuaded to drink daily four Glaſſes of Tar-water, which, with God's Bleſſing, reſtored his Strength and completed his Recovery.

I have here given the general Sum and Subſtance rather than a regular and complete Diary, containing all the particular Circumſtances of this extraordinary Caſe, which it had been impoſſible to recollect at the Diſtance of ſo many Months.

169. *An*

169. *An Extract of a Letter from the Honourable Colonel* John Custis, *of* Williamsburgh *in* Virginia, *and one of the Council of that Province. Dated from* Williamsburgh July 10, 1745.

Mr. *Custis* writes, that he unfortunately got a great Cold, which threw him into the Chin or Hooping Cough, which caused cruel Fevers; that when the Cough was gone, he was troubled with a prodigious Spitting; that he took great Doses of Elixir Vitriol to allay his intense Thirst in his burning Fever, which so relaxed his salival Glands, that he feared they would never come to their due Tone again, nor perform their proper Offices; they are the Sluices that cast off the vitiated Lympha: That he had studied and read Physick more than forty Years, that he had the Opinion of Doctor *Brown*, of *Maryland*, deemed the greatest Physician in *America*, that the Seat of his Distemper lay in his salivary Glands, and that it was dangerous to stop the Spitting, which he well knew by woful Experience, having stopt it by taking an Ounce of Diacodium going to Bed, which flung him into Fevers, Faintings, and many other Disorders, so that he was obliged to procure the Spitting again; he was once so reduced, that he could not get up when down, nor was able to put on his Cloaths, and had no Appetite to any Sort of Food. But, to use his own Words, he writes, that reading one Day in the *Magazine*, I found the Virtues of Tar-water, which I verily believe saved my Life, I had not taken it a Week, before I began to have an Appetite to Victuals, and continued taking it three Months, Night and Morning, which miraculously restored me; so that I can now eat heartily any Thing my Palate has a mind to, tho' I cannot taste any Thing, but what is salt, sweet, or sour, and I bless God, I am much mended. But my Spitting continues with a great Discharge, but eating supports that

that Difcharge, and I refolve to take nothing that may leffen my Stomach, the Saliva not performing its due Office, keeps my Palate and Throat always hot and dry, tho' I have not any Fever, which the Doctors tell me I muft bear; but I hope Time and Tar-water will entirely free me from that Uneafinefs.

This Letter was fent from *Virginia*, to Mr. *Peter Collinfon* of *Grace-church-ftreet*, *London*, who was pleafed to tranfmit the fame hither, giving this Reafon for doing fo, That he was perfuaded, that the reading fome Parts of this Letter would not be difagreeable to the good Bifhop to find that his laudable Endeavours to benefit Mankind, are attended with fuch great Succefs, and perhaps not more remarkably fo, than in the uncommon Cafe of the faid Colonel *Cuftis*.

170. The Reverend Mr. *Syon Hill*, Chaplain to the Work-houfe in *Dublin*, having had great Opportunities of trying and knowing the Effects of Tar-water, both in the faid Houfe, and all over the City, where he had difperfed above a thoufand Gallons of the Water to thofe who had occafion to call upon him for it, and having fet down in writing the Particulars thereof, as the Facts came to his Knowledge, he has been pleafed to communicate the fame to me in the following Narrative, entitled,

A fhort Account of fome remarkable Cafes, with their Succefs, by GOD's *Bleffing, on Tar-water.*

171. In *April* 1744, after reading the Treatife on Tar-water, Curiofity as well as Humanity, prompted me to make tryal of the Effects of the Water, and if I fhould find it anfwer the Character given of it in *Siris*, to make ufe of it on feveral Occafions that offered; having it greatly in my Power, as Chaplain to the Work-houfe, to make Experiments on a great many Subjects, who, fince I came there, were long troubled

troubled with cutaneous, ſcrophulous, and chronical Diſorders.

172. For this End, I picked out of the many in the Work-houſe, four of the moſt afflicted, to whom, for four Days, I adminiſtered Tar-water: And indeed the Succeſs ſo ſurprized me, that being at that Time, ſeverely attacked with an Hoarſeneſs, and ſore Throat, I ventured to take it alſo; and with ſome Pain (my Throat being inflamed) I got down about the Quantity of a Naggin; after which, I felt no Pain in that Part, but could ſwallow without the leaſt Difficulty. From this welcome and aſtoniſhing Experiment, I naturally conceived future joyful Hopes of this powerful Medicine; accordingly, I took it for three Days after, twice each Day with Pleaſure; which ſo wrought me the third Day, I was not able to ſit, by Reaſon of the Acrimony of the Diſcharge. Notwithſtanding, I ſtuck to my Medicine, and the fourth Day, I perceived myſelf much better without any Manner of Complaint; and, I thank GOD, have continued ſo ever ſince; whereas, before I took Tar-water, I was ſubject to a Head-ach, Cramps, Pains in ſeveral Parts, more eſpecially in the Kidneys, very acute from any Wheel-carriage; I was tormented alſo with an Heart-burning, all which Diſorders, I now aſſure you are perfectly vaniſhed, and I am reſtored, bleſſed be GOD, as it were, to a new Life, having a keen Appetite, good Digeſtion, Spirits ſufficient to bear me through all Fatigues, with ſound and eaſy Sleep, tho' now on the Borders of Sixty.

173. The great Benefit I received from Tar-water, induced me for the general Good, to make it for other poor People; who had it ſince laſt *April* 1744, and ſhall always have it Gratis, while I make it, to whom I have diſtributed, with others, above a thouſand Gallons, without any Complaint yet, but with great Acknowledgments, as by the Sequel will appear.

appear. Having diſpatched my own Caſe, I beg Leave to lay before you thoſe others, with their Succeſs, which I durſt not do till *October* was paſt, becauſe ſome predicted frightful Conſequences at that Time to all ſuch, who ventured on this Medicine. But now *May* 1745, being paſt, and ſtill no bad Symptoms appearing on thoſe Adventurers, I look now on this Prediction as a *Brutum Fulmen*.

174. I have now been eight Years Chaplain to the City Work-houſe, in all which Time the Children of that Houſe, have been ſorely afflicted with an inflammatory Itch, or Scurvy, of which we could never get them entirely cured. This I have often complained of to the proper Officer, who once aſſured me, all the Druggs in the Apothecary's Shop would not cure them; nay more, that it was not in his Power to cleanſe them, whilſt the Children were continued on an Oat-meal Diet: On this frank and helpleſs Confeſſion, I imagined I might without Offence, try Tar-water on thoſe poor Incurables, as well for their Relief, as the Good of others; accordingly, I did ſo, and really I obſerved the joyful Succeſs exceeded my Expectations: For above a hundred Children variouſly affected, were for the moſt Part comfortably relieved in one Month's Time, at my own Expence; each Day adminiſtering eight Gallons, often with my own Hands, with three Pounds of Liquorice-ball, cut into little Bits given to the Children, to render the Water agreeable.

175. At this Time, there was a Girl about nine Years old in the Work-houſe, by Name, *Mary Mac Culla*, confined to her Bed for ſome Time, with a moſt violent Scurvy; ſhe had little or no Appetite, full of Pain, becauſe flay'd in ſeveral Parts by repeated Rubbings of Brimſtone; at laſt the Girl fell into a moſt languiſhing Way, taking neither ſufficient Food, nor Reſt to ſupport Nature, every Day declining, ſo look'd on by all who came to ſee her, as

as paſt all Hope. Nevertheleſs, by taking Tar-water a Week, the Girl recovered wonderfully; and by continuing the Uſe of the Water her Sores ſoon dried and ſcaled off, and ſhe looked as one out of the Small-pox, but her Appetite returning, ſhe revived immediately, and is at this Day, *May* the 6th, 1745, one of the ſtrongeſt Children in our Houſe, reads well, and is worth all my Expence and Trouble.

176. The next Subject was *John Hall*, about nine Years old, who in *April* 1744, could neither ſleep, nor eat what was ſufficient to keep the Child alive, as his Mother informed me, ſtill moaning, and complaining of his Belly, which was greatly ſwelled, and in all human Probability, would ſoon have died, had the Child not been relieved ſeaſonably by Tar-water, which cauſed the Child to void a large Quantity of Worms, ſince which Diſcharge, is well, and I hear of no Complaints as formerly: This Child's Mother, *Mary Hall*, then a Nurſe in the Work-houſe, being called on by the Governors for her ſolemn Teſtimony in this Matter, ſwore, that her Son, ſoon after taking Tar-water, voided a Chamber-pot full of Worms, ſome of which, ſhe obſerved to be alive; and further ſwore, that ſhe herſelf was relieved from a violent Pain in her Side and Stomach, by a wonderful Diſcharge both Ways, cauſed by two Quarts of Tar-water taken in four Days, and from no Appetite before, ſhe then, *May* the 10th, 1744, enjoyed a very good one.

177. The next was *James Ellis*, now in the Work-houſe, a Lad of above thirteen Years old, whoſe Hands for a long Time were in a manner uſeleſs by a running Evil, but are now perfectly cured by this Medicine. Nay, there is another Boy in the ſame Houſe, by Name, *George Dorton*, whoſe Glands beneath the Chin, were greatly ſwelled and inflamed, ever oozing forth putrid Matter, moving a Nauſea in all Beholders. This Boy took Tar-water one Month

2 only,

only, which greatly dried up his Sores, and is now very well.

178. A similar Case like this is that of a young Woman, named *Mary-Ann Empty*, in the Parish of *Glandorkin*, about four Miles from *Dublin*, who was of late frightfully afflicted with an Evil in many Parts, especially her Face; she was some Time ago recommended to me by her Parish Minister, and is greatly relieved, of which I am an Eye-witness: Her Mother gave me the following Account of her Cure: That by drinking Tar-water, her Daughter's Ulcers dried up, which so affected her Face and Jaws, that she cold neither eat nor swallow, but the Ulcers in the Girl's Face burst as she slept, making a large Discharge. The Mother overjoyed at her Daughter's unexpected Relief, was curious to examine the Filth which lately tormented her Daughter, and she assured me, she found in the Filth that was discharged, a flat Bone about an Inch long, not quite so broad, both black and jagged: This I suppose stopt the Vent of the Ulcers in the Face, because, when removed, the Discharges for some Time were very large, after which the Maid grew well, and is very little disfigured, and by continuing to drink Tar-water, the Girl is now, in *December* 1745, perfectly cured of the Evil.

179. Another Cure like this was performed on a Lad, Son to a Servant of Alderman *Kane*. This Lad received a Contusion in one of his Hands; the Cure not perfected, the Sore broke out again on the Back of the same Hand; moreover, another Ulcer broke out at the same Time in the Lad's Heel, both Ulcers submitted to this Medicine, tho' for a long Time obstinate, and before the Lad took Tar-water thought incurable.

180. *Ann Maddin*, Sister to a Woman who nurses for Mr. *Putland*, had a very sore Hand so swelled and inflamed, that the Surgeons believed it mortified, and

and ſo doomed it to be cut off; yet the Doctor that attended, as I am informed, adviſed before taking this laſt Extremity, to try Tar-water, which we did; and when I viewed the young Woman's Hand ſome Time ago, it looked kindly from a ſhapeleſs black Lump; and I am informed by a Relation of the young Woman, that ſhe is in a manner well, having no Pain in that Part, and can uſe it like the other Hand.

181. *Peter Evard*, Stocking-weaver, to be heard of at the Ship, in *Old Corn-market*, was ſo ulcerated all over his Body, and in many Parts eat away with the Scurvy, that he could not work: Tho' all Methods were uſed by the Infirmary ſeveral Months, but in vain; ſo reckoned amongſt the Incurables; on this he took this Medicine, and immediately recovered, now follows his Trade, and comfortably provides for himſelf and others. His Mother, an aged Woman, long afflicted with an Aſthma, took with her Son part of his Medicine, which relieved her of her Aſthma, tho' an old Diſorder.

182. A Gentleman bred an Apothecary, (and therefore will not mention his Name,) came one Evening into our Hall in a very melancholy Way with an inflamed ſore Throat; he ſaid he could not ſwallow his Spittle; and that he had a great Lump in his Throat, which he muſt get launced, immediately, or it would choak him; with much a-do, I prevailed on the young Man to take a little Tar-water, which relieved him immediately, and he felt no more of his frightful Lump, but continues both eaſy and well. From this and many other Inſtances, I find nothing ever relieved a ſore Throat ſo ſoon and ſo effectually as this Medicine.

183. Mrs. *Catharine Williams*, who ſells Earthen-ware near the End of *Dirty-lane*, *Thomas ſtreet*, had one of her Legs ſo long ulcerated, that it was doomed to be cut off, after great Expence and moſt

H acute

acute Pain; yet that very Leg was restored to Ease and perfect Soundness by this powerful Medicine in a short Time without any external Application.

184. *Mary Philips*, now in the Work-house, for a long Time had lost in a manner, the Use of a Leg, with a constant Numbness or Tingling, as if it were asleep; she could not walk on it but with Difficulty, but if she stirred quick ever so little, she then felt most acute Pain, and in frosty Weather, would often be forced to sit up in Bed many an Hour by Night, moaning and rubbing it; but by Tar-water that Numbness is entirely gone, and tho' she walks ever so quick or long, she feels no manner of Pain in that Part, the sure Consequence (before Tar-water) of such Motion.

185. A Son of Mr. *B——y*, Iron-monger, in *Thomas-street*, was infected with a dry Scurf in the Scarf-skin, for some Time, much like a Leprosy; no Expence, no Advice, was either with-held, or wanting, yet the Youth found no Relief: On this the tender Mother asked the Doctor, if she might venture to give the Child Tar-water, so much in vogue about that Time; "Ay, ay," says the Doctor, "if you have a Mind to kill your Son;" to demonstrate which, he gave this Reason, "what "Nature kindly throws out," says he, "you will "certainly cork up by the searing Quality of Tar-"water, and so your Son must inevitably perish;" nevertheless, Tar-water was ventured upon, with the utmost Dread; but behold in a short Time the Lad became perfectly clean and healthy, and still continues so. Of this I am both an Eye and Ear-witness, because the Lady and the Lad paid me a Visit, and acknowledged thankfully this great Blessing, and related the above Story.

186. *Robert Scot*, Tape-weaver, to be heard of at *Paul Johnston*'s in *James*'s-*street*, was cured suddenly by this powerful Medicine, of an old Ulcer in

in the Thigh, and relieved from a consumptive Cough, which so weakened the poor Man, that he was not able to work; but now looks brisk, and gets his Bread comfortably, and to use his own Words, he makes his Paws maintain his Jaws.

187 Mrs. *Bermingham*, then living at Mrs. *Becks* in *James*'s-*street*, labouring for many Years under an acute Pain in her Side; supposed to be an Imposthume, by this Medicine was suddenly reliev-ed by a Discharge of an incredible Quantity of Filth and Matter upwards; since which Time, the Woman, tho' much in Years, enjoys the Comforts of Life, being now both vigorous and easy.

188. *Elizabeth Wood*, at Mr. *Mac Guires*, the Corner of *Meath-street*, was relieved by Tar-water from an old Asthma and Dropsy, with both which the poor Woman seemed every Moment to be ready to expire; both her Ailments are cured by this Water, and she now thinks of living as long as any of her Neighbours, being both hearty and strong.

189. *William Billingsly*, formerly of the Work-house, now living on *Crooked-staff*, was troubled with Swellings and violent Pains in both his Legs and Feet, which suffered him neither to work, nor walk; but after taking this Medicine only one Month, all his Disorders vanished, he grew so strong and hearty, that he wove in the Work-house four Yards of Check-linen each Day; I spoke to him *February* 7, 1744, at which Time he was very well.

190. *John Rose*, now in the Work-house, was a long Time bed-rid, with Cramps all over him, from whence the Pain was so acute and constant, that his piteous Moans both Night and Day, disturbed all about him; but by taking Tar-water one Month, his Disorder vanished, as it were, without the least Return since *May* 1744, and now enjoys his Limbs, tho' not able to stir one Foot before.

H 2 181.

191. *Robert Turnbowl*, a Boy of the ſame Houſe, was brought on a Boy's Back, and laid down at my Chamber-door, not being able to ſtir one Step, yet by uſing this powerful Medicine one Month, recovered his Legs, and now goes tolerably.

192. *John Warburghs*, of the ſame Family, was frightfully afflicted with an Inflammation in his Head, his Eye-lids were ſo ſwelled, that the Boy was led to my Apartment, being as dark as one Stone-blind, and there ſupplicated very ſolemnly and fervently for Tar-water; he obtained his Requeſt, tho' I was then doubtful of Succeſs; yet on taking this Medicine three Days, the Inflammation ſo cooled, that the Boy's Eyes were perfectly reſtored; however, his Forehead, Chin, and the Back of his Head, were covered with a large and ſtrange Eryſipelas; all which in three Days Time ſcaled off, the whole Inflammation cooled, and the Boy continues very well, and free from that Diſorder now upwards of twelve Months.

193. *Richard Keeves*, of this Family, had two bleeding Ulcers in his Thigh, which did not permit him to ſleep, work or walk, both which were cured in a ſhort Time by this Medicine without any outward Application.

194. There is a Gentlewoman on *Arbour-hill*, who ſuffered a great deal a long Time by an Ulcer in her Leg, and after many coſtly Experiments, and painful ones too, was injoined Patience, as being incurable. Then, as her laſt Shift, ſhe fell to Tar-water, by which ſhe is ſo well recovered, that ſhe is now able to go to Church, to return Thanks for ſo great a Bleſſing; nay, walks without Pain or Difficulty any where, tho' before, ſhe could not ſtir a Foot without both.

195. There is an Officer in the Barracks, who for a long Time felt, after walking a little Way, a grievous Pain in the Back-ſinews of his Legs, but on

on drinking Tar-water, all Complaints there are perfectly vanished, tho' he walks ever so much and fast, having made the Experiment; and this I had from his own Mouth.

196. *Matthew Lynch*, an old Man, seventy Years at least, now living at Mr. *Floyde*'s in *Kilmainham*, was lately asthmatick to a great Degree, and so afflicted with the Piles, that he was always scared to Death, whenever he had a Call that Way, the Pain was so great; but now by the powerful Help of this Medicine, he can do every natural Office with Ease, and is not only relieved from all his old Disorders, but seems to have regained new Life and Vigour.

197. The present Reader in *Christ Church*, was attacked with an Hoarseness a considerable Time, and assured me he was frightened at its Continuance, but is now so cleared up by Tar-water, that he is able now to sing, *O be joyful.*

198. Mr. *John Purcell*, Son to the present Treasurer of the Work-house, seemed for some Time to be in a decling Way, from a consumptive Cough and frequent Stitches; but by taking this Restorative, he revives daily, and no Wonder, for from Time to Time, the Lad voided several large Worms, accidentally discovered, and many probably we know nothing of.

199. *Jane Hamilton*, now in the Work-house, *Dublin*, being grievously afflicted with a scald Head, for which she was four Years under Cure in *Mercer*'s Hospital, but without Effect, was after admitted into the Work-house, where for several Years all Methods of Cure were pursued, but to as little Purpose: On which Account, she was sent to me as an obstinate Case, to try what Tar-water would do. I accordingly took the Girl in Hand, and gave her nothing but Tar-water, Morning and Evening for a Month; then I had her Head washed and rubbed twice a Day with a Spunge dipp'd in warm

H 3 strong

ſtrong Tar-water, made of a Quart of Tar, and two Quarts of boiling Water, till all the Scurf came off; by which Method, the Girl is now perfectly clean, healthy and ſtrong, with a thick Head of Hair, as if nothing had ever ailed her, to the Admiration of all, who once knew her in a moſt miſerable Condition.

200. One Mrs. *Eager*, now living at *Mullineback*, near *New-row*, *Thomas-ſtreet*, threw up from time to time, ſuch vaſt Quantities of Blood that ſhe was as pale as a Ghoſt, and ſo feeble, that ſhe could ſcarce ſtand: But after taking Tar-water, the bloody Diſcharge ceaſed, and ſhe improved daily, till now ſhe is become a hearty ſtrong Woman.

201. Mr. *William Dickiſon*, oppoſite *James*'s Church, was for ſome Time very Deaf; he took Tar-water, on which his Chin broke out, after which he could hear as well as ever, and continues to do ſo, though upwards of two Years ago.

There are a great many more Caſes, very aſtoniſhing for their Succeſs, which I muſt paſs by in Silence, not being permitted for ſome Reaſons to mention the Names of the Parties concerned; yet there is one ſo remarkably true and aſtoniſhing, that I cannot omit it, without Detriment to the Publick: On which Account, I hope the Perſons concerned will take no Offence, ſince deſigned only for the Benefit of others.

A moſt remarkable Caſe.

202. The third of *November* laſt, a Surgeon of this City paid me a Viſit, in order, (as he ſaid) to thank me for a moſt wonderful Cure performed by my Tar-water: This made me curious to know the Caſe, he aſſured me, a Perſon in this Town had laboured for ſome Time under the foul Diſorder, which had ſo infected the whole Maſs, that Part of the

the unhappy Creature's Nose was lost, before he was called in; so that the Infection by that Time was spread from Top to Toe; for in one of the Calves of the poor Creature's Leg, he could thrust his Fist, and the whole Back was as bare as a cased Rabbet; as also the Head and Glands were so inflamed, he often spent two Hours about this one Subject; but says he, to shorten my Story, having some Time tried in vain all Methods in Practice for such a Disorder, I then gave my Patient your Tar-water; the sensible and sudden Effects of which, astonished me; all the Ulcers appearing more cool and kindly; I then began (continues he) to conceive some Hope of my Patient, though before in good Truth, I had none at all. After my Patient had taken a Gallon of your Tar-water, as I came in one Morning, I found my Patient full of Complaints, seemingly very fretful, and uneasy; on asking the Cause, my Patient protested very solemnly, never to touch one Drop more of Tar-water, because the last Night's Operation caused by Tar-water, was so violent and searching; I strove to get the better of this rash Dislike, by shewing plainly the true Reason and future Benefit of this strong Operation, but to no Purpose; so Tar-water was omitted forty-eight Hours, at the End of which Time, all the Sores and Ulcers became once more putrid, and inflamed very sensibly, plainly demonstrating an absolute Necessity of returning to our old Medicine; after some Struggle with my Patient's obstinate Prejudice, we did so, and now I am able to assure you, Sir, says the Surgeon, my Patient is perfectly recovered, the Nose excepted; and this whole Cure, as strange as it is, was accomplished by your Tar-water, and no other Medicine; now, Sir, continues he, I must confess, that a Principle of Gratitude is not the only Motive of this Visit and frank Confession, but also to intreat you, to inform me of your Sort of Tar, and how you make your Water: Which I imagine, says he, will be of great Service to the most wretched of Mankind: Accordingly I informed him of the Sort of *Norway* Tar I made use of, and how I prepared the Water.

203. A Gentleman now lodging on *Arbour-hill*, was so afflicted with inward Pains, and emaciated to such a Degree, that he was obliged to part with an honourable and profitable Commission, when commanded lately abroad. When all other Medicines and Advice failed, he drank for some time Tar-water of his own making, which he assured me had almost poisoned him, without any manner of Ease or Relief. On this Disappointment, by Advice of a Friend, he sent to me for some of my Tar-water: On taking which for some time, his Pains immediately vanished, and never returned, though upwards of four Months, he still continuing the Use of the Water. Moreover the Night passes now insensibly, whereas before he drank my Tar-water, he generally reckoned by the Clock every Hour of the Night, from which comfortable Composure, his natural Appetite returned, and he is now become an hail brisk strong Man.

204. Mrs. *Dickson*, now living at Mrs. *Ford*'s at *Island-bridge*, laboured a long time under a Complication of Disorders, but more especially, a frequent Colic, and inveterate Scurvy, which affected her whole Body, and her Face particularly, which are now all cured by this Medicine only.

205. Miss *Martha Dowers*, living opposite to the Cock and Bowl in *Plunket-street*, was long afflicted with an inveterate Scurvy over her whole Body, and for Years continued incurable, tho' all Methods were tryed, that the young Woman could either purchase or think of; at last she took Tar-water, which effectually cured her; of which I am

an

an Eye-witneſs, being with me at the Work-houſe the 26th of *November* 1745, to acknowledge the Bleſſing ſhe received, and to return Thanks, not having the leaſt Speck or Spot, and looking healthy and well.

206. Mr. *William Foſter*, Brother to Mr. *Foſter*, Brewer in *James's-ſtreet*, *Dublin*, came to Town the Beginning of *November* 1745, ſorely afflicted with a Swelling in both his Legs, together with a ſevere Cough, for which he took but one Gallon of Tar-water, and this Day *November* 26, I am aſſured by his Nephew, that the Swelling is gone, and alſo the Cough, and he who ſeemed to be in a languiſhing Condition when he came to Town lately, revives daily, and ſeems to be reſtored to a new State of Health.

207. Meſſieurs *Maſſy* and *Boucher*, of the County of *Limerick*, from long Confinement, and other Misfortunes, contracted ſuch ill Habits of Body, that their Phyſicians gave Teſtimony that they could not live, if confined in the Place where they were, ſo were brought into my Neighbourhood to preſerve their Lives: By which happy Accident, hearing of Tar-water, they immediately ſent for ſome, which they drank, and were reſtored ſurprizingly in a ſhort time, after every other Method preſcribed by the beſt Phyſicians had failed. The 5th of this Inſtant *November* 1745, I ſpoke to them both, and they aſſured me, that they have been well ever ſince they took Tar-water, now upwards of ſix Months.

208. A Gentlewoman of my Acquaintance, was attacked *September* laſt 1745, with a ſevere Ague-fit, about three in the Morning, which ſhook her upwards of two Hours. On this I gave her about a Naggin of Tar-water, which compoſed her immediately, and ſhe took a refreſhing Nap for ſome time; at Nine the ſame Morning preparing to riſe, ſhe could

could not ſtir her left Leg, being very ſtiff and ſore, and greatly ſwelled and inflamed. On this a Surgeon was called in, who aſſured it was a moſt violent Diſorder, nor could he foreſee the Conſequence; being thus alarmed, ſhe kept her Bed for ſome time, and ſtuped her Leg with Spirits of Wine, but took no Medicine inwardly but Tar-water, by which Means, ſhe had no other Ague-fit, and her Leg is now neither ſwelled nor inflamed, but in all Appearance, and by its eaſy natural Uſe, as well and as ſound as the other.

209. *A moſt remarkable Cure of a Gentleman's Daughter about nine Years old, lately in the Small-pox.*

Miſs *Hannah Hartnell*, now living at Mrs. *Green*'s in *Ransford-ſtreet*, the 6th of *November* 1745, fell ill of the Small-pox, her Parents having, from reading *Siris*, a good Opinion of Tar-water, were willing to make uſe of it; accordingly I ordered the Quantity of a Naggin of Tar-water to be given to the Child warm every ſixth Hour; the Child took it, and it ſat well on her Stomach, till the third Day, but then ſhe threw it up in a ſhort Time after it was down with a Load of Filth and Phlegm; by which Means all Oppreſſion and Pain in the Child's Stomach ceaſed, of which ſhe continually complained before. Moreover, on that Day, (*viz.* the third) ſhe had a violent Lax, which continued about twenty Hours, ſtill ſhe took her Tar-water as before, but obſerving ſhe threw up all or moſt of it, I then ordered a third of warm Water to be mixt with it, to make it weaker, which cauſed it to ſit, for ſhe never threw it up after, nay was not ſo much as ſick, or made the leaſt Complaint, until *Monday* the 17th of *November*, being the 13th Day; at which Time, when I payed my Viſit in the Morning, I found the Child in a moſt hopeleſs Way; the

the Discharge at her Nose and Eyes was stopt, which before that time was very large (the Disorder on the Child's Face being confluent, and never filled, the *Pus* discharging itself that way) the Small-pox on her Hands appeared black or livid; the Child grew cold, with little or no Pulse, together with an hard Hoarseness, and a continual Cough. Those deadly Symptoms and sudden Alteration astonished me greatly, having left the Child the Evening before in a very promising Way. I then strictly examined how this frightful Alteration happened, and found, that by Accident, Water was spilt in the Child's Bed, out of which she was taken, tho' in a cold frosty Day, and continued so for some considerable Time, because she was not put into Bed till all the wet Things were dried and adjusted. From that Instant, all our former Hopes of the Child's Recovery vanished, and as for my Part, I did not imagine she could struggle twelve Hours, from the Obstructions in both Head and Throat, which appeared most stubborn and obstinate, the Child being able neither to speak, swallow, or breathe freely: However, tho' my Hope was indeed but very small, immediately I warm'd a Naggin of Tar-water, without any Mixture, and obliged the poor Child with some Difficulty to sip it, little by little, till in some considerable Time, she got all down, and it staid with her. On this I ordered some healthy careful Person to be put into Bed, and to take the Child into their Arms, to infuse Heat if possible. The tender Mother readily obeyed, in some time the Child grew warm and easy, fell into a fine Sweat, and slept for about two Hours, after which, the former Discharge from both Nose and Eyes burst forth a-new, and appeared as large, if not larger for some time than ever; which greatly promoted the Child's speedy Recovery from this most imminent Danger. Being now up and well, with a keen Appetite, good Digestion,

Digeſtion, and what is moſt aſtoniſhing in the whole Proceſs, for the Space of twenty-one Days, ſhe was not once ſick, or made the leaſt Complaint, the 3d and 13th Days excepted. Now I beg Leave to aſſure the Publick, that this Child took no manner of Medicine, but only Tar-water, not one Drop of Sack or Sack-whey, her common Drink was two-milk Whey, or boiled Milk and Water, of which ſhe took plentifully, and always warm: By a Bleſſing on which Method, ſhe is now livelier and heartier than before ſhe lay down, being only the 23d Day, this 28th of *November* 1745.

210. Mr. *William Charleton*, in *November* 1745, was attacked with a violent Fever, of which he ſeem'd to get the better, but relapſed immediately, under which he languiſhed for ſome Time, and ſeem'd paſt Hope; as an Addition to his Diſorder, an inflamed Ulcer ſo affected his Throat inwardly, that he could not ſwallow; upon this he ſent to me for Tar-water; on taking which his Ulcer vaniſhed, his Appetite returned, his Fever entirely left him, without any bad Symptom, and the young Gentleman is now, I thank God, both lively and ſtrong, from a very languiſhing dangerous State: All which, this Morning *December* 24, he thankfully acknowledged in my Room, where he took with me a Cup of Tar-water with the greateſt Alacrity. He lodges at Mr. *Silk*'s oppoſite the Work-houſe.

211. *John Mac Donald*, now in the Work-houſe, was miſerably eat away with the King's-evil in many Parts of his Body, it conſumed half his Face, ſo that he was nauſeous both to himſelf and others. This firſt happened to him in the Country: In Hopes of Relief, he ſet out for this City, and by Accident met the Biſhop of *Cloyne*, who adviſed him to Tar-water, and gave him ſome Money to provide it. The Lad neglected this good Advice, but obtained Admiſſion into one of the Infirmaries, where

where being twice ſalivated, but nothing better, he was turned out as incurable; being in great Diſtreſs, he came into the Work-houſe as a Vagabond, where he was ſalivated alſo, but his Evil ſtill continued obſtinate, without the leaſt Sign of Relief, tho' reduced in a manner to a Shadow; as he was crawling about, I took notice of him, and adviſed him to Tar-water, he complied, and in the Space of a Fortnight, he found moſt ſenſible Relief, ſo continued taking Tar-water about ſix Weeks longer, which cured all the Ulcers of his Body; but where the Sores were, the Skin is drawn up in Wrinkles, tho' without any Weakneſs or Pain. Thus far Mr. *Hill.*

212. *An Extract of a Letter from a Gentleman of Veracity and Credit, relating to his own Caſe; dated the 10th of* December 1745.

It is ſomewhat more than a Year ago I firſt meddled with Tar-water, only playing with it. I found it good for a ſlow Digeſtion, and a Strengthener of a weak Stomach. At Times I was wont to be troubled with the Piles, and with a Pain in the lower Part of my Back, in both which Caſes it befriended me. But afterward being pretty well at Eaſe, I thought but little of Tar-water, till the Beginning of *July* laſt, when the ſame Pain in the lower Part of my Back afflicted me ſo violently, as to cauſe me to apply to a Phyſician, from whom I gathered, that what I had deemed to be of the Gravel-kind, was gouty. However, I determined with myſelf to go into the Uſe of Tar-water in earneſt; which I have regularly done ſince that Time, only with ſhort Intermiſſions now and then; and, by the divine Bleſſing, with much Advantage to my Health and Strength, Freedom of Spirits and Chearfulneſs. When I came into the regular Uſe of it, I took a Reſolution to oblige myſelf to as cool and mild Diet

as

as I could well bear, and to deal leſs than formerly in Fleſh-meat, and Malt-liquor, or Wine, or Cyder: And many Times, I believe, much leſs than a Pound of Fleſh, and a Quart of thoſe Liquors put together, had ſerved me a Week. This I did on Account of its being warm, as I ſuppoſed, and Cordial in its Nature, concluding it would ſufficiently ſupport the Conſtitution, as the Effect has proved. Indeed, I find little or no Inclination to drink except at Meals, and then leſs than formerly, nor find the want of Cordial, whilſt in the Uſes of Tar-water.

I was near thirty Years old, when an ulcerous Ailment came upon me in my Seat; and 'tis now ſomewhat more than thirty Years, that it hath been a running Grief or Iſſue, more or leſs, to be ſure ſome time in every Moon pretty plentifully diſcharging a purulent Matter; but this Diſcharge is now ſtopped by the Means of Tar-water.

This Gentleman, though perfectly freed from all his Ailments, yet is apprehenſive, that the ſtopping and healing up his Ulcer, may be attended with bad Conſequences, under the Notion, that the want of ſuch a Diſcharge, which he has been ſo long accuſtomed to, may occaſion ſome Diſorder elſe-where, and therefore would be adviſed about continuing the Uſe of Tar-water; and at the ſame time, ſays, that having found it ſo friendly, he is afraid of being adviſed to forbear the Uſe of it, as long as the Benefit received is manifeſt in the Enjoyment of a better State of Health and Eaſe, unattended with any preſent Inconvenience. It is pleaſant to ſee how this Patient is frighted at his being cured of a running Ulcer, which had infeſted him for thirty Years: He could not be perfectly cured, unleſs his Ulcer was healed, and there is nothing to fear from thence, as the peccant Humour was not repelled, or driven to other Parts, but corrected and mended; ſuch is the wonderful Force of Tar-water in ſweetening the Blood and Juices.

213. In

213. *In* September 1745, *the two following Gentlemen gave me at their respective Houses in* Cloyne, *an Account of the Benefits they received by the Use of Tar-water.*

Mr. *James Hanning*, by catching Cold, was seized with a violent Fever in *November* 1743, his Feet and Legs were at first extreamly cold, his Head much disturbed, and he lost all Appetite, being judged by all to be in a dangerous Condition by the Height of his Fever; he had Recourse to Tar-water, which he drank in Plenty, and took nothing else; in ten Days drinking, his Fever, and all other bad Symptoms went off, and in a Fortnight's Time he was perfectly recovered.

214. Mr. *Clement Foster*, who deals much there in the Worsted-trade, was in Summer 1744, seized with a Fever, which greatly affected him, and made him incapable to do any Business: He was advised to drink Tar-water, which had such an Effect, that in ten Days his Fever turned to an Ague, which was so easy, that on the first taking the Bark, he was perfectly cured; he informed me also, that he used to be troubled with one or two Fits of the Gout every Year for several Years past, but that he had no Return of it, since he began to drink Tar-water.

215. *Robert Dillon* of *Clonbrock* in the County of *Galway*, Esq; Member of Parliament, was pleased to give me the following Account in *January* 1745, that he had been afflicted with the Gout above fifteen Years, which became more violent every Year, that he used to be confined in the Fits for many Months together, with great Pain, and such Weakness in his Limbs, that he could hardly walk; that when he was out of the Fits, he was troubled in the Morning especially, with a great uneasiness and loathing in his Stomach, and a Discharge of a great deal of Phlegm, that he had no Relief from any

any Medicine he took; but that in Summer 1744, he began to drink Tar-water, which he has continued for a Year and half without Intermiſſion, taking conſtantly half a Pint in the Morning, and as much every Night, which he was encouraged to do by the Benefit he received by it; all the Loathing in his Stomach is quite gone, and though he has now and then ſome Fits of the Gout, yet they happen but ſeldom, and laſt but a ſhort time with little or no Pain, and he now enjoys good Appetite and Spirits, though his Limbs are ſtill weak, and he thinks himſelf happy in compariſon of his former Condition.

216. *Henry Leſtrange* of the *King*'s County, Eſq; Member of Parliament, informed me in *January* 1745, that he had been troubled with the Gout for ten Years paſt, that about four Years ago he was ſeized with the Small-pox, from which he recovered with great Difficulty, that for a Year after he had no Return of the Gout, but that for the laſt three Years, the Gout returned upon him with more Violence, ſo that he had a Fit every Autumn and Spring; that the Fit in the laſt Spring laſted three Months, which deprived him of Reſt, Appetite, and Spirits; that being adviſed to drink Tar-water, he began to drink it in Summer 1745, which he has continued the Uſe of ever ſince, with ſuch good Effect, that he has had no Return of the Gout in the uſual Seaſon, nor any Symptom of it, and now enjoys a good Appetite, Flow of Spirits, and Freedom from all Uneaſineſs, and has the full Uſe and Strength of his Limbs as much as ever, and reſolves to drink Tar-water conſtantly, to which he imputes all his Recovery.

217. Colonel *Charles Tottenham* of *Tottenham-green*, in the County of *Wexford*, Eſq; Member of Parliament, informed me on the 30th of *January* 1745, that he had been afflicted with a dead Ague for five Years,

Years, and had not any cold Fits, but that his hot Fits were very violent, being constantly attended with prodigious Sweats, which wasted and weakened him greatly; he had lost his Appetite and Spirits, and though he took great Quantities of the Bark, he found himself the worse for it. In this decaying Condition, he consulted the Physicians in *Dublin*, and took their Prescriptions without any Relief. But in Summer, 1744, he had Recourse to Tar-water, which he drank cold, half a Pint in the Morning, and as much at Night, for a Month or six Weeks, and found that the Tar-water griped him very much, and gave him no Relief; upon which he discontinued the Use of it: but finding that his Disorder still grew worse, and hearing that it was advised in Cases of Agues, Colics, and Fevers, to drink Tar-water warm, and in smaller Quantities at a Time, he followed that Advice, and from the Moment he drank it Milk-warm, he found it agree with his Stomach, and got immediate Relief, and continuing to drink it plentifully in that Form, he has entirely got the better of his dead Ague, and is quite free from all Symptoms of it; he has recovered his Appetite, Spirits, and Rest, and attributes his Recovery altogether to Tar-water, which he still drinks and resolves always to drink, as it is no way disagreeable to him, and so very useful.

218. Mr. *William Willan*, Tape-weaver in *Thomas-street*, *Dublin*, informed me in *January*, 1745, that for many Years he had been afflicted with the Gout, which gave him much Pain, and frequently confined him to his Chamber; that being advised to drink Tar-water, he did so in the regular Manner, which gave him Spirits, Appetite, and Ease, by which, he is now able to attend all his Business abroad without Pain from the Gout; and though he has still a Weakness in his Limbs, he imputes that to the Necessity of walking much abroad, which his

I Affairs

Affairs frequently require, and acknowledges the great Benefit he received by drinking-Tar-water.

219. Captain *Solomon Debrisay*, of the City of *Dublin*, favoured me with the following Detail of his Case in *January*, 1745. He was troubled with a scorbutical Disorder above twenty Years, for which he took several Medicines in *England*, *France*, and *Ireland*; and though he sometimes had some Abatement of his Disorder, yet at last it grew very violent, breaking out into running Sores, and Scruff, and attended with great Pain, so that he could hardly ride or walk without great Uneasiness. In this Condition in *September*, 1744, he got an Inflammation of the Lungs and violent Cough, by catching cold, for which he was blooded and vomited; and when he had got the better of the Inflammation, he took Tar-water to remove his Cough, at the Rate of a Pint a Day, which in a little Time carried off his Cough; and finding the Water to agree with him, and that it made him easier in the Scurvy, he continued the drinking of it for six Months, by which Means, he was entirely cured of the Scurvy, without the least Sore or Spot remaining, and has had no Return of it since that Time, though he has left off the Use of the Water, as having no farther Occasion for it.

220. Mr. *George Rumford*, aged seventy-five Years, who lives at the *Black-pits*, *Dublin*, was in the Year 1744, seized with a most violent Cough, attended with a continual Spitting of corrupt Stuff and Phlegm. In this dangerous Condition he made Use of every Thing the Doctors had ordered, without receiving the least Benefit, upon which they gave him up as past all Hopes of Cure. But a Friend of his coming to see him, and finding him given over, begg'd he would drink Tar-water, which he did in the Quantity of a Pint each Day, till he made use of three Gallons of Tar-water; in which Time,

Time, he was quite recovered, freed from his violent Cough and Spitting, and reſtored to a good Appetite, and is now in a great Flow of Spirits, and as well as he could wiſh for one of his Years, and he verily believes, that, had it not been for Tar-water, he ſhould have been dead long ago, and that he owes his Life to the Uſe of it.

221. *James Reyly*, Servant to Mr. *Phepoe* Brewer in *Mill-ſtreet*, was in the Year 1745 afflicted with an Aſthma, Shortneſs of Breath, and great Cough, and at the ſame Time, his Belly, Thighs, and Legs were ſwollen to a monſtrous Size, ſo that he could not walk or breath but with great Difficulty, and he loſt all Appetite; he made uſe of many Things preſcribed for him without receiving any Benefit, and he continued in this miſerable Way for ſome Time; but hearing of the Effects of Tar-war, and what Relief others had received from it, he began immediately to drink it, about a Pint a Day, until he had made uſe of a Gallon, by which Time his Breath was reſtored, his Cough was gone, and all the Swellings in his Body and Limbs fell away, and he recovered a good Appetite, and could eat three Times for once he could before. He had alſo at the ſame Time a great Scurvy in his Face, which was alſo carried off by drinking Tar-water, and he is now hearty and well, and able to go through his Buſineſs as well as ever.

222. Mr. *Enoch Maſon*, who lives with Mr. *Burſiquot*, Clothier, near *Eſſex-bridge*, gave me the following Particulars of his Diſorder, on the 31ſt of *January*, 1745. He had been troubled with rheumatick Pains in his Joints for fifteen Years, which he could not remove by any of the Medicines he took; but in 1744, his Diſorder appeared in a new Form; he had great Difficulty of breathing, inſomuch, that he could not lye down in his Bed for ſix Weeks, his Belly was drawn up, and he ſuffered great Pains;

I 2 the

the Physician called it a Contraction of the Bowels; he could not sleep by Reason of his Pains and Difficulty of breathing, and though he took many composing Draughts, which made him doze, yet he got no Refreshment: he went thorough the common Course of Physick, vomiting, and other Prescriptions, which giving him no Relief, his Case was judged to be desperate, and accordingly, he was advised to go into the Country and drink Milk, which might possibly prolong his Life for some Time, but without any Hopes that he could last long. At this Time, he heard much of Tar-water, and was advised to drink it, which he did at the Rate of a Pint a Day; which in a little Time removed the Contraction in his Belly, restored him to a Freedom of breathing, and brought him to a good Appetite, so that he mended every Day, and continued to drink the Water, obtained a perfect Recovery from his Rheumatism, and all his other Disorders, which he attributes altogether to the Use of Tar-water.

223. Mr. *John Wilkinson*, Clerk in the Surveyor General's Office in the Castle of *Dublin*, informed me the first of *February*, 1745, that he had the Misfortune to break his Leg by a Slip in the Street, which confined him for three Months; that by laying so long on his Back in Bed, he got the Gravel, which gave him great Uneasiness; that at the same Time, by catching Cold, he lost his Hearing, and was so deaf, that he could not hear the Drums, that beat near his Chamber in the Castle. To ease him of his Gravel, he was advised to drink Tar-water, and he had not drunk above a Gallon, when, to his Surprize, he found his Deafness carried off, and he could hear as well as ever he did, and continuing to drink Tar-water, which he found very diuretick, he voided a small rough craggy Stone, and, by Degrees, a great Deal of Gravel; and he is now entirely

2 tirely

tirely free from all Pains or Symptoms of the Gravel, and hears perfectly well.

224. *Matthew Haynes*, Sword Cutler, at the *Black Lyon* on the *Blind-quay*, oppoſite to Mr. *Thomas*'s Mohogany Ware-houſe, informed me on the firſt of *February*, 1745, that he was for fifteen Months ill of a Decay. He was ſo ſore and ſtreightened all over his Body, that he could not bear his Apron or his Cloths on without much Pain; he had loſt all Appetite and Reſt, and was brought ſo low, that he was not able to work at his Trade, or even to go up or down Stairs without Help; and though he was oppreſſed with Phlegm, and could hardly breath, yet he dared not cough or ſpit, on Account of the great Pain cauſed thereby in his Breaſt and Body. Being in this miſerable Condition, he was adviſed by Mr. *Bradiſh*, who employed him, to drink Tar-water, and being reſolved to try any thing recommended to him, he incautiouſly drank near a Pint of cold Tar-water at once, which he inſtantly threw up with great Violence, together with a great deal of Phlegm. He then thought himſelf a dead Man, and was for ſending for a Clergyman to pray with him for the laſt Time, as he thought; but in a few Minutes after he found himſelf much eaſier in his Stomach and Cheſt, and mended all the Day. This good Effect reconciled him to Tar-water, and made him reſolve to drink it in ſmaller Quantities and Milk-warm, which he did twice a Day, half a Pint each Time, and, by continuing to drink it that Way for ſome Time, all the Sores in his Breaſt and Body went away, he breathed with Eaſe, and recovered his Reſt and Appetite, and eats a hearty Breakfaſt, which he never could do before in his beſt State of Health. He is able to work at his Trade as formerly, and is perſuaded that he owes his Life to Tar-water.

225. *An Extract from a Letter of* William Pleaſants *of* Knockbeg, *in the County of* Carlow, *Eſq*; *to* Thomas Prior *Eſq*; February 4, 1745.

The Perſon who received ſuch great Benefit by drinking Tar-water, was a Boy who drove my Plough; he laboured under what was judged, by moſt who ſaw him, a ſcrophulous Diſorder, or Kings-evil; he had ſeveral ulcerous Sores about his Jaws and Neck, which continued running for great Part of ſome Years. His Mother, who had ſome Knowledge in Herbs, applyed different Kinds to his Sores, which eaſed a little, but had no other Succeſs.

I recommended him to a Friend in *Dublin*, who prevailed on ſome Gentlemen of Skill, to endeavour to cure him. They had Compaſſion on the Creature, and gave him Medicines, but they alſo proved ineffectual. My Friend then gave him Tar-water; when he had taken a ſmall Quantity, he found more Relief from it, than he had done from all that had been done for him before. He returned to his Mother, and I ſupplyed him with Tar-water; and, as well as I can remember, he had not taken a Gallon of it, when the Ulcers began to dry, and his Face, which was very much ſwollen with his Diſtemper, began to reaſſume its natural Form. He left me laſt Spring, and ſtayed from me till Harveſt. At his Return, he told me, that Tar-water had cured him, and that his Diſorder had given him no Uneaſineſs, the Time he was abſent from me. I am

Your moſt humble Servant,
William Pleaſants.

226. Mr. *Patrick Butler*, Shoemaker in *Crane-lane*, *Dublin*, informed me on the 5th of *February*, 1745, that he had been afflicted with the Rheuma-tiſm

tiſm for ſeveral Years; that about two Years ago, the Fits were ſo violent, that he was layed up three Months together; that for eight Days in that Time, he could not ſtir Hand or Foot, and was turned in his Head by other People, the rheumatick Pains having ſeized his whole Body; that when the Violence of the Fit abated in 1744, he made uſe of Tar-water, which encouraged him to perſiſt in the Uſe of it ever ſince, with ſuch good Effect, that all his rheumatic Pains are gone, and he has had no Return of them ſince he began to drink the Water: he has got the full Strength of his Limbs, Appetite, and Spirits, and reſolves to drink Tar-water conſtantly, finding that if he gets any twitching in his Limbs by cold or ſharp Weather, Tar-water immediately relieves him.

227. *William Heany*, Shoemaker, Journeyman to the ſaid Mr. *Butler*, was in 1744, ſeized with ſuch violent Pains in his Legs, that he could not walk, reſt, or work at his Trade. He was adviſed to drink Tar-water, which he did, and found in a little Time all his Pains go off, and was reſtored to the full Uſe of his Limbs, and able to get his Bread by his Trade, though before, he was apprehenſive that he ſhould not be able to ſubſiſt, having no other Means to ſupport him but his Labour, which the Violence of his Pains diſabled him from performing.

228. Mrs. *Bonvillet*, who lives in *Kings-ſtreet*, near *Stephen's-green*, informed me on the 3d of *February*, 1745, that near twenty-eight Years ago ſhe had the Misfortune to fall down Stairs, and pitched upon her Shoulder, which occaſioned a Contuſion in that Part, but as the Pain ſoon went off, ſhe did not then take any Care about it. She afterwards obſerved a Sort of Pimple in that Part, but finding no Pain in it, ſhe ſtill neglected it.

I 4 However,

However, it ſtill increaſed every Year, without any Manner of Pain, till in the Year 1744, it had formed a Wen of an enormous Size, which ſpread from her Shoulders to one of her Ears, and under her Arm-pit, as large as the Mould of a Hat; ſo that ſhe was obliged to enlarge her Cloaths to cover it, and hide the Deformity; but as ſhe had no Pain with it, ſhe neglected all Thoughts of preventing its Progreſs, which might have been eaſily effected in the Beginning: but in 1744, ſhe found herſelf troubled with other Ailments, with Vapours, Lowneſs of Spirits, want of Appetite and Reſt, which greatly reduced her; for removing theſe laſt Diſorders, ſhe was adviſed to drink Tar-water, which ſhe did regularly for a conſiderable Time. The firſt Effect was, that in a little Time ſhe recovered her Appetite, got Reſt and Spirits, and was freed from all her Vapours and Diſturbance in her Stomach, and has continued well from thoſe Diſorders ever ſince; as ſhe found that Tar-water did her ſo much Service, ſhe ſtill drank it for ſeveral Months, and obſerved, that in ſome Time, the great Wen on her Shoulders began to grow ſoft and fall away. This encouraged her to continue the drinking of the Water, and in a few Months after the Wen was reduced to a Fourth of its firſt Size, and daily grew ſofter, and ſeemed to have ſome floating Roots in it: finding herſelf eaſy, and in ſo good a Way, ſhe laid aſide Tar-water for ſome Months before the Wen was quite diſperſed, and then found that it began to grow hard and ſwell again; upon which, ſhe has of late reſumed her Tar-water, of which ſhe drinks near a Quart a Day, and finds that the Hardneſs and Swelling have already greatly abated; and ſhe reſolves to perſiſt in the conſtant Uſe of it, in full Hopes that in ſome Time ſhe will quite get rid of her Wen. And her Hopes are the greater, conſidering the Benefit which a *French* Gentlemen received

ceived by it in a parallel Caſe: This Gentleman had, as ſhe informed me, a great Lump, that by Degrees grew on the Crown of his Head, which became at laſt as large as an Egg, inſomuch, that he could hardly keep his Hat on his Head, and though it was not attended with Pain, it was very troubleſome. The Gentleman took Tar-water for ſome other Diſorder, from which he was relieved, and found at the ſame Time, that this Lump or Wen ſoftened and waſted by Degrees, and that at laſt it quite melted away and vaniſhed.

229. Mr. *John Wilme*, Silver-ſmith, who lives in *Coles-alley*, near *Caſtle-ſtreet*, informed me on the 5th of *February*, 1745, that by an Accident he got a Hurt in his Shin-bone, which cauſed a Running and Swelling, and being laid open by a Surgeon, was in ſome Time healed; yet he after found, that a Humour flowed to and ſwelled the Part, and gave him great Uneaſineſs. He had at the ſame Time, a Lump or Excreſcence on the Crown of his Head, which grew to the Size of a ſmall Egg, at leaſt an Inch high, and was ſo angry and ſore, that the leaſt Thing that touched it, gave him great Pain, and he could hardly bear a Hat on his Head. His Mother had alſo the like Lumps on her Head. He was adviſed to take Tar-water for the firſt Ailment, which he did for three Months, and though he drank ſcarce half a Pint a Day, yet he ſoon found a great Abatement of the Swelling and Uneaſineſs in his Leg; and to his great Surprize the Excreſcence on his Head grew eaſy and melted away, and became as flat as any Part of his Head, and finding ſuch Benefit from the Water, he reſolves to take it in greater Quantity for the future.

230. Mrs. *Morgan*, Wife of Mr. *Morgan*, Patten-maker at *Nicholas-gate*, *Dublin*, informed me on the 3d of *February*, 1745, that ſhe had been troubled

troubled with a paralytic Diſorder for ſome Time; that her Fingers were ſo drawn up, that ſhe could hardly open them, that ſhe was hardly able to walk in the Streets, her Feet were ſo tottering and weak, and very cold and ſtiff; and ſhe was apprehenſive that ſhe would quite loſe the Uſe of them, and have a Palſy all over her Body, as nothing that ſhe took gave her any Relief; and hearing that Tar-water was uſeful in many Diſtempers, ſhe reſolved to try it in her own Caſe, and ſoon found a ſenſible Benefit; in ſix Weeks drinking ſhe recovered the Uſe of her Fingers and Hands, got Strength, Warmth, and Suppleneſs in her Limbs, and by continuing the drinking of the Water, ſhe has recovered the full Uſe of them, and now walks with Eaſe. She laid aſide Tar-water for ſeveral Months, and, if ſhe finds herſelf out of Order at any Time, ſhe has Recourſe to the Tar-water, which always gives her Relief.

231. Mr. *Hewetſon*, between ſeventy and eighty Years old, who lives in *Schoolhouſe-lane*, informed me the 3d of *February* 1745, that he had been for many Years troubled with the Gout, during which Time, he was ſure of having a Fit the Beginning of every Winter, which laid him up for ſeveral Months; but that in Summer 1744, he drank Tar-water for ſeveral Months running, and the Effect was, that he had no Fit of the Gout in the Winter 1744, and got a good Stomach and Spirits and walked tolerably well without Pain; in Summer 1745, he drank ſome Tar-water, and then laid it quite aſide for ſix Months together, but in Winter 1745, on catching cold, he had a Return of the Gout, attended with great Weakneſs in his Limbs, though with little Pain; and it is probable, that, had he continued taking Tar-water all long in ſufficient Quantity, and avoided catching cold, he would either have had no Fit at all, or a ſlight one. In ſuch Caſes, Tar-water ſhould be drank warm before the

the Fit, in the Fit, and after the Fit, at leaſt a Pint a Day, or a Quart, which would be much better, without any Danger from the Quantity, and with great Comfort to the Patient.

232. Mr. *Francis Watſon*, Sadler in *Capel-ſtreet*, informed me on the 4th of *February* 1745, that he had been troubled with a Stuffing, Wind and Oppreſſion in his Stomach for five or ſix Years paſt, attended at Night-time with a Difficulty of breathing, and with a great Cough in the Mornings, which made him ſtrain and heave, and deprived him of his Stomach and Digeſtion; that in 1743, he was firſt ſeized with the Gout, and had another Fit in 1744, which was followed by a Fit of the Gravel. That in *October* 1744, he began to drink Tar-water at about half a Pint a Day, which he continued to do till *Chriſtmas* following, with ſuch good Effect, that in three Weeks Time he found great Benefit, and ſoon after he was free from the Wind and Oppreſſion in his Stomach, breathed freely, recovered his Appetite, loſt his Cough, and diſcharged a great deal of Gravel without Pain, and has had no Return of the Gout ever ſince; and he now continues perfectly well, and free from all his former Diſorders, and at Times ſtill drinks Tar-water.

233. Mr. *Paſqualino* the Muſician, now in *Dublin*, informed me on the 8th of *February* 1745, that having played a Part in Mr. *Handel*'s grand Oratorio of *Deborah*, which was performed on *Thurſday* the 23d of *January* 1745, for the Support of the Charitable Infirmary on the *Inns quay*, and being in a great Heat and Sweat, was after the Performance expoſed to a very cold Air near half an Hour, by the Footmen breaking into the Room where he was; by which he was immediately ſtruck with a cold ſhivering, and was ſo much out of Order that he could not ſleep one Wink that Night. In the Morning, on *Friday*, he had a violent Head-ach, Colic

Colic Pains, and great Heat all over his Body, which obliged him to keep his Bed. By four o'Clock in the Afternoon, 'his Fever grew ſo high and violent, that he became a little delirious; his Wife had a mind to ſend for a Phyſician, but as he had been cured of a Fever ſome Time before by drinking Tar-water, he ordered, that Tar-water ſhould be got for him in plenty, and nothing elſe; which he began to drink about five o'Clock, Milk-warm, near half a Pint every Quarter of an Hour, and continued to drink at that Rate till eight o'Clock next Morning, on *Saturday*, bating ſome little Intermiſſions, when he got a little Sleep; though he had given Directions to his Servant, to awake him if he ſhould happen to ſleep, and make him drink the Water; and he computed, that in the ſaid Space of Time, he drank eight Quarts: And the Effect was, that during the whole Night, he was in high Spirits, had a great Perſpiration, and by eight o'Clock in the Morning, his Heat and Fever had quite left him, and he was perfectly eaſy, and very hungry. On *Saturday* he kept his Bed by way of Precaution againſt catching cold, free from all Symptoms of a Fever; and on *Sunday*, went abroad, and took the Air, being perfectly recovered.

234. A Gentlewoman near *Sycamore-Alley*, *Dublin*, informed me on the 12th of *February* 1745, that ſhe had been troubled with Fits for ſome Time, which came upon her all at once without any previous Symptom, and deprived her of her Senſes for three, four, or five Minutes at a Time; that theſe Fits became more frequent, and diſordered her Spirits and Mind, and ſhe was apprehenſive, that ſhe would be carried off in one of them. She took ſeveral Things to prevent their Return, without any Effect. She was adviſed to drink Tar-water, and though ſhe had no Opinion of it, yet ſhe complyed to

to satisfy the Desires of her Friends in trying every Thing they recommended. She drank near a Pint a Day for five Days, in *July* 1745, and found no Return of her Fits, and got a good Appetite and Spirits; at the End of five Days she observed a great Itching all over her Body, and soon after, a great Number of black Spots appeared all over her Arms, Shoulders, and Body, as black as Ink. She then thought that she was poisoned by Tar-water, and exclaimed against it; but her Friend who recommended Tar-water, came to see her in this Condition, and finding that she was in good Spirits, and otherwise very well, told her, that since the Water had driven that Humour out on the Surface of her Body, it was so far from doing her Harm, that it did her all the Service imaginable; and encouraged her to persist in drinking it, since it has so good an Effect, which she continued to do for two or three Months in small Quantities; and she found in a little Time, that all the black Spots first became yellow, and by Degrees disappeared one after another, so that she became entirely freed from them, and has had no Return of the Fits since she began to drink Tar-water, but found, that, by getting a greater Appetite, she has grown much fatter than she was before.

235. A Captain of a Man of War in 1744, informed me, that he had been troubled with the Scurvy several Years, and had taken many Medicines, and went to *Bath*, and drank the Waters, but all to no Purpose; his Disorder rather increased, and broke out in Sores, and Scurff over his Arms and other Parts of his Body, especially his Head, which he could not suffer to be shaved; but that by taking Tar-water six Weeks, all the Sores, Spots and Scurff went off, and he became as hail and clean as ever he was, with a great Increase of Appetite.

I shall

I ſhall now give an Account of ſome Caſes communicated to me from Gentlemen of Character and Veracity, who aſſured me of the Truth of the Facts, but did not think proper to mention the Names of the Patients, moſt of them being of the female Sex.

236. Two Siſters in this Kingdom, at the ſame Time drank Tar-water, the one for a Strangury, the other for a Diabetes, and both were cured, in a little Time, of thoſe oppoſite Diſorders.

237. A Gentlewoman had a Deafneſs, which daily increaſed, ſo that ſhe was apprehenſive of quite loſing her Hearing; ſhe had drank Tar-water in ſmall Quantities ſeveral Weeks with no Effect; but being adviſed to take double the Quantity of the Water every Day, ſhe did ſo, and was ſoon after cured of her Deafneſs.

238. One Gentleman was cured of an habitual Coſtiveneſs by Tar-water, and another was made coſtive by it.

239. Two Gentlewomen near *Youghall*, were likewiſe affected in different Ways, one was made coſtive, and the other looſe by Tar-water.

240. An old Beggar-Woman with a moſt ſhocking cancerated Breaſt, was in a few Days much better by drinking and waſhing the Sores with Tar-water.

241. A Woman that was twice married, and yet never was with Child, took Tar-water for a Diſorder ſhe laboured under, and conſtantly drank it for a conſiderable Time, which removed her Ailment. She ſoon after became pregnant, and ſhe imputes her Pregnancy to Tar-water. I deſired to know whether her Huſband alſo drank Tar-water, and I was aſſured that he drank it at the ſame Time. Many other Inſtances have been mentioned to me of Perſons who unexpectedly became with Child, which they verily believe was owing to the Uſe of Tar-water.

242.

242. A young Lady was cured by Tar-water of violent Head-achs, to which ſhe had been long ſubject.

243. A poor Woman, whoſe Legs were monſtrouſly ſwollen, and deformed with Ulcers, was adviſed to apply Tar as a Salve or Poultice, and to drink Tar-water at the ſame Time, which ſhe did, and was ſoon perfectly cured, having before in vain uſed many Things preſcribed for her.

244. A Gentleman's Servant had the Misfortune of having a Coach-wheel run over his Foot, which was thereby terribly bruiſed and ſwollen to a great Size with much Pain. A Poultice of Tar was applied to the Part, which ſoon put an End to both the Swelling and Pain.

245. A Maid Servant, who for many Years had a Tetter in her Arm, conſulted a Country Practitioner, who applied the blue Stone, upon which her Arm ſwelled up to her Shoulder, and was pained to ſuch a Degree, that her Maſter apprehended ſhe might loſe it. He then made her waſh and foment it with hot ſtrong Tar-water, and apply a Plaiſter or Poultice of warm Tar, which ſpeedily cured both the Ulcer and Swelling.

246. A Gentleman in an eminent Station, was troubled with a fixed Pain in his Side for two Years, be took ſeveral Medicines without Benefit. He was adviſed to drink Tar-water, which he did for a conſiderable Time; and he aſſured me of late, that his Pain is quite removed, and that he is at perfect Eaſe from that Diſorder.

247. A Perſon ill of the Ague, was cured in *January* 1745, by drinking two Quarts of Tar-water warm in the cold Fit.

248. Many Parts of the Country have been of late infeſted with ſore Throats, whereby ſeveral Children have died, but thoſe, who drank a Gallon of warm Tar-water a Day, immediately recovered of

of it, without any other Application, as I am aſſured by a Perſon of Credit.

249. Many Inſtances have been communicated to me of the great Succeſs and Efficacy of Tar-water in the Cure of venereal Diſorders, Gleets, *&c.* but in ſuch Caſes, Names are not to be mentioned. But in Charity to thoſe unhappy Creatures who labour under ſuch Ailments, it may be proper to hint ſo much, and to recommend to them the ſole conſtant copious drinking of Tar-water, *viz.* one Quart a Day at ſix or eight Glaſſes, which without any other Medicine, but only a prudent Regimen, avoiding the catching of Cold, and eating of improper Food, has been found in many Inſtances to work a perfect Cure.

250. A Gentlewoman in the Country had hurt her Leg, which being neglected, grew exceeding bad; a Gangrene was apprehended; ſhe had a Phyſician and Surgeon from *Cork* to attend her. After ſome Months phyſicking, cutting and tenting, they abandoned her, declaring ſhe muſt never hope to recover the Uſe of her Leg, which was waſted and uſeleſs, and left her with a running Ulcer kept open with Tents. Her Son came to the Gentleman, who gave me this Information, to know whether ſhe might not take Tar-water with the Bark, which had been preſcribed by the Doctor. She was adviſed to abſtain from the Bark, from the Surgeon's Fomentation, and every other Thing but ſimply Tar-water; whereof ſhe ſhould take three Pints daily in nine Glaſſes, which in three Weeks quite cured her, to the Surprize of all the Neighbourhood. She had a Houſe full of Children, who depended on her Care, and who had deſpaired of her Life.

251. A Maid Servant was ſeized with a vehement Fever and Stitch, on the 19th of *April* 1744, in the Morning; her Face as red as Crimſon, her Pulſe

Pulse exceeding high, scarce able to utter a Word for the great Oppression about her Heart, and her Blood and Flesh hot in an extreme Degree, with other Symptoms declarative of the worst Kind of Fever and Pleurisy. Her Case was looked upon as desperate from the Manner of her falling ill; which was, that the Night before, after hard Work in the House, being in a Heat and Sweat, she drank a great Quantity of cold small Liquor, and after that sat abroad in the open cold Evening Air in her Sweat. In this threatening Case, she was ordered to drink five Quarts of Tar-water in ten Hours, which she did with such good Effect, that the next Morning her Fever left her, and she was so well recover'd, that she put on her Cloaths, and was ready to go to work, but she was ordered to keep quiet in Bed for a Day or two longer. This last Caution is found necessary to prevent a Relapse, which Patients in such Cases are subject to by catching the least Cold; for as they find themselves in high Spirits, and free from the Fever, they imagine themselves to be quite recovered before they are out of Danger, and therefore 'tis found necessary, that the Patient should keep quiet in Bed for a Day or two longer, in which Time the Danger of a Relapse may be over. There is nothing so much to be apprehended in Fevers cured by Tar-water, as an Opinion of their being relieved and quite out of Danger before they are really so.

252. On *Wednesday*, the 1st of *August* 1744, a young Boy about nine Years old, was seized with a dangerous Illness, a Peripneumony or Inflammation of the Lungs, short Coughs, Pain, Soreness in the Throat and Thorax, Difficulty of Breathing, glazed Eyes, Scarlet Cheeks, and burning Heat. In this Condition he was put to Bed, and drank Tar-water five Pints the first Day, and about two Quarts the second, at a Glass every half Hour. The first

K Day,

Day it produced an extraordinary Discharge by Urine; the second, it threw him into moist Perspirations, and sometimes Sweats; every Glass put Life into him, eased his Symptoms, and kept him in continual high Spirits and good Appetite; on *Friday*, which was two Days following, he was past all Danger. It was remarkable, that on drinking Water coloured with Milk (which he desired) he constantly relapsed, and was as immediately eased upon taking a Glass of pure Tar-water. The Child was so sensible of this, that he cried out, " Mamma, " What is this Tar-water made of, that it is such a " sudden Cure?" It was of this Disorder that the late Bishops of *Offory* and *Elphin* died: There is no Distemper more threatening and sudden, than a Pleurisy or an Inflammation of the Lungs. The most copious Bleedings are prescribed by Physicians, even to seventy or eighty Ounces; but without bleeding blistering, or any other Medicine, Tar-water alone effects the Cure; were the World sufficiently apprized of its Virtue in acute Cases, that alone would preserve a Multitude of Lives. To induce the Child to drink plentifully of Tar-water, they gave him a Groat a Glass, and he earn'd half a Guinea in two Days. This is the only Way to prevail on young Children to drink it, and 'tis surprizing how soon they recover Strength and Spirts, who are recovered from Fevers by the sole Use of Tar-water.

253. A Boy was seized with a violent Fever in *September*, 1744, having wetted his Shoes and Stockings (a new Thing to him) and suffered them to dry on his Feet. The Attack was violent, first a shivering cold Fit, then blood-shot Eyes, wild Look, burning Heat all over his Body; he drank a Gallon of Tar-water, which made him vomit, after that he slept and sweated most copiously for sixteen Hours, and when he awoke, was outragiously hungry

gry; and in very high Spirits, every Symptom reduced very low, and the Fever almost gone the third Day; but was kept in Bed two Days longer, to prevent a Relapse.

254. In *October* 1744, a Boy was seized with a violent Fever, and being put to Bed, he drank near two Quarts of Tar-water the first Hour, and continued drinking very copiously. The next Day, he was in Appearance very well, but he was kept quiet from all Company, and confined in Bed one Day longer; after the third Day, he was as well as ever.

255. Another young Lad in *October* 1744, was seized with a violent racking Pain all over his Body, attended with a hot Fever; about Noon, he was put to Bed, and at a Groat a Glass, he drank in nine Hours twenty-five Half-pint-glasses of Tar-water; with all which (what is very singular) he did not sweat, but vented it all by Urine; and his Pain and Fever left him at nine a Clock at Night; and next Day, was hearty, merry, and in as good a Temper, as ever in his Life. It is wonderful in this Medicine, that it works as an emetic, diuretic, diaphoretic, sudorific or cordial, as the Case and Constitution requires, and that this alone should, as one may say, in the twinkling of an Eye, cure all those Fevers of different Kinds.

256. In *January* 1744, a young Woman was miserably tormented with a Pain and Swelling in her Side, which threw her into a Feverish Disorder. She drank Tar-water copiously, and in a short time found herself easy and well. It is to be noted, that she applied a Plaister of Tar and Honey to the Part, which ripened, broke, and then healed it, she drinking Tar-water all the Time.

257. A Gentleman in *February* 1744, had the Gout five Days; at first he drank Sack Whey, and his Pain and Fever were violent, so as to pass a

K 2 whole

whole Night awake and reſtleſs. From that Time he drank nothing ſtrong, but doubled or trebled his Doſes of Tar-water; this made him ſleep ſound every Night after, and kept up his Appetite and Spirits, ſo that he then reckoned his Gout as good as over, and in a few Days after, was free from it.

258. Mr. *Foulks*, Captain in the Army; Mr. *Philips*, who lodges at the Watch-maker's in *Crane-lane*, and ſeveral others have informed me, that having had frequent Fits of the Gout, they drank Tar-water; and though they took it but in ſmall Quantities, they found great Benefit from it; their Fits either not returning at the uſual Time they expected them, and when they did, they had leſs Pain and ſhorter Fits.

259. One of my Correſpondents informed me in *February* 1744, that his Daughter being ſeized with the Small-pox, he gave her no other Medicine than Tar-water, which ſhe drank all the time, and that ſhe had it very favourably with little or no Sickneſs.

260. A Boy was very ill of a Worm-fever in *February* 1744, when the Small-pox ſeized him; both Evils joined, made his Caſe extremely bad. He was treated as only ill of Worms, the Small-pox not being then apprehended. He was reduced to the loweſt State, without Senſe or Motion, and many Cordials were applied to bring him to himſelf; but all to no Purpoſe, till a few Spoonfuls of Tar-water poured down his Throat without his Knowledge, brought him from Death to Life; and by continuing the drinking Tar-water, the Child recovered daily, and was ſoon perfectly well. My Correſpondent ſays, that they never had a ſtronger Inſtance of the Efficacy of Tar-water, (and its Superiority to all other Cordials) than in this Child's

Child's extreme Illneſs, much heightened by the uncommon and fierce Severity of the Weather.

261. In *March* 1744, a Boy complained heavily of a Stitch about eight a Clock in the Morning; he was immediately put to Bed, and in about an Hour drank eight Glaſſes of Tar-water, at three Glaſſes to a Pint; then fell into a ſound Sleep, and againſt three a Clock in the Afternoon was up, dreſt and well, as if nothing had ailed him.

262. In *April* 1745, a Labourer in the Country, having been taken ill, was bled a little, only one Plate; he afterwards grew very ill of a violent Pleuriſy, attended with ſpitting of Blood; he then betook himſelf to his Bed, and drank copiouſly of Tar-water, which quite recovered him, when his Caſe had been thought deſperate.

263. A Gentlewoman in *April* 1745, took the Air in a cold dry windy Day; that Afternoon, ſhe was taken with ſomething like a Palſy, not being able to walk or ſtand upright. She went to Bed, grew feveriſh, and drank immenſely of Tar-water, a moderate Glaſs every Quarter of an Hour, which ſhe continued to drink the next Day in ſmaller Quantity; the Morning following, ſhe could turn eaſily in her Bed, (which ſhe could not do before) and her Fever and blunt Pain in her Back and Limbs left her, and the Day following ſhe was quite recovered.

264. A Man Servant had a pleuritic Stitch, which he concealed, and went about the Houſe with it for two Days. After this he was violently ill, went to Bed in a Fever, and ſpit Blood. Then he drank Tar-water plentifully, which threw him into a great Sweat; being impatient under this Sweat, in order to cool and dry himſelf, he flung off his Shirt, and lay almoſt naked, which had like to have killed him. But Tar-water copiouſly taken, recovered him intirely. I have had many Inſtances of Perſons

K 3 recovered

recoved from pleuretic Fevers, without bleeding, or any Medicine whatſoever, by the ſole copious conſtant drinking of Tar-water warm, one Pint, or even a Quart in an Hour. They cannot drink too much in ſuch Caſes; they will be ſooner well, and ſtrong without that Weakneſs, which attends thoſe copious Bleedings, which ruin a Conſtitution, and entail chronical Diſeaſes.

265. A Lawyer of my Acquaintance in *Dublin*, and two young Ladies, have been cured of Fevers by the copious drinking of Tar-water only.

266. I have had ſeveral Inſtances communicated to me of Perſons of both Sexes, who have been cured of the Piles, ſome by the bare drinking of Tar-water, others by ſitting at the ſame time on a Cloſe-ſtool filled with very hot ſtrong Tar-water, which with anointing the Parts with the Oil ſkummed off from the Tar-water, ſoon healed the Sores, and removed the Diſorder.

267. In *December* 1744, a *Prolapſus Uteri, &c.* given over as incurable by the Surgeous, was perfectly cured by Tar-water.

268. My Correſpondent informs me of two Perſons given over, one ill of a Palſy at *Bath*, and the other of a Cancer at *York*, who were both cured in a ſhort time by Tar-water.

269. A Gentleman's Son in the County of *Limerick*, was cured of a ſpitting of Blood by Tar-water.

270. An Infant had a Cough from its Birth, and ſhewed no Sign of Apprehenſion; thoſe who ſaw it, thought it could not live, or if it did, that it would be ſtupid; the Mother was adviſed to give the Child Tar-water, and to make the Nurſe drink it alſo, which being done, the Child got rid of the Cough, and came to its Apprehenſion, and is now lively.

271. A Gentleman writes in the following Words from *England*. I know ſome Inſtances, where Tar-

Tar-water has done Wonders, particularly on a Lady, who has long had a Cancer in her Breast, and suffered greatly; and by taking Tar-water, the only Thing she has found good from, is freed from Pain, and in a fair Way of Recovery.

272. A Gentleman in the County of *Limerick*, as I am informed, was cured by Tar-water of an Imposthume in his Head, for which he had tried Waters, and consulted Physicians in *England* to no Purpose.

273. A Lady was cured of a Megrim and inveterate Head-ach by Tar-water. Several other Persons have informed me, that they used to be seized with a Dizziness in their Heads on walking in the Streets, so that they were obliged to catch hold of the Rails as they went along to prevent falling; and that since they took Tar-water, they have had no Uneasiness of that Kind.

274. I am well informed, that a Ship being bound from *Portobello* to *Jamaica*, and being detained long in the Passage, the Men on board were reduced to great Distress from the Want of Water, which threw many of them into the bileous or yellow Fever. But to their great Comfort, a heavy Rain fell, which set all their Hands to Work to catch all the Water they could; and the Deck of the Ship and Cordage having been new dawbed with Tar to preserve them against the Heat of the Climate, all the Water they got was impregnated with the Tar; notwithstanding which, they drank plentifully of it, and it had this good Effect, that all those who were ill of the bileous Fever, and drank it, recovered in a short Time from their Fevers, to the great Surprize of them all, as it is reckoned the most fatal Distemper in that Part of the World.

275. A Boy had a Sore in his Leg, which Leg was also inflamed and hard; and being advised to wash it with Tar-water, and apply the Oil of Tar, he was soon recovered.

K 4. 276. A

276. A Man of *Youghall*, was deaf for many Years, but by drinking Tar-water for ſome Time, he is much improved in his Hearing, and though not quite cured, yet has Hopes of Relief by a longer Uſe of it. Any Relief is an Advantage, and many Reliefs may at laſt come up to a Cure.

277. A Gentleman who had a Pain in his right Side for fifteen Years, conſulted many Phyſicians, and took a World of Drugs to no Purpoſe; but on taking Tar-water, (and that but a very indifferent Sort) for five Weeks, found himſelf greatly relieved. At the ſame time, it cauſed a Pain a-croſs his Diaphragm, and alſo in his other Side, which he judged to be a Sign of the Efficacy of Tar-water in diſlodging the peccant Humour, which being once ſet a-float, may afterwards be eaſily worked off.

278. I have an Account of a remarkable Cure performed by Tar-water, on a Woman, who was given over. Her Diſorder was owing to the Retention of the After-birth, by the unſkilful Management of the Midwife in her Delivery. The Caſe was attended with the worſt Symptoms, and accounted deſperate; and when all other Things had failed, ſome adviſed Tar-water, rather from not knowing what elſe to do, than from any Hopes of the Patient's Recovery; ſhe nevertheleſs recovered by that Medicine, contrary to all Expectation.

279. *Margaret Maſterſon*, a young Woman, who lives at Doctor *Wynne*'s Houſe at *Harold's-croſs*, near *Dublin*, came to me the 21ſt of *February* 1745, and gave me the following Account of the remarkable Benefit ſhe received by Tar-water in the Cure of an Ulcer in the Bladder. She informed me, that one Day in the Spring about five Years ago, ſhe walked very faſt from *Harold's-croſs* to *Crumlin* Church, which is about two Miles, and being in a great Heat and Sweat, ſhe ſat on the cold Ground in the Church-yard for above half an Hour, which gave

her

her a great Cold, and threw her immediately into Diſorders. She grew worſe every Day, having great Pains in her Right-ſide, and lower Parts of her Belly; her Pain was ſo exquiſite, that ſometimes, for twenty Days together, ſhe could not get the leaſt Sleep; ſhe loſt her Fleſh and Appetite, and was reduced to a Skeleton. She could not ſtand upright, and walked double, nor could ſhe bear any Carriage, every Motion put her to the Rack, and ſhe was forced to confine herſelf for the moſt Part to her Bed, and, even there, was not able to ſtir a Limb, when her Pains came upon her. Nothing that ſhe took did her any Service. She was ſent to *Mercers* Hoſpital, where ſhe ſtayed three Months, without any Benefit, tho' ſhe had the Advice and Aſſiſtance of ſeveral Phyſicians and Surgeons there, who for ſome time thought ſhe was troubled with a Stone, but they were all of Opinion afterwards, that ſhe had an Ulcer in the Bladder. After ſhe left the Hoſpital, ſhe was ſalivated, and took many Things by the Advice of Phyſicians; but nothing gave her any Relief or Eaſe, and ſhe was judged to be incurable. She continued in this miſerable Condition a long Time, ſhe had alſo a Sort of Diabetes or involuntary and almoſt conſtant Diſcharge of Water. But in Summer 1744, her Brother hearing that Tar-water had wrought many Cures, adviſed her to drink it, which ſhe did for two or three Months together. On the firſt drinking of it, ſhe found it agreed with her Stomach, and gave her ſome Eaſe; in a few Days, ſhe received great Benefit, and mended daily, and in a few Weeks, all her Pains and other Ailments went off; ſhe recovered her Appetite, Fleſh and Reſt, and got the Uſe of her Limbs, and walked as well as ever, to the great Surprize of the Surgeons, and others, who had her under their Care, and who thought ſhe could never recover. She then laid aſide Tar-water, thinking ſhe had no farther Occaſion for

for it, and has continued free from her Pains ever ſince, except now and then ſhe has ſome Twitches on catching cold, which ſhe imputes to her Diſuſe of Tar-water for eight or ten Months paſt; but reſolves to take it again, to remove the Remains of her Ailments. I have obſerved in ſeveral Inſtances, that ſome who had received great Benefit by Tar-water, laid it aſide too ſoon, thinking themſelves quite recovered, before they were really ſo, and that afterwards their Ailments returned upon them in ſome ſmall Degree, which they totally removed by perſiſting longer in the Uſe of it.

280. A Tradeſman in the Earl of *Meath*'s Liberty, was in the Year 1744, greatly afflicted with a Diſcharge of bloody Urine, which was ſometimes ſo violent, that what came from him appeared as clear Blood as any that comes from a Vein on bleeding; and this was attended with great Torture. He could not walk a Quarter of a Mile, but in great Pain, and he waſted away. He continued in this Condition ſeveral Months together, and took many Things for a Cure, without any Effect; but hearing of the great Good that Tar-water had done in ſeveral Caſes, he drank it, and ſoon found Benefit from it, which encouraged him to continue the drinking of it, with ſuch good Succeſs, that he was ſoon perfectly recovered of his Ailment. His Diſcharge of Blood ceaſed, and he made his Water as clear as ever, without the leaſt Colour or Tincture of Blood, and without any Pain, all the Parts being healed, and in *February* 1745, he continues very well, and attributes his Cure wholly to Tar-water.

281. A Gentlewoman, who lives in the Country not far from *Dublin*, was for many Years afflicted with a Cancer in her Breaſt, which had been cut by Surgeon *Dobbs*, but it ſtill grew again, became hard, and was exceſſively painful; and notwithſtanding the great Danger and Torture that attends the Operation,

ration, ſhe reſolved to undergo another Cutting to get rid of her conſtant Pain, and came to Town for that Purpoſe; but the Surgeon finding that ſhe had got a freſh great Cold, and a violent Cough with it, he would not venture to cut her Breaſt till her Cough was removed, and adviſed her to go to the Country to be cured of her Cough. She was there perſuaded to drink Tar-water on that Account, which ſhe did with ſuch Effect, that ſhe ſoon got rid of her Cough; and finding that Tar-water agreed with her Stomach, and that it alſo made her Breaſt eaſier, ſhe continued the drinking of it for a conſiderable Time, by which Means her Breaſt grew eaſy and ſoft, and ſhe mended daily to her great Comfort and Surprize; and ſhe got ſo much Relief, that ſhe laid aſide the Water for ſome time. In what State ſhe now continues I am not informed.

282. *A Copy of a Letter from the Reverend Mr.* Thomas Dawſon, *of* Tallow, *in the County of* Waterford, *to* Thomas Prior, *Eſq*; *dated* February 25, 1745.

I take leave to ſend you the two following Caſes, wherein, among ſeveral others in my Neighbourhood, Tar-water has proved ſucceſsful; and as the Diſorders therein mentioned are common and often fatal, ſo a Publication of the Cure of them may be of Service to Mankind, whoſe general Good ſeems to be the Deſign and End of your Enquiries.

283. *The Caſe of Mrs.* Guinane, *Wife of* John Guinane, *of* Tallow, *in the County of* Waterford, *Merchant.*

The ſaid Mrs. *Guinane*, was violently ſeized with hyſteric Fits in the Year 1744, attended with Laughing, Crying, and frequent Swoonings, which continued for ſeveral Months, though Phyſicians by various Medicines endeavoured to cure her of them.

them. She went to the Salt-water, and bathed therein, purſuant to their Advice, for a conſiderable Time; but received very little Benefit thereby. At laſt ſhe betook herſelf to the drinking of Tar-water, purſuant to the Directions of the Author of *Siris*, and by regularly and conſtantly drinking the ſame for about the Space of three Months, ſhe perfectly recovered her Health, and has been free from the ſaid hyſteric Fits ever ſince, though ſhe deſpaired of being ever cured of them.

284. *The Caſe of Mr.* Thomas Lowris, *of* Tallow, *in the County of* Waterford.

The ſaid Mr. *Lowris* was in a deep Conſumption for four or five Years, and ſo greatly emaciated, and ſo yellow, that all who ſaw him, ſeemed to deſpair of his Life. About two Years ago, he began to drink Tar-water, and having in a few Months received great Benefit thereby, he continued ever ſince to drink the ſame regularly, and has perfectly recovered his Health and Complexion, to the great Surprize of all that knew him.

285. A Gentleman near *Caple-ſtreet*, informed me on the 22d of *February* 1745, that for ſeveral Years he uſed to be troubled with Fits, which gave him great Uneaſineſs in his Stomach, and were attended with a violent Pain, which ran along the Bottom of his Belly, and fixed it ſelf in his left Hip, with a great Inclination to puking. Theſe Pains continued for two or three Days, while the Fits laſted. He thought his Ailment was a windy Colic; and accordingly he took many Things, but without any Benefit. He found that he grew worſe, and that his Fits returned upon him more frequently and with more Violence. He uſed alſo to have Fits of the Gout in his Feet, without any great Violence. But having read the Treatiſe on Tar-water in *April* 1744, he reſolved to drink it, and he had not

not taken it above three Weeks, before he had a sensible Benefit, and, continuing to drink it, he in a little time after, to his great Surprize, discharged two Stones near as big as Peas, and then, and not till then, he discovered that his Disorder was the Stone and Gravel; upon which the Pain in the Bottom of his Belly went off, he got Ease in his Stomach, and recovered his Appetite and Rest. He has since voided Gravel at several Times, and of late, three smaller Stones, which gave him Pain in their Passage, and he does not doubt, but that he voided Gravel and small Stones formerly, without knowing it, when he had those violent Fits. But now that he knows what his Disorder is he can better guard against it. These Fits of the Gravel and Stone return now and then upon him, and are likely to do so, till they are all carried off; for which Purpose, he finds Tar-water to be very useful. He assured me, that, since he began to drink Tar-water, which he constantly doth, he has not been confined one Day with the Gout. He has had some Twitches of it now and then, but they go off soon without Pain; and as he has received so much Benefit by Tar-water, he often recommends the Use of it to others.

286. I am informed, that a Gentleman, who had gone through a Course of *Stephens*'s Medicines, took Tar-water, which he found more successful in the Gravel.

287. Some Gentlemen, who, on catching the least Cold, used to be troubled with sore chopp'd Lips, which they could not heal or cure by any of the Salves prescribed for them, were eased of that Disorder by bathing their Lips with Tar-water, which soon healed them; and they who had sore and running Nostrils received the same Benefit, by bathing them with the Water. These slight Instances are mentioned, only to shew the healing Quality of Tar-water: and it is also found by Experience

perience that a Plaister of Tar is a safe and effectual Cure for Sores and Swellings in the Backs of Horses. And now I am upon this Topick, I shall beg Leave to mention that several Gentlemen informed me of, that they gave two or three Quarts of Tar-water a Day to some of their Horses which had great Colds and Disorders, and received no Benefit by the Drenches of Farriers, so that they were afraid of losing them, and the Effect was, that they soon recovered. And perhaps it may be advisable in all Distempers of Brute Creatures, where the Blood is corrupted, as in Glanders in Horses, and in Infections of the horned Cattle and Sheep, which are thought to be incurable, to give them Tar-water warm in plenty, as it is found by Experience in so many Instances to correct and sweeten the Blood and Juices of the Body, remove Obstructions, and invigorate the Spirits. At least it may be proper to make Tryal when the Case is desperate.

288. The Small-pox having proved very mortal last Season, some were advised to give their Children Tar-water warm, and the Effect was, that they who drank it before they were seized with the Small-pox, generally had it favourably; but they who took it during the Time of the Sickness also, came off still better, there was no Appearance of Danger, the Pock generally distinct, little or no Sickness, and no Marks left by it. These Accounts I had from several Persons of Credit, and in particular, that in and about *Clonmell*, the Small-pox was so very fatal last Summer, that above three Hundred dyed of it, for the most Part of the confluent Kind. Some were at last advised and prevailed upon to give their Children Tar-water warm, and in plenty, as Mr. *Gordon*, an eminent Brewer there, did to four or five of his Children, who all came off very well. This encouraged Mrs. *Powel* to give it to three of her Children, who had the like Success, and had

had it ſo favourably, that they were hardly ſick. Whereas others, who were treated in the common Way, were for the moſt part carried off by the Malignity of the Diſtemper; and I can't hear, that any, who took Tar-water miſcarried. For which Reaſon, many now fall into the Uſe of it with great Benefit, and do not apprehend ſuch Danger from that fatal Diſtemper as formerly they did. Such is the Power and Efficacy of Tar-water in aſſwaging and curing Fevers and inflammatory Diſorders.

289. The Reverend Mr. *Skelton*, Miniſter of *Newry*, made his Son about thirteen Years old, drink Tar-water, before he had the Small-pox, and when he was lately ſeized with it, he gave him a full Wine-glaſs of it every two Hours, during the Time he was ill of the Diſorder; by practiſing on him in this Manner, the Child was hardly ſick, the Pock filled very well, and left no Marks. When Children are treated after this Manner in the Small-pox, and drink plentifully of the Water warm, they generally have it very favourably.

290. Several Inſtances have been communicated to me by Perſons of Credit, of wonderful and unexpected Cures performed by Tar-water in Diſorders peculiar to the Female Sex at the Times of their Delivery; and alſo in provoking the Menſes in ſome where they were wanted, and in reſtraining them in others, when they became immoderate. But in theſe Caſes, Names are not to be publiſhed.

291. There are ſeveral Gentlewomen in this Town, whoſe Names I ſhall forbear to mention, who, having been troubled with Rheumatic Pains, Oppreſſion and Load in their Stomachs, Want of Appetite and Reſt, Streightneſs in their Cheſts, Cough, and ſcorbutical Diſorders, were cured or greatly relieved by the Uſe of Tar-water, though drank but in ſmall Quantities. Several Gentlemen of my Acquaintance were affected the ſame Way, and

and received the like Benefit. But it would be endleſs to enumerate all of them, or to wait for more Caſes, which come every Day to our Knowledge. If any new remarkable Inſtances ſhould happen for the Future, of Cures performed by Tar-water, in any of the Diſorders mentioned in this Narrative; or if any Diſcoveries ſhould be made of it's Succeſs in other Diſtempers; it is to be hoped that they, who ſhall receive the Benefit, will be ſo good and grateful, as to communicate the Particulars of their Caſes, and that others will be found, who will give themſelves the Trouble to collect and publiſh them for the good of Mankind, with or without the Names of the Patients, as the Patients themſelves ſhall deſire. And this Requeſt is deſired not only in the Caſe of Tar-water, but of every other Medicine, which may have the ſame good Effects.

292. Having now ſwelled this Narrative to a Size far beyond my firſt Intentions, I ſhall forbear troubling the Reader with any more Caſes. A great Number of others have been mentioned to me from Time to Time; but the Want of Leiſure, or Opportunity of getting a particular Account from the Patients themſelves, who lived at a Diſtance, and were Strangers to me, and the Shyneſs of others in communicating their Ailments and Recoveries, leſt their Names ſhould be publiſhed, (though I always declared that when I ſhould publiſh the Caſe of any one, I would forbear mentioning their Names if they deſired it) for theſe Reaſons, I neglected to make a Collection of more Caſes; and indeed, there was the leſs Occaſion for doing ſo, as every City and large Town in the Kingdom can furniſh many Inſtances of great and unexpected Cures performed by Tar-water alone, which every one may be ſatisfied of the Truth of, who will give himſelf the leaſt Trouble of enquiring. Beſides, as I was already furniſhed with a great Number of remark-

remarkable Cases and Cures in several Distempers, I had the less Reason to take Notice of others of the same Kind. But as the Power and Efficacy of Tar-water, in curing many Disorders, is happily experienced by great Numbers, and stands sufficiently confirmed by the many authentic Instances produced in this Narrative, which the World hath not been yet acquainted with, it would be a Prejudice to Mankind to defer any longer the Publication of them; it being reasonable to expect, that others, in the like Disorders, may receive equal Benefit by the same Means. It has often grieved me, to hear of several Persons dying of acute Disorders, which were suddenly and effectually cured by Tar-water alone, as appears from several Instances in this Narrative; and it is probable, they might have received the same Benefit, if the same Medicine had been made use of; at least, it was proper to try it, when the Case was desperate. For the Reasons aforesaid, it was high Time to publish this Narrative, that every one may be fully apprized of the Power of this Water, and make tryal of it in parallel Cases.

293. The Gentlemen of the Faculty, who are Men of superior Skill and Abilities, can and will, without Doubt, apply and improve these Hints and Experiments. But though I am no Physician, yet I hope I may be allowed to relate Matters of Fact in this Narrative, and to give an historical Account of the Effects of Tar-water, as they were communicated to me by Letters from the Patients themselves, and in their own Words, or from other Gentlemen, who had their Informations from the Patients, at the same Time mentioning their Names and Places of Abode. I took from others the Particulars of their Cases from their own Mouths, and for greater Exactness, read them over to them, when they were written down. I have mentioned some Cases, where the Names of Persons and Places are omitted; but

L these

these Cases I had from Gentlemen of Integrity and Credit, who assured me of the Truth of the Facts, in the Letters which they sent me, at the Times the Cases happened, and when every Circumstance was fresh in their Memories, which Letters are now in my Custody; they were not willing to mention the Names of Patients, particularly, of the Female Sex, without their Consent, which could hardly be obtained. But I have not the least Reason to doubt of the Truth of the Facts, which are so well attested. But if any Person should be desirous to know the Names, or Places of Abode, of any of the Patients, whose Names are omitted, I shall, for their private Satisfaction, gratify them in that Particular.

294. Having closed my Register of Cases, I shall beg Leave to make some Remarks, which occurred to me from reading those Cases, and from the Observations of my Correspondents.

I. It must be Matter of Surprise, to find, that in the Space of one Year and an half, such a Number and Variety of Distempers have been cured, or greatly relieved by this one Medicine. Thousands have received Benefit, and daily do receive Benefit in *England*, *Ireland*, *Holland*, *France*, *Portugal*, and *Germany*, by the Use of Tar-water. The Letters sent to me signify the same; the least Enquiry may satisfy others of the Truth thereof; this Narrative shews it, and the *Index* hereunto annexed points out the various Sorts of Ailments, wherein it has proved successful. The Treatise on Tar-water, called *Siris*, has been translated into the *French*, *Low Dutch*, *German* and *Portuguese* Languages, and Extracts thereof have been published in the *Magazines*. By so general a Publication, the Use of Tar-water, as a Medicine, came to be universally known, and being strongly recommended by the Author, from his own Experience, for the Cure of several Distempers,

ſtempers, many were induced to make Trial of it, and found immediate Relief: This encouraged others to make Uſe of it alſo, and they received the ſame Benefit thereby. And ſuch was the growing Credit of this Medicine, that ſeveral, who had been long afflicted with grievous Ailments, without receiving any Relief by the Preſcriptions of Phyſicians, though they never heard that Tar-water was made uſe of in the like Diſorders, yet were willing to try, and ſoon found a wonderful and unexpected Relief. Some who had taken Tar-water for one Diſorder, were at the ſame time affected with another, and both were removed by this powerful Medicine. Some of the Virtues of Tar-water were thus accidentally diſcovered, and by many ſubſequent Trials, on others, fully confirmed.

295. The happy Diſcovery of the Efficacy of Tar-water, in curing moſt Kinds of Fevers and Pleuriſies, is a Thing of ſingular and moſt extenſive Benefit to Mankind, and confirmed by ſo many Trials, that they who are acquainted with this Practice, think themſelves in little Danger from Fevers; and it is found, by Experience, that the larger the Quantity of Tar-water that is taken in Fevers by the Patient, the ſooner he recovers. If he takes but two or three Quarts a Day, the Fever may laſt four or five Days; but if four, five, or ſix Quarts, or more, be drank warm in twenty-four Hours, they often find the Fever quite carried off in a Day or two. And what is very remarkable, there is no Inſtance of Danger or Harm done by any Quantity taken; on the contrary, Patients in Fevers are in higher animal Spirits, the more they drink, the Water paſſing through their Bodies by Urine or Perſpiration, as faſt as it is taken in, and thereby carrying off the noxious Humours, and Venom of the Diſtemper the ſooner. The Patients at the ſame Time get ſound Sleep, and a better Appetite than is

is uſual in Fevers. My Correſpondents farther aſſure me, that they never knew an Inſtance where warm Tar-water was given betimes in a Fever, and in due Quantity, that it failed of Succeſs. It is judged, that the greater Part of grown People, who die in their Beds, die of ſome Kind of Fever or other: Therefore, if Reſpect were only had to this one Article of Fevers, wherein Tar-water is ſo ſucceſsful, it would ſeem to follow, that nothing is more beneficial to the Life of Man, or that would ſave more Lives, than this Water duly prepared and taken.

296. II. The next Obſervation I ſhall make is, on the Variety of Diſtempers cured by Tar-water, and even ſuch as are oppoſite in their Natures. This has been judged to be impoſſible by ſome, who have decried the Uſe of Tar-water: Though Fact and Experience, the ſureſt Guides for knowing the Force of any Medicine, are entirely againſt them; not only in the Caſe of Tar-water, but of ſeveral other Medicines, which frequently produce contrary Effects in different Conſtitutions, and ſometimes different Effects in the ſame Conſtitution. Some who firſt wrote and ſpoke againſt Tar-water, at the ſame Time frankly owned, that they had never made any trial of it. How then could they form any Judgment of the good or bad Qualities of it, or expect that others ſhould be ſwayed by their Opinions, when no Way ſupported by Experiment, the only ſure Rule to go by? A Gentleman of the Faculty, one Day, aſked me, if Tar-water was a Panacea, or a Cure for all Diſtempers. I told him, that I thought no Body could anſwer that Queſtion, but a Perſon who had tried it in all Diſtempers, and in Variety of Caſes of every Diſtemper, which I had not done, and I believe no Body living had yet done; and that until Trial had been made, no Judgment could be formed in what Caſes it was good

good or not. I then deſired leave to aſk him the following Queſtion, In what Diſorder Tar-water was not good? this I ſaid, becauſe I was amply furniſhed with many Inſtances of Cures performed by Tar-water in all the common Diſtempers in *Dublin*, to which I could refer him for his Satisfaction, if he ſhould mention any of them: but after conſidering ſome time, he aſked me, if it was good for the Stone? I anſwered, that I had not yet heard that it was made Uſe of for the Stone, but that I could give him many Inſtances, where it was of great Uſe in the Gravel, and I thought what was good for the Gravel, might alſo be good for the Stone. But that in all theſe Caſes, nothing but Experience and undoubted Facts can or ought to determine our Opinions. Some who were offended to find Tar-water recommended for ſo many different Diſtempers, for that very Reaſon were for exploding it, as of no Uſe in any Caſe whatſoever; without conſidering that whatever corrects and ſweetens the Blood, mends the Stomach and removes Obſtructions, as Tar-water manifeſtly doth, muſt be of Uſe in all Diſtempers, and thereby aſſiſt Nature to make a perfect Cure. The univerſal Medicine as well as the Philoſophers-ſtone have been always treated as vain Attempts: But if the former be poſſible in Nature, no Medicine ſeems to bid ſo fair for that Character as Tar-water: but without making any Pretenſions to ſuch an extraordinary Prerogative, I ſhall only obſerve, that it is happy for the World to be poſſeſſed of a Medicine that has done and daily doth great Service in ſo many different Maladies, without repining, that it cannot do the ſame in all.

297. III. The third Remark I ſhall make, is on the Safety of this Medicine. Some Phyſicians adviſe and preſcribe it. Others ſay, that it is good in many Caſes, and that they do not find it do Harm in any. Some ſay, that it is neither good nor bad,

L 3 while

while others suggest, that it is dangerous in inflammatory Cases, by an over-heating Quality: But the contrary thereof is manifest, from its curing Fevers, Pleurisies, Small-pox, and other inflammatory Disorders, in a short Space of Time; and it is so far from increasing Inflammations, that it wonderfully assuages them. Some Patients, on drinking Tar-water, were immediately seized with a Vomiting, which much alarmed them; but they soon found that Tar-water, by thus discharging a great deal of foul Stuff out of their Stomachs, gave them immediate Relief, and the Vomiting soon after stopped. Others had a Purging for a Day or two, on taking Tar-water, which they also did not like; but the Purging soon ceased, when it carried off the peccant Humours, and they received great Benefit by the Operation. Some Patients, who were troubled with violent scorbutical Disorders, Eruptions, Itch, Blotches, running Sores, found, on the drinking Tar-water a few Days, that their Sores, Itchings, and Eruptions grew more troublesome, and increased on the Surface of their Bodies, in greater Quantity and Violence, and then thought Tar-water did them Harm; some were so imprudent as to stop drinking the Water, when it was doing them all the Good imaginable, by driving from the Blood all the noxious Humours to the Surface of the Body; while others, who persisted in drinking, soon found the Scurvy, Eruptions, and other Blotches on their Bodies, die away and heal, to their great Relief. Some, on whom Tar-water works by Perspiration, found that it made them Costive, and heated them; upon this, they laid it aside; others, who in the like Case persisted in drinking it, soon found, that, after the Tar-water had done its Work by Perspiration, they returned to their natural State, and got the Relief they expected. Nature does not work two different Ways at the same Time; if it works by Stool, Perspiration ceases

ceaſes for the Time; if by Perſpiration, then the other ſtops. If both thoſe Channels are ſtopped, there is no Way left for Nature to diſcharge the vitiated Humors, but by Urine: And this is the way that Tar-water generally operates. Theſe are for the moſt Part the Caſes, wherein Tar-water has been imagined to do Harm. But it is hard, that Tar-water ſhould be charged with doing Hurt in ſuch Caſes, when it was doing the greateſt Service to the Patients. It is true, that very bad Tar and Tar-water have often been made Uſe of, and as true, that ſeveral Perſons at the Time they drank Tar-water, indulged themſelves in the Uſe of ſtrong Liquors, and Spirits; and therefore, it is no Wonder, if they did not receive the Benefit that otherwiſe they might have got. On the whole, I do not find any Inſtance, where Tar-water ever did any real Harm, which cannot be ſaid of any other Medicine.

298. IV. Chronical Diſorders, wherein the whole Maſs of Blood and Juices of the Body have been long vitiated, require a Length of Time and Patience to effect a Cure; and if they be very grievous, the Quantity of Tar-water to be taken in ſuch Caſes ſhould be encreaſed from a Pint to a Quart a Day, beginning with a Noggin or a Quarter of a Pint, to find how it agrees with the Stomach; and ſo continuing to drink it often in ſmall Quantities; it being found by Experience, that the more the Patients drink in ſuch Caſes, the ſooner they recover.

299. Scurvies make a great Part of the Ailments of People, in this Part of the World, and yet we find by the many Inſtances produced in this Narrative that the worſt kinds of them, attended with running Sores, Blotches, Scruff, *&c.* were perfectly cured by Tar-water, which heals up all the Sores, and in ſome Meaſure, embalms ſcorbutic Bodies alive.

300. The ſame Succeſs has attended internal Ulcers in the Bladder, Lungs, urinary Paſſages, venereal Taints, and in Ulcers on the outward Parts of the Body, owing to the healing Quality of Tar-water. Even the King's Evil, and other ſcrophulous Diſorders, which are commonly reckoned incurable, have yielded to the Power of this Water, as may be ſeen by ſeveral Caſes in this Collection; inſomuch, that we have Reaſon to believe, that any King's Evil may be cured by Tar-water; having never heard that it failed of Succeſs, when regularly and plentifully taken, and eſpecially when at the ſame Time the Sores were anointed with the Oil ſkimmed from the Tar-water.

301. Scald Head, inveterate Itch, and even Cancers, have yielded to the healing Quality of Tar-water.

302. Though nervous Caſes require a long time to perfect a Cure, yet we find that Hyſterics, Fits, and Palſies have been cured by Tar-water alone. Mr. *Hanning*'s Daughter mentioned in the Collection, who was ſeized with a Palſy, ſo that ſhe could neither ſpeak nor move a Limb in *November* laſt, is now in *March* following, briſk and lively, and perfectly well, notwithſtanding the Severity of the Weather. And I am informed, that a Woman, who was troubled with Fits for above a Twelvemonth, which often returned, and cauſed her to lye ſpeechleſs and ſenſeleſs a long Time together, being adviſed to take Tar-water, a Quart a Day; on doing ſo, ſhe had but one Fit in three Weeks paſt, and that occaſioned by a Fright. I know of others, who having been long troubled with Fits, have had no Return of them ſince they began to drink Tar-water. It is adviſed in ſuch Caſes, to give it freely and boldly.

303. Many Inſtances are produced of Perſons who have been cured or greatly relieved of Diſorders

ders in the Bowels, Colics, Megrims, inveterate Head-achs, Agues, Rheumatiſms, exceſſive Thirſt, and fixed Pains in ſome Parts of the Body. Others, who were tortured with exceſſive Pains, on taking Tar-water, unexpectedly diſcovered that their Ailment was owing to the Stone and Gravel, in diſcharging which, they found Tar-water to be very uſeful.

304. Many who laboured under a Lowneſs of Spirits, Diſorders in their Stomachs, want of Appetite and Sleep, found thoſe Diſorders carried off by the Uſe of Tar-water.

305. Many are the Inſtances of thoſe who being long afflicted with Aſthmas, Shortneſs of Breath, and Difficulty of Breathing, violent Coughs, Wheezing, Stuffings and Decays, ſore Throats and Squinancy, have been either entirely cured, or greatly relieved by Tar-water.

306. As to the Gout, the Diſeaſe of the Rich, we find that ſome, greatly afflicted with that Diſorder, by the conſtant and regular Uſe of Tar-water, have had no Return of their Fits ſince they began to drink the Water; occaſioned by a kindly Perſpiration in their Limbs, which they never had before, and which recovered the Uſe of them, and removed all their Pains. Others, on drinking the Water, found the ſame Benefit; but by laying aſide the Uſe of it too ſoon, their Fits returned upon them, though later than uſual, yet with this Advantage, that they were not ſo violent nor laſting. Others grown in Years and much enfeebled with the Gout, though they got Spirits, Appetite, and Reſt, and ſome Relaxation of their Pains by the Uſe of Tar-water, yet, as this Liquor was not to their Taſte, they either diſcontinued the Uſe of it, or took it in ſuch ſmall Quantities, that the Weakneſs in their Limbs ſtill continued, and their Fits returned on Change of Weather, or on catching Cold. And now

now we find by Experience, that the surest Way of dealing with the Gout, is not only to drink the Water before and after the Fit, but during the whole Time of the Fit, and that in the Quantity of a Quart a Day, warm, which gives such a Discharge by Perspiration or Urine, as relieves Nature and removes the Pains. But if Gentlemen will continue in the Use of strong Liquors, and high Feeding, it must be presumed, that the same Cause will still produce the same Effects.

307. As to the Small-pox, with which nine Parts in ten of all People are seized in one Part or other of their Lives in this part of the World, I shall only observe, that the great Number of Negroes cured on the Coast of *Guinea* of the Small-pox by Tar-water as mentioned in this Narrative, and many others who have been cured in this Kingdom the latter End of last Season, when it was so rife and mortal, by the same Means, evidently shew, that Tar-water is a sovereign, safe, and efficacious Medicine for the Cure of this fatal Distemper, by giving it warm, and in Plenty both before, and in the whole Time of the Illness. And I do not doubt, but that others, who will put it in Practice, will find the same surprizing Success.

308. But the greatest and most useful Discovery of this, or perhaps any other Age, is that of Tar-waters curing so suddenly and effectually, all Sorts of Fevers, Pleurisies, and inflammatory Distempers, whereby two Thirds of Mankind are carried off before their natural Time. These Maladies destroy more of the human Species, than all the Artillery great and small in the World can do, and yet are themselves easily subdued by Tar-water.

This late Discovery of the Virtues of Tar-water stands so confirmed by the authentic Proofs mentioned in the Narrative, that no body can doubt the Truth thereof, who doth not at the same Time deny

ny Facts, which are ſo many, and ſo well atteſted. But this may be put on a ſhort Iſſue, it is in the Power of any one, and every one is concerned in the Event to make a fair Tryal of the Truth or Falſhood of this Diſcovery, and ſee whether Tar-water taken in due Time and Quantity, before the Fever has utterly deſtroyed the Craſis and Conſtitution of the Blood, will not entirely ſubdue and carry off the Fever in a few Days, of any kind whatever.

309. But then to give Tar-water fair Play, the following Caution ſhould be obſerved, which has been found neceſſary in many Inſtances, *viz.* That the Water be good in its kind, that it be adminiſtered to the Patient lying in Bed, in the Beginning of the Fever, and that warm, in the Quantity of half a Pint or more every half Hour, according to the Age and Strength of the Perſon, till the Patient takes ſix or eight Quarts in the Space of twenty four Hours; and that no other Medicine be taken with it; that Care be taken againſt catching Cold; that when the Fever abates, no Nouriſhment be given but what is very light, and cooling; and that when the Fever is gone, the Patient keep his Bed a Day or two longer, free from Noiſe and People's talking, to prevent a Relapſe. It is found by Experience in many Inſtances, that Patients in Fevers cannot drink too much Tar-water, there is no Danger from Exceſs, the more they drink the ſooner they are cured; it hath been often obſerved, that the Heat and Thirſt they have on ſuch Occaſions ſo reconciles the Water to them, that they can drink a great Quantity without diſguſt; they have generally a great flow of Spirits during the whole Time they drink, get Intervals of Sleep, and when the Fever abates, they have commonly keen Appetites, which ought not to be indulged too ſoon or too much. It is amazing to ſee with what Speed and Succeſs

Succefs Tar-water taken copioufly, as above-mentioned, cures the moft violent Pleurifies, without Blifters or Medicines, and without bleeding, which in the common Practice is exceffive. It is faid, the late Honourable Mr. *Hamilton*, Collector at *Cork*, had 150 Ounces taken from him in a pleuretic Diftemper of which he died. It is proper to repeat and inculcate the Advantage of being cured by a Cordial, rather than by Evacuations, which at beft often leave a Patient weak and languifhing for Years together. Nothing is fo dangerous as neglecting the Beginnings of Fevers. *Principiis obfta*, is a good Maxim with Refpect to the natural as well as political Body: Some People are apt to hold out as long as they can, and go abroad with Fevers upon them; By thus expofing themfelves, they inflame their Diforders, and render them very dangerous. The beft Courfe to take in fuch Cafes, is to go to Bed and drink Tar-water. The Efficacy of Tar-water in curing Fevers, evidently fhews, that it is not of an inflaming or heating Nature. And yet fome have thought themfelves heated by Tar-water, who at the fame Time drank too freely of ftrong Liquors. And I am credibly informed, that fome noted Drinkers of Whifky complained that Tar-water gave them the Megrim, a Diforder which in others, it is known to have cured. If therefore any one complains of being heated by Tar-water, let it be enquired at the fame Time, whether he doth not indulge himfelf in the Ufe of fermented or diftilled Liquors.

310. Some People cannot comprehend, that a Medicine, which in flow gradual Courfe removes chronical Difeafes, fhould be proper in acute Cafes which require Difpatch. But nothing hinders, why the fame Medicine, which drank daily in fmall Quantities proves a leifurely Cure for chronical Ills, may not alfo, if drank copioufly, and in very large Quantities,

Quantities, prove a ſpeedy Cure for acute Caſes, ſuch as all Kinds of Fevers.

311. Having thus recapitulated ſeveral Maladies in which Tar-water has been found ſucceſsful, I ſhall beg Leave to recommend the Uſe of it in a particular Manner to ſeafaring Men, who are ſo uſeful to every trading Nation, and whoſe Lives ought therefore to be preſerved with the utmoſt Care. They are ſubject to many Diſtempers, beſides thoſe common to other Men at Land, which they contract at Sea, by the Change and Inclemency of the Weather in long Voyages, by the Heat or Cold of the Climate, by great Fatigues, ſalt Proviſions, cloſe ſuffocating Air in the Ships, *&c.* which produce Fevers, Calentures, Scurvies of ſeveral Kinds, Ulcers, running Sores, Looſeneſs of their Teeth, and many other Diſorders, for which they commonly have little or no Proviſion of Medicines or Accommodation, or any Perſon on board of Skill to aſſiſt them, by which Means great Numbers of them periſh miſerably. Now as it is found by Experience, that Tar-water cures thoſe Diſorders, it is recommended, that in every Ship, Proviſion be made of ſeveral Barrels of good Tar, and that a Veſſel of Tar-water be always prepared to be given in Plenty to ſuch of the Crew, who happen to labour under any of thoſe Diſtempers; by which Means, the Lives of Thouſands may be ſaved. Spruce-Beer, which is a great Antiſcorbutic, and a-kin to Tar-water, would alſo be very uſeful in Sea Voyages.

312. Since Tar-water is ſo ſafe and cheap a Medicine, and found by Experience to cure many chronical Diſtempers as well as ſlight Diſorders, it is recommended to provide Tar and Tar-water in every Hoſpital, Infirmary, and Work-houſe; and that a Barrel of Tar-water be always at hand for every one to repair to, who may be afflicted with ſuch Maladies, to drink thereof, as much, and as often

as

as there is Occaſion. By theſe Means, the Lives of Numbers may be ſaved, and the Patients either cured or greatly relieved. From many Tryals of the good Effects of this Medicine, we find that the Uſe of Tar-water is introduced into the Hoſpitals at *Liſbon*, with great Advantage. We have many Inſtances in this Narrative of People, who were kept a long Time in the Infirmaries, in Order to be cured, and were afterwards tnrned out as Incurable, and yet thoſe very People, were in ſome Time after perfectly recovered by Tar-water, to the Surprize of thoſe who had them under their Care before. Beſides, this Method would ſave great Sums to the Hoſpitals in the Expence for Medicines. And as all Hoſpitals and Infirmaries are ſupported at the Charge of the Public or by private Donations and voluntary Contributions, it ſhould be the Buſineſs of thoſe concerned in the Government of them, to leſſen the Expence as much as poſſible, conſiſtent with the Health and Lives of the Patients. And I am inclined to believe, that many of thoſe who are lodged in *Guy*'s and other Hoſpitals as Incurables, may be cured or greatly relieved by Tar-water, and ſo make room for others to be admitted. Whereas at preſent, little Care is taken of their Recovery, as being deemed incurable, and they ſtay there only to ſpend a wretched Life. Though it is believed that ſome of them would be ſorry to be cured, and thereby be obliged to leave the Hoſpital, where they live in tolerable Eaſe, to get a Livelihood abroad by their own Labour. This deſerves the Attention of the Public.

"313. It is recommended to all Gentlemen who live in the Country and Market-towns, that in Compaſſion for their poor Tenants, Neighbours and Servants, they will be ſo good and humane, as to provide Quantities of Tar, and make Tar-water thereof, and diſtribute the ſame liberally to ſuch as want

want it, and are deſtitute of all Means, which are proper to cure them of the Diſorders they are frequently afflicted with.

314. The Uſe of Tar-water is alſo recommended to ſedentary Perſons, which by its diuretic Quality, greatly prevents Head-ach, Bloating, Dropſy, Stone and Gravel, which ſedentary People are ſubject to from the want of Exerciſe.

315. V. In all odd and new Caſes, where People are at a loſs what to do, and even in deſperate Caſes where Patients are given over, and no Hopes left, it is recommended to try Tar-water, which has been found in ſeveral Inſtances to recover Patients from the Brink of Death.

316. I have an Account, that Tar-water is in great Vogue at *Paris*, notwithſtanding the Endeavours of ſome intereſted Perſons againſt it. An *Iriſh* Phyſician preſcribes it to his *French* Patients with great Succeſs, and has got into good Buſineſs thereby.

Since I have mentioned foreign Practice, it comes into my Thoughts to inſert the Teſtimony or Atteſtation of two foreign Phyſicians, againſt the Notion of an inflaming Heat in Tar-water, entertained by ſome among us who would decry that Medicine. Doctor *De Linden* a *German* Phyſician now in *London*, wrote a Letter about ſix Months ago, from which are taken the following Extracts. It ſeems that learned Foreigner had miſtaken the Senſe of *Siris*, as attributing ſuch Heat to Tar-water, which Opinion both he and his foreign Correſpondent, ſet themſelves to refute. *I myſelf* (ſaith Doctor *De Linden*) *have drank about twenty five Gallons of Tar-water conſtantly every twenty-four Hours three Pints, and that of the Colour of* Spaniſh *Wine, and I never found any Effect that we may call a phyſical Heat in the Blood, notwithſtanding that I am of a very ſanguine Temperament, and the leaſt Thing can occaſion*

occasion in me an Inflammation. He adds, *I would not have taken the Freedom to acquaint you with this if I had not in this Point been attacked by the first Physician to a certain great crowned Head in* Germany, *and President of a most illustrious* Collegium Medicum. After which, Doctor *De Linden*, sets down Part of this Correspondent's Letter, containing the following Words: *I am glad we have got into our Faculty a Reverend Divine, but I am still more pleased with his Discovery; and I agree in every Thing with him, because I have experienced Tar-water myself; but there is one Error committed.* He then proceeds to refute the Error, supposed to be in *Siris*, viz. *that Tar-water is Heating.* After which, he subjoins these Words: *In Reality, Tar-water is of such a mild Nature, that it never can inflame, nor create an Inflammation in the Blood. I agree with every Thing else, and blessed Thanks be to the Bishop for his valuable Discovery.* It is probable, Foreigners might mistake *warming* for *heating*; and so conceive that when Tar-water was said in *Siris* to warm, it was understood to heat. But certain it is, that in many Parts of that Treatise, all inflaming Heat is expressly denied to be in Tar-water. Thus in the seventy-fourth Section it is said; *The Salts, the Spirits, the Heat of Tar water, are of a Temperature congenial to the Nature of Man, which receives from it a kindly Warmth, but no inflaming Heat.* And in the following Section, Tar-water is affirmed to be *so far from increasing a feverish Inflammation, that it is on the contrary, a most ready Means to allay and extinguish it.* There are so many other Passages to the same Effect, throughout the whole Book of *Siris*, that it would be endless, as well as needless to enumerate them.

318. I should not omit to take Notice, that several Ladies, who had received great Benefit by Tar-water, at the same Time recovered their Complexions

plexions and Bloom, and that others, who had ſqueamiſh Stomachs, and could not bear to take Tar-water in the Morning before Breakfaſt, yet found it to agree well with them an Hour or two after eating. An old Lady has been greatly relieved by drinking conſtantly every Day, no more than one Wine-glaſs in the Morning.

319. A great Deal depends on the Goodneſs of Tar-water. Tar being looked upon as a Naval Store, could not be imported without Riſque and Difficulty in time of War: Hence for ſome time no Tar could be got that was fit for making Tar-water; ſome was adulterated with the Mixture of other Stuff, and Retailers frequently ſold for freſh Tar, that which had been formerly uſed. By theſe Means ſeveral have been diſappointed and abuſed by bad Tar-water; ſuch Tar-water, as is of a brown Colour or ſweetiſh flat Taſte, is bad, but they who have once drank good Tar-water, can eaſily diſtinguiſh the bad, which has no Spirit. Liquid Tar, which is the firſt running from the Billets, from whence the Tar flows by ſmothering Heat of Fire, is generally the beſt. And yet no certain Judgment can be formed of the Goodneſs of Tar, by the Colour or Conſiſtence, till Trial be made, by making Tar-water of it. When a Veſſel of Tar has ſtood long on an End, a Sediment often falls to the Bottom, which Sediment ſhould not be made Uſe of for Tar-water.

320. The adding artificial Helps to plain ſimple Remedies, often diſturbs their Operation, and render thoſe Medicines ineffectual: I have an Account of two Caſes, where the Phyſicians preſcribed the Bark with Tar-water: But the Patients found not the Benefit, till they took Tar-water alone. Some have put a Drop of the Oil of Nutmegs to a Glaſs of Tar-water, which made it more palatable; others have added a ſmall Spoonful of Mead, White-wine,

M or

or Cyder, which made the Draught more agreeable; but it were better no Spirits ſhould be taken with it, or any Thing elſe that might weaken the Vertue of the Water, and it is therefore more adviſeable to take it pure, and a little Uſe will reconcile it to the Palate.

Fir-trees grow naturally in moſt Parts of the World, in hot Countries as well as cold, but chiefly in the mountainous Parts of both. After this Manner, Providence furniſhes in great Plenty, the Means of preſerving Health and Life by the ſimpleſt Medicines.

321. It is proper to warn thoſe who expect the whole Benefit of Tar-water, to be very temperate in the Uſe of ſtrong Liquors fermented or diſtilled. They weaken and fruſtrate the Powers of Tar-water, which of itſelf is a ſufficient Cordial. It has a great Effect upon the Nerves and Spirits, animates the Heart without diſordering the Brain, and is an Antidote againſt Cold, Fatigue, and Thirſt. That is certainly the beſt Cordial which encreaſes the animal Spirits, without inflaming the Blood, or diſturbing the Nerves, as all inebriating Liquors never fail to do. If this be the Effect of Tar-water, as I am aſſured it is, it may be of Uſe in our Armies and Fleets.

322. I have no View in giving myſelf this Trouble, but to promote the good of Mankind, without any Deſire to incroach on the Province of Others. They who railed and argued againſt Tar-water on the firſt Publication of *Siris*, inſiſted that particular Caſes, with all their Circumſtances, ſhould have been exhibited to the Publick, that they might examine into the Truth of the Caſes, and be better able to judge of the Effects of this Water. The Names of Perſons, who were alledged as Inſtances of the Vertues thereof, were not mentioned in *Siris*. On this Omiſſion they triumphed, and treated the Whole with Ridicule. But this Narrative ſufficiently

ently ſupplies that Defect, and is the beſt Anſwer to all their Objections. Such a Number of Caſes ſo fully deſcribed and atteſted, muſt be the beſt Refutation of all their Railleries and Reaſonings, which are directly againſt Matter of Fact, the only ſafe Rule to judge by.

323. It is very probable, that I ſhall be judged, and even condemned by ſome, for being ſo ſanguine, and ſo greatly prepoſſeſſed in Favour of Tar-water. I own I am, but it is for the beſt Reaſon in the World. I am fully convinced of the Efficacy of Tar-water in curing a great Number of Diſtempers of the moſt grievous and dangerous Kinds, by the many Inſtances, Caſes, and Matters of Fact, produced in this Narrative, and communicated to me from time to time, by a great Number of Gentlemen and others of good Credit and Integrity from all Parts; who had no other View in ſo doing, than that others might receive the ſame Benefit they had obtained themſelves. And all this ſo well atteſted, that I have not the leaſt doubt of the Truth thereof. If there are any, who have any Doubts, they may repair to the Patients themſelves, whoſe Names and Places of Abode, are herein mentioned for that very Purpoſe, and be fully ſatisfied of the Truth of all, or any of the Caſes herein related. I have recommended Tar-water myſelf to many; ſeveral of them were perfectly cured of their Diſorders; hardly one that did not receive Benefit, and none that got Harm by it. What greater Proof can be given of the Truth or Certainty of any Matter of Fact? Or what better Criterion or Rule can be choſen for determining the Uſe or Power of any Medicine, than many and frequent Trials and Experiments, well atteſted and vouched, and open to all the World? Such Proofs and Evidences are produced in behalf of Tar-water. Some few Inſtances of Cures wrought by Tar-water, being communicat-

M 2 ed

ed to me in the Beginning, induced me to make farther Inquiries into the Effects of it; the more I enquired, the more I was satisfied of the extraordinary Vertues of Tar-water: And found many as ready to communicate their Cases, as I was to receive them. From these Informations, this Narrative has been formed, and has swelled to the Size the Reader sees it in. I had promised to publish such Cases as occurred to me; they who sent them, as well as others, expected it from me, and it would have been very wrong, and even criminal in me, to have stifled or suppressed them.

324. The Variety of Examples in the Collection will direct any Persons, where to find their Cures in particular Cases for which they might not otherwise think of Tar-water. And for this Purpose, an alphabetical Index or Table is annexed to this Narrative, which points out the several Distempers mentioned in this Collection, wherein Tar-water has proved successful, with a Reference to the Sections, where those Distempers are taken Notice of.

325. After the foregoing Sheets were printed off, the following Instances of curing the King's-evil by Tar-water came to my Knowledge, and are therefore inserted in this Place.

A particular Gentleman having informed me of three Persons cured of the King's-evil, he brought to my House at my Desire, on the 12th of *March* 1745, two of the Patients, and a Gentlewoman, who is a near Relation of the Third, who gave me the following Account of their Cases.

326. *Martha Quarle*, about eleven Years old, late of *Glasnevin*, and now living in *Dolphins-barn-lane*, near the Rose and Crown, soon after the hard Frost was afflicted with running Sores, and Holes in one of her Hands and Arms, and under one of her Eyes, which continued to increase, insomuch that it infected her upper Jaw; in this Condition she was

was ſent to *Mercers* Hoſpital, where ſhe ſtayed three Weeks, in which time the Sore under her Eye was a little healed, and ſtopped Running; but in a Fortnight after ſhe left the Hoſpital, it broke out again, and a Splinter of a Bone came off from her Hand. But in 1744 her Parents were adviſed to give her Tar-water, half a Pint a Day, and to apply a Plaiſter of Tar to all the Sores, and a large Tent covered with the Plaiſter to the Hole under her Eye: In a little time, a large Piece of her Jaw-bone, with ſome of her Teeth, came off, and by drinking the Water, and applying the Plaiſters for near three Months, all her Sores healed, and ſhe perfectly recovered, and has continued well this Year and half paſt.

327. *William Murray*, about twelve Years old, Son of *Matthew Murray*, in *Black-horſe-lane*, had running Sores in his Hands and Legs ſoon after the great Froſt, ſo that he was not able to ſtir a Foot, and had great Pains in his Head for a Year. The Boy drank Tar-water, which in a Fortnight's Time carried of the Pains in his Head and then applied the Tar Plaiſter to the Sores a little before laſt *Chriſtmas*, whereby all the Sores are healed up, leaving a great many Marks in his Arm. And the Boy ſtill continues to drink Tar-water, and finds himſelf very hearty.

328. A young Gentlewoman, aged 21 Years, from the Time ſhe was three Years old had a running Evil in one of her Hands, and her Jaws, and ſhe continued in this State many Years without Relief: She was at the Waters of *Loughleah*, in the County of *Cavan*, and was long under the Care of Surgeons without Benefit. Splinters of Bone came from her Hands. But in 1744 ſhe drank Tar-water in ſmall Quantities, and applied the Plaiſter of Tar, which in four Months Time healed them up, and ſhe is now perfectly well.

M 3 329. And

329. And on the 13th of *March* 1745, *James Moony*, Shoe-maker, Son of *Arthur Moony*, who lives at the *Bull's-head* in *Stafford-ſtreet*, came to me at the Deſire of a Gentleman to give me his Caſe which is as follows: In the Winter after the great Froſt, he was afflicted with running Sores, which broke out in many Parts of his Left-hand, and in his Back, and quite diſabled him from following his Trade, and for which he tryed many Things without any Benefit. He attended at the Infirmary on the *Inns-quay*, for two Months, where many Surgeons practiſed upon him; but he got no Relief by any Thing they did, and was at laſt told by them, that there was no other Remedy than to cut off his Hand above the Wriſt: Upon which, he attended no more at the Infirmary. But in *Auguſt* 1745, he was adviſed to drink Tar-water; which he did for two Months, about a Pint a Day, and waſhed the Sores with the ſame Liquor, and the Effect was, that he found the Sores begin to heal in the ſecond Month, and moſt of them were healed up in the End of that Month, and he recovered his Appetite and Spirits, which he had loſt before, and then laid aſide Tar-water, before he was perfectly cured, having two ſmall Sores not quite healed; but he has began to drink the Water again, and finds himſelf much better already, and hopes to perfect his Cure in a little Time.

330. It is very probable that theſe Patients, would have been ſooner cured, if they had taken Tar-water in greater Plenty; half a Pint a Day was too ſmall a Quantity to effect a Cure in a ſhort time: In ſuch grievous Caſes, a Quart a Day ſhould have been taken which might have recovered the Patients in leſs than half the Time as we find to have happened in other Inſtances; and the Water ſhould not be laid aſide, till they were perfectly cured.

331. In ſome Hoſpitals and Infirmaries, where Patients

Patients have had their Hands, Arms, or Legs, ſwollen and inflamed with terrible running Sores, which ate into, and rotted the Bones, and which could not be cured by any of their Medicines, the Surgeons in ſuch Caſes, for fear of a Gangrene or Mortification, ſometimes cut off the Limb; which, if it doth not end with the Death of the Patient, reduces him at leaſt to Want and Beggary. Such Operations ſhould not be attempted, but in the laſt Extremity. And we have Reaſon to ſuſpect, that it is ſometimes done without ſuch Neceſſity; in Regard we find ſeveral Patients mentioned in this Narrative, who were condemned to be ſerved the ſame Way; as the only Means to ſave their Lives, and being told ſo much, and terrified, ran away, or quitted the Hoſpital; yet thoſe very Patients were afterwards recovered by the Uſe of Tar-water, and perfectly reſtored to the Uſe of their Limbs, without any ſuch Mutilations. It is to be hoped that for the future, we ſhall hear but little of ſuch Amputations, ſo ſhocking to Nature, ſince we find that Tar-water not only prevents thoſe Ailments from coming to a dangerous Height but cures them when they do, and when all other Hopes are loſt. And indeed, it is reaſonable to believe, when the whole Maſs of Blood is corrupted, that the cutting off a Limb will not cure the Corruption, which will be apt to break out in ſome other Part.

332. The Murrain, which has lately raged in many Parts of *Europe*, among the horned Cattle, and now prevails in ſome Parts of *England*, ſhould engage our Attention to prevent the ſpreading of ſo deſtructive a Malady. And as this Diſtemper appears by its Symptoms to be a Kind of Fever, it is recommended that Tar-water be tryed in the following Manner. Let the ſick Beaſt have poured down its Throat a Quart of warm Tar-water, made ſtronger than uſual, by ſtirring each Gallon eight or

ten Minutes, and this to be repeated every Hour or two for the firſt Day, while the Beaſt is awake. On the ſecond, let one Half of the former Quantity be given, and on the third Day, half of that which was given on the ſecond: Which laſt Quantity is to be continued till the Cure is perfected; during which time, the Beaſt ſhould be houſed and lie warm. I have no Experience of the Succeſs of this Method, as there is no Infection of that Kind in this Kingdom, but recommend it from the analogous Effects that Tar-water hath in curing Fevers and Infections. It is worth while to try it for the good of the Publick, the Expence being but a Trifle. It may be adviſeable alſo to dawb the Noſtrils, Ears, *&c.* of all the Cattle whether infected or not, to prevent catching or communicating the Infection by the Air. And alſo to make the Beaſt ſwallow one Egg-ſhell full or two of crude Tar.

333. I ſhall add no more, but only ſubjoin to this Treatiſe two Letters from the Author of *Siris*; the firſt addreſſed to me, containing ſome farther Remarks on the Virtues of Tar-water, and the Methods for preparing and uſing it, which was firſt publiſhed in the Year 1744; and the ſecond, lately ſent to me from the ſame Author, containing ſome farther Diſcoveries, Obſervations and Reflections on the Vertues and Effects of Tar-water.

A LET-

ESSAY III.

Of the AUTHORITY *of our* SENSES.

IN a former essay are pointed out some instances, in which our senses may be called deceitful *. They are of two sorts. One is, when the deception is occasioned by indisposition of the organ, remoteness of place, grossness of the medium, or the like; which distort the appearances of objects, and make them be seen double, or greater or less, than they really are. In such instances, the perception is always faint, obscure or confused: and they noway invalidate the authority of the senses, in general, when, abstracting from such accidental obstructions, the perception is lively, strong and distinct. In the other sort, there is a deception established by the laws of nature; as in the case of secondary qualities, taken notice of in that essay; whence it was inferred, that nature does not always give us such correct perceptions, as correspond to the philosophic truth

* Essay upon liberty and necessity.

truth of things. Notwithſtanding of which, the teſtimony of our ſenſes ſtill remains, as a ſufficient ground of confidence and truſt. For, in all theſe caſes, where there is this ſort of eſtabliſhed deception, nature furniſhes means for coming at the truth. As in this very inſtance of ſecondary qualities, philoſophy eaſily corrects the falſe appearances, and teaches us, that they are rather to be conſidered, as impreſſions made upon the mind, than as qualities of the object. A remedy being thus provided to the deception, our belief, ſo far as it can be influenced by reaſon, is the more confirmed, with regard to our other ſenſations, where there is no appearance of illuſion. But this is not the whole of the matter. When any ſenſe preſents to our view, an appearance that may be called deceitful, we plainly diſcover ſome uſeful purpoſe intended. The deceit is not the effect of an imperfect or arbitrary conſtitution; but wiſely contrived, to give us ſuch notice of things, as may beſt ſuit the purpoſes of life. From this very conſideration, we are the more confirmed ed in the veracity of nature. Particular inſtances, in which, our ſenſes are accommodated to the uſes of life, rather than to the ſtrictneſs of truth, are rational exceptions, which ſerve, the more firmly, to eſtabliſh the general rule. And, indeed, when we have nothing but our ſenſes to direct our conduct, with regard to external objects, it would be ſtrange, if there ſhould be any juſt ground, for a general diſtruſt of them. But there is no ſuch thing. There is nothing to which all mankind are more neceſſarily determined, than to put confidence in their ſenſes. We entertain no doubt of their authority, becauſe we are ſo conſtituted, that it is not in our power to doubt.

WHEN the authority of our ſenſes is thus founded on the neceſſity of our nature, and confirmed by conſtant experience, it cannot but appear ſtrange, that it ſhould come into the thought of any man to call it in queſtion. But the influence of novelty is great; and when a bold genius, in ſpite of common ſenſe,

ſenſe, and common feelings, will ſtrike out new paths to himſelf, 'tis not eaſy to foreſee, how far his airy metaphyſical notions may carry him. A late author, who gives us a treatiſe concerning the principles of human knowledge, by denying the reality of external objects, ſtrikes at the root of the authority of our ſenſes, and thereby paves the way to the moſt inveterate ſcepticiſm. For what reliance can we have upon our ſenſes, if they deceive us in a point ſo material? If we can be prevailed upon, to doubt of the reality of external objects, the next ſtep will be, to doubt of what paſſes in our own minds, of the reality of our ideas and perceptions. For we have not a ſtronger conſciouſneſs, nor a clearer conviction of the one, than of the other. And the laſt ſtep will be, to doubt of our own exiſtence; for it is ſhown in the eſſay immediately foregoing, that we have no certainty of this fact, but what depends upon ſenſe and feeling.

IT

It is reported, that doctor Berkeley, the author of the abovementioned treatise, was moved to adopt this whimsical opinion, to get free of some arguments, urged by materialists against the existence of the Deity. If so, he has been unhappy in his experiment; for this doctrine, if it should not lead to universal scepticism, affords, at least, a shrewd argument in favours of Atheism. If I can only be conscious of what passes in my own mind, and if I cannot trust my senses, when they give me notice of external and independent existences; it follows, that I am the only being in the world; at least, that I can have no evidence from my senses, of any other being, body or spirit. This is certainly an unwary concession; because it deprives us of our principal, or only, inlet to the knowledge of the Deity. Laying aside sense and feeling, this learned divine will find it a difficult task, to point out by what other means it is, that we make the discovery of the above important truth. But of this more afterwards.

WERE there nothing elſe in view, but to eſtabliſh the reality of external objects, it would be ſcarce worth while, to beſtow much thought, in ſolving metaphyſical paradoxes againſt their exiſtence, which are better confuted by common ſenſe and experience. But, as the above doctrine appears to have very extenſive conſequences, and to ſtrike at the root of the moſt valuable branches of human knowledge; an attempt to re-eſtabliſh the authority of our ſenſes, by detecting the fallacy of the arguments that have been urged againſt it, may, it is hoped, not be unacceptable to the public. The attempt, at any rate, is neceſſary in this work, the main purpoſe of which is, to ſhow that our ſenſes, external and internal, are the true ſources, from whence the knowledge of the Deity is derived to us.

IN order to afford ſatisfaction upon a ſubject, which is eaſier felt than expreſt, it will be proper, to give a diſtinct analyſis of the operations of thoſe ſenſes, by which we perceive

ceive external objects. And, if this be once clearly apprehended, it will not be a matter of difficulty, to anſwer the ſeveral objections, which have been urged againſt their exiſtence.

THE impreſſions of the external ſenſes are of different kinds. Some we have at the organs of ſenſe, ſuch as ſmelling, taſting, touching. Some are made upon us as from a diſtance, ſuch as hearing and ſeeing. From the ſenſe of feeling, are derived the impreſſions of body, ſolidity and external exiſtence. Laying my hand upon this table, I perceive a thing ſmooth and hard, preſſing upon my hand, and which is perceived as more diſtant from me, than my hand is. From the ſight, we have the impreſſions of motion and of colour; and from the ſight as well as from the touch, thoſe of extenſion and figure. But it is more material to obſerve, upon the preſent ſubject, that from ſight as well as touch, we have the impreſſion of things

as

as having an independent and continued or permanent exiſtence.

LET us endeavour to explain this modification of independency and permanent exiſtence of the objects of ſight and touch, for it is a cardinal point. To begin with the objects of ſight. I caſt my eye upon a tree, and perceive colour, figure, extention, and ſometimes motion. If this be a complete analyſis of the perception, ſubſtance is not diſcoverable by ſight. But upon attentively examining this perception, to try if there be any thing more in it, I find one circumſtance omitted, that the above particulars, are not perceived as ſo many ſeparate exiſtences, having no relation to each other, but as cloſely united and connected. When looking around on different objects, I perceive colour in one quarter, motion in a ſecond, and extenſion in a third; the appearance theſe make in my mind, are in nothing ſimilar to the impreſſion made by a tree, where the extenſion, motion, and other qualities, are introduced

introduced into the mind, under the modification of an intimate connection and union. But in what manner are they united and connected? Of this, every person can give an account, that they are perceived as inhering in, or belonging to some *substance* or *thing*, of which they are *qualities*; and that, by their reference to this substance or thing, they are thus closely united and connected. Thus it is, that the impression of *substance*, as well as of *qualities*, is derived from sight. And it is also to be attended to, as a part of the total impression, that as the qualities appear to belong to their substance, and to inhere in it, so both the substance and its qualities, which we call the tree, are perceived as altogether independent of us, as really existing, and as having a permanent existence.

A SIMILAR impression is made upon us, by means of the sense of feeling. It is observed above, that, from the touch, we have the impressions, of body, solidity and exter-

nal

nal exiſtence; and we have, from the ſame ſenſe, the impreſſions of ſoftneſs and hardneſs, ſmoothneſs and roughneſs. Now, when I lay my hand upon this table, I have an impreſſion, not only of ſmoothneſs, hardneſs, figure and extenſion, but alſo of a thing I call *body*, of which the above are perceived as *qualities*. Smoothneſs, hardneſs, extenſion and figure are felt, not as ſeparate and unconnected exiſtences, but as inhering in and belonging to ſomething I call *body*, which is really exiſting, and which has an independent and permanent exiſtence. And it is this body, with its ſeveral qualities, which I expreſs by the word *table*.

THE above analyſis of the impreſſions of ſight and touch, will be beſt illuſtrated, by a compariſon with the impreſſions made by the other ſenſes. I hear a ſound, or I feel a ſmell. Attending to theſe impreſſions, I perceive nothing but ſound or ſmell. They are not perceived as the qualities or properties of any body, thing or ſubſtance. They

They make their appearance in the mind as ſimple exiſtences; and there is no impreſſion made of independency, or permanent exiſtence. Did ſeeing and feeling carry us no further, we never could have the leaſt conception of ſubſtance.

'Tis not a little ſurpriſing, that philoſophers, who diſcourſe ſo currently of *qualities*, ſhould affect ſo much doubt and heſitation about *ſubſtance*; ſeeing theſe are relative ideas, and imply each other. For what other reaſon do we call figure a quality, but that we perceive it, not as a ſeparate exiſtence, but as belonging to ſomething that is figured; and which thing we call *ſubſtance*, becauſe it is not a property of any other thing, but is a thing which ſubſiſts by itſelf, or has an independent exiſtence. Did we perceive figure, as we perceive ſound, it would not be conſidered as a quality. In a word, a quality is not intelligible, unleſs upon ſuppoſition of ſome other thing, of which it is the quality. Sounds indeed, and ſmells are alſo con-

considered as qualities. But this proceeds from habit, not from original perception. For, having once acquired the distinction betwixt a *thing* and its *qualities*, and finding sound and smell, more to resemble *qualities* than *substances*, we readily come into the use of considering them as qualities.

ANOTHER thing is to be observed with regard to those things, which are perceived as qualities by the sight and touch; that we cannot form a conception of them, independent of the beings to which they belong. It is not in our power, to separate, even in imagination, colour, figure, motion and extension from body or substance. There is no such thing as conceiving motion by itself, abstracted from some body which is in motion. Let us try ever so often, our attempts will be in vain, to form an idea of a triangle independent of a body which has that figure. We cannot conceive a body that is not figured; and we can as little conceive a figure without a body; for this would be to conceive

ceive a figure, as having a ſeparate exiſtence, at the ſame time, that we conceive it, as having no ſeparate exiſtence; or to conceive it, at once, to be a quality, and not a quality. Thus it comes out, that *ſubſtance*, as well as *quality*, makes a part, not only of every perception of ſight and touch, but of every conception we can form, of colour, figure, extenſion and motion. Taking in the whole train of our ideas, there is not one more familiar to us, than that of *ſubſtance*, a being or thing which has qualities.

When theſe things are conſidered, I cannot readily diſcover, by what wrong conception of the matter, Mr. *Locke* has been led, to talk ſo obſcurely and indiſtinctly of the idea of ſubſtance. 'Tis no wonder, he ſhould be difficulted, to form an idea of ſubſtance in general, abſtracted from all properties, when ſuch abſtraction is altogether beyond the reach of our conception. But there is nothing more eaſy, than to form an idea of any particular ſubſtance with its pro-

Ii perties,

perties. Yet this has ſome how eſcaped him. When he forms the idea of a horſe or a ſtone, he admits nothing into the idea, but a collection of ſeveral ſimple ideas of ſenſible qualities †. "And becauſe, ſays he, we "cannot conceive how theſe qualities ſhould "ſubſiſt alone, nor one in another, we ſup-"poſe them exiſting in, and ſupported by "ſome common ſubject; which ſupport, we "denote by the name *ſubſtance*, tho' it be "certain, we have no clear or diſtinct idea "of that thing we ſuppoſe a ſupport." A ſingle queſtion would have unfolded the whole myſtery. How comes it, that we cannot conceive qualities to ſubſiſt alone, nor one in another? Mr. *Locke* himſelf muſt have given the following anſwer, that the thing is not conceiveable; becauſe a property or quality cannot ſubſiſt without the thing to which it belongs; for, if it did, that it would ceaſe to be a property or quality. Why then does he make ſo faint an inference, as that we ſuppoſe qualities exiſting in, and ſupported by ſome common ſubject? It is

† Book 2d, chap. 23.

is not a bare ſuppoſition: it is an eſſential part of the idea: it is neceſſarily ſuggeſted to us by ſight and touch. He obſerves that we have no clear nor diſtinct idea of ſubſtance. If he means, that we have no clear nor diſtinct idea of ſubſtance abſtracted from its properties, the thing is ſo true, that we can form no idea of ſubſtance at all, abſtracted from its properties. But it is alſo true, that we can form no idea of properties, abſtracted from a ſubſtance. The ideas both of ſubſtance and of quality are perfectly in the ſame condition, in this reſpect; which, 'tis ſurpriſing, philoſophers ſhould ſo little attend to. At the ſame time, we have clear and diſtinct ideas, of many things as they exiſt; tho' perhaps we have not a complete idea of any one thing. We have ſuch ideas of things, as ſerve to all the uſeful purpoſes of life. 'Tis true, our ſenſes don't reach beyond the external properties of beings. We have no direct perception of the eſſence and internal properties of any thing. Theſe we diſcover from the effects produced. But had we ſenſes directly to perceive the eſſence and

internal

internal properties of things, our idea of them would indeed be more full and complete, but not more clear and diſtinct, than at preſent. For, even upon that ſuppoſition, we could form no notion of ſubſtance, but by its properties internal and external. To form an idea of a thing abſtracted from all its properties, is impoſſible.

THE following is the ſum of what is above laid down. By ſight and touch, we have the impreſſions of ſubſtance and body, as well as of qualities. It is not figure, extenſion, motion, that we perceive; but a thing figured, extended and moving. As we cannot form an idea of ſubſtance abſtracted from qualities, ſo we cannot form an idea of qualities abſtracted from ſubſtance. They are relative ideas, and imply each other. This is one point gained. Another is, that the idea of ſubſtance or body, thus attained, comprehends in it, independent and permanent exiſtence; that is, ſomething which exiſts independent of our perceptions, and remains the ſame, whether we perceive it or not.

In

In this manner are we made ſenſible of the real exiſtence of things without us. The feeling is ſo ſtrong, and the conviction which makes a part of the feeling, that ſceptical arguments, however cunningly deviſed, may puzzle, but can never get the better: for ſuch is our conſtitution, that we can entertain no doubt of the authority of our ſenſes, in this particular. At the ſame time, every ſort of experience confirms the truth of our perceptions. I ſee a tree at a diſtance, of a certain ſhape and ſize. Walking forward, I find it in its place, by the reſiſtance it makes to my body; and, ſo far as I can diſcover by touch, it is of the ſame ſhape and ſize, which my eye repreſents it to be. I return day after day, year after year, and find the ſame object, with no other variation, but what the ſeaſons and time produce. The tree is at laſt cut down. It is no longer to be ſeen or felt.

To overthrow the authority of our ſenſes, a few particular inſtances, in which they appear

appear fallacious, are of no weight. And to confirm this branch of the argument, we need but compare the evidence of our senses, with the evidence of human testimony. The comparison cannot fail to afford satisfaction. Veracity, and a disposition to rely upon human evidence, are corresponding principles, which greatly promote society. Among individuals, these principles are found to be of different degrees of strength. But, in the main, they are so proportioned to each other, that men are not often deceived. In this case, it would be but a bad argument, that we ought not to give credit to any man's testimony, because some men are defective in the principle of veracity. The only effect such instances have, or ought to have, is to correct our propensity to believe, and to bring on a habit of suspending our belief, 'till circumstances be examined. The evidence of our senses, rises undoubtedly much higher, than the evidence of human testimony. And if we continue to put trust in the latter, after many instances of being deceiv-

ed,

ed, we have better reaſon to put truſt in the former, were the inſtances of being deceived equally numerous; which is plainly not the fact. When people are in ſound health of mind and body, they are very ſeldom miſ-led by their ſenſes.

If I have been ſo lucky, as to put this ſubject in its proper light, it will not be a difficult task to clear it of any doubts which may ariſe, upon peruſing the above mentioned treatiſe. The author boldly denies the exiſtence of matter, and the reality of the objects of ſenſe; contending, that there is nothing really exiſting without the mind of an intelligent being; in a word, reducing all to be a world of ideas. "It is an "opinion ſtrangely prevailing among men, "(ſays he) that houſes, mountains, rivers, "and, in a word, all ſenſible objects, have an "exiſtence, natural or real, diſtinct from "their being perceived by the underſtand-"ing." He ventures to call this a manifeſt contradiction; and his argument againſt the reality

reality of these objects, is in the following words. " The forementioned objects are " things perceived by sense. We cannot " perceive any thing, but our own ideas or " perceptions; therefore, what we call men, " houses, mountains, &c. can be nothing " else but ideas or perceptions." This argument shall be examined afterwards, with the respect that is due to its author. It shall only be taken notice of by the way, that, supposing mankind to be under so strange and unaccountable a delusion, as to mistake their ideas for men, houses, mountains, &c. it will not follow, that there is in this, any manifest contradiction, or any contradiction at all. For deception is a very different thing from contradiction. But he falls from this high pretension, in the after part of his work, to argue more consistently, " that, suppos- " ing solid, figured, and moveable substan- " ces, to exist without the mind, yet we " could never come to the knowledge of " this *." Which is true, if our senses bear

* Sect. 18.

bear no teſtimony of the fact. And he adds *, " that, ſuppoſing no bodies to exiſt " without the mind, we might have the ve- " ry ſame reaſons for ſuppoſing the exiſtence " of external bodies, that we have now:" which may be true, ſuppoſing only our ſen-ſes to be fallacious.

THE doctor's fundamental propoſition is, that we can perceive nothing but our own ideas or perceptions. This, at beſt, is an ambiguous expreſſion. For, taking percep-tion or ſenſation in its proper ſenſe, as ſigni-fying every object we perceive, it is a mere identical propoſition, *ſciz.* that we perceive nothing but what we perceive. But, taking the doctor's propoſition as he intended it, that we can have no perception or conſciouſ-neſs of any thing, but what exiſts in our own minds, he had certainly no reaſon to take this aſſertion for granted; and yet he has never once attempted a proof of it: tho', in ſo bold an undertaking, as that of annihilat-

Kk ing

* Sect. 20.

ing the whole univerſe, his own mind excepted, he had no reaſon to hope, that an aſſertion, ſo ſingular, and ſo contradictory to common ſenſe and feeling, would be taken upon his word. It may be true, that it is not eaſy to explain, nor even to comprehend, by what means we perceive external objects. But our ignorance is, in moſt caſes, a very indifferent argument againſt matter of fact. At this rate, he may take upon him equally to deny the bulk of the operations in the natural world, which have not hitherto been explained by him, or others. And at, bottom, 'tis perhaps as difficult to explain the manner of perceiving our own ideas, or the impreſſions made upon us, as to explain the manner of perceiving external objects. The doctor, beſides, ought to have conſidered, that by this bold doctrine, he, in effect, ſets bounds to the power of nature, or of the Author of nature. If it was in the power of the Almighty, to beſtow upon man, a faculty of perceiving external objects, he has certainly done it. For, ſuppoſing the exiſtence of of external objects, we have no conception, how they could be otherways manifested to us, than in fact they are. Therefore, the doctor was in the right to assert, that a faculty in man to perceive external objects, would be a contradiction, and consequently a privilege not in the power of the Deity to bestow upon him. He perceived the necessity of carrying his argument so far; at the same time, sensible that this was not to be made out, he never once attempts to point at any thing like a contradiction. And if he cannot prove it to be a contradiction, the question is at an end; for, supposing only the fact to be possible, we have the very highest evidence of its reality, that our nature is capable of, no less than the testimony of our senses.

It has been urged in support of the above doctrine, that nothing is present to the mind, but the impressions made upon it, and that it cannot be conscious of any thing but what is present. This difficulty is easily solved. For

For the propoſition, that we cannot be conſcious of any thing but what is preſent to the mind, or paſſes within it, is taken for granted, as if it were ſelf-evident. And yet the direct contrary is an evident fact, *ſciz.* that we are conſcious of many things which are not preſent to the mind; that is, which are not, like impreſſions and ideas, within the mind. Nor is there any manner of difficulty to conceive, that an impreſſion may be made upon us, by an external object, in ſuch a manner, as to raiſe a direct perception of the external object itſelf. When we attend to the operations of the external ſenſes, the impreſſions made upon us by external objects, are diſcovered to have very different effects. In ſome inſtances we feel the impreſſion, and are conſcious of it, as an impreſſion. In others, being quite unconſcious of the impreſſion, we perceive only the external object. And to give full ſatisfaction to the reader, upon the preſent ſubject, it may perhaps not be fruitleſs, briefly to run over the operations of the ſeveral exter-

nal

nal ſenſes, by which the mind is made conſcious of external objects, and of their properties.

And firſt, with regard to the ſenſe of ſmelling, which gives us no notice of external exiſtences. Here the operation is of the ſimpleſt kind. It is no more but an impreſſion made at the organ, which is perceived as an impreſſion. Experience, 'tis true, and habit, lead us to aſcribe this particular impreſſion to ſome external thing as its cauſe. Thus, when a particular impreſſion is made upon us, termed the ſweet ſmell of a roſe, we learn to aſcribe it to a roſe, tho' there is no ſuch object within view, becauſe that peculiar impreſſion upon the organ of ſmelling, is always found to accompany the ſight and touch of the body, called a roſe. But that this connection is the child of experience only, will be evident from the following conſiderations; that, when a new ſmell is perceived, we are utterly at a loſs, what cauſe to aſcribe it to; and, that when a child feels a ſmell, it is not led to aſſign it

to

to any cauſe whatever. In this caſe, there can be no other difficulty, but to comprehend, in what manner the mind becomes conſcious of an impreſſion, made upon the body. Upon which, it ſeems ſufficient to obſerve, that we are kept entirely ignorant, in what manner the ſoul and body are connected; which is no ſingular caſe. But, from our ignorance of the manner of this connection, to deny the reality of external exiſtences, reducing all to a world of ideas, is in reality not leſs whimſical, than if one, after admitting the reality of external exiſtences, ſhould go about to deny, that we have any perception of them; merely becauſe we cannot fully account for the manner of this perception, nor how a material ſubſtance can communicate itſelf to the mind, which is ſpirit and not matter. The ſame obſervations may be applied to the ſenſe of hearing; with this difference only, that a ſound is not perceived, at leaſt not originally, as an impreſſion made at the organ, but merely as an exiſtence in the mind.

IN

In the ſenſes of taſting and touching, we are conſcious not only of an impreſſion made at the organ, but alſo of a body which makes the impreſſion. When I lay my hand upon this table, the impreſſion is of a hard ſmooth body, which reſiſts the motion of my hand. In this impreſſion, there is nothing to create the leaſt ſuſpicion of fallacy. The body acts where it is, and it acts merely by reſiſtance. There occurs not, therefore, any other difficulty in this caſe, than that mentioned above, *ſciz.* after what manner an impreſſion made at an organ of the body, is communicated to, or perceived by the mind. We ſhall only add upon this head, that touch alone, which is the leaſt intricate of all our feelings, is ſufficient to overthrow the doctor's whole pompous ſyſtem. We have, from that ſenſe, the fulleſt and cleareſt perception of external exiſtences, that can be conceived, ſubject to no doubt, ambiguity, nor even cavil. And this perception, muſt, at the ſame time, ſupport the

the authority of our ſenſes, when they give us notice of external exiſtences.

WHAT remains to be examined, is the ſenſe of ſeeing, which, 'tis preſumed, the doctor had principally an eye to, in arguing againſt the reality of external exiſtences. And indeed, the operation of perceiving objects at a diſtance, is ſo curious, and ſo ſingular, that it is not ſurpriſing, a rigid philoſopher ſhould be puzzled about it. In this caſe, there is a difficulty, which applies with ſome ſhew of ſtrength, and which poſſibly has had weight with our author, tho' it is never once mentioned by him. It is, that no being can act but where it is, and that a body, at a diſtance, cannot act upon the mind, more than the mind upon it. I muſt candidly own, that this argument appears to evince the neceſſity, of ſome intermediate means, in the act of viſion. One means is ſuggeſted by matter of fact. The image of a viſible object, is painted upon the retina of the eye. And it is not more difficult to con-

conceive, that this image may be ſome how conveyed to the mind, than to conceive the manner of its being painted upon the retina. This circumſtance puts the operation of viſion, in one reſpect, upon the ſame footing, with that of touching; both being performed by means of an impreſſion made at the organ. There is indeed this eſſential difference, that the impreſſion of touch is felt as ſuch, whereas the impreſſion of ſight is not felt: we are not conſcious of any ſuch impreſſion, but merely of the object itſelf, which makes the impreſſion.

AND here a curious piece of mechaniſm preſents itſelf to our view. Tho' an impreſſion is made upon the mind, by means of the image painted upon the retina, whereby the external object is perceived; yet nature has carefully concealed this impreſſion from us, in order to remove all ambiguity, and to give us a diſtinct feeling of the object itſelf, and of that only. In touching and taſting, the impreſſion made at the organ, is ſo cloſe-

L l ly

ly connected with the body which makes the impreſſion, that the perception of the impreſſion, along with that of the body, creates no confuſion nor ambiguity, the body being felt as operating where it really is. But were the impreſſion of a viſible object felt, as made at the retina, which is the organ of ſight, all objects behoved to be ſeen as within the eye. It is doubted among naturaliſts, whether outneſs or diſtance is at all diſcoverable by ſight, and whether that appearance be not the effect of experience. But bodies, and their operations, are ſo cloſely connected in place, that were we conſcious of an organic impreſſion at the retina, the mind would have a conſtant propenſity to place the body there alſo; which would be a circumſtance extremely perplexing, in the act of viſion, as ſetting feeling and experience in perpetual oppoſition; enough to poiſon all the pleaſure we enjoy by that noble ſenſe.

For ſo ſhort-ſighted a creature as man, it is the worſt reaſon in the world for denying any

any well attested fact, that we cannot account for the manner by which it is brought about. It is true, we cannot explain, after what manner it is, that, by the intervention of the rays of light, the beings, and things around us, are laid open to our view; but it is mere arrogance, to pretend to doubt of the fact, upon that account; for it is, in effect, maintaining, that there is nothing in nature, but what we can explain.

THE perception of objects at a distance, by intervention of the rays of light, involves no inconsistency nor impossibility. And unless this could be asserted, we have no reason nor foundation to with-hold that assent to a matter of fact, which is due to the authority of our senses. And after all, this particular step of the operation of vision, is, at bottom, not more difficult to be conceived or accounted for, than the other steps, of which no man entertains a doubt. It is, perhaps, not easy to explain, how the image of an external body is painted upon the *retina tunica*.

ca. And no perſon pretends to explain, how this image is communicated to the mind. Why then ſhould we heſitate about the laſt ſtep, to wit the perception of external objects, more than about the two former, when they are all equally ſupported, by the moſt unexceptionable evidence. The whole operation of viſion far ſurpaſſes human knowledge: but not more, than the operation of magnetiſm, electricity, and a thouſand other natural appearances; and our ignorance of the cauſe, ought not to make us ſuſpect deceit in the one caſe, more than in the other.

We ſhall conclude this ſubject, with the following reflection. Whether our perception of the reality of external objects, correſponds to the truth of things, or whether it be a mere illuſion, is a queſtion, which, from the nature of the thing, cannot admit of a ſtrict demonſtration. One thing is certain, that, ſuppoſing the reality of external objects, we can form no conception of their being diſplayed to us, in a more lively and con-

convincing manner, than in fact is done. Why then call a thing in doubt, of which we have as good evidence, as human nature is capable of receiving? But we cannot call it in doubt, otherways than in speculation, and even then, but for a moment. We have a thorough conviction of the reality of external objects; it rises to the highest certainty of belief; and we act, in consequence of it, with the greatest security of not being deceived. Nor are we in fact deceived. When we put the matter to a trial, every experiment answers to our perceptions, and confirms us more and more in our belief.

ESSAY

Thus, again, I know the general nature, the real essence, of justice, and am able to define it in very clear propositions, tho' I am not able to frame any general idea or notion of it abstracted from all particulars, and containing them all. It is

I 2 not,

not, most certainly, to do as we would be done by; for that is more properly a definition of benevolence, than of justice, as every one, who considers the constant force and the occasional injustice of self-love, must admit. But it consists in a disposition to give to every one what is his own, where there is property; to deal by others according to the natural fitness or unfitness of things where there is no property; and in other distinct notions, which will altogether amount to a definition, if we may be said to define when we only enumerate particular notions: and we can do nothing more when we set about to explain the general nature of justice; for which I may appeal to every man who has meditated well on this subject. To conclude; I know the general nature, and the real essence of likeness, and am able to explain it by a very short definition; for it consists in that relation which arises from an uniformity of appearance in things that are distinct in existence. But still I have no general idea nor notion of this relation, abstracted from all my particular ideas of things so related *.

* THESE disputes about abstraction may be deemed after all, perhaps, to be purely verbal. A loose determination of the word idea may have given occasion to them. A proper distinction between ideas and notions may help to reconcile them. These two words are commonly used by inadvertency and habit, or authority, as if they were synonimous. Mr. LOCKE, and even his antagonist in this dispute, the bishop of CLOYNE, have used them so. I have done the same in all I have writ to you. But I think that the example before us shews how necessary it is to distinguish them, in order to maintain a philosophical precision of terms.

WHAT

WHAT advances now do we make in general knowledge by this expedient which the art of the

THE word idea should, I presume, be held to signify one single perception of the mind, whether simple or complex, whether produced by the impressions of outward objects, or by the operations of our own minds, by sensation or reflection. These ideas are preserved in the memory by frequent repetitions of the same impressions, and the same operations. But those of them which can be painted, as it were, on the canvass of the mind, like single objects of internal sight, and like pictures of the original impressions which were made on it, or of the original forms which were raised in it, are best preserved and most steadily determined. They are all particular, and have no generality but that of application. They represent to the mind that which does, or may exist. Of that which neither does, nor can exist, we can have no idea. The ideal man, or the ideal horse, which the mind perceives, is a particular idea that represents all the men, and all the horses that exist, or ever did exist; and the ideal triangle is as truly a particular idea that represents all the triangles that exist, or can exist in the mind, or out of it. The mind indeed has a power of varying, without destroying the idea: for instance, it adds wings to the man, and to the horse; one becomes an angel, the other an hippogriph; and as it can represent the ideal man to be white or black, crooked or strait, so it can represent the triangle to be rectangle, oblique, equilateral, equicrural, or scalenon. Thus far the mind can generalise it's ideas: and I think myself sure that mine can generalise them no further. But when we have been accustomed to call every thing an idea that is an object of the mind in thinking, we fall easily into that confusion of language, whereby men are led very often, as I apprehend that they are in the present case, to dispute, and to mean the same thing. We might avoid it, I presume, if we distinguished between ideas and notions, if we conceived the former to be particular in their nature, and general only by their application, and the latter to be general in their nature, and particular only by their application; in short, if we considered how notions succeed ideas, and how they become the immediate instruments of general knowledge, when these can be such no longer. Particular ideas of actual, or possible existence, are made ge-

I 3 mind

mind has invented? Nor such as philosophers would have believed, but some however. Tho' we

neral in some sort, that is, in their effect, as it has been said, and as it is allowed on all hands. But the power of generalising ideas is so insufficient, that it goes no further. We make one phantasm of a man stand for all men, and one of an horse for all horses; but here our progress by ideas, that is, by single perceptions of the mind, stops. We have none of humanity, nor of horseity, and much less have we any of animality. Just so the phantasm of a particular triangle stands for every triangle of that species, but we have no idea of triangularity, and much less of figure. We make a particular stand for a general idea in this case, as in the two former; but in no case can we make ideas that are particular, and that can represent only what does, or may exist, become ideas of general natures that cannot exist. There is however a great difference between cases of the former, and cases of the latter kind. The essences of substances are absolutely unknown to us, but the essences of complex modes are perfectly known, so that we have clear and distinct notions, tho' we cannot have clear and distinct ideas, nor indeed any ideas at all of them. From the contemplation of particular triangles we collect a notion of their general nature. We do more; by contemplating the various terminations of finite extension, we collect a notion of the general nature of figure. We have ideas of these no more than we have ideas of humanity or animality, but we know what we mean, and are able to explain our meaning when we speak of these, which we are not when we speak of the others.

Much more might be said to shew the difference between complex ideas and notions, and between general and abstract ideas, and the advantage that those (in the conception of which, internal sense, and in the communication of which, external sense help intellect) have over such as are merely objects of intellect. I might expose, even to ridicule, the stir that is made about the pains and skill our masters pretend that they take to form the supposed idea of triangularity, for instance, that they may teach their scholars to know a triangle when they see it; tho' the meanest of their scholars, who have

cannot

cannot by any power of the mind frame ideas of general natures and eſſences, which neither do nor can exiſt ſeparately from particulars, yet is it ſome advance to be able to comprehend, under one conſideration, a great number of particulars, by appropriating general names to the ſeveral lots, if the term may be allowed me, into which the mind has ſorted it's ideas and notions. The expedient facilitates extremely, as every man who thinks muſt obſerve, not only the communication of our thoughts to others, but the progreſs of them in their ſeveral trains, and all the operations of the mind about it's ideas; for tho' theſe general names have no abſtract ideas annexed to them, nor, ſtrictly ſpeaking, any ideas or notions, yet are they not unaccompanied by ideas and notions. That would be to have no meaning at all, whereas they have a meaning, a plain and uſeful meaning or intention. What they have not, they borrow. They create no ideas in the mind, but they give occaſion to the mind to collect and apply ſuch ideas and notions as are there already. They call them forth, they marſhal them, as it were: and by the manner in which, and by the occaſions on which, they do ſo, theſe names produce all the effect they are deſigned to produce, and

been uſed to contemplate particular triangles, will have made this notable diſcovery, "that every triangle is a ſpace comprehended by three lines, and containing three angles," without any help of theirs, or ſkill or pains of his own. All the merit of our maſters ſeems to be this, they begin to learn at the right, they begin to teach at the wrong, end; which is an obſervation that may be enforced by what Mr. LOCKE himſelf ſays about maxims.

I 4 carry

carry us towards general knowledge as far as our feeble intellect can crawl with their assistance, and much further than we could advance without it.

Here now the word force, of which we are to speak, comes into play, and serves as a sign of the unknown causes of the phænomena both of nature and of art; for effects are produced in the works of art by an imitation of those of nature, whereof the causes are unknown even to the artificer. When we employ the word alone, it is of very vague signification, and imports nothing more than some determining power, intellectual or corporeal. But the mind takes two methods to give it greater precision, when that is necessary. We annex it sometimes to words which signify that whereof we would, on such occasions, denote the power in general to produce effects in physics, in mechanics, in ethics; and thus we say the force of wind, the force of a mill, or the force of habit. We annex at other times to it words, that, referring to particular known effects, serve to fix on every occasion the meaning of it; just as we annex the words hot or cold, to signify certain supposed qualities of body; and as intelligibly at least as we use the names of substances. Thus we speak of attractive, repelling, impelling force, of the force

of

2

of gravitation, of coheſion, and even of inactivity. Our NEWTON, who has opened, by the help of theſe ſure guides, experiment and geometry, ſo large a field of knowledge and enquiry to preſent and future philoſophers, concerning the greateſt and the leaſt phænomena of nature, was far from pretending to determine the efficient cauſe of his attraction, or what that force is which makes bodies, and every particle of body, mutually tend to one another, and thereby give us an idea of attracting, according to what has been taken notice of already. He diſtinguiſhed ſo carefully between the particular attractions of the ſchools, and his meaning in the uſe of this word, that nothing could be more deſpicable than the ignorance or malice of thoſe who would have confounded them, and have made him an aſſerter of occult qualities, who diſcovered the moſt univerſal and the leaſt occult quality, if I may have leave to call it ſo for once, that ever was, ſince it intercedes the whole corporeal ſyſtem. To this and to the ſeveral kinds of it, he referred all the phænomena that cannot be accounted for by impulſe: and they are many, tho' many of thoſe, which were aſcribed to a ſort of attraction by the ancients, are on better foundations aſcribed to impulſe by the moderns. But neither for the cauſe of impulſe, nor of attraction, nor of any action of body even the moſt ſenſible, can philoſophy account. They, therefore, who uſe the word force as the ſign of an unknown cauſe, whilſt they apply themſelves ſolely to diſcover the laws by by which this cause acts, and the effects it produces, make a proper use of the word. They who affect to talk in any other manner, either physical or metaphysical, about force, abuse the word most impertinently, and pervert into artifice a very useful art of the mind.

But this is not the only method by which this art of the mind is perverted. It degenerates into artifice, likewise, by the use which they make of it, who invent words to point out causes, they suppose unknown, of effects whose real causes are known. In the former method men are led into error by affecting knowledge; in this by affecting ignorance. Whatever force is, it is the cause of effects, that are known, but cannot be ascribed to any cause that is known. In this the propriety of the word consists: for if they could be ascribed to any cause known and denominated, it would be improper, and the use of it could only serve to mislead. But there may be more than error, there may be fraud, in this case; for, to borrow an image from the application of the word chance, the fair gamester, who should see a raffle of sixes thrown several times together, might ascribe it to chance, that is, to an unknown cause, very properly; but the sharper, who had loaded the dice, or who knew that they were loaded, would ascribe it to chance fraudulently as well as improperly.

I could wish that Alciphron and Lysicles had made this observation to Euphranor, and had

had applied it to shew him why they admitted the word force, and rejected the word grace. The task would not have been hard, since it would not have been hard to shew him real causes sufficiently known, and sufficiently marked by words, of the effects ascribed by him to a cause supposed unknown, and marked by a distinct word appropriated to this purpose. They might have shewn these causes to be the influence of a religious education, a warm head, and a warmer heart; hope, fear, grief, joy, strong passions turned by prejudice and habit to devotion, devotion itself nursing it's own principles, the effect in it's turn becoming a cause uniform and constant, or redoubling it's force, on the least failure, in acts of attrition, contrition, mortification, and repentance. They might have proved not only by probable reasons, but by indubitable facts, the sufficiency of these and other known causes to produce all the effects commonly ascribed to grace, even the most astonishing that ever appeared in saints, confessors, or martyrs. Nay, they might have shewn that effects more astonishing, and many of them better vouched, than most of these, have been, and are still daily, produced in men, whom it would be blasphemous to repute under the divine influence. Alciphron might have illustrated this argument in his serious character, by quoting the saints, confessors, and martyrs of idolatry and heresy; and Lysicles in his gayer character, by quoting those of atheism, and of the most abominable vices, as well as the most

most indifferent customs; of paederasty, for instance, and of long beards.

I AM thinking what EUPHRANOR would have replied to the minute philosophers; and can discover no reply worthy of that solidity and that candor which render him equally admirable and amiable. He might have said indeed that he was misunderstood by them, that the parity he insisted on was not meant to "consist in a "proof of grace, as well as force, from the "effects; that it was only meant to answer an "objection against the doctrine of grace, suppo-"sing it proved from revelation, and not to "prove it's existence; that therefore if the pa-"rity was sufficient to prove the possibility of "believing grace without an idea of it, the "objection they had made was answered, and "he aimed at no more." But I think that, as minute philosophers as I am willing to allow ALCIPHRON and LYSICLES to have been, they would have maintained very easily the pertinence of their objection, and the insufficiency of EUPHRANOR's answer.

THEY might have said, there is not even the parity you now suppose between force and grace. Our objection against the latter did in effect anticipate your reply: and if we allowed your reply to be a good one, it would neither strengthen your cause, nor weaken ours. The parity between force and grace, which you confine now to a possibility of believing one as well as the other, is not sufficient; because it is not real. The possibility of believing force, is nothing more than the possibility of believing that every effect has a cause, tho' the cause be unknown to us, and the propriety of the word consists in the application of it to no other cause. The disparity and impropriety do not arise from our having no idea of grace; for it is true that we have none of force: but they arise from hence, that there is not the same possibility of believing a cause, whereof we have no idea, and which cannot be ascertained by it's effects, as there is of believing one whereof we have no idea indeed, but which may be ascertained by it's effects. You assume grace as a cause of one particular kind, an immediate influence of God on the mind; and you apply it to effects that may have causes of several kinds. Should a word be invented to signify a moral cause of effects purely physical, or a physical cause of effects purely moral, you would laugh at the invention; and you would be in the right. But is it a jot less ridiculous to assign a particular cause, either natural or supernatural, of effects that may be produced by any, or all, of these; and to think to save the absurdity by saying that the word, invented to denote this cause, has no idea attached to it, no more than that of force?

The use of the word force can have no equivocal consequence: the use of the word grace may. The testimony, nay, the conviction, of men, that they felt the influence of this unknown cause, would

would not take off the equivocation. How ſhould it, after all the examples that may be brought from daily experience? A real enthuſiaſt doubts no more of his perceptions of the operations of grace, informing his mind, and determining his will, than he doubts of his perceptions of the action of outward objects on his ſenſes, and perhaps leſs.

ANOTHER thing, which I imagine that the minute philoſophers would have ſaid to EUPHRANOR, is this. Since the parity you endeavour to eſtabliſh between force and grace, cannot be ſo eſtabliſhed as to anſwer your purpoſe on any principles of reaſon; it remains that the notion of grace cannot be received, nor the word employed, on any other authority, than that of implicit faith in the revelation by which you ſuppoſe the exiſtence of grace proved. That authority obliges us to believe an action or an influence of God on his elect, the manner of which no human idea can reach: but on what authority, EUPHRANOR, do you anſwer our "objection againſt the doc-"trine of grace, by ſuppoſing it proved by re-"velation?" If you have proved this fact, that the Chriſtian revelation, in which the doctrine of grace is contained, was made by God to mankind, as all facts, and eſpecially one of this importance, ought to be proved, for every other kind of proof proves nothing; we will agree, tho' there be not the ſame reaſon for admitting grace as for admitting force, that both are to

N 2 be

be received alike. Our objection was insufficient; but your answer then was unnecessary: for surely nothing can be more unnecessary, than to go about to establish on probable arguments what is already established on demonstration: and the real existence of grace has been already demonstrated, if the truth of the revelation, in every part of it, has been so; since no proposition can be more demonstrated than this, that a doctrine taught by infinite wisdom and truth is a true doctrine. If you have not proved this fact, and we think you have scarce attempted it, by the proper proofs, your argument is a pure sophism. When we urge that the doctrine of grace, or any other Christian doctrine, is inconceivable, or that it is pregnant with absurd consequences, and therefore unworthy of God; this is urged, in strictness, ex abundantia; for we do not give up the fundamental point, which is, that the authenticity of your scriptures, in the whole and in every part of them, and the truth by consequence of your revelation, has not been yet proved. When you suppose the contrary, therefore, in disputing with us, you beg the question about a principle, in order to confirm a consequence. Thus it seems to me that the dispute between EUPHRANOR and the minute philosophers would have ended. What I have said upon it can be scarce called a digression; since this comparison of force and grace serves admirably well to exemplify what has been said concerning the art and artifice of the mind in the proper

proper and improper uſe of words, to which no determinate ideas are annexed.

APPENDIX.

Concerning Dr. BERKLEY's *Scheme, That there is no material World.*

IN considering this scheme, we shall

I. Propose the scheme itself, and the arguments by which it is supported.

II. Examine the objections brought against it.

III. Consider how far our enquiries into natural philosophy are affected by it.

SECT. I. The scheme itself is not, that sensible objects have *no real existence*; or that all is but a waking dream: he disclaims both these, his principle is, that no sensible object exists *unperceived*; or more plainly, that *there is no material world*, and that *primary*, as well as secondary qualities, do only exist in the mind perceiving them; so that if all minds were annihilated, all bodies would be annihilated too; and the difference between dreaming and perceiving, is only that the latter is more active, regular and vivid than the former.

The arguments by which the Doctor supports this system are these.

1. The existence of a material world cannot be demonstrated; because an almighty power can always produce such sensations without any archetype, and it is plain in dreams he does so.

Ans. This will not prove that he *has* done it. We assert not that matter is a necessary being; but its actual existence may nevertheless be proved, as well as that of a created mind.

2. It is an useless incumbrance; because a divine influence is necessary to produce ideas from material archetypes.

Ans. The divine power may be illustrated in such a harmony; and the actual support of bodies seems an act of great power, as well as the union of the soul and body, of great wisdom.

3. The supposition of it is very inconvenient, as it introduces disputes about the production and subsistance of bodies, the infinite divisibility of matter, the union of body and mind, &c.—But it may be replied, that if giving occasion to disputes could disprove the thing disputed about, we must also give up the existence of spiritual and immaterial beings.

4. It implies a contradiction. Sensible objects are the things we perceive by our senses; but we can perceive only our own ideas and sensations: now it is plainly repugnant, that any of our own sensations should exist unperceived, and therefore that sensible objects should so exist.

Ans. This is plainly taking the question for granted; yet he triumphs greatly in this argument, and says, the bare possibility of the existence of any extended

6 move-

moveable substance, or in general any idea, or any thing like an idea, but in a thinking mind, is absurd. But this triumph is extremely ill grounded; because if it were granted him, that sensible objects are in fact only the things which our senses immediately perceive, *i. e.* that they are our own ideas, (which is, as we observed above, begging the question) it will not follow from thence, that it is impossible there should be, or should have been, any external archetypes of them.

Berkley's Princ. § 22.

5. The various appearances of the same object to different persons at the same time, prove that it exists only in a perceiving mind; else the same thing must have different magnitudes, colours, *&c.*

Ans. The various circumstances in which it is, seems to account for its different appearance; and if the object were material, it must be so.

6. The best philosophers have granted it as to *secondary* qualities, but the case is the same as to *primary.*—This is denied.

Sect. II. The objections against it are these.

1. To deny the possibility of matter, is plainly limiting the power of God.

2. This hypothesis which supposes us under a continual deception, reflects upon the divine veracity.—He answers, the same objection will lie against supposing the earth to move about the sun.

3. The senses give us such an evidence, that if it is possible they may be true notices of what passes without us, we must certainly believe they are so.

4. Our ideas can have no parts; but the objects of them have parts: therefore the objects are something different from the ideas themselves.

5. Every thing real is banished out of the world.—This *Berkley* expresly denies.

6. Things on this supposition are continually annihilated and created anew. —He answers, the school-men allow a continual creation. But that is a weak reply. If *Adam* and *Eve* both slept, the sun for that time was annihilated: if it be said, it existed in the divine mind; it may be answered, so it did from all eternity, and at that rate all creatures must be eternal.

7. It makes all the apparatus of nature in the organization of plants and animals vain.

Ans. Not vainer than upon the supposition of a continued divine concurrence, asserted *Prop.* 32. they are rules which God has laid down, according to which he directs his own operations.

8. This doctrine destroys all the evidence of the existence of other created spirits; some also add, of the divine existence; but I think not: yet it certainly weakens some proofs of it, especially that taken from the *vis inertiæ* of matter.

Sect. III. How far our inquiries into natural philosophy are affected by it.

1. It cuts off a great part of our present inquiries.

2. In a strict sense, it would change a great part of our language.

3. Never-

3. Nevertheleſs, it leaves room for the obſervation of the phænomena of nature, and the connection between cauſes and effects, in many inſtances. On the whole, it is a ſcheme deſtitute of proof; the moſt we can aſſert is, that it is *poſſible*; and we are led every moment, whether we will or no, into an apprehenſion of the contrary. If we believe it to be true, we ought to act in every inſtance, and on every occaſion, juſt as if it were falſe.—We conclude with obſerving, that as ſome have denied all *material*, and others all *immaterial* ſubſtances, each aſſerting one or the other *only* to be real, we may reaſonably believe them *both* to be ſo.

Berkley's Princ. & Dial. paſſ.
Collier's Immat. World.
Baxter on the Soul, vol. ii. § 2. *Oct.*
Hume's Eſſ. on the Princ. of Morality and Nat. Rel. part ii. *Eſſ.* iii.

PART

S E C T. VII.

Of the exiſtence of a material world.

IT is beyond our power to ſay, when or in what order we came by our notions of theſe qualities. When we trace the operations of our minds as far back as memory and reflection can carry us, we find them already in poſſeſſion of our imagination and belief, and quite familiar to the mind: but how they came firſt into its acquaintance, or what has given them ſo ſtrong a hold of our belief, and what regard they deſerve, are no doubt very important queſtions in the philoſophy of human nature.

Shall we, with the Biſhop of Cloyne, ſerve them with a *Quo warranto*, and have them

them tried at the bar of philoſophy, upon the ſtatute of the ideal ſyſtem? Indeed, in this trial they ſeem to have come off very pitifully. For although they had very able counſel, learned in the law, *viz.* Des Cartes, Malebranch, and Locke, who ſaid every thing they could for their clients; the Biſhop of Cloyne, believing them to be aiders and abetters of hereſy and ſchiſm, proſecuted them with great vigour, fully anſwered all that had been pleaded in their defence, and ſilenced their ableſt advocates; who ſeem for half a century paſt to decline the argument, and to truſt to the favour of the jury rather than to the ſtrength of their pleadings.

Thus, the wiſdom of *philoſophy* is ſet in oppoſition to the *common ſenſe* of mankind. The firſt pretends to demonſtrate *a priori*, that there can be no ſuch thing as a material world; that ſun, moon, ſtars, and earth, vegetable and animal bodies, are, and can be nothing elſe, but ſenſations in the mind, or images of thoſe ſenſations in the memory and imagination; that, like pain and joy, they can

T have

have no exiſtence when they are not thought of. The laſt can conceive no otherwiſe of this opinion, than as a kind of metaphyſical lunacy; and concludes, that too much learning is apt to make men mad; and that the man who ſeriouſly entertains this belief, though in other reſpects he may be a very good man, as a man may be who believes that he is made of glaſs; yet ſurely he hath a ſoft place in his underſtanding, and hath been hurt by much thinking.

This oppoſition betwixt philoſophy and common ſenſe, is apt to have a very unhappy influence upon the philoſopher himſelf. He ſees human nature in an odd, unamiable, and mortifying light. He conſiders himſelf, and the reſt of his ſpecies, as born under a neceſſity of believing ten thouſand abſurdities and contradictions, and endowed with ſuch a pittance of reaſon, as is juſt ſufficient to make this unhappy diſcovery: and this is all the fruit of his profound ſpeculations. Such notions of human nature tend to ſlacken every nerve of the ſoul, to put every

very noble purpoſe and ſentiment out of countenance, and ſpread a melancholy gloom over the whole face of things.

If this is wiſdom, let me be deluded with the vulgar. I find ſomething within me that recoils againſt it, and inſpires more reverent ſentiments of the human kind, and of the univerſal adminiſtration. Common ſenſe and reaſon have both one author; that Almighty author, in all whoſe other works we obſerve a conſiſtency, uniformity, and beauty, which charm and delight the underſtanding: there muſt therefore be ſome order and conſiſtency in the human faculties, as well as in other parts of his workmanſhip. A man that thinks reverently of his own kind, and eſteems true wiſdom and philoſophy, will not be fond, nay, will be very ſuſpicious, of ſuch ſtrange and paradoxical opinions. If they are falſe, they diſgrace philoſophy; and if they are true, they degrade the human ſpecies, and make us juſtly aſhamed of our frame.

To what purpoſe is it for philoſophy to decide againſt common ſenſe in this or a-

T 2 ny

ny other matter? The belief of a material world is older, and of more authority, than any principles of philoſophy. It declines the tribunal of reaſon, and laughs at all the artillery of the logician. It retains its ſovereign authority in ſpite of all the edicts of philoſophy, and reaſon itſelf muſt ſtoop to its orders. Even thoſe philoſophers who have diſowned the authority of our notions of an external material world, confeſs, that they find themſelves under a neceſſity of ſubmitting to their power.

Methinks, therefore, it were better to make a virtue of neceſſity; and, ſince we cannot get rid of the vulgar notion and belief of an external world, to reconcile our reaſon to it as well as we can: for if Reaſon ſhould ſtomach and fret ever ſo much at this yoke, ſhe cannot throw it off; if ſhe will not be the ſervant of Common Senſe, ſhe muſt be her ſlave.

In order therefore to reconcile reaſon to common ſenſe in this matter, I beg leave to offer to the conſideration of philoſophers theſe two obſervations. Firſt, That

That in all this debate about the exiſtence of a material world, it hath been taken for granted on both ſides, that this ſame material world, if any ſuch there be, muſt be the expreſs image of our ſenſations; that we can have no conception of any material thing which is not like ſome ſenſation in our minds; and particularly, that the ſenſations of touch are images of extenſion, hardneſs, figure, and motion. Every argument brought againſt the exiſtence of a material world, either by the Biſhop of Cloyne, or by the author of the *Treatiſe of human nature*, ſuppoſeth this. If this is true, their arguments are concluſive and unanſwerable: but, on the other hand, if it is not true, there is no ſhadow of argument left. Have thoſe philoſophers then given any ſolid proof of this hypotheſis, upon which the whole weight of ſo ſtrange a ſyſtem reſts? No. They have not ſo much as attempted to do it. But, becauſe ancient and modern philoſophers have agreed in this opinion, they have taken it for granted. But let us, as becomes philoſophers, lay aſide authority;

authority; we need not ſurely conſult Ariſtotle or Locke, to know whether pain be like the point of a ſword. I have as clear a conception of extenſion, hardneſs, and motion, as I have of the point of a ſword; and, with ſome pains and practice, I can form as clear a notion of the other ſenſations of touch, as I have of pain. When I do ſo, and compare them together, it appears to me clear as day-light, that the former are not of kin to the latter, nor reſemble them in any one feature. They are as unlike, yea as certainly and manifeſtly unlike, as pain is to the point of a ſword. It may be true, that thoſe ſenſations firſt introduced the material world to our acquaintance; it may be true, that it ſeldom or never appears without their company: but, for all that, they are as unlike as the paſſion of anger is to thoſe features of the countenance which attend it.

So that, in the ſentence thoſe philoſophers have paſſed againſt the material world, there is an *error perſonæ*. Their proof touches not matter, or any of its qualities;

qualities; but ſtrikes directly againſt an idol of their own imagination, a material world made of ideas and ſenſations, which never had nor can have an exiſtence.

Secondly, The very exiſtence of our conceptions of extenſion, figure, and motion, ſince they are neither ideas of ſenſation nor reflection, overturns the whole ideal ſyſtem, by which the material world hath been tried and condemned: ſo that there hath been likewiſe in this ſentence an *error juris.*

It is a very fine and a juſt obſervation of Locke, That as no human art can create a ſingle particle of matter, and the whole extent of our power over the material world, conſiſts in compounding, combining, and disjoining the matter made to our hands; ſo in the world of thought, the materials are all made by nature, and can only be variouſly combined and diſjoined by us. So that it is impoſſible for reaſon or prejudice, true or falſe philoſophy, to produce one ſimple notion or conception, which is not the work of nature, and the reſult of our conſtitution. The conception

conception of extenſion, motion, and the other attributes of matter, cannot be the effect of error or prejudice, it muſt be the work of nature. And the power or faculty by which we acquire thoſe conceptions, muſt be ſomething different from any power of the human mind that hath been explained, ſince it is neither ſenſation nor reflection.

This I would therefore humbly propoſe as an *experimentum crucis*, by which the ideal ſyſtem muſt ſtand or fall; and it brings the matter to a ſhort iſſue: Extenſion, figure, motion, may, any one, or all of them, be taken for the ſubject of this experiment. Either they are ideas of ſenſation, or they are not. If any one of them can be ſhown to be an idea of ſenſation, or to have the leaſt reſemblance to any ſenſation, I lay my hand upon my mouth, and give up all pretence to reconcile reaſon to common ſenſe in this matter, and muſt ſuffer the ideal ſcepticiſm to triumph. But if, on the other hand, they are not ideas of ſenſation, nor like to any ſenſation, then the ideal ſyſtem is

a

a rope of ſand, and all the laboured arguments of the ſceptical philoſophy againſt a material world, and againſt the exiſtence of every thing but impreſſions and ideas, proceed upon a falſe hypotheſis.

If our philoſophy concerning the mind be ſo lame with regard to the origin of the cleareſt, moſt ſimple, and moſt familiar objects of thought, and the powers from which they are derived, can we expect that it ſhould be more perfect in the account it gives of the origin of our opinions and belief? We have ſeen already ſome inſtances of its imperfection in this reſpect: and perhaps that ſame Nature which hath given us the power to conceive things altogether unlike to any of our ſenſations, or to any operation of our minds, hath likewiſe provided for our belief of them, by ſome part of our conſtitution hitherto not explained.

Biſhop Berkeley hath proved, beyond the poſſibility of reply, that we cannot by reaſoning infer the exiſtence of matter from our ſenſations: and the author of

U the

the *Treatiſe of human nature* hath proved no leſs clearly, that we cannot by reaſoning infer the exiſtence of our own or other minds from our ſenſations. But are we to admit nothing but what can be proved by reaſoning? Then we muſt be ſceptics indeed, and believe nothing at all. The author of the *Treatiſe of human nature* appears to me to be but a half-ſceptic. He hath not followed his principles ſo far as they lead him: but after having, with unparallelled intrepidity and ſucceſs, combated vulgar prejudices; when he had but one blow to ſtrike, his courage fails him, he fairly lays down his arms, and yields himſelf a captive to the moſt common of all vulgar prejudices, I mean the belief of the exiſtence of his own impreſſions and ideas.

I beg therefore to have the honour of making an addition to the ſceptical ſyſtem, without which I conceive it cannot hang together. I affirm, that the belief of the exiſtence of impreſſions and ideas, is as little ſupported by reaſon, as that of the exiſtence of minds and bodies. No man

man ever did, or could offer any reason for this belief. Des Cartes took it for granted, that he thought, and had sensations and ideas; so have all his followers done. Even the hero of scepticism hath yielded this point, I crave leave to say, weakly and imprudently. I say so, because I am persuaded that there is no principle of his philosophy that obliged him to make this concession. And what is there in impressions and ideas so formidable, that this all-conquering philosophy, after triumphing over every other existence, should pay homage to them? Besides, the concession is dangerous: for belief is of such a nature, that if you leave any root, it will spread; and you may more easily pull it up altogether, than say, Hitherto shalt thou go, and no further; the existence of impressions and ideas I give up to thee; but see thou pretend to nothing more. A thorough and consistent sceptic will never, therefore, yield this point; and while he holds it, you can never oblige him to yield any thing else.

U 2 To

To ſuch a ſceptic I have nothing to ſay; but of the ſemi-ſceptics, I ſhould beg to know, why they believe the exiſtence of their impreſſions and ideas. The true reaſon I take to be, becauſe they cannot help it; and the ſame reaſon will lead them to believe many other things.

All reaſoning muſt be from firſt principles; and for firſt principles no other reaſon can be given but this, that, by the conſtitution of our nature, we are under a neceſſity of aſſenting to them. Such principles are parts of our conſtitution, no leſs than the power of thinking: reaſon can neither make nor deſtroy them; nor can it do any thing without them: it is like a teleſcope, which may help a man to ſee farther, who hath eyes; but without eyes, a teleſcope ſhews nothing at all. A mathematician cannot prove the truth of his axioms, nor can he prove any thing, unleſs he takes them for granted. We cannot prove the exiſtence of our minds, nor even of our thoughts and ſenſations. A hiſtorian, or a witneſs, can prove nothing, unleſs it is

taken

taken for granted, that the memory and ſenſes may be truſted. A natural philoſopher can prove nothing, unleſs it is taken for granted, that the courſe of nature is ſteady and uniform.

How or when I got ſuch firſt principles, upon which I build all my reaſoning, I know not; for I had them before I can remember: but I am ſure they are parts of my conſtitution, and that I cannot throw them off. That our thoughts and ſenſations muſt have a ſubject, which we call *ourſelf*, is not therefore an opinion got by reaſoning, but a natural principle. That our ſenſations of touch indicate ſomething external, extended, figured, hard or ſoft, is not a deduction of reaſon, but a natural principle. The belief of it, and the very conception of it, are equally parts of our conſtitution. If we are deceived in it, we are deceived by him that made us, and there is no remedy.

I do not mean to affirm, that the ſenſations of touch do from the very firſt ſuggeſt the ſame notions of body and its qualities,

qualities, which they do when we are grown up. Perhaps Nature is frugal in this, as in her other operations. The paſſion of love, with all its concomitant ſentiments and deſires, is naturally ſuggeſted by the perception of beauty in the other ſex. Yet the ſame perception does not ſuggeſt the tender paſſion, till a certain period of life. A blow given to an infant, raiſes grief and lamentation; but when he grows up, it as naturally ſtirs reſentment, and prompts him to reſiſtance. Perhaps a child in the womb, or for ſome ſhort period of its exiſtence, is merely a ſentient being: the faculties, by which it perceives an external world, by which it reflects on its own thoughts, and exiſtence, and relation to other things, as well as its reaſoning and moral faculties, do poſſibly unfold themſelves by degrees; ſo that it is inſpired with the various principles of common ſenſe, as with the paſſions of love and reſentment, when it has occaſion for them.

SECT.

SECT. VIII.

Of the systems of philosophers concerning the senses.

ALL the systems of philosophers about our senses and their objects have split upon this rock, of not distinguishing properly sensations, which can have no existence but when they are felt, from the things suggested by them. Aristotle, with as distinguishing a head as ever applied to philosophical disquisitions, confounds these two; and makes every sensation to be the form, without the matter, of the thing perceived by it. As the impression of a seal upon wax has the form of the seal, but nothing of the matter of it; so he conceived our sensations to be impressions upon the mind, which bear the image, likeness, or form of the external thing perceived, without the matter of it. Colour, sound, and smell, as well as extension, figure, and hardness, are, according to him, various forms of matter: our sensations are the same forms imprinted on the mind, and

and perceived in its own intellect. It is evident from this, that Aristotle made no distinction between primary and secondary qualities of bodies, although that distinction was made by Democritus, Epicurus, and others of the ancients.

Des Cartes, Malebranch, and Locke, revived the distinction between primary and secondary qualities. But they made the secondary qualities mere sensations, and the primary ones resemblances of our sensations. They maintained, that colour, sound, and heat, are not any thing in bodies, but sensations of the mind: At the same time, they acknowledged some particular texture or modification of the body, to be the cause or occasion of those sensations; but to this modification they gave no name. Whereas, by the vulgar, the names of colour, heat, and sound, are but rarely applied to the sensations, and most commonly to those unknown causes of them; as hath been already explained. The constitution of our nature leads us rather to attend to the things signified by the sensation, than to the

the ſenſation itſelf, and to give a name to the former rather than to the latter. Thus we ſee, that with regard to ſecondary qualities, theſe philoſophers thought with the vulgar, and with common ſenſe. Their paradoxes were only an abuſe of words. For when they maintain as an important modern diſcovery, that there is no heat in the fire, they mean no more, than that the fire does not feel heat, which every one knew before.

With regard to primary qualities, theſe philoſophers erred more groſsly: they indeed believed the exiſtence of thoſe qualities; but they did not at all attend to the ſenſations that ſuggeſt them, which having no names, have been as little conſidered as if they had no exiſtence. They were aware, that figure, extenſion, and hardneſs, are perceived by means of ſenſations of touch; whence they raſhly concluded, that theſe ſenſations muſt be images and reſemblances of figure, extenſion, and hardneſs.

The received hypotheſis of ideas naturally led them to this concluſion: and in-

X deed

deed could not conſiſt with any other; for according to that hypotheſis, external things muſt be perceived by means of images of them in the mind; and what can thoſe images of external things in the mind be, but the ſenſations by which we perceive them?

This however was to draw a concluſion from a hypotheſis againſt fact. We need not have recourſe to any hypotheſis to know what our ſenſations are, or what they are like. By a proper degree of reflection and attention we may underſtand them perfectly, and be as certain that they are not like any quality of body, as we can be, that the toothach is not like a triangle. How a ſenſation ſhould inſtantly make us conceive and believe the exiſtence of an external thing altogether unlike to it, I do not pretend to know; and when I ſay that the one ſuggeſts the other, I mean not to explain the manner of their connection, but to expreſs a fact, which every one may be conſcious of; namely, that, by a law of our nature, ſuch a conception and belief conſtantly and immediately follow the ſenſation.

Biſhop

Bishop Berkeley gave new light to this subject, by showing, that the qualities of an inanimate thing, such as matter is conceived to be, cannot resemble any sensation; that it is impossible to conceive any thing like the sensations of our minds, but the sensations of other minds. Every one that attends properly to his sensations must assent to this; yet it had escaped all the philosophers that came before Berkeley: it had escaped even the ingenious Locke, who had so much practised reflection on the operations of his own mind. So difficult it is to attend properly even to our own feelings. They are so accustomed to pass through the mind unobserved, and instantly to make way for that which nature intended them to signify, that it is extremely difficult to stop, and survey them; and when we think we have acquired this power, perhaps the mind still fluctuates between the sensation and its associated quality, so that they mix together, and present something to the imagination that is compounded of both. Thus in a globe or cylinder, whose opposite sides are quite unlike in colour, if you turn it slowly, the colours are perfectly distinguishable, and their dissimilitude is manifest; but if it is turned fast, they lose their distinction, and seem to be of one and the same colour.

No succession can be more quick, than that of tangible qualities to the sensations with which nature has associated them: but when one has once acquired the art of making them separate and distinct objects of thought, he will then clearly perceive, that the maxim of Bishop Berkeley above mentioned, is self-evident; and that the features of the face are not more unlike to a passion of the mind which they indicate, than the sensations of touch are to the primary qualities of body.

But let us observe what use the Bishop makes of this important discovery: Why, he concludes, that we can have no conception of an inanimate substance, such as matter is conceived to be, or of any of its qualities; and that there is the strongest ground to believe that there is no existence in nature but minds, sensations,

tions, and ideas: if there is any other kind of exiſtences, it muſt be what we neither have nor can have any conception of. But how does this follow? Why thus: We can have no conception of any thing but what reſembles ſome ſenſation or idea in our minds; but the ſenſations and ideas in our minds can reſemble nothing but the ſenſations and ideas in other minds; therefore, the concluſion is evident. This argument, we ſee, leans upon two propoſitions. The laſt of them the ingenious author hath indeed made evident to all that underſtand his reaſoning, and can attend to their own ſenſations: but the firſt propoſition he never attempts to prove; it is taken from the doctrine of ideas, which hath been ſo univerſally received by philoſophers, that it was thought to need no proof.

We may here again obſerve, that this acute writer argues from a hypotheſis againſt fact, and againſt the common ſenſe of mankind. That we can have no conception of any thing, unleſs there is ſome impreſſion, ſenſation, or idea, in our

our minds which reſembles it, is indeed an opinion which hath been very generally received among philoſophers; but it is neither ſelf-evident, nor hath it been clearly proved: and therefore it had been more reaſonable to call in queſtion this doctrine of philoſophers, than to diſcard the material world, and by that means expoſe philoſophy to the ridicule of all men, who will not offer up common ſenſe as a ſacrifice to metaphyſics.

We ought, however, to do this juſtice both to the Biſhop of Cloyne and to the author of the *Treatiſe of human nature*, to acknowledge, that their concluſions are juſtly drawn from the doctrine of ideas, which has been ſo univerally received. On the other hand, from the character of Biſhop Berkeley, and of his predeceſſors Des Cartes, Locke, and Malebranch, we may venture to ſay, that if they had ſeen all the conſequences of this doctrine, as clearly as the author before mentioned did, they would have ſuſpected it vehemently, and examined it more carefully than they appear to have done.

The theory of ideas, like the Trojan herſe,

horſe, had a ſpecious appearance both of innocence and beauty; but if thoſe philoſophers had known that it carried in its belly death and deſtruction to all ſcience and common ſenſe, they would not have broken down their walls to give it admittance.

That we have clear and diſtinct conceptions of extenſion, figure, motion, and other attributes of body, which are neither ſenſations, nor like any ſenſation, is a fact of which we may be as certain, as that we have ſenſations. And that all mankind have a fixed belief of an external material world, a belief which is neither got by reaſoning nor education, and a belief which we cannot ſhake off, even when we ſeem to have ſtrong arguments againſt it, and no ſhadow of argument for it, is likewiſe a fact, for which we have all the evidence that the nature of the thing admits. Theſe facts are phenomena of human nature, from which we may juſtly argue againſt any hypotheſis, however generally received. But to argue from a hypotheſis againſt facts, is contrary to the rules of true philoſophy.

CHAP.

SECT. II.

Of the Non-existence of Matter.

IN the preceding ſection I have taken a ſlight ſurvey of the principles, and method of inveſtigation, adopted by the moſt celebrated promoters of modern ſcepticiſm. And it appears, that they have not attended to the diſtinction of reaſon and common ſenſe, as explained in the firſt part of this Eſſay, and as acknowledged by mathematicians and natural philoſophers. Erroneous, abſurd, and ſelf-contradictory notions, have been the conſequence. And now, by entering into a more particular detail, we might eaſily ſhow, that many of thoſe abſurdities that diſgrace the philoſophy of human nature, would never have exiſted, if men had acknowledged and attended to this diſtinction ; regulating their inquiries by the criterion above-mentioned, and never proſecuting any chain of argument beyond the ſelf-evident principles of common ſenſe. We ſhall confine ourſelves to two inſtances ; one of which is connected with the evidence of external ſenſe, and the other with that of internal.

That

That matter or body hath a real, ſeparate, independent exiſtence *; that there is a real ſun above us, a real air around us, and a real earth under our feet,—has been the univerſal belief of all men who were not mad, ever ſince the creation. This is believed, not becauſe it is or can be proved by argument, but becauſe the conſtitution of our nature is ſuch that we muſt believe it. There is here the ſame ground of belief, that there is in the following propoſitions: I exiſt; whetever is, is; two and two make four. It is abſurd, nay, it is impoſſible, to believe the contrary. I could as eaſily believe, that I do not exiſt; that two and two are equal to three, that whatever is, is not; as believe, that I have neither hands, nor feet, nor head, nor cloaths, nor houſe, nor country, nor acquaintance; that the ſun, moon, and ſtars, and ocean, and tempeſt, thunder, and lightning, mountains, rivers, and cities, have no exiſtence but as ideas or thoughts in my mind, and independent on me and my faculties, do not exiſt at all, and could not poſſibly exiſt if I were to be annihilated; that fire, and burning, and pain, which I feel, and the recollection of pain that is paſt, and the idea of pain which I never felt, are all in the ſame ſenſe ideas or perceptions in my mind, and nothing elſe; that the qualities of matter are not qualities of matter, but affections of ſpirit; and that I have no evidence that any being exiſts in nature but myſelf. Philoſophers may ſay what they pleaſe; and the world, who are apt enough to admire what is monſtrous, may give

* By *independent exiſtence,* we mean an exiſtence that does not depend on us, nor, ſo far as we know, on any being, except the Creator. BERKELEY, and others, ſay, that matter exiſts not but in the minds that perceive it; and conſequently depends, in reſpect of its exiſtence, upon thoſe minds.

give them credit; but I affirm, that it is not in the power, either of wit or madnefs, to contrive any conceit more inconfiftent, more abfurd, or more nonfenfical, than this, That the material world hath no exiftence but in my mind.

Des Cartes acknowledges, that every perfon muft be perfuaded of the exiftence of a material world: but he does not allow this point to be felf-evident, or fo certain as not to admit of doubt; becaufe, fays he, we find in experience, that our fenfes are fometimes in an error, and becaufe in dreams we often miftake ideas for external things really exifting. He therefore begins his philofophy of bodies with a formal proof of the exiftence of body *.

But however imperfect, and however fallacious, we acknowledge our fenfes to be in other matters, it is certain, that no man ever thought them fallacious in regard to the exiftence of body; nay, every man of a found mind, is, by the law of his nature, convinced, that, in this refpect at leaft, they are not, and cannot be miftaken. Men have fometimes been deceived by fophiftical argument, becaufe the human underftanding is in fome, and indeed in many, refpects fallible; but does it follow, that we cannot, without proof, be certain of any thing, not even of our own exiftence, nor of the truth of a geometrical axiom? Some difeafes are fo fatal to the mind, as to confound men's notions even of their own identity; but does it follow, that I cannot be certain of my being the fame perfon to-day I was yefterday, and twenty years ago, till I have firft proved this point by argument? And becaufe we are fometimes deceived by our fenfes, does it therefore follow, that we never are certain of our not

* Cartefii Principia, part 1, § 4. part 2. § 1.

not being deceived by them, till we have firſt convinced ourſelves by reaſoning that they are not deceitful?—If a Carteſian can prove, that there have been a few perſons of ſound underſtanding, who, from a conviction of the deceitfulneſs of their ſenſes, have really diſbelieved, or ſeriouſly doubted, the exiſtence of a material world, I ſhall allow a conviction of this deceitfulneſs to be a ſufficient ground for ſuch doubt or diſbelief, in one or a few inſtances; and if he can prove, that ſuch doubt or diſbelief, hath at any time been general among mankind, I ſhall allow that it may poſſibly be ſo again: but if it be certain, as I think it is, that no man of a ſound mind, however ſuſpicious of the veracity of his ſenſes, ever did or could really diſbelieve or ſeriouſly doubt, the exiſtence of a material world, then is this point ſelf-evident, and a principle of common ſenſe, even on the ſuppoſition that our ſenſes are as deceitful as DES CARTES and MALEBRANCHE chuſe to repreſent them. But we have formerly proved, that our ſenſes are never ſuppoſed to be deceitful, except when we are conſcious, that our experience is partial, or our obſervation inaccurate; and that, even then, the fallacy is detected, and rectified, only by the evidence of ſenſe placed in circumſtances more favourable to accurate obſervation. In regard to the exiſtence of matter, there cannot poſſibly be a ſuſpicion, that our obſervation is inaccurate, or our experience partial; and therefore it is not poſſible, that ever we ſhould diſtruſt our ſenſes in this particular. If it were poſſible, our diſtruſt could never be removed either by reaſoning or by experience.

As to the ſuſpicion againſt the exiſtence of matter that is ſuppoſed to ariſe from our experience of the delusions

delusions of dreaming, we observe, in the first place, that if this be allowed a sufficient ground for suspecting, that our waking perceptions are equally delusive, there is at once an end of all truth, reasoning, and common sense. That I am at present awake, and not asleep, I certainly know; but I cannot prove it: for there is no criterion for distinguishing dreaming fancies from waking perceptions, more evident, than that I am now awake, which is the point in question; and, as we have often remarked, it is essential to every proof, to be more evident than that which is to be proved. That I am now awake, must therefore carry its own evidence along with it; if it be evident at all, it must be self-evident. And so it is: we may mistake dreams for realities, but no rational being ever mistook a reality for a dream. Had we the command of our understanding and memory in sleep, we should probably be sensible, that the appearances of our dreams are all delusive: which in fact is sometimes the case; at least I have sometimes been conscious, that my dream was a dream; and when it was disagreeable, have actually made efforts to awake myself, which have succeeded. But sleep has a wonderful power over all our faculties. Sometimes we seem to have entirely lost our moral faculty; as when we dream of committing, without scruple or remorse, what we could hardly think of when awake without horror. Sometimes memory is extinguished; as when we dream of conversing with our departed friends, without remembering any thing of their death, tho' it was perhaps one of the most striking incidents we had ever experienced, and is seldom or never out of our thoughts when we are awake. Sometimes our understanding seems to have quite forsaken us; as when we dream of talking with a dead friend, remembering at the same time that he is dead, but

but without being conſcious of any thing abſurd or unuſual in the circumſtance of converſing with a dead man. Conſidering theſe and the other effects of ſleep upon the mind, we need not be ſurpriſed, that it ſhould cauſe us to miſtake our own ideas for real things, and be affected with thoſe in the ſame manner as with theſe.——But the moment we awake, and recover the uſe of our faculties, we become ſenſible, that the dream was a deluſion, and that the objects which now ſolicit our notice are real. To demand a reaſon for the implicit confidence we repoſe in our waking perceptions; or to deſire us to prove, that things are as they appear to our waking ſenſes, and not as they appear to us in ſleep, is as unreaſonable as to demand a reaſon for our belief in our own exiſtence: in both caſes our belief is neceſſary and unavoidable, the reſult of a law of nature, and what we cannot in practice contradict, but to our ſhame and perdition.

If the deluſions of dreaming furniſh any reaſonable pretence for doubting the authenticity of our waking perceptions, they may, with equal reaſon, make me doubtful of my own identity: for I have often dreamed that I was a perſon different from what I am; nay, that I was two or more diſtinct perſons at one and the ſame time.

Further: If DES CARTES thought an argument neceſſary to convince him, that his perception of the external world was not imaginary, but real, I would aſk, how he could know that his argument was real, and not imaginary. How could he know that he was awake, and not aſleep, when he wrote his Principles of Philoſophy, if his waking thoughts did not, previous to all reaſoning, carry along with them undeniable evidence of their reality? *I am awake*, is a principle which

which he must have taken for granted, even before he could satisfy himself of the truth of what he thought the first of all principles, *Cogito, ergo sum.*—To all which we may add, that if there be any persons in the world who never dream at all, * (and some such I think there are,) and whose belief in the existence of a material world is not a whit stronger than that of those whose sleep is always attended with dreaming; this is a proof from experience, that the delusions of sleep do not in the least affect our conviction of the authenticity of the perceptions we receive, and the faculties we exert, when awake.

The first part of DES CARTES' argument for the existence of bodies, would prove the reality of the visionary ideas we perceive in dreams; for they, as well as bodies, present themselves to us, independent on our will. But the principal part of his argument is founded in the veracity of God, which he had before inferred from our consciousness of the idea of an infinitely perfect, independent, and necessarily-existent being. Our senses inform us of the existence of body; they give us this information in consequence of a law established by the divine will: but God is no deceiver; therefore is their information true. I have formerly given

* "I once knew a man," says Mr. LOCKE, "who was bred "a scholar, and had no bad memory, who told me, that he had "never dreamed in his life, till he had that fever he was then newly recovered of, which was about the five or six and twentieth "year of his age. I suppose the world affords more such in"stances."

Essay on Human Understanding, book 2. ch. 1.

A young gentleman of my acquaintance told me, a few days ago, that he never dreams at all, except when his health is disordered.

given my opinion of this argument, and ſhown that it is a ſophiſm, as the author ſtates it. We muſt believe our faculties to be true, before we can be convinced, either by proof, or by intuitive evidence. If we refuſe to believe in our faculties, till their veracity be firſt aſcertained by reaſoning, we ſhall never believe in them at all. *

MALEBRANCHE || ſays, that men are more certain of the exiſtence of God, than of the exiſtence of body. He allows, that DES CARTES hath proved the exiſtence of body, by the ſtrongeſt arguments that reaſon alone could furniſh; nay, he ſeems to acknowledge thoſe arguments to be in every reſpect unexceptionable: ‡ yet he does not admit, that they amount to a full demonſtration of the exiſtence of matter. In philoſophy, ſays he, we ought to maintain our liberty as long as we can, and to believe nothing whatſoever, but

* See the preceding ſection.

|| Recherche de la Verité, tom. 3. p. 30. A Paris, chez Pralard, 1679.

‡ Mais quoque M. DES CARTES ait donné les preuves le plus fortes que la raiſon toute ſeule puiſſe fournir pour l'exiſtence des corps; quoiqu' il ſoit evident, que Dieu n'eſt point trompeur, et qu'on puiſſe dire qu'il nous tromperoit effectivement, ſi nous nous trompions nous-mêmes en faiſant l'uſage que nous devons faire de nôtre eſprit et des autres facultez dont il eſt l'auteur; cependant on peut dire que l'exiſtence de la matiere n'eſt point encore parfaitement demontrée. Car, enfin, en matiere de philoſophie, nous ne devons croire quoique ce ſoit, *que lorſque l'evidence nous y oblige.* Nous devons faire uſage de nôtre liberté autant que nous le pouvons.——Pour être pleinement convaincus qu'il y a des corps, il faut qu'on nous demontre, non ſeulement qu'il y a un Dieu, et que Dieu n'eſt point trompeur, mais encore que Dieu nous a aſſuré qu'il en a effectivement crée: ce que je ne trouve point prouvé dans les ouvrages de M. DES CARTES.

Tom. 3, *p.* 37, 38, 39.

but when evidence compels us to believe. To be fully convinced of the exiſtence of bodies, it is neceſſary that we have it demonſtrated to us, not only that there is a God, and that God is no deceiver, but alſo that God hath aſſured us, that he hath actually created ſuch bodies; and this, ſays he, I do not find proved in the works of M. DES CARTES.

There are, according to MALEBRANCHE, but two ways in which God ſpeaks to the mind, and compels (or obliges) it to believe; to wit, by evidence, and by the faith. "The faith obliges us to believe that bo-" dies exiſt; but as to the evidence of this truth, it "certainly is not complete; and it is alſo certain, "that we are not invincibly determined to believe, "that any thing exiſts, but God, and our own mind. "It is true, that we have an extreme propenſity to be-" lieve that we are ſurrounded with corporeal beings; "ſo far I agree with M. DES CARTES: but this pro-" penſity, natural as it is, doth not force our belief "by evidence; it only inclines us to believe by im-" preſſion. Now we ought not to be determined, in "our free judgments, by any thing but light and evi-" dence; if we ſuffer ourſelves to be guided by the "ſenſible impreſſion, we ſhall be almoſt always "miſtaken." †——Our author then propoſes, in brief, the

† Dieu en parle à l'eſprit, et ne l'oblige à croire qu'en deux manieres; par l'evidence, et par la foi. Je demeure d'accord, que *la foi oblige à croire* qu'il y a des corps: mais pour l'evidence, il eſt certain, qu'elle n'eſt point entiére, et que nous ne ſommes point invinciblement portez à croire qu'il y ait quelqu' autre choſe que Dieu et nôtre eſprit. Il eſt vray, que nous avons un penchant extrême à croire qu'il y a des corps qui nous environnent. Je l'accorde à M. DES CARTES: mais ce penchant, tout naturel qu'il eſt, *ne nous y force* point par evidence; il nous y incline ſeulement

the ſubſtance of that argument againſt the exiſtence of body, which BERKELEY afterwards took ſuch pains to illuſtrate; and diſcovers, upon the whole, that, as a point of philoſophy, the exiſtence of matter is but a probability, to which we have it in our power either to aſſent, or not to aſſent, as we pleaſe. In a word, it is by the faith, and not by evidence, that we become certain of this truth.

This is not a proper place for analyſing the paſſage above quoted, otherwiſe it would be eaſy to ſhow, that the doctrine (ſuch as it is) which the author here delivers, is not perfectly reconcileable with other parts of his ſyſtem. But I only mean to obſerve, that what is here aſſerted, of our belief in the exiſtence of body being not neceſſary, but ſuch as we may with-hold if we pleaſe, is contrary to my experience. That my body, and this pen and paper, and the other corporeal objects around me, do really exiſt, is to me as evident, as that my ſoul exiſts; it is indeed ſo evident, that nothing is or can be more ſo; and though my life depended upon the conſequence, I could not, by any effort, bring myſelf to entertain a doubt of it, even for a ſingle moment.

I muſt therefore affirm, that the exiſtence of matter can no more be diſproved by argument, than the exiſtence of myſelf, or than the truth of a ſelf-evident axiom in geometry. To argue againſt it, is to ſet

K reaſon

ſeulement par impreſſion. Or nous ne devons ſuivre dans nos jugemens libres que la lumiere et l'evidence; et ſi nous nous laiſſons conduire à l'impreſſion ſenſible, nous nous tromperons preſque toujours. *Tom.* 3. *p.* 39.—*La foi* I tranſlate *The faith*, becauſe I ſuppoſe the author to mean the *Chriſtian* or *Catholic faith*. If we take it to denote *faith* or *belief in general*, I know not how we ſhall make ſenſe of the paſſage.

reaſon in oppoſition to common ſenſe; which is indirectly to ſubvert the foundation of all juſt reaſoning, and to call in queſtion the diſtinction between truth and falſhood. I am told, however, that a great philoſopher hath actually demonſtrated, that matter does not exiſt. Demonſtrated! truly this is a piece of ſtrange information. At this rate any falſhood may be proved to be true, and any truth to be falſe. For it is abſolutely impoſſible, that any truth ſhould be more evident to me than this, that matter does exiſt. Let us ſee, however, what BERKELEY has to ſay in behalf of this extraordinary doctrine. It is natural for demonſtration, and for all ſound reaſoning, to produce conviction, or at leaſt ſome degree of aſſent, in the perſon who attends to it, and underſtands it. I read *The Principles of Human Knowledge*, together with *The Dialogues between Hylas and Philonous*. The arguments, I acknowledge, are ſubtle, and well adapted to the purpoſe of puzzling and confounding. Perhaps I will not undertake to confute them. Perhaps I am buſy, or indolent, or unacquainted with the principles of this philoſophy, or little verſed in your metaphyſical logic. But am I convinced, from this pretended demonſtration, that matter hath no exiſtence but as an idea in the mind? Not in the leaſt; my belief now is preciſely the ſame as before.——Is it unphiloſophical not to be convinced by arguments which I cannot confute? Perhaps it may, but I cannot help it: you may, if you pleaſe, ſtrike me off the liſt of philoſophers, as a non-conformiſt; you may call me unpliant, unreaſonable, unfaſhionable, and a man with whom it is not worth while to argue; but till the frame of my nature be unhinged, and a new ſet of faculties given me, I cannot believe this ſtrange doctrine, becauſe it is perfectly incredible. But if I were

were permitted to propoſe one clowniſh queſtion, I would fain aſk, Where is the harm of my continuing in my old opinion, and believing, with the reſt of the world, that I am not the only created being in the univerſe, but that there are a great many others, whoſe exiſtence is as independent on me as mine is on them? Where is the harm of my believing, that if I were to fall down yonder precipice, and break my neck, I ſhould be no more a man of this world? My neck, Sir, may be an idea to you, but to me it is a reality, and an important one too. Where is the harm of my believing, that if, in this ſevere weather, I were to neglect to throw (what you call) the idea of a coat over the ideas of my ſhoulders, the idea of cold would produce the idea of ſuch pain and diſorder as might poſſibly terminate in my real death? What great offence ſhall I commit againſt God or man, church or ſtate, philoſophy or common ſenſe, if I continue to believe, that material food will nouriſh me, though the idea of it will not; that the real ſun will warm and enlighten me, though the livelieſt idea of him will do neither; and that, if I would obtain true peace of mind and ſelf-approbation, I muſt not only form ideas of compaſſion, juſtice, and generoſity, but alſo really exert thoſe virtues in external performance? What harm is there in all this?—O! no harm at all, Sir;—but the truth, the truth,—will you ſhut your eyes againſt the truth?—No honeſt man ever will: convince me that your doctrine is true, and I will inſtantly embrace it.—Have I not convinced thee, thou obſtinate, unaccountable, inexorable——? Anſwer my arguments, if thou canſt.—Alas, Sir, you have given me arguments in abundance, but you have not given me conviction; and if your arguments produce no conviction, they are worth nothing to me. They are like counterfeit bank-bills; ſome of which are ſo dextrouſly forged, that neither your eye nor mine can detect them; but yet a thouſand of them would go for nothing at the bank; and even the paper-maker would allow me more handſomely for a parcel of old rags. You need not give yourſelf the trouble to tell me, that I ought to be convinced: I ought to be convinced only when I feel conviction; when I feel no conviction, I ought not to be convinced. It has been obſerved of ſome doctrines and reaſonings, that their extreme abſurdity prevents their admitting a rational confutation. What! am I to believe ſuch doctrine? am I to be convinced by ſuch reaſoning? Now, I never heard of any doctrine more ſcandalouſly abſurd, than this of the non-exiſtence of matter. There is not a fiction in the Perſian tales that I could not as eaſily believe; the ſillieſt conceit of the moſt contemptible ſuperſtition that ever diſgraced human nature, is not more ſhocking to common ſenſe, is not more repugnant to every principle of human belief. And muſt I admit this jargon for truth, becauſe I cannot confute the arguments of a man who is a more ſubtle diſputant than I? Does philoſophy require this of me? Then it muſt ſuppoſe, that truth is as variable as the fancies, the characters, and the intellectual abilities of men, and that there is no ſuch thing in nature as common ſenſe.

But all this, I ſhall perhaps be told, is but childiſh cavil, and unphiloſophical declamation. What if, after all, this very doctrine be believed, and the ſophiſtry (as you call it) of BERKELEY be admitted as ſound reaſoning, and legitimate proof? What then becomes of your common ſenſe, and your inſtinctive convictions?—What then do you aſk? Then indeed I acknowledge the fact to be very extraordinary; and

I cannot

I cannot help being in ſome pain about the conſequences, which muſt be important and fatal. If a man, out of vanity, or from a deſire of being in the faſhion, or in order to paſs for wonderfully wiſe, ſhall ſay, that BERKELEY's doctrine is true, while at the ſame time his belief is perciſely the ſame with mine, it is well; I leave him to enjoy the fruits of his hypocriſy, which will no doubt contribute mightily to his improvement in candour, happineſs, and wiſdom. If a man profeſſing this doctrine act like other men in the common affairs of life, I will not believe his profeſſion to be ſincere. For this doctrine, by removing body out of the univerſe, makes a total change in the circumſtances of men; and therefore, if it is not merely verbal, muſt produce a total change in their conduct. When a man is only turned out of his houſe, or ſtripped of his cloaths, or robbed of his money, he muſt change his behaviour, and act differently from other men, who enjoy thoſe advantages. Perſuade a man that he is a beggar and a vagabond, and you ſhall inſtantly ſee him change his manners. If your arguments againſt the exiſtence of matter have ever carried conviction along with them, they muſt at the ſame time have produced a much more extraordinary change of conduct; if they have produced no change of conduct, I inſiſt on it, they have never carried conviction along with them, whatever vehemence of proteſtation men may have uſed in avowing ſuch conviction. If you ſay, that, though a man's underſtanding be convinced, there are certain inſtincts in his nature which will not permit him to alter his conduct; or, if he did, the reſt of the world would account him a mad-man; by the firſt apology, you acknowledge the belief of the non-exiſtence of body to be inconſiſtent with the laws of nature; by the fecond, to be inconfiftent with common fenfe.

But if a man be convinced, that matter hath no exiftence, and believe this ftrange tenet as fteadily, and with as little diftruft, as I believe the contrary; he will, I am afraid, have but little reafon to applaud himfelf on this new acquifition in fcience; he will foon find, it had been better for him to have reafoned, and believed, and acted, like the reft of the world. If he fall down a precipice, or be trampled under foot by horfes, it will avail him little, that he once had the honour to be a difciple of BERKELEY, and to believe that thofe dangerous objects are nothing but the ideas in the mind. And yet, if fuch a man be feen to avoid a precipice, or to get out of the way of a coach and fix horfes at full fpeed, he acts as inconfiftently with his belief, as if he ran away from the picture of an angry man, even while he believed it to be a picture. Suppofing his life preferved by the care of friends, or by the ftrength of natural inftinct urging him to act contrary to his belief;. yet will this belief coft him dear. For if the plaineft evidence, and fulleft conviction, be certainly fallacious, I beg to be informed, what kind of evidence, and what degree of conviction, may reafonably be depended on. If Nature be a juggler by trade, is it for us, poor purblind reptiles, to attempt to penetrate the myfteries of her art, and take upon us to decide, when it is fhe prefents a true, and when a falfe appearance! I will not fay, however, that this man runs a greater rifk of univerfal fcepticifm, than of univerfal credulity. Either the one or the other, or both, muft be his portion; and either the one or the other would be fufficient to imbitter my whole life, and to difqualify me for every duty of a rational creature. He who can believe againft common fenfe, againft the cleareft cleareſt evidence, againſt the fulleſt conviction, in any one caſe, may do the ſame in any other; conſequently he may become the dupe of every wrangler who is more acute than he; and then, if he is not entirely ſecluded from mankind, his liberty, virtue, and happineſs, are gone for ever. Indeed a chearful temper, ſtrong habits of virtue, and the company of the wiſe and good, may ſtill ſave him from perdition, if he have no temptations nor difficulties to encounter. But it is the end of every uſeful art to teach us to ſurmount difficulties, not to diſqualify us for attempting them. Men have been known to live many years in a warm chamber, after they were become too delicate to bear the open air; but who will ſay, that ſuch a habit of body is deſirable? what phyſician will recommend to the healthy ſuch a regimen as would produce it?

But that I may no longer ſuppoſe, what I maintain to be impoſſible, that mankind in general, or even one rational being, could, by force of argument, be convinced, that this abſurd doctrine is true;—what if all men were in one inſtant deprived of their underſtanding by almighty power, and made to believe, that matter hath no exiſtence but as an idea in the mind, all other earthly things remaining as they are? Doubtleſs this cataſtrophe would, according to our metaphyſicians, throw a wonderful light on all the parts of knowledge. I pretend not even to gueſs at the number, extent, or quality, of aſtoniſhing diſcoveries that would then ſtart forth into view. But of this I am certain, that in leſs than a month after, there could not, without another miracle, be one human creature alive on the face of the earth.

Berkeley foreſaw, and has done what he could to obviate, ſome of theſe objections. There are two points which he has taken great pains to prove. The firſt is, That his ſyſtem differs not from the belief of

K 4 the

the reſt of mankind; the ſecond, That our conduct cannot be in the leaſt affected by our diſbelief of the exiſtence of a material world.

1. As to the firſt, it is certainly falſe. Mr. HUME himſelf ſeems willing to give it up. I have known many who could not anſwer BERKELEY's arguments; I never knew one who believed his doctrine. I have mentioned it to ſome who were unacquainted with philoſophy, and therefore could not be ſuppoſed to have any bias in favour of either ſyſtem; they all treated it as moſt contemptible jargon, and what no man in his ſenſes ever did or could believe. I have carefully attended to the effects produced by it upon my own mind; it appears to me at this moment, as when I firſt heard it, incredible and incomprehenſible. I ſay incomprehenſible: for though, by reading it over and over, I have got a ſet of phraſes and arguments by heart, which would enable me, if I were ſo diſpoſed, to talk, and argue, and write, "about it and about it;" yet, when I lay ſyſtems and ſyllogiſms aſide, when I enter on any part of the buſineſs of life, or when I refer the matter to the unbiaſſed deciſion of my own mind. I plainly ſee, that I had no diſtinct meaning to my words when I ſaid, that the material world hath no exiſtence but in the mind that perceives it. In a word, if this author had aſſerted, that I and all mankind acknowledge and believe the *Arabian Nights Entertainment* to be a true hiſtory, I could not have had any better reaſon for contradicting that aſſertion, than I have for contradicting this, "That BERKELEY's "principles, in regard to the exiſtence of matter, "differ not from the belief of the reſt of man-"kind."

2. In behalf of the ſecond point he argues, "That "nothing gives us an intereſt in the material world, except

" except the feelings pleaſant or painful which accom-" pany our perceptions; that theſe perceptions are the " ſame, whether we believe the material world to exiſt " or not to exiſt; conſequently that our pleaſant or " painful feelings are alſo the ſame; and therefore " that our conduct, which depends on our feelings and " perceptions, muſt be the ſame, whether we believe " or diſbelieve the exiſtence of matter."

But if it be certain, that by the law of our nature we are unavoidably determined to believe that matter exiſts, and to act upon this belief, (and nothing, I think, is more certain,) how can it be imagined, that a contrary belief would produce no alteration in our conduct and ſentiments? Surely the laws of nature are not ſuch trifles, as that it ſhould be a matter of perfect indifference, whether we act and think agreeably to them or not? I believe that matter exiſts;—I muſt believe that matter exiſts;—I muſt continually act upon this belief; ſuch is the law of my conſtitution. Suppoſe my conſtitution changed in this reſpect, all other things remaining as they are;—would there then be no change in my ſentiments and conduct? If there would not, then is this law of nature, in the firſt place, uſeleſs, becauſe men could do as well without it; ſecondly, inconvenient, becauſe its end is to keep us ignorant of the truth; and, thirdly, abſurd, becauſe inſufficient for anſwering its end, the Biſhop of Cloyne, and others, having, it ſeems, diſcovered the truth in ſpite of it. Is this according to the uſual œconomy of Nature? Does this language become her ſervants and interpreters? Is it poſſible to deviſe any ſentiments or maxims more ſubverſive of truth, and more repugnant to the ſpirit of true philoſophy?

Further: All external objects have ſome qualities in common; but between an external object and an idea,

K 5 or

or thought of the mind, there is not, there cannot poſſibly be, any reſemblance. A grain of ſand, and the globe of the earth; a burning coal, and a lump of ice; a drop of ink, and a ſheet of white paper, reſemble each other, in being extended, ſolid, figured, coloured, and diviſible; but a thought or idea hath no extenſion, ſolidity, figure, colour, nor diviſibility: ſo that no two external objects can be ſo unlike, as an external object and (what philoſopers call) the idea of it. Now we are taught by BERKELEY, that external objects (that is, the things we take for external objects) are nothing but ideas in our minds; in other words, that they are in every reſpect different from what they appear to be. This candle, it ſeems hath not one of thoſe qualities it appears to have: it is not white, nor luminous, nor round, nor diviſible, nor extended; for to an idea of the mind, not one of thoſe qualities can poſſibly belong. How then ſhall I know what it really is? From what it ſeems to be, I can conclude nothing, no more than a blind man, by handling a bit of black wax, can judge of the colour of ſnow, or the viſible appearance of the ſtarry heavens. The candle may be a lump of ice, an Egyptian pyramid, a mad dog, or nothing at all: it may be the iſland of Madagaſcar, Saturn's ring, or one of the Pleiades, for any thing I know, or can ever know to the contrary, except you allow me to judge of its nature from its appearance; which, however, I cannot reaſonably do, if its appearance and nature are in every reſpect ſo different and unlike as not to have one ſingle quality in common. I muſt therefore believe it to be, what it appears to be, a real, corporeal, external object, and ſo reject BERKELEY's ſyſtem; or I never can, with any ſhadow of reaſon, believe any thing whatſover concerning it. Will it yet be ſaid, that the belief of this ſyſtem cannot

in

in the leaſt affect our ſentiments and conduct? With equal truth may it be ſaid, that Newton's conduct and ſentiments would not have been in the leaſt affected by his being metamorphoſed into an ideot, or a pillar of ſalt.

Some readers may perhaps be diſſatisfied with this reaſoning, on account of the ambiguity of the words *external object* and *idea*; which, however, the aſſertors of the non-exiſtence of matter, have not as yet fully explained. Others may think that I muſt have miſunderſtood the author; for that he was too acute a logician to leave his ſyſtem expoſed to objections ſo deciſive, and ſo obvious. To gratify ſuch readers, I will not inſiſt on theſe objections. That I may have miſunderſtood the author's doctrine, is not only poſſible, but highly probable; nay, I have reaſon to think, that it was not perfectly underſtood even by himſelf. For did not BERKELEY write his *Principles of human Knowledge*, with this expreſs view, (which does him great honour,) to baniſh ſcepticiſm both from ſcience and from religion? Was he not ſanguine in his expectations of ſucceſs? Hath not the event proved, that he was egregiouſly miſtaken? For is it not evident, from the uſe to which later authors have applied it, that his ſyſtem leads directly to atheiſm and univerſal ſcepticiſm? And if a machine diſappoint its inventor ſo far as to produce effects contrary to thoſe he wiſhed, intended, and expected; may we not, without breach of charity, conclude, that he did not perfectly underſtand his plan? At any rate, it appears from this fact, that our author did not foreſee all the objections to which his theory is liable. He did not foreſee, that it might be made the foundation of a ſceptical ſyſtem; if he had, we know he would have renounced it with abhorrence.

This

This one objection therefore, (in which I think I cannot be miſtaken,) will fully anſwer my preſent purpoſe: Our author's doctrine is contrary to common belief, and leads to univerſal ſcepticiſm. Suppoſe it, then, univerſally and ſeriouſly adopted; ſuppoſe all men diveſted of all belief, and conſequently of all principle; would not the diſſolution of ſociety, and the deſtruction of mankind, neceſſarily enſue?

Still I ſhall be told, that BERKELEY was a good man, and that his principles did him no hurt. I allow it; he was indeed a moſt excellent perſon; none can revere his memory more than I. But does it appear, that he ever acted according to his principles, or that he thoroughly underſtood them? Does it appear, that, if he had put them in practice, no hurt would have enſued to himſelf, * or to ſociety? Does it appear, that he was a ſceptic, or a friend to ſcepticiſm? Does it appear, that men may adopt his principles without danger of becoming ſceptics? The contrary of all this appears with uncontrovertible evidence.

Surely,

* Let it not be pretended, that a man may diſbelieve his ſenſes without danger of inconvenience. Pyrrho (as we read in Diogenes Laertius) profeſſed to diſbelieve his ſenſes, and to be in no apprehenſion from any of the objects that affected them. The appearance of a precipice or wild beaſt was nothing to Pyrrho; at leaſt he ſaid ſo: he would not avoid them; he knew they were nothing at all, or at leaſt that they were not what they ſeemed to be. Suppoſe him to have been in earneſt; and ſuppoſe his keepers to have in earneſt adopted the ſame principles; would not their limbs and lives have been in as great danger, as the limbs and life of a blind and deaf man wandering by himſelf in a ſolitary place, with his hands tied behind his back? I would as ſoon ſay, that our ſenſes are uſeleſs faculties, as that we might diſbelieve them without danger of inconvenience.

Surely pride was not made for man. The moſt exalted genius may find in himſelf many affecting memorials of human frailty, and ſuch as often render him an object of compaſſion to thoſe who in virtue and underſtanding are far inferior. I pity BERKELEY's weakneſs in patroniſing an abſurd and dangerous theory; I doubt not but it hath overcaſt many of his days with a gloom, which neither the approbation of his conſcience, nor the natural ſerenity of his temper, could entirely diſſipate. And though I were to believe, that he was intoxicated with this theory, and rejoiced in it; yet ſtill I ſhould pity the intoxication as a weakneſs: for candour will not permit me to give it a harſher name; as I ſee in his other writings, and know by the teſtimony of his contemporaries, particularly Pope and Swift, that he was a friend to virtue, and to human nature.

We muſt not ſuppoſe a falſe doctrine harmleſs, merely becauſe it hath not been able to corrupt the heart of a good man. Nor, becauſe a few ſceptics have not authority to render ſcience contemptible, nor power to overturn ſociety, muſt we ſuppoſe, that therefore ſcepticiſm is not dangerous to ſcience or mankind. The effects of a general ſcepticiſm would be dreadful and fatal. We muſt therefore, notwithſtanding our reverence for the character of BERKELEY, be permitted to affirm, what we have ſufficiently proved, that his doctrine is ſubverſive of man's moſt important intereſts, as a moral, intelligent, and percipient being.

After all, though I were to grant, that the diſbelief of the exiſtence of matter could not produce any conſiderable change in our principles of action, and reaſoning, the reader will find in the ſequel,

quel, * that the point I have chiefly in view would not be much affected even by that conceſſion. I ſay not this, as being diffident or ſceptical in regard to what I have advanced on the preſent ſubject. Doctrines, which I do not believe, I will never recommend to others. I am abſolutely certain, that to me the belief of BERKELEY's ſyſtem would be attended with the moſt fatal conſequences; and that it would be equally dangerous to the reſt of mankind, I cannot doubt, ſo long as I believe their nature and mine to be the ſame.

Though it be abſurd to attempt a proof of what is ſelf-evident, it is manly and meritorious to confute the objections that ſophiſtry may urge againſt it. This, with reſpect to the ſubject in queſtion, hath been done, in a deciſive and maſterly manner, by the learned and ſagacious Dr. Reid; † who proves, that the reaſonings of BERKELEY, and others, concerning primary and ſecondary qualities, owe all their ſtrength to the ambiguity of words. I have proved, that, though this fundamental error had never been detected, the philoſophy of BERKELEY is in its own nature abſurd, becauſe it ſuppoſeth the original principles of common ſenſe controvertible and fallacious: a ſuppoſition repugnant to the genius of true philoſophy; and which leads to univerſal credulity, or univerſal ſcepticiſm; and conſequently to the ſubverſion of knowledge and virtue, and the extermination of the human ſpecies.

It is proper, before we proceed to the next inſtance, to make a remark or two on what hath been ſaid.

1. Here

* Part 2. chap. 3.

† Inquiry into the Human Mind on the Principles of Common Senſe.

1. Here we have an inſtance of a doctrine advanced by ſome philoſophers, in direct contradiction to the general belief of all men in all ages.

2. The reaſoning by which it is ſupported, though long accounted unanſwerable, did never produce a ſerious and ſteady conviction. Common ſenſe ſtill declared the doctrine to be falſe: we were ſorry to find the powers of human reaſon ſo limited, as not to afford a logical confutation of it: we were convinced it merited confutation, and flattered ourſelves, that one time or other it would be confuted.

3. The real and general belief of this doctrine would be attended with fatal conſequences to ſcience, and to human nature: for this is a doctrine according to which a man could not act nor reaſon in the common affairs of life, without incurring the charge of inſanity or folly, and involving himſelf in diſtreſs and perdition.

4. An ingenious man, from a ſenſe of the bad tendency of this doctrine, applies himſelf to examine the principles on which it is founded; diſcovers them to be erroneous; and proves, to the full conviction of all competent judges, that from beginning to end it is all a myſtery of falſhood, ariſing from the uſe of ambiguous expreſſions, and from the gratuitous admiſſion of principles which never could have been admitted if they had been thoroughly underſtood.

SECT.

SECTION V.

Dr. Reid's *position, that sensation implies the belief of the present existence of external objects and his view of* Berkley's *theory, particularly considered.*

HAVING replied to our author's capital objections to Mr. Locke's, or the common hypothesis, concerning sensations, ideas and objects, I come to consider what he has farther to advance in support of his own. Now one would imagine *a priori,* that a man who should have assumed the airs and tone that Dr. Reid has given himself through the whole of this treatise, as if he had utterly demolished all the preceding systems of the

the mind, and erected another quite different from any thing that was ever heard or thought of before, would be able to produce something like *positive evidence* for it. But, behold, when we have got to the end of these *negative arguments*, he has, in fact, nothing more to offer, besides his own very confident assertions (repeated indeed without end, if that would give them any weight) that the thing must certainly be as he represents it.

Now though I, who do not pretend to advance any hypothesis of my own, might very reasonably imitate his example; and, having shewn the futility of his objections to the commonly received hypothesis, content myself with leaving things in *statu quo*; yet for the greater satisfaction of my readers, I shall make a few more observations on the subject of our author's instinctive principles, selecting for a more particular examination that by which he says *our perceptions necessarily imply the belief of the present existence of external objects*. There is no one article of of his whole ſyſtem of common ſenſe that he can leſs ſcruple to ſubmit to this examination; for there is no one thing that he repeats ſo often, or ſeems to triumph in ſo much, as this; imagining that his method of conſidering the ſubject is an effectual antidote, and the only effectual antidote to all the ſcepticiſm of the preſent age.

Now excepting what our author has ſaid about the abſurdity of Mr. Locke's principles, of which I think I have offered a ſufficient vindication, and of the peculiarly abſurd and dangerous conſequences which he aſcribes to Berkley's theory, and which I ſhall preſently ſhow to be no better founded, all that he ſays amounts to nothing more than this; that he cannot, in his own mind, ſeparate the belief of the exiſtence of external objects from his ſenſations, as thoſe of taſte, touch, ſight, &c. With reſpect to this I would make the following obſervations.

1. There

1. There are many opinions which we know to be acquired, and even founded on prejudice and miſtake, which, however, the fulleſt conviction that they are void of all real foundation cannot eraſe from the mind; the groundleſs *belief*, and *expectation*, founded upon it, being ſo cloſely connected with the idea of certain circumſtances, that no mental power of which we are poſſeſſed can ſeparate them.

Though, for inſtance, Dr. Reid, no doubt, as well as other philoſophers, believes the earth to be ſpherical, and conſequently is ſenſible that no one part of its ſurface can be *uppermoſt* and another part under it; or, that if there were ſuch a thing as an uppermoſt part, every part muſt become ſo in its turn; yet he always conſiders the place on which he ſtands as conſtantly uppermoſt, and conceives of his antipodes as hanging with their heads downwards. Nay he cannot help having an idea of their having a tendency to fall down into the void ſpace below the earth. He

He may talk as a philoſopher, but I am confident he conceives and thinks as the vulgar do; and though in many things our author appeals to the ſentiments of the vulgar as the teſt of truth, in oppoſition to the philoſophers, I think he will hardly chuſe to do ſo in this caſe. He cannot, however, poſſibly ſeparate in his imagination the idea of a tendency to fall from his idea of the ſituation of the antipodes. Now why may not this be the caſe with reſpect to Berkley's theory, ſo that though we cannot ſeparate the idea of the real exiſtence of external objects and our ſenſations; it may, like the other, be no more than a prejudice, void of all real foundation. As we cannot pretend to diſtinguiſh between our feelings in theſe two caſes, and one of them we know to be fallacious, why may not the other be fallacious alſo? There muſt be ſome *other kind* of evidence beſides *feeling*, to prove that it is not ſo.

Secondly, This ſcheme of Dr. Reid's ſuppoſes that an extraordinary proviſion is is made for a *kind* of faith, that is by no means neceſſary for the purpoſe of it, viz. with reſpect to the conduct of life. For a very high degree of probability, not to be diſtinguiſhed in feeling from abſolute certainty, is attainable without it. Now ſince it cannot be denied but that the divine being leaves us to be governed by a kind of faith far inferior to mathematical certainty in things of infinitely more conſequence (in this, however, I do not appeal to Dr. Oſwald) it is abſolutely incredible that he ſhould have implanted in us a peculiar inſtinctive principle, merely for the ſake of giving us a *plenary conviction* with reſpect to this buſineſs, which is comparatively of very trifling conſequence.

Thirdly, Our author's ſcheme has this farther untoward circumſtance attending it, that it ſuppoſes the divine being to have formed us in ſuch a manner, as that we muſt neceſſarily believe what, by our author's own confeſſion, *might not have been true.* For 'no man,' ſays he, p. 85, 'can

'can ſhow by any good argument, that 'all our ſenſations might not have been 'as they are, though no body or quality 'of body had ever exiſted.' Now this I ſhould think to be, upon the face of it, ſo very unlikely to be true, that no perſon who conſiders the caſe can admit of it. For this is very different from thoſe deceptions which neceſſarily ariſe from general laws, and to which all mankind are ſubject; but with reſpect to which it is in their power, by the proper uſe of their faculties, to relieve themſelves.

It appears, therefore, that confident as our author is of the truth and importance of his ſyſtem, he acknowledges it to be founded not on *abſolute* but *relative truth*, ariſing from his conſtitution, which (contrary to what is advanced by his followers Dr. Beattie and Dr. Oſwald) is eſſentially different from that kind of evidence by which we are ſatisfied that two and two are four, which is independent of any *arbitrary conſtitution* whatever.

I wonder

I wonder it ſhould not have a little ſtaggered Dr. Reid, to conſider that his whole ſyſtem muſt fall at once before the fainteſt ſuſpicion, that God may think proper that mankind ſhould be ſubject to deceptions for their good, at which my mind does not ſhudder, when I ſee it to be the neceſſary conſequence of the moſt excellent general laws. Do we not ſee that the bulk of mankind live and die in the belief that the ſun moves round the earth, and of other things in which they are deceived by the teſtimony of their ſenſes? Now let Dr. Reid aſſign a *good reaſon*, why the ſame being who permits his creatures to believe that the ſun moves round the earth, might not permit them to believe that there was a ſun, though, in reality, there ſhould be no ſuch thing; at the ſame time that, by his own immediate power, without the aid of any real ſun, he ſhould afford them all the benefit of light and heat which they had falſely aſcribed to that luminary. I allow it to be as *improbable* as any perſon pleaſes, but the ſuppoſition is certainly not directly

directly abſurd and *impoſſible*, and this is the only thing in debate.

Fourthly, I wonder that our author ſhould not have attempted ſome ſolution of the phenomena of *dreams*, *reveries*, and *viſions* upon his hypotheſis. In all theſe circumſtances it cannot be denied that men imagine themſelves to be ſurrounded with objects which have no real exiſtence, and yet their ſenſations are not to be diſtinguiſhed from thoſe of men awake; ſo that if *ſenſations, as ſuch*, neceſſarily draw after them the belief of the preſent exiſtence of objects, this belief takes place in dreams, reveries, and viſions, as indeed is the caſe; and if there be a fallacy in theſe caſes, it is certainly *within the compaſs of poſſibility*, that there may be a fallacy in the other alſo.

Notwithſtanding theſe obvious difficulties with which our author's ſcheme is clogged, and which a genius of any order leſs than *the moſt daring* would think to be inſuperable, nothing can exceed the

E confidence

confidence with which he expresses his full persuasion of the truth of it, from the supposed impossibility of believing the contrary, or the supercilious and cavalier manner in which he treats all objections to it.

'I am aware,' says he, p. 291, 'that 'this belief which I have in perception 'stands exposed to the strongest batteries 'of scepticism. But they make no great 'impression upon it. The sceptic asks 'me, why do you believe the existence 'of the external object which you per- 'ceive? This belief, Sir, is none of my 'manufacture; it came from the mint of 'nature; it bears her image and super- 'scription; and if it is not right, the fault 'is not mine. I even took it upon trust, 'and without suspicion. Reason, says 'the sceptic, is the only judge of truth, 'and you ought to throw off every opi- 'nion, and every belief, that is not 'grounded on reason. Well, Sir, why 'should I believe the faculty of reason 'more than that of perception? They 'both

'both came out of the ſame ſhop, and 'were made by the ſame artiſt; and if he 'puts one piece of falſe ware into my 'hands, what ſhould hinder him from 'putting another?'

'Perhaps the ſceptic will agree to diſ-'truſt reaſon, rather than give any credit to 'perception. For, ſays he, ſince by your 'own confeſſion, the object which you 'perceive, and that act of your mind by 'which you perceive it are quite different 'things, the one may exiſt without the 'other; and as the object may exiſt with-'out being perceived, ſo the perception 'may exiſt without an object. There is 'nothing ſo ſhameful in a philoſopher as 'to be deceived, and deluded, and there-'fore you ought firmly to withhold your 'aſſent, and throw off this belief of ex-'ternal objects, which may be all delu-'ſion. For my part, I will never attempt 'to throw it off, and although the ſober 'part of mankind will not be very anxious 'to know any reaſons, yet if they can be 'of uſe to any ſceptic, they are theſe.'

E 2 'Now,

Now, as I do not pretend to rank myſelf with thoſe whom Dr. Reid will call the *ſober part of mankind*, I frankly acknowledge that I have had a little curioſity to look at theſe reaſons.

The firſt I find is, that it is not in his power to believe otherwiſe, which I preſume I have conſidered ſufficiently above.

His ſecond argument is derived from the dangerous conſequences which he aſcribes to Berkley's hypotheſis, and which he expreſſes in that ludicrous and contemptuous manner in which the greateſt part of this *philoſophical treatiſe* is written.

'I think,' ſays he, p. 291, 'it would 'not be prudent to throw off this belief, 'if it were in my power. If nature in'tended to deceive me, and impoſe upon 'me by falſe appearances, and I, by my 'great cunning and profound logic, have 'diſcovered the impoſture, prudence 'would

'would dictate to me in this case even to 'put up this indignity done me, as quietly as I could, and not to call her an 'impostor to her face, lest she should be 'even with me in another way. For 'what do I gain by resenting this injury? 'You ought, at least, not to believe what 'she says. This, indeed, seems reasonable, if she intends to impose upon me. 'But what is the consequence. I resolve 'not to believe my senses. I break my 'nose against a post that comes in my 'way; I step into a dirty kennel; and 'after twenty such wise and rational actions, I am taken up, and clapt into a 'mad-house. Now I confess I had rather 'make one of the credulous fools whom 'nature imposes upon, than of those wise 'and rational philosophers, who resolve 'to withhold assent at all this expence.'

But all this profusion of genuine wit and humour turns upon a gross misrepresentation of Berkley's theory; and it is really a pity that what is so excellent in its kind should be thrown away, by being misplaced.

E 3 This

This misrepresentation and abuse is exactly the conduct of many divines, who charge one another with actually maintaining the supposed consequences of their respective opinions. But this is no *fair* consequence. Berkley did not exclude from his system *sensations* and *ideas*, together with matter, the *necessary connections* that subsist among them, or our *power* over them. He only ascribed them to a *different origin*; so that all the rules of conduct depending upon them are the same on his scheme as on ours. Our philosophical language only is different.

I say there is a post in my way, and I must turn aside, lest I hurt myself by running against it. He, in the same situation, is as apprehensive of danger as myself, though he says he has only the idea of a post before him; for if he do not introduce the idea of avoiding it, he is sensible that he shall experience a very painful sensation, which may bring on other sensations, till death itself ensue. I may smile at his language, but he is consistent

consistent with himself, and his fears have as much foundation as mine.

This representation of Berkley's theory, which is common to Dr. Reid, Dr. Beattie, and Dr. Oswald, and with which they often make themselves and their readers foolishly merry, is exceedingly unjust; but when considered by philosophers, the laugh must rebound upon themselves.

The third reason, as our author is pleased to call it, why he believes in the existence of a material world, or the evidence of his senses, is that he does not find that he has been imposed upon by this belief. 'I find,' says he, p. 293 'that 'without it I must have perished by a 'thousand accidents. I find that without 'it I should have been no wiser now than 'when I was born' &c. &c. &c. But all this goes upon the same misrepresentation with the former argument, and is not, in fact, at all different from it. Besides, a reasonable degree of evidence, which may be attained without this extraordinary, inſtinctive, abſolute, and as our author calls it, *inſpired belief*, is juſt as uſeful for any real purpoſe.

SECTION VI.

Mr. Locke's *doctrine not ſo favourable to* Berkley's *theory as Dr.* Reid's.

IT is by an evident abuſe and perverſion of Mr. Locke's doctrine that Dr. Reid pretends that it is favourable to Biſhop Berkley's notion of there being no material world; when, in reality, our author's own principles are much more favourable to that notion than Mr. Locke's.

'If,' ſays he, p. 42, 'impreſſions and 'ideas are the only objects of thought, 'then heaven and earth, and body and 'ſpirit, and every thing you pleaſe, muſt 'ſignify only impreſſions and ideas, or 'they muſt be words without any meaning.'

But

But it was never ſuppoſed by Mr. Locke, or any other advocate for ideas, that they were more than the *immediate* object of our thoughts, the things of which we are properly ſpeaking *conſcious*, or that we know in the *firſt inſtance*. From them, however, we think we can *infer* the real exiſtence of other things, from which thoſe ideas are derived; and then we can reaſon about thoſe *objects*, as well as about the *ideas* themſelves. In fact, ideas being only the ſigns of external things, we reaſon about the external things themſelves, without ever attending to the ideas which repreſent them, and even without knowing that there are any ſuch things in the mind, till we come to reflect upon the ſubject. In like manner, a perſon may ſee perfectly without ever thinking of his eyes, or indeed knowing that he has any ſuch organs.

Mr. Locke would not, indeed pretend to ſuch an abſolute *demonſtration* of the reality of an external world as Dr. Reid pleads for; but neither is that ſtrict de-monſtration

monſtration neceſſary. It is quite ſufficient if the ſuppoſition be the eaſieſt hypotheſis for explaining the origin of our ideas. The evidence of it is ſuch that we allow it to be barely poſſible to doubt of it.; but that it is as certain as that two and two make four, we do not pretend.

Strongly attached as our autnor is to this material world of ours, let us ſee whether his own ſyſtem, in other reſpects, be ſufficiently adapted to it. Now it appears to me that his notions of mind, ideas, and external objects, are ſuch as are hardly compatible with one another, that he puts an impaſſable gulph between them, ſo as intirely to prevent their connection or correſpondence; which is all that the biſhop could wiſh in favour of his doctrine.

I take it for granted,' ſays Dr. Reid, p. 381, 'upon the teſtimony of common 'ſenſe, that my mind is a ſubſtance, that 'is, a permanent ſubject of thought, and 'my 'my reaſon convinces me that it is an un-'extended and indiviſible ſubſtance; and 'hence I infer that there cannot be in it any 'thing that reſembles extenſion.' But with equal appearance of truth he might infer that the mind cannot be *affected* by any thing that has extenſion; for how can any thing act upon another but by means of ſome common property? Though, therefore, the divine being has thought proper to create an external world, it can be of no proper uſe to give us ſenſations or ideas. It muſt be he himſelf that impreſſes our minds with the notices of external things, without any *real inſtrumentality* of their own; ſo that the external world is quite a ſuperfluity in the creation. If, therefore, the author of all things be a *wiſe* being, and have made nothing in vain, we may conclude that this external world, which has been the ſubject of ſo much controverſy, can have no exiſtence.

If then we wiſh to preſerve this external world, which is very convenient for many purpoſes, we muſt take care to entertain notions

notions of mind and ideas more compatible with it than thoſe of Dr. Reid.

Our author's fallacious argument from the want of reſemblance between our ideas and external objects leads him into many difficulties. It makes him, in ſeveral reſpects, allow too much to Dr. Berkley, and to come nearer to him than he is aware. And in ſpite of his averſion to the union, and of every thing that he can do or ſay, their common principles will bring them together. 'Our ſenſations' he ſays, p. 305, 'have no reſemblance to external objects, nor can we diſcover by our reaſon any neceſſary connection between the exiſtence of the former and that of the latter. No man,' ſays he, p. 85, 'can ſhew by any good argument, that all our ſenſations might not have been as they are, though no body or quality of body had ever exiſted.' He even ſays, p. 304, 'that when we conſider the different attributes of *mind* and *body*, they ſeem to be ſo different, and ſo unlike, that we can find 'no 'no handle by which one may lay hold 'of the other.'

According to our author, therefore, Berkley's theory is at least *possible*; and if, as he says, p. 117, 'sensations and 'ideas in our minds can resemble nothing 'but sensations and ideas in other minds,' it may well appear *probable*, that they are transferred (as Malebranche, I think, supposes) immediately from the divine mind to ours, without any real agency of a material world. If I could admit Dr. Reid's premises, I think I could hardly help drawing this conclusion from them; especially as nothing can be pleaded for the existence of this same material world, but a mere *unaccountable persuasion* that it *does* exist. This persuasion Dr. Reid says arises from a branch of his new common sense. But if I cannot discover or imagine any *end* or *reason* why it should exist; common sense, in its old and familiar acceptation, would tell me that it does not exist at all.

SEC-

Of the Senſe of SEEING. *to* 332.

DR. BERKLEY, in his New Theory of Viſion, one of the fineſt examples of philoſophical analyſis that is to be found, either in our own, or in any other language, has explained, ſo very diſtinctly, the nature of the objects of Sight: their diſſimilitude to, as well as their correſpondence and connection with thoſe of Touch, that I have ſcarcely any thing to add to what he has already done. It is only in order to render ſome things, which I ſhall have occaſion to ſay hereafter, intelligible to ſuch readers as may not have had an opportunity of ſtudying his book, that I have preſumed to treat of the ſame ſubject, after ſo great a Maſter. Whatever I ſhall ſay upon it, if not directly borrowed from him, has at leaſt been ſuggeſted by what he has already ſaid.

That the objects of Sight are not perceived as reſiſting or preſſing upon the organ which perceives them, is ſufficiently obvious. They cannot therefore ſuggeſt, at leaſt in the ſame manner,

ner, as the objects of Touch, the externality and independency of their exiſtence.

We are apt, however, to imagine that we ſee objects at a diſtance from us, and that conſequently the externality of their exiſtence is immediately perceived by our Sight. But if we conſider that the diſtance of any object from the eye, is a line turned endways to it; and that this line muſt conſequently appear to it, but as one point; we ſhall be ſenſible that diſtance from the eye cannot be the immediate object of Sight, but that all viſible objects muſt naturally be percived as cloſe upon the organ, or more properly, perhaps, like all other Senſations, as in the organ which perceives them. That the objects of Sight are all painted in the bottom of the eye, upon a membrane called the *retina*, pretty much in the ſame manner as the like objects are painted in a Camera Obſcura, is well known to whoever has the ſlighteſt tincture of the ſcience of Optics; and the principle of perception, it is probable, originally perceives them, as exiſting in that part of the organ, and nowhere but in that part of the organ. No Optician, accordingly, no perſon who has ever beſtowed any moderate degree of attention upon the nature of Viſion, has ever pretended that diſtance from the eye was the immediate object of Sight. How it is that, by means of our Sight, we learn to judge of ſuch diſtances, Opticians have endeavoured to explain in ſeveral different ways. I ſhall not, however,

however, at present, stop to examine their systems.

The objects of Touch are solidity, and those modifications of solidity which we consider as essential to it, and inseparable from it; solid extension, figure, divisibility, and mobility.

The objects of Sight are colour, and those modifications of colour which, in the same manner, we consider as essential to it, and inseparable from it; coloured extension, figure, divisibility, and mobility. When we open our eyes, the sensible coloured objects, which present themselves to us, must all have a certain extension, or must occupy a certain portion of the visible surface which appears before us. They must too have all a certain figure, or must be bounded by certain visible lines, which mark upon that surface the extent of their respective dimensions. Every sensible portion of this visible or coloured extension must be conceived as divisible, or as separable into two, three, or more parts. Every portion too of this visible or coloured surface must be conceived as moveable, or as capable of changing its situation, and of assuming a different arrangement with regard to the other portions of the same surface.

Colour, the visible, bears no resemblance to solidity, the tangible object. A man born blind, or who has lost his Sight so early as to have no remembrance

remembrance of viſible objects, can form no idea or conception of colour. Touch alone can never help him to it. I have heard, indeed, of ſome perſons who had loſt their Sight after the age of manhood, and who had learned to diſtinguiſh, by the Touch alone, the different colours of cloths or ſilks, the goods which it happened to be their buſineſs to deal in. The powers by which different bodies excite in the organs of Sight the Senſations of different colours, probably depend upon ſome difference in the nature, configuration, and arrangement of the parts which compoſe their reſpective ſurfaces. This difference may, to a very nice and delicate touch, make ſome difference in feeling, ſufficient to enable a perſon, much intereſted in the caſe, to make this diſtinction in ſome degree, though probably in a very imperfect and inaccurate one. A man born blind might poſſibly be taught to make the ſame diſtinctions. But though he might thus be able to name the different colours, which thoſe different ſurfaces reflected, though he might thus have ſome imperfect notion of the remote cauſes of theſe Senſations, he could have no better idea of the Senſations themſelves, than that other blind man, mentioned by Mr. Locke, had, who ſaid that he imagined the Colour of Scarlet reſembled the Sound of a Trumpet. A man born deaf may, in the ſame manner, be taught to ſpeak articulately. He is taught how to ſhape and diſpoſe of his organs, ſo as to pronounce each letter, ſyllable, and word. But

ſtill,

ſtill, though he may have ſome imperfect idea of the remote cauſes of the Sounds which he himſelf utters, of the remote cauſes of the Senſations which he himſelf excites in other people; he can have none of thoſe Sounds or Senſations themſelves.

If it were poſſible, in the ſame manner, that a man could be born without the Senſe of Touching, that of Seeing could never alone ſuggeſt to him the idea of Solidity, or enable him to form any notion of the external and reſiſting ſubſtance. It is probable, however, not only that no man, but that no animal was ever born without the Senſe of Touching, which ſeems eſſential to, and inſeparable from, the nature of animal life and exiſtence. It is unneceſſary, therefore, to throw away any reaſoning, or to hazard any conjectures, about what might be the effects of what I look upon as altogether an impoſſible ſuppoſition. The eye when preſſed upon by any external and ſolid ſubſtance, feels, no doubt, that preſſure and reſiſtance, and ſuggeſts to us (in the ſame manner as every other feeling part of the body) the external and independent exiſtence of that ſolid ſubſtance. But in this caſe, the eye acts, not as the organ of Sight, but as an organ of Touch; for the eye poſſeſſes the Senſe of Touching in common with almoſt all the other parts of the body.

The

The extenſion, figure, diviſibility, and mobility of Colour, the ſole object of Sight, though, on account of their correſpondence and connection with the extenſion, figure, diviſibility, and mobility of Solidity, they are called by the ſame name, yet ſeem to bear no ſort of reſemblance to their nameſakes. As Colour and Solidity bear no ſort of reſemblance to one another, ſo neither can their reſpective modifications. Dr. Berkley very juſtly obſerves, that though we can conceive either a coloured or a ſolid line to be prolonged indefinitely, yet we cannot conceive the one to be added to the other. We cannot, even in imagination, conceive an object of Touch to be prolonged into an object of Sight, or an object of Sight into an object of Touch. The objects of Sight and thoſe of Touch conſtitute two words, which, though they have a moſt important correſpondence and connection with one another, bear no ſort of reſemblance to one another. The tangible world, as well as all the different parts which compoſe it, has three dimenſions, Length, Breadth, and Depth. The viſible world, as well as all the different parts which compoſe it, has only two, Length and Breadth. It preſents to us only a plain or ſurface, which, by certain ſhades and combinations of Colour, ſuggeſts and repreſents to us (in the ſame manner as a picture does) certain tangible objects which have no Colour, and which therefore can bear no reſemblance to thoſe ſhades and combinations of Colour. Thoſe ſhades and combinations

tions ſuggeſt thoſe different tangible objects as at different diſtances, according to certain rules of Perſpective, which it is, perhaps, not very eaſy to ſay how it is that we learn, whether by ſome particular inſtinct, or by ſome application of either reaſon or experience, which has become ſo perfectly habitual to us, that we are ſcarcely ſenſible when we make uſe of it.

The diſtinctneſs of this Perſpective, the preciſion and accuracy with which, by means of it, we are capable of judging concerning the diſtance of different tangible objects, is greater or leſs, exactly in proportion as this importance to us. We can judge of the diſtance of near objects, of the chairs and tables, for example, in the chamber where we are ſitting, with the moſt perfect preciſion and accuracy; and if in broad daylight we ever ſtumble over any of them, it muſt be, not from any error in the Sight, but from ſome defect in the attention. The preciſion and accuracy of our judgment concerning ſuch near objects are of the utmoſt importance to us, and conſtitute the great advantage which a man who ſees has over one who is unfortunately blind. As the diſtance increaſes, the diſtinctneſs of this Perſpective, the preciſion and accuracy of our judgment gradually diminiſh. Of the tangible objects which are even at the moderate diſtance of one, two, or three miles from the eye, we are frequently at a loſs to determine which is neareſt, and which remoteſt. It is ſeldom of much

much importance to us to judge with precifion concerning the fituation of the tangible objects which are even at this moderate diftance. As the diftance increafes, our judgments become more and more uncertain; and at a very great diftance, fuch as that of the fixed ftars, it becomes altogether uncertain. The moft precife knowledge of the relative fituation of fuch objects could be of no other ufe to us than to fatisfy the moft unneceffary curiofity.

The diftances at which different men can by Sight diftinguifh, with fome degree of precifion, the fituation of the tangible objects which the vifible ones reprefent, is very different; and this difference, though it, no doubt, may fometimes depend upon fome difference in the original configuration of their eyes, yet feems frequently to arife altogether from the different cuftoms and habits which their refpective occupations have led them to contract. Men of letters, who live much in their clofets, and have feldom occafion to look at very diftant objects, are feldom farfighted. Mariners, on the contrary, almoft always are; thofe efpecially who have made many diftant voyages, in which they have been the greater part of their time out of fight of land, and have in day-light been conftantly looking out towards the horizon for the appearance of fome fhip, or of fome diftant fhore. It often aftonifhes a land-man to obferve with what precifion a failor can diftinguifh in the Offing, not only the

X appearance

appearance of a ſhip, which is altogether inviſible to the land-man, but the number of her maſts, the direction of her courſe, and the rate of her ſailing. If ſhe is a ſhip of his acquaintance, he frequently can tell her name, before the land-man has been able to diſcover even the appearance of a ſhip.

Viſible objects, Colour, and all its different modifications, are in themſelves mere ſhadows or pictures, which ſeem to float, as it were, before the organ of Sight. In themſelves, and independent of connection with the tangible objects which they repreſent, they are of no importance to us, and can eſſentially neither benefit us nor hurt us. Even while we ſee them we are ſeldom thinking of them. Even when we appear to be looking at them with the greateſt earneſtneſs, our whole attention is frequently employed, not upon them, but upon the tangible objects repreſented by them.

It is becauſe almoſt our whole attention is employed, not upon the viſible and repreſenting, but upon the tangible and repreſented objects, that in our imaginations we are apt to aſcribe to the former a degree of magnitude which does not belong to them, but which belongs altogether to the latter. If you ſhut one eye, and hold immediately before the other a ſmall circle of plain glaſs, of not more than half an inch in diameter, you may ſee through that circle the moſt extenſive

tenſive proſpects; lawns and woods, and arms of the ſea, and diſtant mountains. You are apt to imagine that the Landſcape which is thus preſented to you, that the viſible Picture which you thus ſee, is immenſely great and extenſive. The tangible objects which this viſible Picture repreſents, undoubtedly are ſo. But the viſible Picture which repreſents them can be no greater than the little viſible circle through which you ſee it. If while you are looking through this circle, you could conceive a fairy hand and a fairy pencil to come between your eye and the glaſs, that pencil could delineate upon that little glaſs the outline of all thoſe extenſive lawns and woods, and arms of the ſea, and diſtant mountains, in the full and exact dimenſions with which they are really ſeen by the eye.

Every viſible object which covers from the eye any other viſible object, muſt appear at leaſt as large as that other viſible object. It muſt occupy at leaſt an equal portion of that viſible plain or ſurface which is at that time preſented to the eye.—Opticians accordingly tell us, that all the viſible objects which are ſeen under equal angles muſt to the eye appear equally large.—But the viſible object, which covers from the eye any other viſible object, muſt neceſſarily be ſeen under angles at leaſt equally large as thoſe under which that other object is ſeen. When I hold up my finger, however, before my eye, it appears to cover the greater part of the viſible

X 2 chamber

chamber in which I am ſitting. It ſhould therefore appear as large as the greater part of that viſible chamber. But becauſe I know that the tangible finger bears but a very ſmall proportion to the greater part of the tangible chamber, I am apt to fancy that the viſible finger bears but a like proportion to the greater part of the viſible chamber. My judgment corrects my eyeſight, and, in my fancy, reduces the viſible object, which repreſents the little tangible one, below its real viſible dimenſions; and, on the contrary, it augments the viſible object which repreſents the great tangible one a good deal beyond thoſe dimenſions. My attention being generally altogether occupied about the tangible and repreſented, and not at all about the viſible and repreſenting objects, my careleſs fancy beſtows upon the latter a proportion which does not in the leaſt belong to them, but which belongs altogether to the former.

It is becauſe the viſible object which covers any other viſible object muſt always appear at leaſt as large as that other object, that Opticians tell us that the ſphere of our viſion appears to the eye always equally large; and that when we hold our hand before our eye in ſuch a manner that we ſee nothing but the inſide of the hand, we ſtill ſee preciſely the ſame number of viſible points, the ſphere of our viſion is ſtill as completely filled, the retina is as entirely covered with the object which is thus preſented to to it, as when we ſurvey the moſt extenſive horizon.

A young gentleman who was born with a cataract upon each of his eyes was, in one thouſand ſeven hundred and twenty-eight, couched by Mr. Cheſelden, and by that means for the firſt time made to ſee diſtinctly. "At firſt, ſays "the operator, he could bear but very little "Sight, and the things he ſaw he thought ex-"tremely large; but upon ſeeing things larger, "thoſe firſt ſeen he conceived leſs, never being "able to imagine any lines beyond the bounds "he ſaw; the room he was in, he ſaid, he knew "to be but part of the houſe, yet he could not "conceive that the whole houſe would look big-"ger." It was unavoidable that he ſhould at firſt conceive, that no viſible object could be greater, could preſent to his eye a greater number of viſible points, or could more completely fill the comprehenſion of an organ, than the narroweſt ſphere of his viſion. And when that ſphere came to be enlarged, he ſtill could not conceive that the viſible objects which it preſented could be larger than thoſe which he had firſt ſeen. He muſt probably by this time have been in ſome degree habituated to the connection between viſible and tangible objects, and enabled to conceive that viſible object to be ſmall which repreſented a ſmall tangible object; to be great, which repreſented a great one. The great objects did not appear to his Sight greater than the

the ſmall ones had done before; but the ſmall ones, which, having filled the whole ſphere of his viſion, had before appeared as large as poſſible, being now known to repreſent much ſmaller tangible objects, ſeemed in his conception to grow ſmaller. He had begun now to employ his attention more about the tangible and repreſented, than about the viſible and repreſenting objects; and he was beginning to aſcribe to the latter, the proportions and dimenſions which properly belonged altogether to the former.

As we frequently aſcribe to the objects of Sight a magnitude and proportion which does not really belong to them, but to the objects of Touch which they repreſent, ſo we likewiſe aſcribe to them a ſteadineſs of appearance, which as little belongs to them, but which they derive altogether from their connection with the ſame objects of Touch. The chair which now ſtands at the farther end of the room, I am apt to imagine, appears to my eye as large as it did when it ſtood cloſe by me, when it was ſeen under angles at leaſt four times larger than thoſe under which it is ſeen at preſent, and when it muſt have occupied, at leaſt, ſixteen times that portion which it occupies at preſent, of the viſible plain or ſurface which is now before my eyes. But as I know that the magnitude of the tangible and repreſented chair, the principal object of my attention, is the ſame in both ſituations, I aſcribe to the viſible and repreſenting chair (though

(though now reduced to lefs than the fixteenth part of its former dimenfions) a fteadinefs of appearance, which certainly belongs not in any refpect to it, but altogether to the tangible and reprefented one. As we approach to, or retire from, the tangible object which any vifible one reprefents, the vifible object gradually augments in the one cafe, and diminifhes in the other. To fpeak accurately, it is not the fame vifible object which we fee at different diftances, but a fucceffion of vifible objects, which, though they all refemble one another, thofe efpecially which follow near after one another; yet are all really different and diftinct. But as we know that the tangible object which they reprefent remains always the fame, we afcribe to them too a famenefs which belongs altogether to it: and we fancy that we fee the fame tree at a mile, at half a mile, and at a few yards diftance. At thofe different diftances, however, the vifible objects are fo very widely different, that we are fenfible of a change in their appearance. But ftill, as the tangible object which they reprefent remains invariably the fame, we afcribe a fort of famenefs even to them too.

It has been faid, that no man ever faw the fame vifible object twice; and this, though, no doubt, an exaggeration, is, in reality, much lefs fo than at firft view it appears to be. Though I am apt to fancy that all the chairs and tables, and other little pieces of furniture in the room where

where I am ſitting, appear to my eye always the ſame, yet their appearance is in reality continually varying, not only according to every variation in their ſituation and diſtance with regard to where I am ſitting, but according to every, even the moſt inſenſible variation in the altitude of my body, in the movement of my head, or even in that of my eyes. The perſpective neceſſarily varies according to all, even the ſmalleſt of theſe variations; and conſequently the appearance of the objects which that perſpective preſents to me. Obſerve what difficulty a portrait painter finds, in getting the perſon who ſits for his picture to preſent to him preciſely that view of the countenance from which the firſt outline was drawn. The painter is ſcarce ever completely ſatisfied with the ſituation of the face which is preſented to him, and finds that it is ſcarcely ever preciſely the ſame with that from which he rapidly ſketched the firſt outline. He endeavours, as well as he can, to correct the difference from memory, from fancy, and from a ſort of art of approximation, by which he ſtrives to expreſs as nearly as he can, the ordinary effect of the look, air, and character of the perſon whoſe picture he is drawing. The perſon who draws from a ſtatue, which is altogether immoveable, feels a difficulty, though, no doubt, in a leſs degree, of the ſame kind. It ariſes altogether from the difficulty which he finds in placing his own eye preciſely in the ſame ſituation during the whole time

time which he employs in completing his drawing. This difficulty is more than doubled upon the painter who draws from a living subject. The statue never is the cause of any variation or unsteadiness in its own appearance. The living subject frequently is.

The benevolent purpose of nature in bestowing upon us the sense of seeing, is evidently to inform us concerning the situation and distance of the tangible objects which surround us. Upon the knowledge of this distance and situation depends the whole conduct of human life, in the most trifling as well as in the most important transactions. Even animal motion depends upon it; and without it we could neither move, nor even sit still, with complete security. The objects of sight, as Dr. Berkley finely observes, constitute a sort of language which the Author of Nature addresses to our eyes, and by which he informs us of many things, which it is of the utmost importance to us to know. As, in common language, the words or sounds bear no resemblance to the things which they denote, so in this other language, the visible objects bear no sort of resemblance to the tangible object which they represent, and of whose relative situation, with regard both to ourselves and to one another, they inform us.

He

He acknowledges, however, that though ſcarcely any word be by nature better fitted to expreſs one meaning than any other meaning, yet that certain viſible objects are better fitted than others to repreſent certain tangible objects. A viſible ſquare, for example, is better fitted than a viſible circle to repreſent a tangible ſquare. There is, perhaps, ſtrictly ſpeaking, no ſuch thing as either a viſible cube, or a viſible globe, the objects of ſight being all naturally preſented to the eye as upon one ſurface. But ſtill there are certain combinations of colours which are fitted to repreſent to the eye, both the near and the diſtant, both the advancing and the receding lines, angles, and ſurfaces of the tangible cube; and there are others fitted to repreſent, in the ſame manner, both the near and the receding ſurface of the tangible globe. The combination which repreſents the tangible cube, would not be fit to repreſent the tangible globe; and that which repreſents the tangible globe, would not be fit to repreſent the tangible cube. Though there may, therefore, be no reſemblance between viſible and tangible objects, there ſeems to be ſome affinity or correſpondence between them ſufficient to make each viſible object fitter to repreſent a certain preciſe tangible object than any other tangible object. But the greater part of words ſeem to have no ſort of affinity or correſpondence with the meanings or ideas which they expreſs; and if cuſtom had ſo ordered it, they might with equal propriety have been made uſe of to expreſs any other meaning or ideas.

Dr.

Dr. Berkley, with that happineſs of illuſtration which ſcarcely ever deſerts him, remarks, that this in reality is no more than what happens in common language; and that though letters bear no ſort of reſemblance to the words which they denote, yet that the ſame combination of letters which repreſents one word, would not always be fit to repreſent another; and that each word is always beſt repreſented by its own proper combination of letters. The compariſon, however, it muſt be obſerved, is here totally changed. The connection between viſible and tangible objects was firſt illuſtrated by comparing it with that between ſpoken language and the meanings or ideas which ſpoken language ſuggeſts to us; and it is now illuſtrated by the connection between written language and ſpoken language, which is altogether different, Even this ſecond illuſtration, beſides, will not apply perfectly to the caſe. When cuſtom, indeed, has perfectly aſcertained the powers of each letter; when it has aſcertained, for example, that the firſt letter of the alphabet ſhall always repreſent ſuch a ſound, and the ſecond letter ſuch another ſound; each word comes then to be more properly repreſented by one certain combination of written letters or characters, than it could be by any other combination. But ſtill the characters themſelves are altogether arbitrary, and have no ſort of affinity or correſpondence with the articulate ſounds which they denote. The character which marks the firſt letter of the alphabet, for example, if cuſtom had

ſo

ſo ordered it, might, with perfect propriety, have been made uſe of to expreſs the ſound which we now annex to the ſecond, and the character of the ſecond to expreſs that which we now annex to the firſt. But the viſible characters which repreſent to our eyes the tangible globe, could not ſo well repreſent the tangible cube; nor could thoſe which repreſent the tangible cube, ſo properly repreſent the tangible globe. There is evidently, therefore, a certain affinity and correſpondence between each viſible object and the preciſe tangible object repreſented by it, much ſuperior to what takes place either between written and ſpoken language, or between ſpoken language and the ideas or meanings which it ſuggeſts. The language which nature addreſſes to our eyes, has evidently a fitneſs of repreſentation, an aptitude for ſignifying the preciſe things which it denotes, much ſuperior to that of any of the artificial languages which human art and ingenuity have ever been able to invent.

That this affinity and correſpondence, however, between viſible and tangible objects could not alone, and without the aſſiſtance of obſervation and experience, teach us, by any effort of reaſon, to infer what was the preciſe tangible object which each viſible one repreſented, if it is not ſufficiently evident from what has been already ſaid, it muſt be completely ſo from the remarks of Mr. Cheſelden upon the young gentleman above-mentioned, whom he had couched for a cataract.

cataract. "Though we say of this gentleman, "that he was blind," observes Mr. Cheselden, "as we do of all people who have ripe cataracts; "yet they are never so blind from that cause but "that they can discern day from night; and for "the most part, in a strong light, distinguish "black, white, and scarlet; but they cannot per-"ceive the shape of any thing; for the light by "which these perceptions are made, being let in "obliquely through the aqueous humour, or the "anterior surface of the crystalline, (by which the "rays cannot be brought into a focus upon the "retina,) they can discern in no other manner "than a sound eye can through a glass of broken "jelly, where a great variety of surfaces so dif-"ferently refract the light, that the several dis-"tinct pencils of rays cannot be collected by the "eye into their proper foci; wherefore the shape "of an object in such a case cannot be at all dis-"cerned, though the colour may: and thus it was "with this young gentleman, who, though he "knew those colours asunder in a good light, "yet when he saw them after he was couched, "the faint ideas he had of them before were not "sufficient for him to know them by afterwards; "and therefore he did not think them the same "which he had before known by those names." This young gentleman, therefore, had some advantage over one who from a state of total blindness had been made for the first time to see. He had some imperfect notion of the distinction of colours; and he must have known that those colours had

had ſome ſort of connection with the tangible objects which he had been accuſtomed to feel. But had he emerged from total blindneſs, he could have learnt this connection only from a very long courſe of obſervation and experience. How little this advantage availed him, however, we may learn partly from the paſſages of Mr. Cheſelden's narrative, already quoted, and ſtill more from the following:

" When he firſt ſaw," ſays that ingenious operator, " he was ſo far from making any judgment " about diſtances, that he thought all objects " whatever touched his eyes (as he expreſſed it) " as what he felt did his ſkin; and thought no ob- " jects ſo agreeable as thoſe which were ſmooth " and regular, though he could form no judg- " ment of their ſhape, or gueſs what it was in any " object that was pleaſing to him. He knew not " the ſhape of any thing, nor any one thing from " another, however different in ſhape or magni- " tude; but upon being told what things were, " whoſe form he before knew from feeling, he " would carefully obſerve, that he might know " them again; but having too many objects to " learn at once, he forgot many of them; and (as " he ſaid) at firſt learned to know, and again for- " got a thouſand things in a day. One particular " only (though it may appear trifling) I will re- " late: Having often forgot which was the cat, " and which the dog, he was aſhamed to aſk; " but catching the cat (which he knew by feeling) " he

" he was obſerved to look at her ſtedfaſtly, and " then ſetting her down, ſaid, So, puſs! I ſhall " know you another time."

When the young gentleman ſaid, that the objects which he ſaw touched his eyes, he certainly could not mean that they preſſed upon or reſiſted his eyes; for the objects of ſight never act upon the organ in any way that reſembles preſſure or reſiſtance. He could mean no more than that they were cloſe upon his eyes, or, to ſpeak more properly, perhaps, that they were in his eyes. A deaf man, who was made all at once to hear, might in the ſame manner naturally enough ſay, that the ſounds which he heard touched his ears, meaning that he felt them as cloſe upon his ears, or, to ſpeak, perhaps, more properly, as in his ears.

Mr. Cheſelden adds afterwards: " We thought " he ſoon knew what pictures repreſented which " were ſhewed to him, but we found afterwards " we were miſtaken; for about two months after " he was couched, he diſcovered at once they " repreſented ſolid bodies, when, to that time, " he conſidered them only as party-coloured " planes, or ſurfaces diverſified with variety of " paints; but even then he was no leſs ſurpriſed, " expecting the pictures would feel like the things " they repreſented, and was amazed when he " found thoſe parts, which by their light and " ſhadow appeared now round and uneven, felt " only

" only flat and like the reſt; and aſked which was " the lying ſenſe, feeling or ſeeing?"

Painting, though, by combination of light and ſhade ſimilar to thoſe which Nature makes uſe of in the viſible objects which ſhe preſents to our eyes, it endeavours to imitate thoſe objects; yet it never has been able to equal the perſpective of Nature, or to give to its productions that force and diſtinctneſs of relief and projection which Nature beſtows upon hers. When the young gentleman was juſt beginning to underſtand the ſtrong and diſtinct perſpective of Nature, the faint and feeble perſpective of Painting made no impreſſion upon him, and the picture appeared to him what it really was, a plain ſurface bedaubed with different colours.—When he became more familiar with the perſpective of Nature, the inferiority of that of Painting did not hinder him from diſcovering its reſemblance to that of Nature.—In the perſpective of Nature, he had always found that the ſituation and diſtance of the tangible and repreſented objects, correſponded exactly to what the viſible and repreſenting ones ſuggeſted to him. He expected to find the ſame thing in the ſimilar, though inferior perſpective of Painting, and was diſappointed when he found that the viſible and tangible objects had not, in this caſe, their uſual correſpondence.

" In a year after ſeeing," adds Mr. Cheſelden, " the young gentleman being carried upon Ep-" ſom-

" som-downs, and observing a large prospect, he " was exceedingly delighted with it, and called it " a new kind of seeing." He had now, it is evident, come to understand completely the language of Vision. The visible objects which this noble prospect presented to him did now appear as touching, or as close upon his eye. They did not now appear of the same magnitude with those small objects to which, for some time after the operation, he had been accustomed, in the little chamber where he was confined. Those new visible objects at once, and as it were of their own accord, assumed both the distance and the magnitude of the great tangible objects which they represented. He had now, therefore, it would seem, become completely master of the language of Vision, and he had become so in the course of a year; a much shorter period than that in which any person, arrived at the age of manhood, could completely acquire any foreign language. It would appear too, that he had made very considerable progress even in the two first months. He began at that early period to understand even the feeble perspective of Painting; and though at first he could not distinguish it from the strong perspective of Nature, yet he could not have been thus imposed upon by so imperfect an imitation, if the great principles of Vision had not beforehand been deeply impressed upon his mind, and if he had not, either by the association of ideas, or by some other unknown principle, been strongly determined to expect certain tangible objects in con-

Y sequence

ſequence of the viſible ones which had been preſented to him. This rapid progreſs, however, may, perhaps, be accounted for from that fitneſs of repreſentation, which has already been taken notice of, between viſible and tangible objects. In this language of Nature, it may be ſaid, the analogies are more perfect; the etymologies, the declenſions, and conjugations, if one may ſay ſo, are more regular than thoſe of any human language. The rules are fewer, and thoſe rules admit of no exceptions.

But though it may have been altogether by the ſlow paces of obſervation and experience that this young gentleman acquired the knowledge of the connection between viſible and tangible objects; we cannot from thence with certainty infer, that young children have not ſome inſtinctive perception of the ſame kind.—In him this inſtinctive power, not having been exerted at the proper ſeaſon, may, from diſuſe, have gone gradually to decay, and at laſt have been completely obliterated.—Or, perhaps, (what ſeems likewiſe very poſſible,) ſome feeble and unobſerved remains of it may have ſomewhat facilitated his acquiſition of what he might otherwiſe have found it much more difficult to acquire.

That, antecedent to all experience, the young of at leaſt the greater part of animals poſſeſs ſome inſtinctive perception of this kind, ſeems abundently evident. The hen never feeds her young by by dropping the food into their bills, as the linnet and the thrush feed theirs. Almost as soon as her chickens are hatched, she does not feed them, but carries them to the field to feed, where they walk about at their ease, it would seem, and appear to have the most distinct perception of all the tangible objects which surround them. We may often see them, accordingly, by the straightest road, run to and pick up any little grains which she shews them, even at the distance of several yards; and they no sooner come into the light than they seem to understand this language of Vision as well as they ever do afterwards. The young of the partridge and of the grouse seem to have, at the same early period, the most distinct perceptions of the same kind. The young partridge, almost as soon as it comes from the shell, runs about among the long grass and corn; the young grouse among long heath, and would both most essentially hurt themselves if they had not the most acute, as well as distinct perception of the tangible objects which not only surround them but press upon them on all sides. This is the case too with the young of the goose, of the duck, and, so far as I have been able to observe, with those of at least the greater part of the birds which make their nests upon the ground, with the greater part of those which are ranked by Linnæus in the orders of the hen and the goose, and of many of those long-shanked and wading birds which he places in the order that he distinguishes by the name of Grallæ.

The young of thoſe birds that build their neſts in buſhes, upon trees, in the holes and crevices of high walls, upon high rocks and precipices, and other places of difficult acceſs; of the greater part of thoſe ranked by Linnæus in the orders of the hawk, the magpie, and the ſparrow, ſeem to come blind from the ſhell, and to continue ſo for at leaſt ſome days thereafter. Till they are able to fly they are fed by the joint labour of both parents. As ſoon as that period arrives, however, and probably for ſome time before, they evidently enjoy all the powers of Viſion in the moſt complete perfection, and can diſtinguiſh with moſt exact preciſion the ſhape and proportion of the tangible objects which every viſible one repreſents. In ſo ſhort a period they cannot be ſuppoſed to have acquired thoſe powers from experience, and muſt therefore derive them from ſome inſtinctive ſuggeſtion. The ſight of birds ſeems to be both more prompt and more acute than that of any other animals. Without hurting themſelves they dart into the thickeſt and moſt thorny buſhes, fly with the utmoſt rapidity through the moſt intricate foreſts, and while they are ſoaring aloft in the air, diſcover upon the ground the little inſects and grains upon which they feed.

The young of ſeveral ſorts of quadrupeds ſeem, like thoſe of the greater part of birds which make theit neſts upon the ground, to enjoy as ſoon as they come into the world the

the faculty of feeing as completely as they ever do afterwards. The day, or the day after they are dropt, the calf follows the cow, and the foal the mare, to the field; and though from timidity they feldom remove far from the mother, yet they feem to walk about at their eafe; which they could not do unlefs they could diftinguifh, with fome degree of precifion, the fhape and proportion of the tangible objects which each vifible one reprefents. The degree of precifion, however, with which the horfe is capable of making this diftinction, feems at no period of his life to be very complete. He is at all times apt to ftartle at many vifible objects, which, if they diftinctly fuggefted to him the real fhape and proportion of the tangible objects which they reprefent, could not be the objects of fear; at the trunk or root of an old tree, for example, which happens to be laid by the road fide, at a great ftone, or the fragment of a rock which happens to lie near the way where he is going. To reconcile him, even to a fingle object of this kind, which has once alarmed him, frequently requires fome fkill, as well as much patience and good temper, in the rider. Such powers of fight, however, as Nature has thought proper to render him capable of acquiring, he feems to enjoy from the beginning, in as great perfection as he ever does afterwards.

The

The young of other quadrupeds, like those of the birds which make their nests in places of difficult access, come blind into the world. Their sight, however, soon opens, and as soon as it does so, they seem to enjoy it in the most complete perfection, as we may all observe in the puppy and the kitten. The same thing, I believe, may be said of all other beasts of prey, at least of all those concerning which I have been able to collect any distinct information. They come blind into the world; but as soon as their sight opens, they appear to enjoy it in the most complete perfection.

It seems difficult to suppose that man is the only animal of which the young are not endowed with some instinctive perception of this kind. The young of the human species, however, continue so long in a state of entire dependency, they must be so long carried about in the arms of their mothers or of their nurses, that such an instinctive perception may seem less necessary to them than to any other race of animals. Before it could be of any use to them, observation and experience may, by the known principle of the association of ideas, have sufficiently connected in their young minds each visible object with the corresponding tangible one which it is fitted to represent. Nature, it may be said, never bestows upon any animal any faculty which is not either necessary or useful, and an instinct of this kind would

would be altogether uſeleſs to an animal which muſt neceſſarily acquire the knowledge which the inſtinct is given to ſupply, long before that inſtinct could be of any uſe to it. Children, however, appear at ſo very early a period to know the diſtance, the ſhape, and magnitude of the different tangible objects which are preſented to them, that I am diſpoſed to believe that even they may have ſome inſtinctive perception of this kind; though poſſibly in a much weaker degree than the greater part of other animals. A child that is ſcarcely a month old, ſtretches out its hands to feel any little play-thing that is preſented to it. It diſtinguiſhes its nurſe, and the other people who are much about it, from ſtrangers. It clings to the former, and turns away from the latter. Hold a ſmall looking-glaſs, before a child of not more than two or three months old, and it will ſtretch out its little arms behind the glaſs, in order to feel the child which it ſees, and which it imagines is at the back of the glaſs. It is deceived, no doubt; but even this ſort of deception ſufficiently demonſtrates that it has a tolerably diſtinct apprehenſion of the ordinary perſpective of Viſion, which it cannot well have learnt from obſervation and experience.

Do any of our other ſenſes, antecedently to ſuch obſervation and experience, inſtinctively ſuggeſt to us ſome conception of the ſolid and reſiſting

resisting substances which excite their respective sensations; though these sensations bear no sort of resemblance to those substances?

The sense of Tasting certainly does not. Before we can feel the sensation, the solid and resisting substance which excites it must be pressed against the organs of Taste, and must consequently be perceived by them. Antecedently to observation and experience, therefore, the sense of Tasting can never be said instinctively to suggest some conceptions of that substance.

It may, perhaps, be otherwise with the sense of Smelling. The young of all suckling animals, (of the Mammalia of Linnæus,) whether they are born with sight or without it, yet as soon as they come into the world apply to the nipple of the mother in order to suck. In doing this they are evidently directed by the Smell. The Smell appears either to excite the appetite for the proper food, or at least to direct the new-born animal to the place where that food is to be found. It may perhaps do both the one and the other.

That when the stomach is empty, the Smell of agreeable food excites and irritates the appetite, is what we all must have frequently experienced. But the stomach of every new-born animal is necessarily empty. While in the womb

womb it is nouriſhed, not by the mouth, but by the navel-ſtring. Children have been born apparently in the moſt perfect health and vigour, and have applied to ſuck in the uſual manner; but immediately, or ſoon after, have thrown up the milk, and in the courſe of a few hours have died vomiting and in convulſions. Upon opening their bodies it has been found that the inteſtinal tube or canal had never been opened or pierced in the whole extent of its length; but, like a ſack, admitted of no paſſage beyond a particular place. It could not have been in any reſpect by the mouth, therefore, but altogether by the navel-ſtring, that ſuch children had been nouriſhed and fed up to the degree of health and vigour in which they were born. Every animal, while in the womb, ſeems to draw its nouriſhment, more like a vegetable, from the root, than like an animal from the mouth; and that nouriſhment ſeems to be conveyed to all the different parts of the body by tubes and canals in many reſpects different from thoſe which afterwards perform the ſame function. As ſoon as it comes into the world, this new ſet of tubes and canals, which the providential care of Nature had for a long time before been gradually preparing, is all at once and inſtantaneouſly opened. They are all empty, and they require to be filled. An uneaſy ſenſation accompanies the one ſituation, and an agreeable one the other. The ſmell of of the ſubſtance which is fitted for filling them, increaſes and irritates that uneaſy ſenſation, and produces hunger, or the appetite for food.

But all the appetites which take their origin from a certain ſtate of the body, ſeem to ſuggeſt the means of their own gratification; and, even long before experience, ſome anticipation or preconception of the pleaſure which attends that gratification. In the appetite for the ſex, which frequently, I am diſpoſed to believe almoſt always, comes a long time before the age of puberty, this is perfectly and diſtinctly evident. The appetite for food ſuggeſts to the new-born infant the operation of ſucking, the only means by which it can poſſibly gratify that appetite. It is continually ſucking. It ſucks whatever is preſented to its mouth. It ſucks even when there is nothing preſented to its mouth, and ſome anticipation or preconception of the pleaſure which it is to enjoy in ſucking, ſeems to make it delight in putting its mouth into the ſhape and configuration by which it alone can enjoy that pleaſure. There are other appetites in which the moſt unexperienced imagination produces a ſimilar effect upon the organs which Nature has provided for their gratification.

The Smell not only excites the appetite, but directs to the object which can alone gratify that appetite. But by ſuggeſting the direction towards that object, the Smell muſt neceſſarily ſuggeſt ſome

ſome notion of diſtance and externality, which are neceſſarily involved in the idea of direction; in the idea of the line of motion by which the diſtance can be beſt overcome, and the mouth brought into contact with the unknown ſubſtance which is the object of the appetite. That the Smell ſhould alone ſuggeſt any preconception of the ſhape or magnitude of the external body to which it directs, ſeems not very probable. The ſenſation of Smell ſeems to have no ſort of affinity or correſpondence with ſhape or magnitude; and whatever preconception the infant may have of theſe, (and it may very probably have ſome ſuch preconception,) is likely to be ſuggeſted, not ſo much directly by the Smell, and indirectly by the appetite excited by that Smell; as by the principle which teaches the child to mould its mouth into the conformation and action of ſucking, even before it reaches the object to which alone that conformation and action can be uſefully applied.

A
CATALOGUE

OF THE

VALUABLE LIBRARY

OF THE LATE

Right Rev. Dr. BERKELEY, LORD BISHOP of CLOYNE.

TOGETHER WITH THE

Libraries of his Son and Grandſon, the late Rev. GEORGE BERKELEY, D. D. PREBENDARY of CANTERBURY, and the late GEORGE MONK BERKELEY, Eſq.

Including a good Collection of Books in *Divinity*, *Foreign* and *Engliſh Domeſtic Hiſtory*, *Voyages*, *Travels*, *Claſſics*, *Belles Lettres*, *Miſcellanies*, *Poetry*, and in almoſt every Branch of Polite Literature, in both the modern and dead Languages.

N. B. Several EDITIONES PRINCIPES in the fifteenth and ſixteenth Centuries.

Which will be Sold by Auction,

By *LEIGH* AND *SOTHEBY*, BOOKSELLERS,

At their Houſe in YORK-STREET, COVENT-GARDEN,

On MONDAY, JUNE 6, 1796, and the Five following Days.

Beginning each Day at TWELVE o'Clock.

To be Viewed to the Time of Sale.

CATALOGUES to be had of the following Bookſellers:

Mr. Walter, Charing Croſs; Mr. Beckett, Pall Mall; Mr. Faulder, Bond-Street; Meſſrs. White, Fleet-Street; Mr. Sewell, Cornhill; and at the Place of Sale.

First Day's Sale.

TWELVES.

1 *STERNHOLD* and *Hopkin's Psalms* — *1642*
2 Testamentum Græcum — *Sedani* 1628
3 Liber Salmorum, Græce — — *Par.* 1618
4 Testamentum Græcum Leusdeni — *L. Bat.* 1716
5 Cardani Arcarna Politia, *mor. gilt leaves* *Elz.* 1635
6 Rami Grammatica. Talæi Rhetorica — *Hanov.* 1622
7 Plauti Comœdiæ — *Amst.* 1630
8 Pindari Opera, *Gr. et Lat.* — *Genev.* 1626
9 Lucan, by May — — 1650
10 *Marino (la Sampogna del)* — *Amst.* 1651
11 *Dante* — — *Lyons* 1551
12 *Marino (l'Adone del)* — — *Amst.* 1651
13 *Bartoli dell Huomo di Lettere, Bologna,* 1646. *Bartoli La Poverta Contenta* — *Milan* 1650
14 D'Alquie Les Memoires du Voyage de la Marquis de Ville an Levant, ou l'Histoire du Siege de Candie, 2 tom. *Amst.* 1671,0
15 *Lalli l'Eneide Travestita* — *Venet.* 1651
16 *La Sofonisba, Tragedia, di Trissino, Venet.* 1595. *Il Re Torrismondo, Tragedia del Tassa, Ferrara,* 1587. *Orbecca, Tragedia di Giraldi Cinthio, Venet.* 1594. *Ifigenia, Tragedia, di Dolce, Veneg. ap. Giolito,* 1551. *Madrigali dell' Valerio Belli, Venet. ap. Ciotti,* 1599, &c. &c.
17 Caussini Tragœdiæ Sacræ — *Par.* 1629
18 Les Funestes Effets de l'Amour, 2 tom. *Luxembourg* 1707
19 Hilperti Disquisitio de Præadamitis, *Amst.* 1656. Ursini Shediasma Novus Prometheus Præadamitarum Plalles, ad Caucasum relegatus et religatus *Francof.* 1656

B 20 Arliquiana

(2)

20 Arliquiniana — — Par. 1694
21 *Gonzalez di Mendozza l'Historia del Gran Regno della China* Vineg. 1587
22 *Tassoni, La Secchia Rapita, Bologna*, 1683. *Prediche Panegiriche del Mattia* — *Parma* 1658
23 *Ripalda Catecismo, y Expoficion Breve de la Doctrina Christiana* — — — *Madrid* 1659
24 Redi de Insectis, *cum fig.* — *Amst.* 1671
25 *Arcadia del Sannazaro, Dolce* *Vineg. ap. Giolito* 1556
26 Fleury du Choix et de la Methode des Etudes *Bruxel.* 1687
27 Gottelow's Charles Stuart and Oliver Cromwell United 1655
28 Æliani Varia Historia, *Gr. et Lat.* *ap Tornæs* 1610
29 Barclai Argenis — *Lug. Bat. ap. Elz.* 1630
30 Bible (Holy) 2 vol. — *Oxf. by Basket* 1739
31 Claudiani Historia — *Amst. ap. Elz.* 1677
32 Strada de Bello Belgico, *cum fig.* 2 tom. *Rom.* 1648
33 Maximus Tyrius, *Gr. et Lat.* — *Oxon.* 1677
34 Bellegarde Reflexions sur le Ridicule — *Hague* 1720
35 Golnitzii Itinerarium Belgico Gallicum *Amst. ap. Elz.* 1655
36 Juvenalis et Persii Satyræ — *ib. ib.* 1651
37 *El Discreto de Lorenzo Gracian* — *Amst.* 1665
38 Owen's Guide to Church-Fellowship — 1778
39 *Il Nipotismo di Roma*, 2 parts en 1 — 1668
40 Platonis Opera, a Ficino, *lineis rubris, corio turcico ac foliis deauratis*, 5 tom. *wants the first vol. Lugdun. ap. Tornæs* 1550
41 Le Sage, Le Diable Boiteux, *avec fig.* 2 tom. en une *Amst.* 1739
42 Biblia Hebraicæ, 4 tom. —
43 Testamentum (Novum) Græcum, *corio turcico, ac foliis deauratis*, 2 tom. *Lutet. ap. Rob. Steph.* 1549
44 Corvini Jus Canonicum — *Amst. ap. Elz.* 1663
45 *Rime del Eustachio Manfredi* — *Bologna* 1713
46 Demosthenis Orationes Selectæ, *Gr. et Lat.* *Lond.* 1746
47 Preces Privatæ *Lond. ap. Seres* 1573
48 Lemnius de Miraculis Occultis Naturæ, *Francof.* 1604. Ejusdem Hebr. Bibl. Explicatio et de Astrologia *Francof.* 1608
49 Montalte Lettres Provinciales — *Colog.* 1657
50 Comines (Les Memoires de Philippe de) *Leide ap. Elz.* 1648
51 Mureti Orationes — — *Col. Agrip.* 1682
52 Caussinus de Symbolica Ægyptiorum Sapientia *ib. ib.* 1623
53 Herodiani Historia, *Gr. et Lat.* ab Huobero *Basil ap. Henrichum Petri* 1549
54 Quintus Curtius, a Maittaire, cum indice *Lond.* 1716
55 *Tasso Gierusalemme liberata* *Venet. ap. Ciotti* 1595
56 Dickinsoni Delphi Phoenicizantes — *Oxon.* 1655

57 Testamentum

57 Testamentum (Novum) Græcum, a Leusdeno *Amst.* 1749
58 Testamentum (Novum) Græcum, *caret tit.*
59 Terentii Comœdiæ, a Maittaire, *cum indice* *Lond.* 1713
60 Pensees de Pascal — — *Par.* 1679
61 *Poesie del Testi* — — *Venet.* 1683
62 Parthenii Piscatoria et Nautica, *cum fig.* *Neapol. Typis Regiis* 1685
63 Leslie's Short Method with the Deists *Canterbury* 1786
64 Lily's Introduction to Latin Grammar — 1784
65 Valerius Flaccus — — *Amst.* 1680
66 *Historia delle Medaglie, con fig.* — *Venet.* 1673
67 Antonii Liberalis Metamorphoses, *Gr. et Lat.* a Berkelio *Lug. Bat. et Amst. ap. Gaasbekios* 1674
68 Crucii Suada Delphica, sive Orationes *Amst.* 1709
69 Menagii Poëmata — *ib.* 1687
70 Montalte Lettres Provinciales — *Cologne* 1683
71 Raleigh's (Sir Walter) Remains — 1681
72 Osborn's (Francis) Advice to a Son — 1658
73 Hierocles in Aurea Carmina Pythagoreorum, *Gr. et Lat.* a Curterio — *Lond.* 1654
74 Phædri Fabulæ, a Maittaire, *cum indice* — *ib.* 1713
75 Macrinus de Vesuvio et Poetica Opuscula *Neapol.* 1693
76 Quintus Calaber, *Græcé* — — *ap. Ald.*
77 *Dialoghi di Amore, per Leone Medico* *Veneg. ap. Ald.* 1545
78 Huart l'Examen des Esprits, par Tourangeau *Lyon* 1608
79 Cornelius Nepos — *Edinb.* 1776
80 *Lally l'Eneide Travestita* — *Rom.* 1634
81 *Proverbi Italiani, e Latini, Raccolti da Lena* *Bologn.* 1694
82 Petronii Arbitri Satyricon et Fragmenta, cum Priapeia *Amst.* 1663
83 Leusdeni Compendium Græcum — *Ultraject.* 1682
84 Aristophanis Comœdiæ, *Gr. et Lat.* a Scaligero *L. Bat.* 1624
85 Crebillon, Le Sopha, Conte Moral, 2 tom. *Francfort* 1751
86 Schotti Itinerarium Italiæ — *Amst.* 1655
87 Bernier Histoire de Revolution des Estats du Grand Mogol, 2 tom. en une — *Par.* 1671
88 Martialis Epigrammata, a Farnabio — *Amst.* 1645
89 Baudii Epistolæ et Orationes, *chart max.* *Amst. ap. Ez.* 1654
90 Crusii Suada Delphica, sive Orationes — *Amst.* 1650
91 *Cole's and the Bishop of Sarum's Letters, occasioned by a Sermon preached by the Bishop before the Quene* — 1560
92 Petronii Arbitri Satyricon — *Lond.* 1707
93 *Tasso, la Gerusalemme Liberata, con fig.* 2 tom. *Parigi ap. Jolly* 1705
94 Butler's Hudibras — — 1779
95 Horace, *Lat. and Eng.* by Smart, 2 vol. *Edinb.* 1777
96 Conciones et Orationes ex Historicis Latinis *Lond.* 1713

B 2 97 *Pallavicino*

97 *Palavicino (Lettere dal Card.)* — *Venet.* 1678

98 Voyage d'Espagne, 3 tom. in une — *Haye* 1693

99 Hattige, or the Amours of the King of Tamaran, a Novel, *with MS. Key* — *Amst.* 1680

100 Misna, *Hebrew*

101 Smith's David's Repentance, or Exposition of the 51st Psalm, *gilt leaves* — 1623

102 Quevedo, (Les Visions de) par de la Geneste *Par.* 1639

103 Oeuvres de Mon. Le Pays, *deux parties* *Amst.* 1677

104 Recueil de Divers Pieces, servans a l'Histoire de Henry III. — *Cologne* 1662

105 Sobrino Grammaire Espagnole — *Brussel* 1697

106 Juvenal and Persius, by Dryden, *plates* *Tonson* 1713

107 Virgile, (Les Oeuvres de) *Lat. et Fr.* 4 tom. *Par.* 1746

108 Le Sage, Les Avantures de Gil Blas, *avec fig.* 3 tom. *Amst.* 1720

109 Vidæ Opera — *Lugdun* 1607

110 Vossius de Studiorum Ratione — *Ultraject* 1651

111 *Pietra del Paragone Politico, con fig.* *In Cosmopol.* 1664

112 *Rimas de Lope de Vega Carpio* — *En Sevilla* 1604

113 Histoire des Diables de Loudun — *Amst* 1693

114 Memoires de la Cour d'Espagne, *deux parties* *Haye* 1692

115 Birago Avogadro Histoire Africane, 2 tom. en une *Par.* 1666

116 Taciti Opera — *Lug. Bat. ap Elz.* 1634

117 Bohours la Maniere de bien Penser *Amst.* 1688

118 Fenelon Nouveaux Dialogues des Morts, *deux parties* *Amst.* 1694

119 Boursault Lettres Nouvelles — *Par.* 1698

120 Naude Apologie des Grands Hommes Accusez de Magie, *Par.* 1669

121 Spon et Wheler Voyage d'Italie, de Dalmatie, de Grece et du Levant, *avec fig.* 2 tom. *Amst.* 1679

122 Sainctyon Histoire du Grand Tamerlan *ib.* 1697

123 Nostradamus (Les Vrayes Centuries et Propheties de Maitre) *Amst.* 1668

124 Bellegarde Modeles de Conversations pour les Personnes Polies — *Haye* 1719

125 Voyage d'Espagne, 3 tom. en une — *ib.* 1692

126 Bruscambille (Les Oeuvres de) — *Rouen* 1629

127 Neri Ars Vitraria, a Merretto *Amst.* 1686

128 Aristophanis Comoediæ Undecim, *Gr. Lat.* a Scaligero, 2 tom. *ibid* 1670

130 Testamentum (Novum) Græcum, a Leusdeno, *Amst.* 1698. Robertson's Hebrew Text of the Psalmes and Lamentations — *Lond.* 1656

131 Andrew's

(5)

131 Andrew's (Bp.) Manual of Private Devotions, by Drake 1674

132 Bernier Histoire des Etats du Grand Mogul, 2 tom. Par. 1670

133 *Poesie Toscane del Senatore da Filicaia* Parma 1709

134 *Nuova Guida per Napoli, con fig.* — Napol. 1716

135 *Boccaccio, I Casi de gl' Huomini Illustri, per Betussi* In Fiorenza 1598

136 *Vita di Marco Aurelio* — Venet. 1622

137 Sorberiana — Par. 1695

138 Plaute (Comedies de) *Lat. et Fr.* par Le Fevre, 3 tom. ib. 1691

139 Motte (Odes de M. de la) — Amst. 1707

140 *Trissino (La Italia Liberata da Gotthi dell) en maroquin, e foglie dorat,* 3 tom. — Roma et Venez 1547. 8

141 Pope's Miscellaneous Poems, 2 vol. — 1722

*142 Piganiol de la Force Description de Paris, Versailles, Marly, &c. &c. *avec fig.* 8 tom. Par. 1742

*143 Neckerus de Secretis, ex variis Authoribus Collecti Basil 1662

*144 Psalmi Davidis, *lineis rubris* Lutet ap Rob. Steph. 1546

*145 Porree des Anciennes Ceremonies Quevilly 1673

*146 Selectæ è Veteri Testamento Historiæ Lond. 1753

*147 *Do Tor and Student* — 1660

*148 Etat des Royaumes de Barbarie, Tripoly, Tunis et Alger Haye 1714

*149 *Malvezzi (Opera del Virgilio)* Venez 1693

*150 Horace, *Lat. et Eng.* by Creech, 2 vol. in 1 1718

*151 Horatii Opera, a Bond Amst. 1628

*152 Sallustii Historia, a Maittaire, *cum indice* Lond. 1713

*153 *Gomara (Lopez de) Historia de la Conquista de Mexico* Anvers 1554

*154 Testament (Le Nouveau) par Quesnel, 4 tom. Brux. 1702

*155 Rudiments of the Latin Tongue — 1759

QUARTO.

142 Dutch Bible — 1685

143 *El Politico de Cielo* Madrid 1637

144 Hero and Leander, a Poem — Glasg. 1783

145 *Crescentio delle Cose, a Bisogni, con figure* Venet. 1561

146 Clavis Talmudica, *Heb. et Lat.* L. Bat. 1634

147 *Filosophia Morale d' Aristotle* Roma 1558

148 Spanhemi Numismata — Amst. 1671

149 Maffei Historia Indicarum — 1589

150 Miege's French Dictionary — 1677

151 Usserius de Christianarum Ecclesiarum — 1613

152 Guicciardini

£ 11

No.	Title	Place	Year	s.	d.	Buyer
152	*Guicciardini delle cose in Europa*	*Veneti*	1565	1	–	Atkinson
153	*El Parnaso Espagnol*	*Madrid*	1648	–	9	Herriere
154	Chamberlayni Oratio Dominica	*Amst.*	1715	7	6	Herriere
155	Somner's Antiquities of Canterbury, *plates*		1640	4	–	Priestley
156	Borough's Treatise of Evils		1654 }	3	–	Bowes
157	Biblia Hebraica		}			
158	Meursii Athenæ Atticæ	*L. Bat.*	1624	–	6	Delongchamp
159	Portius de Dolore	*Florent*	1551	–	6	Bedel
160	Gualtheri Siciliæ Antiquæ Tabulæ			1	–	Leigh
161	~~*De Solis Comedias*~~	*Madrid*	1716			
162	*Alvaro Relatione delle Granda Monarchia*	*Roma*	1643	1	3	Herriere
163	Junius de Pictura	*Amst.*	1637	1	3	Herriere
164	Sturmii Collegium Experimentale Curiosum		1676 }			
165	Clarendon on Hobbes's Leviathan		1676 }	2	9	Walker
166	Campanella on the Spanish Monarchy		1654 }			
167	Behmen's (Jacob) Arrora, or Day Spring		1712 }			
168	Vita del Don Philippo II	*Vicenza*	1605			
169	*Calvetro Poetica d'Aristotele*		1576	1	6	Geddes
170	Scepher Elim, in Hebrew, a Joseph del Medico			4	–	Geddes
171	Campanella Astrologicæ	*Francof.*	1630	–	6	Darcey
172	*Sansovino del Governo*	*Venet.*	1607 }	4	–	Banks
173	*Il Pastor Fido, figuris*	*Venet.*	1602 }			
174	Diodati's Annotations on the Bible		1548	3	–	Bedel
175	*Laynez sobre los Evangelios de la Quaresma*		1625	1	3	Herriere
176	Meurii Creta Rhodus et Cyprus		1675	1	9	Bond
177	Bottoni de Igne Dissertatio		1692 }	3	6	Darcey
178	Charron on Wisdom		1670 }			
179	Le Moyne l'Art des Devises, *avec fig. embl.*	*Par.*	1666	2	6	D. Walker
180	Lock on St. Paul's Epistles		1707			
181	Vossii Observationes		1707 }	2	3	Geddes
182	Florus, *Delph*	*Par.*	1674	3	6	Banks
183	Montfaucon Diarium Italicum	*ib.*	1702			
184	Virgilius, *Delph.*	*Amst.*	1690	4	3	Bond
185	Parker's Eusebius		1720	1	9	Bedel
186	*Boccario il Decameron*	*Venet.*	1638	4	3	Herriere
187	*Glorias de Maria Santissima*	Coimbra	1659	–	9	Herriere
188	Des Cartes de Homine	*Amst.*	1677 }	1	–	Bedel
189	Bates Vita Selectorum Virorum		1681 }			
190	Van Dale super Aristea	*ib.*	1705 }	1	–	Bedel
191	Hale's Golden Remains		1673 }			
192	Frisii Astrologiæ	*Antv.*	1583 }	3	3	J. Walker
193	Buccaniers of America		1684 }			
194	Cornelius Nepos, *Delph.*	*Par.*	1675	2	–	Geddes
195	Heylin's Theological Lectures		1749	–	6	Priestley
196	Pancirolli Rerum Memorabilium			1	–	Bethel
197	Sabellico le Historie Venitiane	*Venet.*	1554 }			
198	*Mattia Metodo Geometrico*	*Anvers*	1715 }			
199	Catalogues					

14 . 10 . 6

199 Catalogus Librorum Bodleianæ — Oxon. 1620
200 Ben Gorionis Historiæ Judaicæ — 1706
201 Tomassini Elogia — 1644
202 Wood's Elements of Jurisprudence — 1783
203 Virgilii Opera, a Valkenier — Amst. 1646
~~204 El Olimpo del Sabio — Barcel. 1691~~

FOLIO.

205 Blackmore's King Arthur — 1697
206 White's Divine Works — 1624
207 Book of Common Prayer — 1662
208 Taylor's Sermons at Golden Grove — 1653
209 Heinsii Exercitationes ad Nov. Testam. L. Bat. 1639
210 Pococke on Hosea — 1685
211 *Bonanni delle Antiche Siracuse, fig.* 2 vol. in 1 — 1717
212 Euclidis Elementa a Commandino — Pisari 1572
213 Taciti Opera, a Lipsio — L. Bat. 1589
214 Polybii Historia, Causoboni, Gr. Lat. Par. 1609
215 Testamentum (Novum) Græcum, a Millio, Oxon. 1707
216 Hooker's Ecclesiastic Politie — 1632
217 Selden on the Dominion of the Sea — 1652
218 *Granada (Luis de) de la Introduccion del Simbolo de la Fé*
219 Petrarchæ Opera — Basil 1554
220 Bion on Mathematical Instruments, by Stone 1723
221 Sanderson's Sermons — 1681
222 Holyoke's Dictionary — 1677
223 Hooker's Ecclesiastical Politie — 1682
224 Cluverii Italia Antiqua, 2 tom. — 1624
225 Stobæi Sententiæ — Francof. 1581
226 Platonis Opera, Ficini, 2 tom. — ib. 1602
227 Gyraldus de Deis Gentium, *fig.* L. Bat. 1696
228 Graduale Romanum suxta Missale Antv. 1620
229 History of Philip de Comines — 1665
230 Seleni Crytographia — 1624
231 Philips's New World of Words — 1658
232 *More's (Sir Thomas) Works* — 1557
233 *Alunno della Fabrica del Mondo* Venet. 1600
234 Machumitis Alcoran — 1550
235 Helvici Theatrum Historicum — 1662
236 Pauli Jovi Vitæ — Florent 1551
237 Firmici Astronomicon — Basil 1551
238 Andrews's (Bishop) Sermons — 1641
239 Cowley's Works — 1681
240 *Leonardo de Argensola Conquista de las Islas Maluccas* 1509
241 Jamblicus de Mysteriis — ap. Ald. 1497
242 Plotini

242 Plotini Opera Philosophica — Basil 1580
243 Schmidii Concordantia in Nov. Testam. Lips. 1717
244 Aristotelis Opera, Græcè, ab Erasmo Basil 1531
245 Chauvin Lexicon Philosophicum — Rotterd. 1692
246 *Sermones de la Passion de Christo* — Madrid 1563
247 Blackmore's Prince Arthur — 1695
248 Sadi Rosarium Politicum, *Pers. et Lat.* Amst. 1651
249 Xenophontis Opera, Leunclavii, *Gr. Lat.* Bas. 1573
250 Josephi Opera, *Græcè* — ib. 1544
251 Eustratii in Aristotelem de Moribus, *Græce* Venet. ap. Ald. 1536
252 El Triompho del Desenganna — Nap. 1632
253 Harris's Lexicon Technicum, 2 vol. 1704
254 Erasmi Adagia — 1629
255 Percivale's Spanish and English Dictionary 1623

Second Day's Sale.

TWELVES.

256 DIARISTE et d'Eugene (les Entretiens) Amst. 1703
257 Browne's *Hydriotaphia*, or Urne Burial 1658
258 *Cervantes Don Quixote*, Spanish, 2 tom. Brucelas 1617
259 *Monteinayer (Diana de George de)* Madrid 1622
260 Observationes Selectæ ad Rem Litterarium, 3 tom. Hal. Magdeb. 1700
261 Bibliotheque des Génies et des Fees, 2 tom. Par. 1765
262 Delitiæ Poetarum Germanorum, 13 tom. Francof. 1612. Poetarum Italorum, 4 tom. 1608. Poetarum Belgicorum, 6 tom. Francof. 1614. Poetarum Gallorum, 2 tom. 1609. Poetarum Hungaricorum, Francof. 1619. Poetarum Scotorum, Amst. 1637. Poetarum Danorum, 2 tom, Lug. Bat. 1693, together 29 vol.

263 Cæsaris

263 Cæfaris Commentaria — Amft. ap. Elz. 1661
264 Scarron, le Virgile Travefty — Par. 1668
265 Galloway's Poems, Epiftles, and Songs, chiefly in the Scottifh Dialect — Glafg. 1788
266 *Elucidario Poetico, Raccolta per Hermano Torrentino, tradotto di Horatio Tufcanella* — Venet. 1565
267 Epiftolæ Indicæ et Japanicæ — Lovan. 1570
268 *Dialoghi del Guazzo* — Venet. 1590
269 *Dialoghi del Guazzo* — ib. 1590
270 Buchanani Paraphrafis Pfalmorum Davidis Poetica, *chart. opt.* — Glafg. 1765
271 Anacreontis Carmina, *Gr. Lat.* a Barnefio Cantab. 1705
272 Dugard Rhetorices Elementa Quæftionibus et Refponfionibus Explicata — Lond. 1721
273 Relandus de Spoliis Templi Hierofolymitani, *cum fig.* Traj. ad Rhen. 1716
274 *Il Petrarca, da Dolce* — Vineg. ap. Giolito 1558
275 Suetonius, Aurelius Victor, Eutropius et Pauli Diaconi libri VIII. ad Eutropii Hiftoriam additi Venet. ap. Ald. 1516
276 Bouhours, la Maniere de Bien Penfer Amft. 1688
277 *Salazar (de) Secretos de la Gramatica Efpañolo* Rouen 1640
278 *Paolo (Opere del Padre)* 5 tom. — Venet. 1677
279 *Xenophonte della Vita di Ciro Re de Perfi, tradotto per Domenichi* — Vineg. ap. Giolito 1558
280 Ciceronis Epiftolæ ad Familiares — Amft. 1645
281 Harrington's Art of Law-Giving — 1659
282 Bouhours Penfées Ingenieufes des Anciens et des Modernes Par. 1692
283 *Tracts.*—Heads of a Difcourfe held in Axbridge, 1650, between John Smith and Charles Carlile on one part and Thomas Collier on the other, 1651. Gomerfall's Levites Revenge, containing Poetical Meditations upon the 19th and 20th Chapter of Judges, 1628, &c.
284 Teiffier Abrege de la Vie de divers Princes, *avec fig.* 1710
285 *Giornale de Letterati d'Italia*, 27 tom. wants the 12th, and 14th vol. — Venez. 1710
286 Ciceronis Opera omnia, 20 tom. — Glafg. 1749
287 Teftament (The) of the 12 Patriarchs the Sons of Jacob, *wood cuts* — 1660
288 Teftamentum (Novum) *Gr. Lat.* — Amft. 1741
289 D'Alembert's Mifcellanies in Literature, Hiftory, &c. Glafg. 1765
290 Religio Medici, cum Annotationibus Argent. 1665
291 Epiftolæ Clarorum Virorum Harling. Frif. 1664
292 Watts on Education — 1769
293 Sadoleti Epiftolæ — Lugdun. ap. Gryph. 1556

C 294 Traitez

1 . 9 . 3

263 — 2 — Hoger
273 — 2 — 6 Field
274 — 9 Madaillon
276 — 1 — Wilbraham
277 — 3 — Madaillon
278 — 6 Madaillon
280–283 — 1 — 3 Madaillon
284 — 4 Madaillon
285 — 4 — 6 Madaillon
286 1 — 10 — Lowe
287 — 1 — 6 Hoger
288 — 6 Cuthel
289 — 9 (1) Edw. Winnington
291 — 6 Cuthel
293 — 1 — 6 Coombe

£ 3 . 10 . 9

294 Traitez des Barometres, Thermometres et Notiometres ou Hygrometres, *avec fig.* — *Amst.* 1688

295 *Cervantes Galatea* — — *Par.* 1611

296 Grotius de Veritate Religionis Christianæ, a Clerico *Hag. Com.* 1718

297 *Dialoghi di Speron Speroni* *Vineg. ap. Giglio* 1558

298 Marivaux le Spectateur François, 2 tom. *Par.* 1752

299 D'Orleans Histoire des Revolutions d'Espagne, 4 tom. *Haye* 1734

300 Rowe's Works, 2 vol. — 1747

301 Réponse a l'Histoire des Oracles de Mr. de Fontenelle *Strasb.* 1707

302 Romaine on the Life of Faith — 1764

303 Palairet Methode pour Apprendre a bien lire *Lond.* —

304 Erasmus de Copia Verborum *Argent. a Knoblochus* 1523

305 Themistoclis Epistolæ, *Gr. Lat.* a Caryophilo cum notis Schoettgenii — *Lips.* 1710

306 Statii Opera — *Ven. ap. Ald.* 1519

307 Thompson's Sailor's Letters, 2 vol. — 1767

308 Horatii Opera, *cum fig.* 2 tom. *Lond, ap. Sandby.* 1749

309 Blair's Synopsis of Lectures on Belles Lettres and Logic *Edinb.* 1781

310 Clayton's (Bp.) Vindication of the Old and New Testament against Bolingbroke, 3 vol. *Dubl.* 1754

311 Les Curiositez de Paris, *avec fig.* 3 vol. *Par.* 1733

312 Gürtleri Historia Templariorum — *Amst.* 1703

313 Fenelon Lettres sur la Religion et la Metaphysique *Par.* 1718

314 *Ariosto (Le Satire de) Il Negromante Comedia, le Leva, Comedia Vineg. per Nicolo d'Aristotile detto Zoppino* 1538,7

315 La Casas la Decouvertes des Indes Occidentales, par les Espagnols — — *Paris* 1697

316 *Parabosco (Lettere Amorose di)* — *Venet.* 1717

317 Damiano a Goes de Æthiopum Moribus, Fides, Religio Moresque — *Paris ap. Wech.* 1541

318 *Ariosto (Satire e Rime di)* — *Lond.* 1716

319 Vigerius de Precipuis Græcis — *Lond.* 1678

320 Pascal (Pensees de) — *Amst.* 1699

321 Decker on Foreign Trade — *Dubl.* 1749

322 Sedulii Poemata Sacra — *Edinb.* 1701

323 Letters from a Persian in England — 1735

324 Hesiodi Opera, Theognidis Sententiæ, &c. *lineis rubris* *Venet.* 1543

325 Cicero de Officiis — *Dublin* 1735

326 Ciceronis Epistolæ, a Sturmio — 1717

327 Satyre Menippee de la Vertu — *Ratisbon* 1690

328 Scotch

328 Scotch Presbyterian Eloquence Displayed 1786
329 Joannis ab Indagine Introductiones Apotelesmaticæ in Physiognomian, &c. *cum fig.* — *Argent* 1630
330 Buxtorf de Abbreviaturis Hebraicis *Basil* 1613
331 Apolinarii interpretatio Psalmorum, versibus Heroicis, *Græcæ* — — *Lond.* 1690
332 Preston's Plain and Familiar Guide to Astronomy
333 Warder's Monarchy of Bees — 1712
334 La Science des Medailles — *Paris* 1692
335 De Luna's Spanish Grammar — *Lond.* 1623
336 Fables Choisies de la Fontaine — *Amst.* 1693
337 Basnage Histoire de la Bible, 3 tom. en 2 *Genev.* 1708
338 *Vegetio del Arte Militare* — *Venet.* 1525
339 Chevigny la Science des Personnes de la Cour, *avec planches*, 2 tom. — *Amst.* 1713
340 La Croze Histoire du Christianisme d'Ethiope et d'Armenie — — *Haye* 1739
341 The Travels of the Imagination — 1773
342 Alvarado's Spanish and English Dialogues 1719
343 Bullokar's English Expositor — 1641
344 *Historia de los Vandos de los Zegris, y Abencerrages Cavelleros Moros de Granada, por Gines Perez de Hita Sevilla* 1625
345 Luciani Opera, *Græcè* — *Hagan.* 1526
346 Goulart Thresor Admirable et Memorables, 4 tom. en 2 *Genev.* 1620,28
347 D'Aristote (la Poetique) par Dacier *Paris* 1692
348 Graunt on the Bills of Mortality *Oxford* 1665
349 Marivaux Pharsamon, ou les Nouvelles Folies Romanesque, 2 tom. en une — *Haye* 1737
350 L'Iliade d'Homere, par la Motte, *avec fig.* *Paris* 1714
351 Letters from Altamont — 1767
352 Valerius Flaccus ab Egentino — *Argent* 1525
353 Albinovani Elegia et Fragmenta — *Amst.* 1703
354 Vernulæi Tragœdiæ Septem — *Lovan* 1631
355 Moliere (Les Oeuvres de) 2 tom. — *Jene* 1750
356 *Cervantes los Trabaios de Persiles* *Bruselas* 1618
357 Buxtorfii Lexicon Hebraicum et Chaldaicum *Basil* 1655
358 Liturgia Anglicana — — *Leyd.* 1703
359 *Boccaccio (Il Philopono di)* — *Vineg.* 1527,(
360 *Guzman de Alfarache* — *Madrid* 1601
361 *Porcacchi, Lettere di XIII. Huomini Illustri* *Venet.* 1582
362 Plaute (Les Oeuvres de) *Lat. & Fr.* par Limiers, 10 tom. *Amst.* 1719
363 Buchanani Historia Rerum Scoticarum *Francof. ad Moen.* 1624
364 Satyre Menippée, *avec fig.* 3 tom. *Ratisbon* 1711
365 Prideaux's Directions to Churchwardens 1716

C 2 366 Gentle-

366 Gentleman's Religion —— 1716
367 *Viaggi di Franceſco Carletti dell' Indie Occidentali e Orientali* *Firenzl* 1701
368 *Nuova della Scienza Chiamata Cavallereſca* *Palermo* 1717
369 Virgilii Opera, ab Erythræo —— *Hanov.* 1608
370 *Gravina della Ragion Poetica* —— *Napol.* 1716
371 Roſſet (De) Hiſtoires Tragiques de Noſtre Temps *Rouen* 1665
372 The Good Man's Preparation for the Sacrament 1704
373 Alciati Emblemata, cum Comment. Claudii Minois, *cum fig.* —— —— *ap Plant.* 1608
374 Ammianus Marcellinus, Trebellius Pollio, Flavius Vopiſcus, Aurelius Victor, Pomponius Lætus, Baptiſta Egnatius de Principibus Romanorum *Par. ap. Rob. Steph.* 1544
375 Blackwall on the Claſſics —— 1728
376 Croix (De la) Hiſtoire du Grand Genghizcan *Par.* 1710
377 Bartolo Thermologia Aragonia —— *Neapol.* 1679
378 Æſchinis Dialogi Tres, *Gr. Lat.* Clerici *Amſt.* 1711
379 Michaelis's Introductory Lectures to the New Teſtament *Edinb.* 1779
380 Holy Bible and Teſtament, *ruled Lond. by Hills and Field* 1660
381 *Hiſtoria de Don Hernando Daualos Marques de Peſcara* *En Anvers* 1570
382 *Il Libro delle Preghiere Publiche ſecondo l'uſo della Chieſa Anglicana* —— *Lond.* 1685
383 Pagnini Epitome Theſauri Linguæ Sanctæ *Antv. ap. Plant.* 1588
384 Hiſtoire des Drogues et Eſpiceries, *avec fig.* *Lyon* 1619
385 Lombardi (Petri) Epiſcopi Pariſienſis Sententiæ *Venet.* 1589
386 Moſis Kimchi *O'doiporia* ad Scientiam, *Heb. et Lat.* ab l'Empereur ab Oppyck *Lug. Bat.* 1631
387 Hubner's Introduction to the Political Hiſtory of all Nations —— —— 1742
388 Gracian l'Homme de Cour, par la Houſſaie *Rott.* 1716
389 Bouhours, la Maniere de bien Penſer *Amſt* 1709
390 Commenii Janua Linguarum —— *Lond.* 1664
*390 *Bentivoglio (Memorie Overo Diario del Card.)* *Amſt.* 1648
*391 *Santos, El Vivo y El Difunto* —— *En Pamplona* 1692
*392 Confeſſions of Faith of Authority in the Church of Scotland —— —— *Edinb.* 1739
*393 *L'Inganno, Dialogo di Gioſeppe Horologgi* *Vineg. ap. Giolito* 1562
*394 Fenelon Dialogues des Morts, 2 tom. *Par.* 1752
*395 Les Solitaires en Belle Humeur —— *ib.* 1722
*396 Buxtorfii

*396 Buxtorfii Epitome Grammaticæ Hebrææ — *Amst.* 1652

*397 *Ariosto Orlando Furioso, di Dolce, con fig.* — *Vineg.* 1595

*398 Gray's Poems — 1776

*399 Hervey's Letters to Wesley — 1765

*400 Frederic, Son of Theodore, King of Corsica, Memoirs of Corsica, *maps* — 1768

*401 Bouhours Recueil de Vers Choisies — *Par.* 1693

*402 Bertii Res Germanicæ, *cum tab. Geograph.* — *Amst.* 1635

*403 Oppiani Opera, *Gr. Lat.* a Lippio — *Ven. ap. Ald.* 1517

*404 Curcellæi Synopsis Ethices — *Lond.* 1684

*405 Juvenalis et Persii Satyræ — *Lugdun* 1557

QUARTO.

391 *De las Casas Vocabulario de las dos Lenguas Toscano y Castellana* — 1570

392 Majemonides de Sacrificiis — *Lond.* 1683

393 Newtoni principia Mathematici — 1687

394 Sales Koran — *Lond.* 1734

395 *Divers Voyages touching the Discoverie of America* — 1582

396 *Agudezas de Juan Owen, traducidas en Metro Castellano, por Francisco de la Torre* — *Madrid* 1674

397 ~~Biblia Hebraica, cum punctis~~

398 Bacon's Elements of the Common Laws — 1639

399 Cæsaris Opera, *Delph.* — *Lut. Par.* 1678

400 Phædrus, *Delph.* — *Par.* 1675

401 Cruden's Concordance — 1738

402 Young's Travels in France — 1792

403 Dimock on the Book of Psalms — 1791

404 Leusdeni Perke Abhoth, *Heb. Lat.* — *Ultraj.* 1665

405 Sheringhamii Codex Talmudicus — 1648

406 ~~Aristotelis Ethicæ, a Victorio, *Gr. Lat.* — *Francof.* 1584~~

407 Delrii Disquisitiones Magicæ — *Venet.* 1610

408 Portius de Rerum Naturalium Principiis — *Neap.* 1561

409 Vossius de Ætate Mundi — 1659

410 Prideaux's Method of Reading History — 1672

411 The English Spaw, or Glory of Knaresborough, by Michael Stanhope — 1649

412 Pontani Opera, 2 vol. — *Venet. ap. Ald.* 1519

413 Papyrii Gemini Elentis Hermathema seu de Eloquentiæ Victoria, *impressum in Alma Cantabrigia, per Jsa. Siberch* — 1522

Note. The above Book is printed on Vellum.

414 Le Clerc Histoire de la Medicine — *Amst.* 1702

415 Gulielmini Opera Mathematica, &c. — *Genev.* 1719

416 Bracton de Legibus — 1640

417 *Alberti Architectura* — *Venet.* 1565

418 Bythneri

418 Bythneri Lyra Prophetica — 1664
419 *Vite di Plutarcho per Dominichi*, 2 tom. *Venet* 1607
420 Merrick's Tranſlation of the Pſalms — 1765
421 Savary Dictionnaire de Commerce, 2 tom. 1726
422 Ovidii Opera Delph. 4 tom. *Lugd.* 1689
423 Plauti Comœdiæ, Delph. 2 tom. — *Par.* 1689
424 Statii Opera *Delph.* 2 tom. — *ib.* 1685
426 Relandi Palæſtina, 2 vol. — *Traj. Batav.* 1714
427 Biblia Hebraica a Vander Hooght — *Lipſ.* 1740
428 Voſſius de Poetis Græcis et Latinis — *Amſt.* 1662
429 Rittangelii Liber Jeſirah — *ib.* 1642
430 Donne's Letters to ſeveral Perſons of Honor 1654
431 Borellus de Motu Animalium, 2 tom. — 1685
432 Newtoni Optice — 1706
433 Voyage de la France Equinoxiale en l'Iſle de Cayenne 1602 *Par.* 1664
434 Molyneux on putting a Teleſcope to a horizontal Dial 1686
435 Spanhemii Diſputationes Theologicæ *Genev.* 1552
436 Lampadii Mellificium Hiſtoricum — 1628
437 Como del Iſtore del ſuo Tempo — *Venet.* 1560
438 Hottingeri Theſaurus Theologicus — 1649
439 Pindari Opera Benedicti, *Gr. et Lat.* *Salmur* 1620
440 Analyſe des Infiniment Petits — *Par.* 1696
441 Buckſtorfi Lexicon Chaldaicum — 1622
442 Morhofus de Scypho Vitreo — 1683
443 Voſſius de Hiſtoricis Græcis et Latinis *Francf.* 1677
444 Bonæ Opera Theologica — *Antv.* 1677
445 Morhofii Polyhyſtor — *Lubec* 1699
446 Caninii Helleniſmi Alphabetum *Par. ap. Morel* 1555
447 Spratt's Hiſtory of the Royal Society — 1667

FOLIO.

448 Pulton's Statutes — — 1670
449 Scapulæ Lexicon — — *Baſil* 1580
450 Leſlie's Works, 2 vol. — 1721
451 Reign of Edward the Second — 1680
452 Sexti Empirici Opera, *Gr. et Lat.* — *Lipſ.* 1718
453 Cooperi Theſaurus Linguæ Romanæ et Britannicæ 1573
454 Cypriani Opera — — *Oxon.* 1682
455 Clarendon's Hiſtory of the Rebellion, with the Heads inſerted from 8vo Edition, 2 vol. — 1707
456 Haweis's Expoſition of the Bible, 2 vol. — 1765
457 Grammatici (Joannis) in Ariſtotelem de Naturali Auſcultatione Comment. Græcè *Venet. ap. Zanetti* 1535
458 Thorndike Lexicon Hebraicum Syriacum, &c. 1635
459 Scapulæ

(15)

43 .. 1 .. 9

459 Scapulæ Lexicon — — *Genev.* 1619 — 4 — Winstanly — 1 .. 3
460 Davenant's Works — — 1673 — 1 - 3
461 Alexandri Aphrodisiensis Naturales, de Anima, Morales Græce — — *Venet.* 1513 — 5 — S.
462 Polybius, by Grimston — 1634 — 1 - 9 Marson
463 Budæi Comment. Linguæ Græcæ — 1529
464 Brown's Anatomy, plates — 1681 — 2 - 3 Marson
465 Concordantæ Græco Latinæ Testamentum Novi 1624
466 Excerpta Dione Historiæ a Xiphilino — 1592 — 2 — Edwd. Winnington
467 Philo Judæus Græce *Par. ap. Turneb.* 1552 — 1 — Madaillon
468 *Labacco Architettura*
469 Illustrium Virorum ut extant in Urbe expressi Vultus *Romæ* 1569 — 2 - 6 Medaillon — 1
470 Lloydii Dictionarium Historicum, &c. *Lond.* 1686 — 1 —
471 Rycaut's History of the Turks — 1680
472 Collection of Statues, *wants title* — 3 - 6 Bruce
473 Bayeri Uranometria omnium Asterismorum Schemata 1639 — 2 - 9 Marson
474 Hammond on the New Testament — 1659 — 5 - 6 Cuthil
475 Lightfoot's Works, 2 vol. — — 1684 — 2 - 6 Madaillon
476 Vignola Architettura di Buanoroti
477 Bramhall's Works — 1676 — 1 — Bruce
478 Spotwood's History of Church and State — 1677 — 1 - 9 Bruce
479 Gilbertus de Magnete — — 1600 — 6 - 6 Cuthil
480 Grew's Anatomy of Plants — 1682 — 1 — Priestly — 1 - 6
481 Burnet on the XXXIX Articles — 1699 — 1 - 6 Hawes
482 Kettlewell's Works — — — 1719
483 Burnet's Theory of the Earth — 1691 — Marson
484 Henry's History of the Bible, 5 vol. — 1737 — 2 - 10 - 3 Weston
485 Baconi Opera — — — 1665 — 1 - 5 — Edwd. Winnington
486 Perry's View of the Levant — 1743 — 5 — Lain
487 Cluverii Germania Antiquæ, figuris — 1631 — 2 - 6 Cuthil
488 Pisonis Indiæ re Naturali et Medica figuris *Amst.* 1653
489 Testamentum Novum, Græce *ap. Rob. Steph.* stained 1550 — 1 — Bruce
490 Gregorii Opera, *Gr. et Lat.* — *Par.* 1630 — 2 — Delongchamps
491 Grew's Rarities of Gresham College — 1681 — 1 - 3 Bruce
492 Bernardi Sancti Opera, 2 tom. — *ib.* 1719 — 10 - 6 Geddes
493 Pitisci Lexicon Antiquetatum Romanorum, 2 tom. *Leovardi* 1713 — 8 — Priestly
494 Salmasii Expercitationes Plinianæ *Traj. Rhen* 1689 — 6 - 6 Priestly
495 Sanctii Opera Theologica — 1621 — 1 - 6 Delongchamps
496 Junius de Pictura Veterum — *Rotterd.* 1694 — 3 - 6 Maltby
497 Pithoei Canones Ecclesiæ Romanæ — *Par.* 1687 — 2 — Priestly
498 Baconi Opus Majus — — 1733 — 5 — D. Walker
499 Digbææ Demonstratio Immortalitatis Animæ Rationalis *ib.* 1651 — 1 - 6 Delongchamps
500 Mischna sive totius Hebræorum Juris a Surenhusio, *Heb. et Lat.* 6 tom. — *Amst.* 1688 1 - 14 — Delongchamps
501 Harduini

£52 .. 11 .. 0

501 Harduini Opera — — *Amst.* 1709
502 Chillingsworth's Works — 1727
503 Innet's Origines Anglicanæ, 2 vol. — 1704
504 Philostrati Opera, *Gr. et Lat.* *Venet. ap. Ald.* 1502
505 Shaw's Travels to the Levant — 1738
506 Simplicii Comment. in Aristotelem de Anima Græce *Venet. ap. Ald.* 1527
507 Poetæ Græci Principes Heroici Carminis *Græce* 1566
508 Liber de Proprietatibus rerum Bartholomei Anglici *Argent* 1485
509 Scammozzi Architettura — *Venezzia* 1714

Third Day's Sale.

TWELVES.

510 PRIOR's Poems, 2 vol. — *Tonson* 1721
511 ——— Poems, 2 vol. — — *Dublin* 1728
512 Voyages de Rabbi Benjamin, par Baratier, 2 tom. *Amst.* 1734
513 Breviarum Romanum — *Embricæ* 1670
514 Architecture de Vitruve Abregé, par Perrault, *avec fig.* *Amst.* 1681
515 La Mecanique du Feu des Cheminées, *avec fig.* *Par.* 1713
516 Les Bons Mots des Orientaux — *Haye* 1694
517 Labat Voyage aux Isles de l'Amerique, *avec fig.* 6 tom. — — — *ib.* 1724
518 Livii Histoira, a Maittaire, *cum indice*, 6 tom. *Lond.* 1722
519 Lafitau Moeurs des Sauvages Ameriquains, *avec fig.* 4 tom. — — — *Par.* 1724
520 Stephanus de Urbibus, *Gr. et Lat.* a Berkelio *L. Bat.* 1674
521 Saint Louys, ou la Sante Couronne Reconquise, Poeme Heroique, par le Moyne, *avec fig.* *Par.* 1666
522 Rousseau

522 Rousseau (J. J.) Eloisa, 3 vol. — *Edinb.* 1773
523 Freigii (Thomæ) Pædagogus — *Basil* 1582
524 Petrarchæ (Franc.) Epistolæ — *Lugdun* 1601
525 Estiene l'Apologie pour Herodote — 1572
526 Sulpicii Severi Historia Sacra, ab Hofmeistero *Tigur* 1708
527 Apollinarii Interpretatio Psalmorum Versibus Heroicis, *Gr. et Lat.* a Sylburgio — *ap. Commelin* 1596
528 Croix (De la) Histoire du Genghizcan *Par.* 1710
529 Lily's Latin and Greek Grammars — *Lond.* 1721
530 Phœdri et Aviani Fabulæ, *chart. max.* *Par. ap. Coustelier* 1742
531 Hutcheson's Moral Philosophy — *Glasg.* 1747
532 Essay on Medals — — 1784
533 Abregé Chronologique de l'Histoire de France *Par.* 1752
534 Dean of Coleraine, 3 vol. — 1780
535 *Tasso, La Jerusalemme Liberata,* 2 tom. *Par. ap. Molini* 1783
536 Lady's Travels into Spain, 2 vol. — 1722
537 *Cinthio (Le Tragedie di Giraldi)* — *Venet.* 1583
538 Sterne's Sentimental Journey — 1784
539 *Delle Cento Novelle, di Sansovino* — *Venet.* 1563
540 Nettleton on Virtue and Happiness — *Edinb.* 1776
541 Buchanan's English Syntax — 1767
542 Account of the Eight Parts of Speech, for Merchant-Taylor's School — — 1770
543 Decerpta ex Ovidii Metamorphoseon, with English Notes, by Willymot — — *Lond.* 1711
544 Analysis of the Law — — — 1713
545 Guion's Method of Prayer, by Brooke — 1775
546 Corderii Colloquia Selecta, *Lat. and Eng.* by Clarke 1771
547 Selectæ e Veteri Testamento Historiæ *Eton* 1765
548 Apology for Mr. Thomas Rhind for separating from the Presbyterian Party — — *Edinb.* 1717
549 Politiani Opera, 2 tom. *Lugdun. ap. Gryph.* 1528
550 Comenii Janua Linguarum Reserata, *Lat. et Eng. Lond.* 1650
551 Sacred Annals, or the Life of Christ, from Locke, Taylor, Cradock, Whiston, &c. &c. — 1776
552 Williams's (Helen Maria) Poems, 2 vol. — 1786
553 Juliani Proverbes et Heures de Recreation, *Fr. Ital. et Span. Par.* 1668
554 Memoires du Compte de Busy Rabutin, 2 tom. en une *ib.* 1697
555 Lucius Florus, a Freinshemio — *Argent.* 1636
556 Blount's (Charles) Miscellaneous Works — 1695
557 *Satire di Ariosto, Bentivogli, Alemanni, &c. &c. &c. Venet.* 1583
558 Claudiani Opera *Par. ap. Colinæum* 1530

D 559 Balzack's

559 Balzack's Letters, by Sir Richard Baker — 1638
560 *Costanzo (Rime di)* — — *Padova* 1666
561 *Santos, Dia y Noche de Madrid, Discursos de lo Mas notable que en el Passa* — *Madrid* 1666
562 Joceline's (Elizabeth). Mother's Legacy to her unborn Child 164
563 Euripidis Tragœdiæ, Græce, 2 tom. *Ven. ap. Ald.* 1503
564 Poiret Fides et Ratio Collatæ Adversus Principia Lockii *Amst.* 1708
565 Procli Paraphrasis in Ptolimæi Libos iv. de Siderum effectionibus, *Gr. et Lat.* ab Allatio *Lug. Bat. ap. Elz.* 1635
566 Cæsaris Commentaria, a Maitaire — *Lond.* 1749
567 Raii Synopsis Methodica Stirpium Britannicarum *ib.* 1690
568 *Gravina (Tragedie Cinque di Vincenzo)* *Napol.* 1717
569 Pagnini Epitome Thesauri Linguæ Sanctæ *Antwerp ap. Plant.* 1588
570 Socini de diversis materiis ad Christianam religionem pertinentibus, Tractatus — *Racov.* 1618
*562 Frauds of Romish Monks and Priests — 1691
*563 Couleii Poemata Latina de Plantis — *Lond.* 1668
*564 Tremblay (Du) Traité des Langues — *Amst.* 1700
*565 Sophoclis Tragœdiæ, *Gr. et Lat.* *Ingolstad.* 1608
*566 Apolonii Rhodii Argonautica, *Græcè, Par.* 1541. Musæus de Herone et Leandro, *Græcè* *Par. ap. Wechel.* 1548
*567 Donne's Poems — — 1669
*568 Silius Italicus, a Nicandro *Florent. ap. Junt.* 1515
*569 *Alberti de l'Architettura* *Vineg. ap. Vangris* 1546
571 Hermogenis de Gravitate Apta. Ejusque tractandi ratione. Demetrius Phalareus de Elocutione. Aristidæ de Genere dicendi civili, *Græcè* — *Argent.* 1556
572 Bülffingeri Specimen Doctrinæ Veterum Sinarum Moralis et Politicæ — *Francof ad Moen.* 1724
573 Serrani Metaphrasis Psalmi Davidis, *Gr. et Lat.* ab Okely, *Lond.* 1770
574 Dodwelli Annales Velleiani, Quintilianei, Statii *Oxon.* 1698
575 Platon (Les Œuvres de) par Dacier, 2 tom. *Amst.* 1700
576 Cæsar (Les Commentaires de) par d'Ablancourt *Par.* 1672
577 Martini Martinii Sinicæ Historia — *Amst.* 1659
578 Prior's Poems — — *Tonson,* 1717
579 Voltaire, Le Micromégas — *Lond.* 1752
580 Moeurs (Les) — — *Amst.* 1748
581 Maurocordatus de Officiis, *Gr. et Lat.* *Lond.* 1724
582 Metoscitæ Institutiones Linguæ Arabicæ *Rom.* 1624
583 Apollinarii Interpretatio Psalmorum, versibus Heroica, *Græcè* *Par. ap. Turnebum* 1552
584 Hill on the Classics — — — 1753

585 Paradin

4 . 6 . 3

1 . 9 Edw Wenington
2 . 6 Heber
2 . 3 Heber
9 Cuthel
6 Madaillon
9 Madaillon
3 . 3 Madaillon
9 Field
3 . 6 Heber
1 . — Field
2 . 3 Heber
1 . 6 Dalrymple
1 . 3 Bond
1 . 9 Madaillon
1 . 6 Dalrymple
1 . 6 Darcey
1 . — Cuthel
1 . — Heber
3 . — Leigh

£ 6 . 7 . 0

585 Paradin Devises Heroiques et Emblemes, par François D'Amboise, *avec fig. Par.* 1622. Devises Royales, par Adrian D'Amboise, *avec fig. Par.* 1621. François D'Amboise Traité de Devises — *Par.* 1620
586 Doddridge's Rise and Progress of Religion in the Soul 1753
587 Le Congrés de Citére — — *a Citére* 1749
588 Voltaire Histoire de Charles XII. 2 tom. en une *Basle* 1731
589 Aristotelis Ethica, *Gr. et Lat.* Riccoboni *Francof.* 1596
590 Teate's (Faithful) Doctrine of the Three Sacred Persons, Father, Son, and Spirit — *Leipzig* 1699
591 Testament (Le Nouveau) 2 tom. — *Mons*
592 *Pinarolo, L'Antichita di Roma, con. fig.* 2 tom. *Roma* 1713
593 *Descrizione di Roma Antica e Moderna, con. fig.* 2 tom. *ib.* 1708
594 L'Etat de la Suisse, traduit de l'Anglois *Amst.* 1714
595 Fontenelle Histoire des Oracles — *Par.* 1713
596 Boileau (Œuvres Diverses du) 2 tom. en une *Amst.* 1697
597 Testamentum (Novum) Græcum, ab Hoole *Lond.* 1653
598 *Delle Guerre di Fiandra, di Giustiniano* — *Milan* 1615
599 Ferrarius de Re Vestiaria, *cum fig.* — *Patav.* 1642
600 Wettenhall Institutio Græcæ Grammaticæ Compendiaria, *Lond.* 1739
601 Parecbolæ sive Excerpta Statutorum Universitatis Oxoniensis *Oxon.* 1784
602 Denina's Revolutions of Literature, by Murdoch *Lond.*
603 Lucien, par D'Ablancourt, *avec fig.* 2 tom. *Amst.* 1709
604 Rollin, Belles Lettres, 4 tom. — *Par.* 1741
605 *Nuova Guida per Pozzuoli, di Parrino, con fig.* *Napol.* 1715
606 Dugard Rhetorices Elementa — *Lond.* 1712
607 Plinii Epistolæ et Panegyricus, a Maittaire, *cum indice*, *ib.* 1722
608 Raynal's Revolution of America — 1781
609 Willymott Decerpta ex Latina Castellionis Novi Foederis Versione — — — *ib.* 1706
610 Dunlop Linguæ Græcæ Institutiones Grammaticæ *Glas.* 1754
612 History (The) of the Chancery — 1726
613 History of some of the Penitents in the Magdalen-house, 2 vol. in one — — — *Dubl.* 1760
614 Independent (The) a novel, 2 vol. — 1784
615 Hervey's Life of Robert Bruce, King of Scots, an Heroic Poem — — *Edinb.* 1768
616 Rabelais's Works, by Ozell, *plates*, 5 vol. 1737
617 Buxtorfii Thesaurus Grammaticus Linguæ Sanctæ Hebrææ *Basil.* 1651
618 Sacy de la Gloire — — *Haye* 1715
619 Turner's Exercises to the Accidence and Grammar. 1740

D 2 620 Vertot

6.7.0
585 — 2 — Madaillon
586 — 9 Lowe
587 — 6 Darcey
588 — 9 Dulos
589 — 6 Heber
590 — 6 Lowe
590 — 2 — 9 Darcey
592 — 2 — Calamy
593 — 4 — 6 Fried
594 — 1 — 6 Madaillon
595 — 1 — Darcey
596 — 6 Madaillon
598–599 — 1 — 9 Heber
602 — 1 — 9 Cuthel
603 — 7 — 6 Cuthel
604 — 1 — Madaillon
608–609 — 9 Heber
612–613 — 1 — 6 Darcey
615 — 15 — 6 Staines
617 — 6 Madaillon
£ 8.14.6

610 Vertot Histoire des Revolutions de la Republique Romaine, 3 tom. *Haye* 1724
621 Man in the Moon, 2 vol. —— 1783
622 Cruden's Nature Spiritualised, in a variety of Poems 1766
623 Vertot Histoire de l'ordre de Malthe, 5 tom. *Par.* 1726
624 D'Arcon's Philosophical Differtations, 2 vol. 1753
625 Martialis Epigrammata, a Maittaire, *cum indice* *Lond.* 1716
626 *Achille Tazio dell' Amore di Clitofonte e Leucippe, tradotto dal Coccio* —— *Fiorenz. ap. Giunt.* 1598
627 Prideaux Directions to Church-wardens — 1716
628 True Grounds of the Benefits of Jesus Christ *Bristol* 1777
629 Millot's Elements of the History of England, by Mrs. Brooke, 4 vol. —— —— 1771
630 D'Orleans Histoire des Revolutions D'Angleterre, *avec fig.* 3 tom. —— —— *Par.* 1724
631 Fenelon Sentimens de Piété —— *ib.* 1737
632 Martine on Thermometers —— *Edinb.* 1780
633 Beveridgius de Linguarum Orientalium *Lond.* 1658
634 Orrery on the Life and Writings of Swift — 1752
635 Wilson (Bishop) on the Sacrament —— 1777
636 Fitzosborne's Letters — — 1772
637 Harper's Accomptant's Companion —— 1779
638 Stockwood's Figures at the End of the Rules of Construction in the Latin Grammar, *Lat. and Eng.* *Lond.* 1738
639 *Contarini della Republica di Venetia* — *Venet.* 1630
640 Gustave Vasa, Histoire de Suede, *deux parties* *Par.* 1725
641 Moretii's Treatise of Artillery, by More, *plates* 1683
642 Scaligeri Poetices —— *ap. Commelin.* 1617
643 Sallustii Historia —— *Dublin* 1747
644 Egerton's Theatrical Remembrancer —— 1788
645 History of the Christian Church, 2 vol. — 1790
646 Justini Historia. Æmylius Probus. Velleius Paterculus, *Florent. ap. Junt.* 1525
647 Seldenus de Diis Syris — — *Lond.* 1617
648 Buxtorfii Lexicon Hebraicum et Chaldaicum *Amst.* 1654
649 Dionysii Opera, *Græcé* —— *ap. Junt* 1516
650 Herodoti Historia, *Gr. et Lat. chart. opt.* 9 tom. *Glas.* 1761
*650 Langbaine's Lives of English Dramatick Poets
*651 Hugenii Poemata, a Barlæo *Hag. Com.* 1655
*652 Devotional Tracts, from the French, by Dr. Heylin 1757
*653 Wesley's Hymns —— *Bristol* 1773
*654 De Modis Verborum Latinis — *Lond.* 1714
*655 Mason's Rudiments of the Italian Language *Edinb.* 1771
*656 Pasoris Grammatica Græca Sacra Novi Testamenti *Groning. Fris.* 1655
*657 Gordon's Distinguishing Graces of the Christian Character —— —— 1778
*658 Pindari

*658 Pindari Opera, *Græcè* — *Basil ap. Cratand.* 1526
*659 Lucretius de Rerum Natura — *Lugdun. ap. Gryph.* 1540
*660 Boileau (Œuvres de) — *Amst.* 1689
*661 Prædium Rusticum, *lineis rubris* *Lutet. ap. Rob. Steph.* 1554
*662 Coventry's Philemon to Hydaspes — *Glasg.* 1761
*663 Demosthenis Orationes, *Græcè* — *ib.* 1762
*664 Herbert's Temple, Sacred Poems — 1695
*665 Goldsmith's Essays and Poems — 1782

QUARTO.

652 Ursini Poemata — *Basil* 1522
653 Borellus de Vero Telescopii Inventore — *Haye* 1655
654 Glauber on Philosophical Furnaces — 1651
655 Limborch de Veritate Religionis — *Goudæ* 1687
656 *Othoboni la Istoria Universale* — *Roma.* 1697
657 Vitringæ Observationes Sacræ — 1691
658 Il Lamberto overo del Parlare, a Patritio
659 Noli me Tangere, and other Tracts, *plates* — 1642
660 Dodwellus de Græcorum Romanorum Cyclis *Oxon.* 1701
661 Martialis Epigrammatica, *Delph.* — *Par.* 1680
662 Parkhurst's Hebrew Lexicon — 1778
663 Newton's Opticks — 1704
664 Macknight's Truth of the Gospel History — 1763
665 Fromondi Meteorologicæ — 1627
666 Hyde de Veterum Persarum Religionis Historia 1700
667 Flecher's Purple Island — 1633
668 Musæi Joviani Imagines, &c. — *Basil* 1577
669 Jones's Philological Disquisitions — 1781
670 Berkley and other Sermons — 1785
671 Smellie on the Society of Antiquaries of Scotland 1782
672 Whitfield on the Hebrew Vowel Points — 1748
673 Butler's Analogy of Religion — 1736
674 Marshami Canon Chronicus Ægyptiacus, Ebraicus, &c. 1676
~~675 Aristotelis Politica, *Gr. et Lat.* a Sylburgio *Francf.* 1587~~
676 Boothby's Discovery, or Description of Madagascar, 1646. Castel's Short Discoverie of the Coasts and Continent of America, 1644. Nova Britannia offering excellent Fruits by planting in Virginia, 1609. Morton's Abstract of New England
~~677 Ciceronis Epistolæ, *Delph.* — *Par.* 1685~~
678 Newton on Daniel — 1733
679 Holy Bible, 6 vol. interleaved — 1715
680 Maimonides de Sacrifiis — 1683
681 Aymon Monumens Authentiques de la Religion de Greece — *Haye* 1708
682 Callimachi Hymni, *Gr. et Lat.* *ap. Hen. Steph.* 1577

683 Homeri

683 Homeri Odyssea, *Gr. et Lat.* Didymi *Amst. ap. Elz.* 1655
684 Marolles Temple de Muses, *figures* — *ib.* 1676
6.. Florilegium Epigrammatum — *ap. Hen. Steph.* 1566
686 Aristophanis Comœdiæ, *Græcè* — *ap. Cratandum* 1532
687 *Mercurialis de Arte Gymnastica* — *Venet.* 1601
688 Theses Medicæ — — *Lug. Bat.* 160..
689 Weil's Symboliographie — — 16..
690 Lactantibus — — *ap. Cratand.* 152..
691 Diogenes Laertius, a Meibomio, 2 tom. *Amst.* 1692
692 Philips's Life of Cardinal Pole, part 1st. — 1764
693 Æschyli Tragœdiæ, a Victorio, *Gr. et Lat. ap. Hen. Steph.* 1557
694 Æliani Variæ Historia, Græce — *Romæ* 1545
695 *Platina Vite de i Pontifici,* 2 tom. — *Venet.* 1513
696 Frankii Exercitationes Anti-Limborchianæ *Kiloni* 1694
697 Parker on the Divine Authority — 1681
698 *Cento Novelle di Cinthio* — — *Venet.* 1608
699 Golii Elementa Astronomica — *Amst.* 1669
700 Acta Canonizationis Sanctorum — — 1669
701 Budæi Epistolæ Græce — — 1574
702 Brightman Illust. of the Revelation of St. John 1644
703 Oudin Dictionaire Francoise et Italiennes
704 Gulielmini Opera Mathematica — *Genev.* 1719
705 Lee's Statute Law of Ireland — 1754
706 Ruæi Carmina — *Lut. Par.* 168..
707 Surenhusii Theologorum Hebræorum — *Amst.* 171..
708 Ammianus Marcellinus Lindenbrogi *Hamb.* 16..
709 Suetonius, Casauboni — — 1595
710 *Il Petracha* — — 1553
711 *La Coltivatiane di Luigi Alamanni Parigi da Roberto Stephano* 1546
712 *Alberti Descrittione D'Italia* — *Vineg.* 1588
713 *Gomez El Siglo Pitagorico y la Vida de Don Gregorio Guadanna Brusselas* 1727
714 Pomponii Læti Romanæ Historiæ Compendium *Venet.* 1500
715 Catalogus Alumnorum e Collegio Regali Beatæ Mariæ de Etona ab anno, 1444, usque ad Annum, 1730 *Eton* 1730
716 *Common Prayer,* wants title—*Psalmes, by Sternhold, Witingham, Hopkins, and others, with Music Lond. by John Daye* 1580
717 *Jornada de Africa y Union del Regno de Portugal, a la Corona de Castilla, por Sebastian de Mesa Barcelona* 1630
718 *Agricoltura, dal Alfonso D'Herrera, tradotta da Mambrino Roseo Venet.* 1568
719 Herberti de Religione Gentilium — *Amst.* 1663
720 Camdeni et Illustrium Virorum Epistolæ, cum ejus Vita, a Smitho — *Lond.* 1691

721 Buxtorfii

721 Buxtorfii Tiberias sive Commentarius Masorethicus, *Heb. et Lat.* — — *Basil* 1665
722 *Kennet's Bibliotheca Americanæ Primordia* *Lond.* 1713
723 *Pardo Discursus Evangelicos para las Solemnidades de los Mysterios de Christo* — *Em. Coimbra* 1662
724 Des-Cartes Opera Philosophica
*725 Van Dale Dissertationes IX. Antiquitatibus quin et Marmoribus, cum Romanis, cum Potissimum Græcis, *cum fig.* *Amst.* 1702
*726 Ferrarius de Re Vestiaria, *cum fig.* *Patav.* 1654
725 Silius Italicus — — *Par.* 1618
726 Justini Historia, Delphini — *ib.* 1677

FOLIO.

727 Themistii Opera, *Græce* — *Venet. ap. Ald.* 1534
728 Oratorum Veteres Orationes *Græcæ* *ap. Hen. Steph.* 1575
729 Constantini Lexicon — — 1607
730 Heylin's Cosmographie — — 1657
731 Eusebii Thesaurus Temporum — 1606
732 Desgodetz Edefices Antiques de Rome *Par.* 1682
733 Herodoti Historia, *Gr. et Lat.* — *Francof.* 1608
734 Appiani Historia — *Lutet.* 1551
735 Suidæ Lexicon — *Venet. ap. Ald.* 1515
736 Dionis Historiæ *Græcè* *Lutet. ap. Rob. Steph.* 1548
737 Euclidis Elementa — — *Basil* 1533
738 Demosthenes *Græce* — *Lutet.* 1570
739 Calderwood's Church of Scotland — 1680
740 Chaucer's Works — — 1602
741 Julii Polucis Vocabularium Græce — *Juntæ* 1521
742 Thucidides Græce — — *Basil* 1540
743 Pausanias Græce, a Xylandro — 1583
744 Isocrates, *Gr. et Lat.* a Wolsio — — 1570
745 Hesychii Lexicon — — *Hag.* 1521
746 *Palladii Architettura* — — *Venet.* 1581
747 Novum Testamentum Bezæ — 1642
748 Athenæi Deipnosophistarum — — 1597
749 Lycophronis Opera, a Pottero, *Gr. et Lat.* 1697
750 Jovii Illust Viror. Elogia — *Florent.* 1551
751 Taciti Opera — — 1689
752 Poetæ Græce Veteres, *Gr. et Lat.* — *Collonia* 1614
753 Dionis rerum Romanarum — *Lutet.* 1551
754 Photii Bibliotheca — *Aug. Vind.* 1606
755 Pauli Æginæti Opera *Græce* *Venet. ap Ald.* 1528
756 Proclus in Platonis Theologiam *Hamb.* 1618
757 Hippocratis Opera, a Foesio, *Gr. et Lat.* *Genev.* 1657
758 Rossi Architettura

759 Pagnini

759 Pagnini Lexicon Hebraicum — *Antv.* 1572
760 Demosthenes et Æschines, *Gr. Lat.* a Wolfio 1604
761 Bellorii Admiranda Romanarum Antiquitatum —
762 Bartoli Colonna Trajana
763 Bellorii Columna Antoni — 1704
764 Schmidii Omnium Vocam Novi Testamenti, *Græci, caret tit.*
765 Gesneri Bibliotheca — 1583
766 Pindari Opera, a West, *Gr. Lat.* — 1698
767 Hale on the Origination of Mankind — 1677

Fourth Day's Sale.

TWELVES.

768 EPIGRAMMATA Græca — *Lond.* 1720
769 Fresnoy (Du) L'Art de Peinture . *Par.* 1684
770 Institutiones Linguæ Græcæ — *Edinb.* 1764
771 Essay on Crimes and Punishments — *ib.* 1778
772 Butler's Hudibras, by Grey, 2 vol. — *ib.* 1779
773 Euclide's Elements, by Barrow 1714
774 Goulart Thresor d'Histoires Admirables et Memorables *Genev.* 1610
775 Liturgia Anglicana — *Lond.* 1759
776 Robbe, Geographie, 2 tom. — *Utrecht.* 1688
777 Enfield's Biographical Sermons — 1777
778 Historia et Præcepta Selecta *Bristol* 1748
779 Cicero de Officiis, a Rachelio *Amst.* 1686
780 Mair's Introduction to Latin Syntax *Edinb.* 1779
781 Herefbachius de Re Rustica *Spiræ Nemetum* 1694
782 Gray's Poems and Life, by Mason, 4 vol. *York* 1778
783 Poiret

(25)

783 Poiret de Eruditione Solida, Superficiaria et Falsa . Amst. 1692 — 9 Maltby

784 Tournefort Histoire des Plantes Par. de l'Imprimerie Royale 1698 — 9 Darcey

785 Fenelon Avantures de Telemaque Haye 1703 — 1 —

786 Sanson l'Etat du Royaume de Perse, avec fig Par. 1695

787 Sans Fard Anti-Rousseau —— Rotterd. 1712 — 1 — Lands.

788 Valla (Laurentius) de Linguæ Latinæ Elegantia . Cantab. 1688

789 Ignatii (S. i) Epistolæ, Gr. Lat. a Sylvio, Antv. ap. Plant. 1572. Annæ Mariæ Schurman Opuscula, Heb. Gr. Lat. Gal. cum effigie Lug. Bat. ap. Elz. 1650 — 4 — Leigh

790 Buchanani Poëmata —— Lond. 1686

791 Gobien (Le) Histoire des Isles Marianes Par. 1700 — 1 — Leigh

792 Camdeni Annales Elizabethæ Amst. ap. Elz. 1677

793 Excerptæ Historiæ ex Ctesia, Agatharcide, Memnone, Appiani Iberica. Item de Gestis Annibalis, Gr. Lat. ab Henrico Stephano, Par. ap. Hen. Steph. 1557 Appiani Hispanica et Annibalica, a Beraldo Par. ap. Hen. Steph. 1560 — 2 6 Lands

794 Ludolf Histoire d'Abissinie, avec fig. Par. 1684 — 4 6 Cox

795 Common Prayer —— — Edinb. 1712 — 1 6 Hayes

796 Orton's Letters to a Young Clergyman Shrewsbury 1791 — 6 Hayes

797 Septuaginta Græca Juxta Exemplar Vaticanum Romæ — 3 9 Marson

798 Fenelon Dialogues des Morts, Contes et Fables, 2 tom. Amst. 1727 — 2 6

799 Sadoleti Epistolæ Lugdun. ap. Gryph. 1560 — 2 — Fael

800 Law's Serious Call, with other Tracts, by Fenelon, &c. &c. Dublin 1762 — 1 — Lands.

801 Ashwellus de Socino et Socinianismo Oxon. 1680

802 Peres (Les Obras y Relaciones de Antonio) Geneva 1676

803 Clergyman's Vade Mecum, 2 vol. —— 1707 — 9 Darcey

804 Sancta Cruz Floresta Espanola, Span. et Fr. Bruxel. 1614

805 Law's Serious Call —— Dubl. 1762 — 2 3 Payne

806 Piacevolissime Notti di Francesco Straparola Venet. 1608 — 1 — Lands.

807 Difesa delle Donne, di Domenico Bruni Firenz. 1552 — 7 6 Cox

808 Martialis Epigrammata —— Lond. 1721

809 Leusdeni Compendium Græcum Novi Testamenti, interfol. —— Lug. Bat. 1688 — 6 Marson

810 Grey's Memoria Technica —— Lond 1756 — 2 — Cuthel

811 Jaquelot de la Vérité et de l'Inspiration des Livres Sacrez Rotterd. 1715

812 Rei Rusticæ Scriptores, corio turcico, ac foliis deauratis, 2 tom. —— Par. ap. Rob. Steph. 1543 — 8 — Cuthel

813 Thucydidis Historia, a Laurentio Valla Francof. ap. Wechel 1589 — 1 — Lands.

814 Histoire Genéalogique des Tatars Leyde 1726

E 815 Hermant

£4 . 1 . 3

815 Hermant Histoire des Ordres de Chevalerie . *Rouen* 1698

816 Oudin Dialogues, *Espag. Ital. Alleman, et Fr.* *Par* 1650

817 L'Imitation de Jesus Christ, en Vers François, par P. Corneille, *avec fig.* ——— *ib.* 1715

818 D'Aristote (La Rhetorique) par Cassandre . *ib.* 1675

819 Histoire de l'Inquisition et son Origine *Cologne* 1693

820 *Cervantes (Novelas de)* ——— *En Brusselas* 1614

821 *Campailla (Emblemi Poesi del Tomaso)* *Palermo* 1716

822 Disquisitio de Mutuo ——— *Lug. Bat.* 1645

823 Letters to Soame Jenyns on Gibbon, Priestley, Lindsey, &c. ——— ——— 1786

824 Thucydidis Historia, *Gr. Lat. chart. opt.* 8 tom. *Glasg.* 1759

825 Histoire Generale du Jansenisme, *avec portraits,* 2 tom. *Amst.* 1700

826 Terence, *Lat.* & *Fr.* par Dacier, *avec fig.* 3 tom. *ib.* 1691

827 Psalmi Davidis, cum translationibus Quatuor, et Paraphrasibus duabus ——— *Argent.* 1545

828 Tilly's Offices of Prayer and Devotion — 1714

829 Sentimental Connoisseur, Prose and Verse ———

830 Child on Trade ——— 1693

831 M'Kennie's Man of Feeling, a Novel 1771

832 *Savonarola (Prediche del)* . ——— 1544

833 Philelphi Epistolæ ——— *Par.* 1513

834 Gradus ad Parnassum ——— *Lond.* 1691

835 Isocratis Orationes, *Græcè* ——— *Basil* 1565

836 Cave's Primitive Christianity ——— 1676

837 Sophoclis Tragœdiæ Septem, *Gr. Lat.* *Cantab.* 1673

838 Spizelius de Vita et Moribus Literatorum *Aug. Vind.* 1680

839 Martin's Voyage to St. Kilda ——— 1698

840 Camerarii Quæstiones de Natura, Moribus, *Gr. Lat.* *Genev.* 1594

841 Constitution of the Primitive Church ——— 171[illegible]

842 Epigrammatum Delectus ——— *Lond.* 17[illegible]

843 Blair's Synopsis or Lectures on Belles Lettres and Logic *Edinb.* 17[illegible]

844 Phædri Fabulæ, à Maittaire, *cum indice* *Lond.* 171[illegible]

845 Excerpta e Corpore Statutorum Universitatis Oxon. *Oxon.* 17[illegible]

846 Addison's Evidences of the Christian Religion *Glasg.* 177[illegible]

847 Gentleman's Religion ——— 1746

848 Selectæ e Profanis Scriptoribus Historiæ *Lond.* 1771

849 Aristæneti Epistolæ, *Gr. Lat.* à Berglero *Lips.* 1715

850 Epistolæ Veterum Græcorum, *Gr. Lat.* à Lubino *ap. Commelin.* 1609

851. Boetius

851 Boetius de Consolatione Philosophiæ *Lug. Bat.* 1656
852 Lycophronis Alexandra, *Gr. Lat.* a Cantero *Genev. ap. Commelin.* 1596
853 Locke on Education 1693
854 Mitford on the Pleadings in the Court of Chancery *Dubl.* 1784
855 Dairval de l'Utilité des Voyages, *avec fig.* 2 tom. en une *Par.* 1686
856 Montesquieu de la Grandeur et Decadence des Romains *ib.* 1750
857 Pontani Opera, *foliis deauratis* *Ven. ap. Ald.* 1533
858 Scaligeri (Julii Cæsaris) Poemata, *corio turcico ac foliis deauratis* *Lugdun.* 1546
859 Antiquitates Ecclesiæ Orientalis *Lond.* 1682
860 Virgilii Opera, 2 tom. *Edinb.* 1755
861 Voyage de France, *avec cartes*, 2 tom. *Par.* 1724
862 Guion (Oeuvres de Madame de) 27 tom. *Cologne* 1715, 13,20,22
863 Guion's Method of Prayer, by Brooke 1775
864 *Vestibulum Technicum* 1684
865 Schickardi Horologium Hebræum *Lond.* 1639
866 Mythologici Latini *ap. Commelin.* 1599
867 Ramsay's Gentle Shepherd, *with music and plates* *Edinb.* 1776
868 The Book of Bertram, or Rathram, Priest and Monk of Corbey *Dubl.* 1753
869 Godignus de Abassinorum Rebus *Lugdun.* 1615
870 Ellis's English Exercises 1782
871 Schola Italica *Col. Agrip.* 1631
872 Junii Animadversa Ejusdemque de Coma Comment. *Rotterd.* 1708
873 Solis Histoire de la Conquête du Mexique, *avec fig.* 2 tom. *Haye* 1692
874 Fenelon, les Avantures de Telemaque, *avec fig.* *Amst.* 1719
875 Desmarais Grammaire Françoise *ib.* 1707
876 Fenelon Vies des Anciens Philosophes *Par.* 1720
877 Fenelon Sermons Choisies *ib.* 1744
878 Fenelon sur la Rhetorique et sur la Poetique *Amst.* 1717
879 Richardson on Shakespeare's Dramatic Characters, of Macbeth, Hamlet, Jacques, Imogen, Richard the IIId. King Lear and Timon of Athens, 2 vol. 1785
880 Williams's Key to the Language of America 1643
881 *Maffei della Scienza Chiamata Cavalleresca, en marochino e foglie dorat.* *Palermo* 1717
882 Holy Bible and Testament, *blue morocco, gilt leaves*, 2 vol. *Edin. by Basket* 1726

E 2 883 Plutarchi

883 Plutarchi Opera, *Gr. Lat.* ab Henrico Stephano, 13 tom. *ap. Hen. Steph.* 1572. Les Oeuvres de Plutarque, par Amyot, 13 tom. *Par. ap. Vascosan*, 1574. *The whole uniformly bound* in 26 vol. *white calf, gilt and marbled leaves*

884 West on the Resurrection — 1747

885 Ovidii Metamorphoses, Delphini — *Lond.* 1744

886 Euripidis Tragœdiæ, *Græcè* *Basil. ap. Hervag.* 1537

887 Polignac Anti-Lucretius, *foliis deauratis* *Par.* 1747

889 Scarron, le Virgile Travesty, *avec fig.* 2 tom. en une *Par.* 1668

890 *Viaggi di Pietro della Valle*, 4 tom. *Bologna* 1672

891 Churchill's Poems, 3 vol. — 1776

892 Relandus de Spoliis Templi Hierosolymitani, *cum fig.* *Traj. ad Rhen.* 1716

893 *Dialoghi del Guazzo* — *Venet.* 1590

894 Galloway's Poems — *Glasg.* 1788

895 Epistolæ Indicæ et Japanicæ — *Lovan.* 1570

896 Buchanani Paraphrasis Psalmi Davidis *Glasg.* 1765

897 *Dialoghi del Guazzo* — *Venet.* 1590

898 Fabricii Codex Pseudepigraphus Veteris Testamenti, et Observationes in Novi Testamenti, 3 tom. *Hamb. & Lipsiæ* 1712,13

899 Anacreontis Opera, *Gr. Lat.* a Barnesio *Cantab.* 1705

900 Petiveri Gazophylacii Naturæ et Artis *Lond.* 1702

901 Luciani Opera, *Græcè*, 2 tom. — *Basil.* 1545

*901 Ciacconius de Triclinio, *cum fig.* *Amst.* 1689

OCTAVO.

902 Bradley's Dictionarium Botanicum, 2 vol. 1728

903 Garnier's Geography made Easy — 1748

904 Toland's Tetradymus and other Tracts — 1720

905 Shaw's Practice of Physic, 2 vol. — 1728

906 Davenant on Trade — 1698

907 Ostervald on the Old and New Testament, 3 vol. 1737

908 Jenkins on the Christian Religion, 2 vol. 1715

909 Prideaux's Connexion, 2 vol. — 1718

910 Oldmixon's British Empire in America, *with maps*, 2 vol. 1708

911 Hutchinson's Works, 12 vol. — 1709

912 Arbuthnot on Aliments — 1732

913 Knowledge of Divine Things from Revelation 1742

914 Boyle's Examination of Bentley on Phalaris's Epistles 1698

915 Glass's Works, 4 vol. — 1761

916 Spectator, vol. 1 and 2 — 1712

917 Tatler, vol. 1 and 2, *large paper* — 1710

918 Causes of the Decay of Christian Piety — 1669

919 Newton's

919 Newton's Opticks — 1730
920 English and Hebrew Grammar — 1771
921 Geographiæ Veteris Scriptores Græci Minores, *Gr. Lat.* ab Hudsono, 4 tom. *Oxon.* 1698, 1703, and 1712
922 Vertot's Roman Republic, 2 vol. — 1724
923 The Confessional — 1767
924 Jones on the Offering of Isaac — 1772
925 Horbery on Future Punishments — 1744
926 Collier's Discourses — 1725
927 Rowe's Life of Pythagoras — 1707
928 Testamentum Græcum, by Hardy, 2 vol. in one 1768
929 Weston on the Miracles — 1746
930 Brevint's Saul and Samuel at Endor — 1674
*930 Horneck's Crucified Jesus — 1700

QUARTO.

931 Turretini Disputationes, 4 tom. — *Genev.* 1691
932 Dallæus de Cultibus Religiosis Latinorum *ib.* 1671
933 *Pollini l'Historia Ecclesiastica della Rivoluzion d'Inghilterra* *Rom.* 1594
934 *Marco Aurelio, per di Guevara, tradotto di lingua Spagnola* *Vineg.* 1553
935 *Rossetti Insegnamenti Fisico-Matematici* *In Livorno* 1669
936 Epistolæ Basilii Magni, Libanii Rhetoris, Chionis Platonici, Æschinis & Isocratis Oratorum, Phalaridis Tyranni, Bruti Romani, Apollonii Tyanensis, Juliani Apostatæ, *Græcè*, EDITIO PRINCEPS *Ven. ap. Ald.* 1499
937 *Machiavelli (l'Opere di)* — 1550
938 *Tracts*—Sentence of the Councell of Warre against Lord Mountnorris in Ireland, in 1635, 1641. *Ordinance of the Parliament for Disarming Popish Recusants*, 1641. General Lesley's Speech in the Parliament of Scotland, 1641, *with frontispiece.* Impeachment of Philip's, the Queene's Confessor, *with his head*, 1641. Religion's Enemies, with a Relation as by Anabaptists, Brownists, Papists, Familists, Atheists and Foolists, sawcily presuming to tosse Religion in a Blanquet, *with frontispiece*, 1641. Thomas Herbert's *Vox secundi Populi*, or the Commons Gratitude to Philip Earl of Pembroke, a Poem, *with Figure of Lord Pembroke*, 1641, and several other very curious
939 *Guicciardini la Historia d'Italia* — *Venet.* 156[illegible]
940 Cæsaris Commentaria, Davisii — *Cantab.* 172[illegible]
941 Johnsoni Quæstiones Philosophicæ, 12mo. *interleaved in quarto, MS. notes* *ib.* 173[illegible]
942 Ortelii Thesaurus Geographicus *Hanov.* 161[illegible]

943 Casaubon[illegible]

943 Casauboni (Isaaci) Epistolæ — *Brunsvig.* 1656
944 *Bembo (De Gliasolani di Pietro) foglie dorat* *Vineg.* 1530
945 *Aste (B[illegible] de) Sermones Varios* — *Madrid* 1671
946 Vossii Variæ Observationes, *chart. max.* *Lond.* 1685
947 *Valguarnera dell' Origine et Antichita di Palermo* *Palermo* 1614
948 Musæus's Hero and Leander, a Poem, by Edward Taylor *Glasg.* 1783
949 *Francisco de Lizana Tesoro Mariano* *Madrid* 1663
950 Beveregii Institutiones Chronologicæ *Lond.* 1669
951 *Fontanini della Eloquenza Italiana* — *Rom.* 1706
952 Cluverii Comment. de Tribus Rheni Alveis, et Ostiis *Lug. Bat.* 1611
953 *Costanzo (Buonfiglio) dell' Historia Siciliana* *Venet.* 1604
954 Fabrettus de Aquis et Aquæductibus Romæ, *cum fig.* *Rom.* 1680
*954 Van Til Malachias Illustratus *Lug. Bat.* 1701
955 Huetius de Situ Paradisi Terrestris *Lips.* 1694
956 Quintius Curtius, Delphini — *Par.* 1678
957 *Doni Compendio del Trattato de' Generi e de' Modi della Musica* *Rom.* 1635
958 Ortelii Deorum Dearumque Capita ex Antiquis Numismatibus Collecta et Historica Narratione illustrata a Sweertio — — *Antverp.* 1602
959 Portii (Simonis) an Homo Bonus vel Malus Volens fiat *Florent.* 1551
960 *Escuela de Discursos, Formada de Sermones varios escritos por deferentes Autores* — *Lisboa* 1639
961 *Nisseno el Gran Padre de los Creyentes Abraham* *ib.* 1636
962 Dering's Works 1614
963 Flaminius de Hominis Felicitate, de Vera & Falsa Voluptate, et de Honore, *foliis deauratis* *Lusar* 1567
964 *Spinosa Dialogo en Laude de las Mugeres, intitulado Ginæcepænos* — *Milan* 1580
965 Hugonis Analysis Geometrica — *Gadibus* 1698
966 *Luis Munos Vida y Virtudes del P. Fr. Luis de Granada* *Madrid* 1639
967 Vitas Patrum — *Venet.* 1505
968 Conringius de Differentiis Regnorum, &c. &c. *Helmestad.* 1655
969 Cosin's Canon of Scripture — 1657
970 *Polano Historia del Concilio Tridentino* *Genev.* 1629
971 *Dante (La Comedia di) di Vellutello, con fig* *Vineg.* 1544
972 Godwyn's Moses and Aaron — 1672
973 Ittigius de Hæresiarchis — *Lips.* 1690
974 Power's Experimental Philosophy, *plate* — 1664
975 Do.

975 *Dell' Istoria di Mantoua, da Mario Equicola d'Alveto* — *Mantoua* 1607
976 Van Dale de Idolotria — *Amst.* 1696
977 Hamilton Sectiones Conicæ — *Dub.* 1758
978 Mosis Majiemonidis Constitutiones de Fundamentis Legis, *Heb et Lat.* a Vorstio, *Amst.* 1638. Abravanel de Capite Fidei, a Vorstio — *Amst.* 1738
979 *Menzini dell' Arte Poetica* — *Firenz.* 1688

FOLIO.

*970 Wilkins Concilia, 4 tom. — 1737
*971 Hickesii Thesaurus, 3 tom. — *Oxon.* 1705
*972 Frearl Parallele de l'Architecture — *Par.* 1702
*973 Homeri Opera, *Græcè*, 4 tom. — *Glasg.* 1756
*974 Barrow's Works, 2 vol. — 1687
*975 Patini Numismata — *Par.* 1696
*976 Wilkins's Essay on Language — 1668
*977 Diodati Biblia Italiana — 1640
*978 Grotii Epistolæ — *Amst.* 1687
*979 Enfield's History of Liverpool — 1773
980 Lorino delle Fortificationi — *Venet.* 1597
981 *Solis Historia de la Conquista de Mexico* — *Barcelonæ* 1691
982 Lipsius de Constantia — *Antv.* 1615
983 Evelyn on Medals — 1697
984 Pearson on the Creed — 1715
985 Heroica Philostrati et Dialogus Stephani Nigri apud Pausaniam, &c. — *Mediol.* 1517
986 Pauli Æmylii Historici de Rebus Gestis Francorum — *Par.* 1544
987 Scapulæ Lexicon — *Amst. Elz.* 1652
988 Chaucer's Works
989 Bellori Pitture Antiche del Sepolchro de Nassonii — *Roma* 1702
990 Thucydides, *Gr. Lat.* — *ap. Hen. Steph.* 1588
991 Bulli Opera — 1703
992 Velseri Opera Historica Sacra et Profana — *Norimb.* 1682
993 Krantzie Rerum Germanicarum — *Francof.* 1575
994 *Agostini Medaglie* — *Roma* 1592
995 Brokelsby's Explication of the Gospel Theism — 1706
996 Fox's Acts and Monuments, *wood cuts*, 3 vol. — 1641
997 Lambecii Bibliotheca Cæsarea, *figuris*, 4 tom. — 1669
998 Du Cange Glossarium ad Scriptores Mediæ et Infimæ, 3 tom. — 1681
999 Fiddes's Body of Divinity, *large paper*, 2 vol. — 1718
1000 Chrysostomi Opera, *Græce*, 8 tom. — *Eton.* 1613
1001 Bibliotheca Fratrum Polonorum, 8 tom. — *Irenopoli* 1656

1002 Aldrovandi

1002 Aldrovandi Opera omnia, 11 tom. *Bonon.* 1640, &c.
1003 Erasmi Opera, 11 tom. —— *L. Bat.* 1703
1004 Petavii Opus Theologicus, 3 tom. *Antv.* 1700
1005 Broughton's Dictionary of all Religions 1742
1006 Burnet's History of the Reformation, 3 vol. *plates* 1681,3 1715
1007 Whitby on the Testament, 2 vol. —— 1703
1008 Paruta della Vita Politica —— *Venet.* 1579
1009 De Brys Collectiones Peregrinationum in Indiam Orientalem et Indiam Occidentalem, *figuris*, 9 *parts in* 3 *vol.* —— 1590, &c.
1010 Ramusii delle Navigazioni et Viaggi, 3 tom. 1613, &c.
1011 Ederi Oeconomia Bibliorum —— 1568
1012 Hilarii Opera —— —— *Par.* 1631
1013 Strabo, *Gr. Lat.* a Xylandro *Lut. Par.* 1620
1014 Galeni Opera, *Græce*, 5 tom. *Venet. ap. Ald.* 1525
1015 Thomasini Lexicon Hebraicum *Par.* 1697
1016 Athænei Deipnosophistæ, *Gr. Lat.* Causoboni, 2 tom. *ap. Comelin* 1597
1017 Lister Historiæ Couchyliorum, *fig.* *Lond.* 1685
~~1018 *Archiesta Performar con Facilita del Cornaro*~~
1019 Fowler on the Troubles of Swethland and Poland 1656
1020 Marianæ Tractatus —— *Col. Agrip.* 1609
1021 Sibbaldi Scotia Illustrata —— 1684
1022 *Maggi e Cartriette della Fortificatione* —— 1583
1023 Cave Historia Litteraria, 2 tom. —— 1688
1024 Schindleri Lexicon Pentaglotton *Hanov.* 1612
1025 *Mariana Historia d'Espagna*, 2 tom. *Madrid* 1678
1026 Montani Communes et Familiares Hebraicæ Linguæ, &c. *Antv.* 1572
1027 Kettlewell's Works, 2 vol. —— 1719
1028 Marollois Opera Mathematica, *avec planches* 1614
~~1029 Buxtorfi Concordantiæ Bibliorum Hebraicæ *Basil* 1632~~

Fifth

Fifth Day's Sale.

OCTAVO.

1030 JUVENAL, *Delphini* — — 1736
1031 Epictetus, *Gr. et Lat.* Simpsoni — 1758
1032 Dodwell's Sick Man's Companion — 1767
1033 *Beveridge's Thesaurus Theologicus*, 4 vol. — 1711
1034 Wall on the Testament — 1730
1035 Millet's Gardeners Dictionary, 3 vol. — 1754
1036 Simpson's Euclid, *wants title*
1037 Clarke on the Attributes — — 1725
1038 Hodges's Christian Plan — — 1755
1039 Burnet's Life of Bedel — — 1736
1040 Clarke on the Evangelists, 2 vol. — 1717
1041 An Appeal to Reason — 1778
1042 Taylor's Worthy Communicant — 1686
1043 Evans's Sermons — — 1789
1044 Scomberg on the Roman Law — — 1785
1045 Bennet on Prayer — — 1708
1046 Allix against the Unitarians — 1699
1047 Rogers's Sermons, 4 vol. — 1740, &c.
1048 Calamy's Sermons — — 1726
1049 Voyages en differens Pays de l'Europe, 2 tom. en une *Suisse* 1778
1050 Cæsaris Commentaria, *Delphini* — 1770
1051 Spencerus de Urim et Thummim — 1669
1052 Clagett's Sermons — — 1689
1053 Johnson's Collection of Ecclesiastical Canons, &c. 2 vol. 1720
1054 Mainwaring's Sermons — — 1780

F 1055 Sheridan's

1055 Sheridan's Art of Reading — — 1781
1056 Davidson's Horace, 2 vol. — — 1746
1057 Henckel's Pyritologia — — 1757
1058 Gordon's Geographical Grammar — — 1749
1059 Boerhaave's Aphorisms — — 1755
1060 Bos Exercitationes Philologicæ — — 1713
1061 Divine Analogy — — — 1733
1062 Prideaux on Tythes — — 1713
1063 Trapp on unsettled Notions in Religion — 1715
1064 Kennicot on the Hebrew Text — 1753
*1064 Minucius Felix, *varior* — *L. Bat.* 1672
1065 Balasii Miscellanea — — 1680
1066 Fielding's Joseph Andrews — — 1767
1067 Aristarchus Anti-Bentleianus — — 1717
1068 Ayliffe's Account of Oxford, 2 vol. — 1714
1069 Saurin Sermons sur Divers Textes, 12 tom. *Lausan* 1759
1070 De Lolme on the English Constitution — 1784
1071 History of the Flagellants — — 1783
1072 Catechisme de Granade, 4 tom. — *Par.* 1665
1073 Taylor on Prophecy — — 1702
1074 Wilkins's Discovery of a New World — 1684
1075 Rymer on Tragedy and Shakespeare — 1693
1076 Burnet on the Church Catechism — 1710
1077 Art of Contentment — — 1694
1078 Norris's Miscellanies — — 1706
1079 Xerxes's Address to the Jews — — 1710
1080 Cole's English Dictionary — — 1676
1081 Phillips on teaching modern and ancient Languages 1750
1082 Johnson's Unbloody Sacrifice, 2 vol. — 1724
1083 Lactantii Opera, a Spark — — 1684
1084 Platonis Dialogi juxta edit. Serani — *Dublin* 1738
1085 Clarke and Leibnitz's Papers — — 1717
1086 Kettlewell's Mesures of Obedience — — 1700
1087 Stephens's Sermons, 2 vol. — — 1737
1088 Care on English Liberties — — 1719
1089 Vossius de Sibyllinis, *Oxon.* 1689. de Poematum Cantu et Viribus Rythmi — — 1673
1090 Plinii Epistolæ — — *Oxon.* 1686
1091 Mason on Shakespeare's Plays — — 1785
1092 Letters to and from the Countess de Barry — 1780
1093 Wollaston's Religion of Nature — — 1759
1094 Dorman's Sermons — — 1743
1095 Adey's Discourses — — 1700
1096 Dodwell against Tole — — 1751
1097 Bennet's Answer to the Dissenters Plea — 1728
1098 Antiquitez de la Ville de Nismes, *avec figures* 1767
1099 Cheyne on Regimen — — 1740
1100 Locke

1100 Locke on Underſtanding, 2 vol. — 1748
1102 Life of Guzman d'Alfrache, *plates*, 2 vol. 1708
1103 Veneroni Maitre Italien — 1774
1104 Robinſon on Animal Œconomy — 1732
1105 Life of St. Ignatius — 1686
1106 Fleetwood Inſcriptionum antiquarum Sylloge 1691
1107 Cæſaris Commentaria, *Delphini* — 1718
1108 Clayton on the Primitive — 1737
1109 Powel's Hiſtory of Wales — 1697
1110 Nelſon's Life of Bull — 1714
1111 Woodford on the Pſalms — 1678
1112 Sherlock on Prophecy — 1732
1113 Bolingbroke on Patriotiſm — 1749
1114 Winſtanley's Chriſtian Calling — 1751
1115 Pinkerton on Literature — 1785
1116 Joannet de la Connoiſance, 2 vol. — *Par.* 1775
1117 Smith's Wealth of Nations, 3 vol. — 1776
1118 Davidſon's Virgil, 2 vol. — 1770
1119 Hutchinſon's Works, 12 vol. — 1749
1120 Eſſais ſur l'Art d'Obſerver
1121 Seneca's Morals, by l'Eſtrange — 1682
1122 Edward's Canons of Criticiſm — 1758
1123 Keil Introductio ad Verum Aſtronomiam 1718
1124 Holloway's Originals — 1751
1125 Macrobii Opera, *varior* — 1694
1126 Campbell's Goſpel Harmony, 2 vol. in one 1759
1127 Bray's Bibliotheca Parochialis — 1707
1128 Smith's Students Vade Mecum — 1770
1129 Grove's Life of Cardinal Wolſey, 4 vol. *plates* 1742
1130 Fry's Poems — 1774
1131 Dorman's Sermons — 1743
1132 Bolingbroke on Parties — 1739
1133 Seneca's Morals, by l'Eſtrange — 1739
1134 Swift's Four laſt Years of Queen Anne — 1758
1135 Bunce's St. Chryſoſtom of the Prieſthood 1759
1136 Jortin's Sermons, 7 vol. *wanting the ſecond* — 1774
1137 Velleius Paterculus, *varior* — 1693
1138 Grenade Traité de l'Oraiſon, 2 vol. *Par.* 1675
1139 Reeves's Apologies of Juſtin Martyr, &c. 2 vol. 1709
1140 Lingendes Concionum in Quadrageſimum, 3 tom. *Par.* 1664
1141 Clarke's Homer's Iliad, 2 vol. — 1735
1142 Buchet ſur les Epitres d'Ovide, 2 tom. 1716
1143 Statutes of Hertford College — 1747
1144 Condillac Cours de l'Etude, 12 tom. *Genev.* 1780
1145 Raikes's Magiſtrates Aſſiſtant — 1784
1146 Letters on Education — 1785

F 2 1147 Annual

1147 Annual Regifter for 1776 and 1777
1148 Original Effays and Tranflations — *Edinb.* 1780
1149 Marigny's Hiftory of the Arabians, 4 vol. 1758
1150 Brett on Church Government — 1710
1151 Warren Haftings's Anfwer — — 1788
1152 Biblia Hebraica Leufdeni, a Vanderhooght, 2 tom. 1705
1153 Steele on Conic Sections — — 1723
1154 Fletcher's Sermons — — 1772
1155 Nature and End of the Sacrament — 1735
1156 The Apochrypha
1157 Fabricii Bibliotheca Latina — 1703
1158 Martialis Epigrammata — — 1740
1159 Epicteti Enchiridion et Cebetis Tabulæ, *Gr. et Lat.* 1670
1160 Creake's Compendious Hiftory — 1754
1161 Martialis Epigrammata, *Delphini* — 1720
1162 Dodwell's Chriftianity not founded on Argument 1743
1163 Knight's Sermons — — 1721
1164 Evidence on the Slave Trade — 1791
1165 Cornelius Nepos, *Delphini* — 1773
1166 Government of the Tongue — 1675
1167 Life of Mary Queen of Scots — 1725
1168 Frifii Hiftoria Belgicorum Tumultuum *L. Bat.* 1619

QUARTO.

1169 Scaligeri Opufcula — *Par.* 1610
1170 *Locatelli Racconto Hiftorico della Veneta Guerra in Levante* *Colon.* 1691
1171 Dygbeius de Arte Natandi, *cum fig. Lond. ap. Thom. Dawfon* 1587
1172 Pugh's Britifh and Out-landifh Prophecies — 1658
1173 *Vettori delle Lodi e della Coltivazione degli Ulioi Firenz.* 1718
1174 Cupani Hortus Catholicus *Neapol.* 1696
1175 *Camillo delle Materie e della Imitatione Venet.* 1544
1176 Selon his Follie, by Beacon — *Oxford* 1594
1177 Mercurialis de Arte Gymnaftica, *cum fig. Venet.* 1587
1178 Suetonii Hiftoria, Delphini — *Par.* 1684
1179 Abelardi et Eloifæ Opera, a Quercetano — *ib.* 1616
1180 Somner's Antiquities of Canterbury, *plates* 1640
1181 Parkhurft's Hebrew and Englifh Lexicon — 1762
1182 Parkhurft's Hebrew and Englifh Lexicon — 1762
1183 Churchill's Rociad, Apology, Night, 1761—Lloyd's Actor — — 1760
1184 Leti Vita del Filippo II. 2 tom. en une *Coligni* 1679
1185 *Malefpina Hiftoria Fiorentina Fiorenz. ap. Giunt.* 1568
1186 Torriano's Italian Tutor — — 1640
1187 Voffius de Quatuor Artibus Popularibus *Amft.* 1660

1188 Biblia

1188 Biblia Sacra, a Tremellio et Junio, *foliis deauratis* *Lond.* 1581
1189 *Boccaccio (Il Decameron di)* —— *Vineg.* 1541
1190 Les Origines de la Langue Françoise *Par.* 1650
1191 *Mendo Principe Perfecto Documentos Politicos, y Morales, en Emblemas, con fig.* —— *Leon* 1662
1192 *Vitruvii dell' Architettura, di Barbaro, con fig.* *Ven.* 1584
1193 Tunstall on Natural and Revealed Religion 1765
1194 Brissonii Opera —— *Francof.* 1592
1195 Liturgiarum Orientalium Collectio, à Renaudotio, 2 tom. in uno —— *Par.* 1716
1196 Collection of Papers relating to the Affairs of England 1688
1197 *Bibliotheca Literaria*, 10 Numbers —— 1722
1198 *Dialogi di Brucioli, foglie dorat.* —— *Venet.* 1545
1199 Cluverii Italia Antiqua, *cum tab. Geograph. Guelferb.* 1669
1200 *Mugnos Raguagli Historici del Vespro Siciliano Palermo* 1669
1201 Camden's Remaines concerning Britaine 1614
1202 Schmidii Collectanea Talmudia, *Heb. et Lat. Lips.* 1670
1203 Origen Contra Celsum, *Græcè*, ab Hoeschelio *Aug. Vind.* 1605
1204 Spanhemii Dubia Evangelia, 3 tom. in duo *Genev.* 1658
1205 *Pindaro, tradotto da Adamari* —— *Pisa* 1631
1206 *Sermones Varios* —— *Lisboa* 1673
1207 Godwyn's Catalogue of Bishops of England 1601
1208 Disputationes Theologicæ —— *Helmæstad.* 1639
1209 [illegible] Antiquitates Romanæ —— *Genev.* 1559
1210 Licetus de Natura et Arte —— *Utini* 1640
1211 *Vasari le Vite Pittori, Scultori et Architetti Bologna* 1647
1212 North's Examen —— 1740
1213 Tollii Epistolæ Itinerariæ, ab Henninio *Amst.* 1700
1214 Robbins's Abridgment of the Irish Statutes *Dubl.* 1736
1215 *Crescimbeni Vite degli Arcadi Illustri*, 3 tom. *Rom.* 1708
1216 Several Pamphlets relative to the English and Dutch at Amboyna, *plates*, 2 vol. —— 1632
1217 *Comedias de Moreto*, 3 tom. —— *Valencia* 1676
1218 *Antonio de Solis Comedias* —— *Madrid* 1716
1219 *Los Libros de las Madre Teresa de Jesus* *Caragoça* 1623
1220 *Varios Eloquentes libros* *Valencia* 1700
1221 *Paiochelli Il Regno di Napoli*, 2 tom. *Napol.* 1703

F O L I O.

1222 De Marca de Concordia Sacerdotii et Imperii *Par.* 1663
1223 A Volume of Newspapers from 1766, &c.
1224 Playfair's System of Chronology —— 1784
1225 Septuaginta Græca, a Grabe, 2 tom. *Oxon.* 1707

1226 Pittura

1226 Pittura Antica nelle Terme di Tito
1227 Triompho del Desenganno — *Napoles* 1632
1228 Nicephori Historiæ Ecclesiasticæ, 2 tom. — 1630
1229 Plutarchi Parallela, *Græce* — *Basil* 1560
1230 Origenis Opera, 2 tom. — *Rothomagi* 1668
1231 Towerson of the Cathechism — 1685
1232 Perkins on the Creed — 1635
1233 Pappi Alexandrini Mathematicæ — 1660
1234 Vossius de Theologia Gentili — *Amst.* 1668
1235 Curcellæi Opera Theologica — *ib.* 1675
1236 Fernilii Universa Medicina — *Lut. Par.* 1567
1237 Cowley's Works — 1672
1238 Mathiolus in Dioscoridem — *Venet.* 1570
1239 Casaubonus in Athenæum — *Lugd.* 1600
1240 Camdenus de Scriptoribus Rerum Angliæ — *Franc.* 1603
1241 Turnebi Opera — *Argent.* 1600
1242 *Finch del Ley, interleaved* — 1613
1243 Diomedis de Arte Grammatica — *Venet. ap. Rubeum* 1511
1244 Martin's Sermons — 1674
1245 Renerii Tabulæ Motuum Cœlestium — 1647
1246 Procopii Historiæ ab Hoeschelio, *Græce* — 1607
1247 Chabræi Stirpium Icones — *Genevæ* 1666
1248 Mede's Works, 2 vol. — 1664
1249 *Davilla Padilla Historia de la Mexico* — *Bruss.* 1625
1250 Wolfii Memorabilia Centenarii XVI. 2 tom. — 1600
1251 Fulke's Remish Testament — 1601
1252 Lindsay's Vindication of the Church of England — 1728
1253 Malpigii Anatome Plantarum
1254 Polydori Vergilii Opera — *Basil* 1534
1255 The Rehearsal, or View of the Times — 1708
1256 Pauli Jovii Historiæ — *Vascosan* 1553
1257 Grew's Cosmologia Sacra — 1701
1258 Marianæ Scholæ in Vet. et Nov. Testamentum — 1619
1259 Scriptores de Chirurgia — *Figur* 1555
1260 Clarendon's Tracts — 1747
1261 Covel's Account of the Greek Church — 1722
1262 Imagini depinte da Rafaelle d'Urbino, *cum figuris*, 2 tom. — *Romæ* 1695
1263 Holy Bible — *by Baskett* 1715
1264 Missale Romanum — *Lugd.* 1685
1265 Da Vinci della Pittura — *Parigi* 1651
1266 King Charles's Works — 1687
1267 Raii Historia Plantarum, 2 tom. — 1686
1268 Watson's Clergyman's Law — 1747
1269 Cluverii Sicilia Antiqua — *L. Bat.* 1619
1270 Index Librorum Prohibitorum, 2 tom. — 1667
1271 Chaucer's Works

1272 Bibliotheca

1272 Bibliotheca Græcorum Patrum — Par. 1672
1273 Theophylacti Opera, *Græcè* — *Romæ* 1542
1274 Helvici Theatrum Historicum — 1529
1275 Grammatici (Joan) Comment. in Aristotelem de Anicenne, *Græce* — *Venet.* 1535
1276 Caleppino Dittionario della Lingua Latina — 1554
1277 Horatii Opera — 1642
1278 Chrysostomi Orationes — *Lutet.* 1604
1279 Pisonis Historia Naturalis Brasiliæ — 1648
1280 Architettura de Serlio di Salvetti — *Venet.* 1680
1281 Comber's Companion to the Temple — 1688
1282 Agricola de Re Metallica — *Basil* 1621
1284 Hackluyt's Voyages, *imperfect*
1285 Bradley's Family Dictionary, 2 vol. in one — 1725
1286 Knowles's History of the Turks — 1631
1287 Neperi Arithmeticæ Logarithmica, a Bridges 1624
1288 Meursii Historia Danica — *Amst.* 1638
1289 Book of Common Prayer — 1683

Sixth Day's Sale.

OCTAVO.

1290 HAWKINS on Scripture Mysteries — 1787
1291 H Report of the Regency — 1789
1292 Wilson's Elements of Hebrew Grammar 1782
1293 Evidence on the Slave Trade — 1791
1294 Clavis Homerica, a Patrick — 1771
1295 Lobo's Voyage to Abyssinia, by Johnson 1789
1296 Halfpenny's Architecture — 1752
1297 Spelman's Life of Alfred the Great, by Hearne 1709
1298 Bateman

17 : –

No.	Title	Date	£	s.	d.	Buyer
1298	Bateman on Tythes	1778		2	6	Cuthel
1299	Hartley's Sermons	1755		1	–	Floyer
1300	Wintle's Sermons	1794		2	9	Bond
1301	Cheyne's English Malady	1734		–	6	Floyer
1302	Duff on original Geniuses in Poetry	1770		1	3	Heber
1303	Cicero de Officiis, a Pearce	1778		2	6	Floyer
1304	Weston Conjecturæ in Athæneum	1784		–	6	Floyer
1305	Martin's Introduction to Newton's Philosophy	1754		1	–	Smith
1306	Sherlock on Death	1776		–	6	Floyer
1307	Poetæ Græce (Selecta ex)	1777		–	9	Heber
1308	Grey's Defence of Ancient and Modern Historians	1725		1	9	Wigstead
1309	Voltaire's Letters on the English Nation	1733		3	6	Marrow
1310	Virgilius, *Delphini*	1777		11	–	Leigh
1311	Needham de re Rustica	1704		–	9	Elphinstone
1312	Lettres de Voltaire, a l'Abbe Moussinet *Par.*	1781		–	6	Fisher
1313	Scott's Christian Life	1683				
1314	Reflections on Polygamy	1737		–	–	Smith
1315	Butler's Hudibras, by Grey, 2 vol. *plates*, by Hogarth	1744	1	14	–	Smith
1316	The Feasts and Fasts	1705		–	6	Floyer
1317	James on Canine Madness	1760		–	9	Wigstead
1318	Secret History of Europe, 2 vol.	1712		–	6	Fisher
1319	Quevedo's Visions, by L'Estrange	1702		–	9	Chapman
1320	Huntingford on Writing Greek, 2 vol.	1772		3	–	Booth
1321	Conybeare's Sermons, 2 vol.	1757		2	–	Smith
1322	Bolingbroke on the Study of History, 2 vol.	1752		5	–	Smith
1323	Universal Dictionary *Edinb.*	1763		3	6	Winstanley
1324	Hawkins on Scripture Mysteries	1787		2	6	Cuthel
1325	Political Life of Charles Fox	1783		–	9	Chapman
1326	Practice of Ecclesiastical Courts, 2 vol.	1749		4	3	Cuthel
1327	Duncomb's Translation of Juvenal, 2 vol.	1784		2	6	Heber
1328	Puffendorf's Introduction to History, 2 vol.	1748		2	–	Hamilton
1329	Chelsum on Gibbon	1785		1	–	Leigh
1330	Portius de Humani Mente Disputatio *Florent.*	1551		1	–	Leigh
1331	Orrery's Pliny, 2 vol.	1752		4	6	Winstanley
1332	Hume's History of England, 8 vol.	1775		19	6	Hamilton
1333	Nelson's Feasts and Fasts	1704				Floyer
1334	Ockley's Saracens	1708				
1335	Echard on the Revolution	1725		1	–	Floyer
1336	Sherlock on a Future State	1704				
1337	Warneford's Sermons, 2 vol.	1757		2	9	Bond
1338	Kays's Philosophical Letters	1718		1	–	Floyer
1339	Antiquities of Westminster Abbey, *plates*, 2 vol.	1722		11	–	Wigstead
1340	Administration of Sir Robert Walpole	1743				
1341	Kennet's Roman Antiquities	1717		2	–	Winstanley
1342	Bennet on the Common Prayer	1709				
1343	Carter's Sermons	1738				

1344 Earl

£ 7 : 13 : 6

No.	Title	Year
1344	Earl of Peterborough's Conduct in Spain	1707
1345	Aristophanis Plutus et Nubes, *Gr. Lat.*	1732
1346	Campbell on the Original of Moral Virtue	1733
1347	Parsons's Directory, by Stanhope —	1703
1348	State of the Case between Newton and Hutchinson	1753
1349	Cæsaris Commentaria, a Clarke —	1720
1350	Puffendorf de Officio Hominis & Civis, a Johnson	1748
1351	Causes of Decay of Christian Piety —	167[illegible]
1352	Chrysostom de Sacerdotio —	171[illegible]
1353	Hawkins on Scripture Mysteries —	178[illegible]
1354	Letters from Europe and the East, 2 vol.	1753
1355	Aristotelis Rhetorica, *Græce, cum var. Lect.* —	
1356	Rudder's Gloucester —	1731
1357	Varenius's Geography, 2 vol. —	1765
1358	Religion of Nature Delineated —	17[illegible]
1359	Essay on the Genius of Pope —	17[illegible]
1360	Poem, by Robert Alves —	1782
1361	Bishop of Cloyne's Miscellanies —	1752
1362	Bates's Dispensatory, by Salmon —	1700
1363	Smith's County of Waterford —	1746
1364	Barclay's Apology —	1701
1365	The 39 Articles —	1739
1366	Skelton's Sermons, 2 vol. —	1734
1367	Sanchoniatho's Phoenician History —	1720
1368	Bennet Grammatica Hebræa —	1731
1369	Ray's Select Remains —	1760
1370	Earse Vocabulary —	
1371	Rawlinson's Method of Studying History, 2 vol.	1730
1372	Spencer's Fairy Queen 2 vol. —	1758
1373	Venn on the Prophecy of Zacharias —	1774
1374	Defence of English Ordinations —	1725
1375	Geddes on the Composition of the Antients	1748
1376	Veneer on the 39 Articles, 2 vol. —	1734
1377	Johnson's English and Hebrew Grammar	1771
1378	Almanack Royal —	1739
1379	Guicciardini's History of Italy, by Goddard, 10 vol.	1753
1380	Memoirs of Bishop Berkeley —	1784
1381	*Del Parere del S. Leonardo di Capoa*, 2 tom. *Cologn.*	1714
1382	Ovidii Opera, *Delph.* —	1765
1383	Virgilii Opera, *Delph.* —	1723
1384	Polyæni Stratagemata, *Gr. Lat.* Causoboni	1691
1385	Ciceronis Epistolæ, a Lambino —	1580
1386	Clavis Homerica —	1727
1387	Lowth de Sacra Poesi Hebræorum —	1763
1388	Verwey Nova Via docendi Græca —	1702
1389	Raii Synopsis Avium —	1713
1390	Berkeley on Violent Innovations —	1785

G 1391 Metricorum

1391 Metricorum Quorundam Monoſtrophicorum ſecunda Collectio

1392 Fabricii Bibliotheca Latina — 1703

1393 Introduction to Grammar — Oxf. 1699

1394 Du Pin's Univerſal Library, 2 vol. — 1709

1395 Johnſon on Genders of Nouns — 1703

1396 Holmes's Greek Grammar — 1739

1397 Johnſon's Grammatical Commentaries — 1706

1398 De Pile's Art of Painting — 1744

1399 Browne's Chriſtianity not Myſterious — 1697

1400 The Clergyman's Intelligencer — 174[illegible]

1401 Hill's (Aaron) Works, 2 vol. — 176[illegible]

1402 Criticiſms on the Roliad — 1785

1403 Goldſmith's Hiſtory of England, 4 vol. 1779

1404 Pope's Works, 9 vol. — 1752

1405 Pope's Iliad and Odyſſey, 11 vol. — 1760

1406 Atterbury's Epiſtolary Correſpondence, 3 vol. 1783

1407 Geddes's Tracts — 1715

1408 Bacon on Good and Evil — 170[illegible]

1409 Eraſmus's Select Coloquies, by l'Eſtrange 1725

1410 Edwards's Preacher — 1705

1411 Conybeare's Sermons, 2 vol. — 1757

1412 Hymns to the Supreme Being — 1780

1413 Biblia Sacra, *Vulg. Edit.* — *ap. Plant.* 1619

1414 Cunningham on Tythes — 1748

1415 Port Royal Greek Grammar — 1748

1416 Devil upon Two Sticks — 1708

1417 Puffendorf's Introduction to the Hiſtory of Europe 1695

1418 Secker's Lectures on the Catechiſm and his Charges, and on the Rebellion, 4 vol. — 176[illegible]

1419 Secker's Sermons, his Lectures and Charges, 9 vol. 1769, &c.

1420 Seed's Sermons, 2 vol. — 1758

1421 Supplement to the 5th edition of Collins's Peerage 1784

1422 Conant's Sermons, 6 vol. wanting the 5th 1699

1423 A Parcel of odd Volumes, *ſmall duodecimo, Lat. Fr. Ital.* —

1424 Ditto, ditto, *duodecimo, Lat. Fr Ital. Eng.* —

1425 Ditto, ditto, *duodecimo, Lat. Fr. Ital. Eng.* —

1426 Ditto, ditto, *duodecimo, Lat. Fr. Gr Eng.* —

1427 Ditto, ditto, *octavo and 12mo. Eng. & Fr.* —

1428 Ditto, ditto, *8vo. & 12mo. Eng. Lat. Fr.* —

1429 Ditto, ditto, *8vo. Engliſh* —

1430 Ditto, of Pamphlets, 8vo. —

1431 Ditto, ditto, 12mo. —

1432 Ditto, Magazines, Reviews, &c. —

QUARTO.

QUARTO.

1433 *Comedias del Calderon*, 9 tom. — *Madrid* 1685

1434 Aristotelis Opera, *Gr. et Lat.* a Sylburgio, 7 tom. *Francof.* 1587

1435 *Caro (Lettere Familiari del Annibal)* 2 tom. en 1 *Venet.* 1591

1436 *Ammirato (Opuscoli del Scipione)* 3 tom. *Fiorenz.* 1640

1437 *Garau El Salbio en Quarenta Maximas Politicas, et Morales, con fig.* 3 tom. — *Barcelona* 1691

1438 Mesnardiere (La Poetique de) — *Par.* 1639

1439 *Sansovino Historia dell' Origine et Origine de Turchi*, 2 tom. *Venet.* 1654

1440 *Salvini Discorsi Accedemici*, 2 tom. *Firenz.* 1713

1441 Biblia Hebræa

1442 *Summonte (Historia della Citta e Regno di Napoli di Antonio)* 4 tom. — — *Napol.* 1675

1443 Fabricii Bibliotheca Græca, 7 tom. *Hamburg.* 1708

1444 Wolfii Bibliotheca Hebræa *Hamb. et Lips.* 1715

1445 Acta Eruditorum, from 1682 to 1701, both inclusive, with Index and Supplements, 24 vol. — *Lips.* 1682

1446 Miscellanea Curiosa, 10 tom. — *Norimb.* 1683

1447 Wood's (Anthony) History of Oxford, by Gutch, vol. 1st 1792

1448 *Siri Il Mercurio Overo Historia de' correnti Tempi*, 13 vol. *Genev.* 1645

1449 Ciceronis Orationes et Epistolæ *Delphini*. 4 tom. *Par.* 1684

1450 Wolfii Bibliotheca Hebræa, 2 tom. *Hamb. et Lips.* 1715

1451 Ptolemæi Geographiæ Universæ, a Patavino, *cum fig.* *Venet.* 1696

1452 Fabri Epistolæ — — *Salmur.* 1673

1453 Willis's History and Antiquities of Buckingham 1755

1454 Miscellanea Curiosa Medico-Physica, *avec fig.* 3 tom. *Lips.* 1670

1455 Peters's Preface to his Dissertation on Job 1757

1456 Du Pin Bibliotheque Ecclesiastique, Historiens, et Prolegomenes sur la Bible, 21 tom en 12 tom. *Par.* 1693

1457 Wittichii Exercitationes Theologicæ, 2 tom. *L. Bat.* 1682

1458 *Segneri (Opere del Padre Paolo)* 4 tom. *Venez.* 1716

1459 Patrick on Joshua, Judges and Ruth — 1702

1460 Heylin's Theological Lectures, 2 vol. — 1749

1461 Spencerus de Legibus Hebreorum, 2 tom. *Lips.* 1705

1462 Boyle's Philosophical Works, 3 vol. — 1725

1463 Græciæ Orthodoxæ, *Gr. et Lat.* 2 tom. *Romæ* 1652

1464 Kircheri Concordantiæ Vetus Test. Græcæ, Ebræis vocibus Respondentes, 2 tom. — *Francof.* 1607

1465 Ciceronis Opera, a Gronovio, 2 tom. *Lug. Bat.* 1692

G 2 1466 Morhophi

1466 Morhophi Polyhistor, 2 tom. — *Lubec* 1714

1467 Altieri's Italian and English Dictionary, 2 tom. 1726

1468 Baretti's Italian Dictionary, 2 tom. —— 1760

1469 Smith's Optics, *plates*, 2 tom. —— *Camb.* 1738

1470 Sharp (Arch.) Relation des Mesures qui furent prise pour introduires la Liturgie Ang. dans la Prusse, &c. *maroquin dorèes* —— — *Lond.* 1767

1471 Bibliotheca Biblica, or Commentary on the Old and New Testament, 6 tom. —— *Oxford* 1720

1472 Smollet's History of England, 4 vol. 1757

1473 Maffei Gemme Antiche, 3 tom. — *Roma* 1707

1474 Hooke's Roman History, 3 vol —— 1757

1475 Arbuthnot's Tables of Ancient Coins, &c. 1727

1476 Telemachus, by Hawksworth, *plates, boards, uncut* 1768

1477 Catullus Tibullus et Propertius — *Tonson* 1702

1478 Ainsworth's Dictionary, by Morell —— 1773

1479 Ecton's Thesaurus Rerum Ecclesiasticarum 1742

1480 Sully's Memoirs by Mrs. Lennox, 3 vol. 1761

1481 Septuaginta Græca, a Brettingero, 4 tom. *Tigur.* 1730

1482 Dalrymple's Memoirs of Great Britain and Ireland 1771

1483 Plinii Historia Naturalis, Delphini, 5 tom. *Par.* 1685

1484 Livii Historia, 6 tom. —— *ib.* 1679

FOLIO,

1485 Waræus de Præsulibus Hiberniæ —— 1665

1486 Sigonii Histor. de Occidentali Imperio *Hanov.* 1618

1487 Thome de Acquino super Libris Boetii *Tholossa.* 1481

1488 Dionis Cassii Historiæ, *Gr. et Lat.* *ap. Hen. Steph.* 1591

1489 Budei Comment. Linguæ Græcæ — *Basil* 1530

1490 Pearson on the Creed —— — 1704

1491 Cœlii Lectiones —— — *Colon.* 1620

1492 Hasted's History of Kent, vol. 3d —— 1790

1493 Mercatoris Atlas ab Hondio —— 1606

1494 Wood Antiquitates Oxoniensis —— 1674

1495 Speed's Maps —— —— 1631

1496 Ainsworth's Dictionary, 2 vol. Russia — 1752

1497 Montfaucon l'Antiquité Expliqué, *avec fig.* large Paper in boards, 10 vol. —— *Par.* 1719

1499 Pitt's English Atlas, on Royal Paper, ruled, coloured, and beautifully illuminated, aud bound superbly in morocco —— —— 1680

1500 Barrows's Universal Dictionary of Arts and Sciences with Supplement, 2 vol. —— 1754

1501 Plutarchi Moralia Opuscula *Græce* — *Basil* 1542

1502 Calasii Concordantiæ, a Romaine, 4 tom. — 1747

1503 Du Chales Cursus Mathematicus, 3 tom. *Lugd.* 1674

1504 Juliani

72.16.6

No.	Title	Place / Date	Price, buyer (manuscript)
1504	Juliani Opera, *Gr. et Lat.*	*Lipſ.* 1696	8 — Priestley
1505	Hall's (Biſhop) Works	1714	3-6 Priestley
1506	*Il Cortegiano*	*ap. Ald.* 1528	2-6 Hamilton
1507	Locke on Underſtanding	1700	
1508	*Hiſtoria de Emperadores de Roma*	*Anvers* 1579	1-6 Priestley
1509	Seldenus de Jure Naturali et Gentium	1640	
1510	Coronica de Los Moros de Eſpagna	*Valencia* 1618	12-6 P.
1511	Hall's Works	1647	2-9 Winstanley
1512	Caſtelli Lexicon, 2 tom.	1669	15 — Chapman
1513	Conciliorum Omnium Generalium et Provintialium Collectio Regia, 37 tom.	*Par.* 1644	4-5 — Wilcher
1514	Babillon de Re Diplomatica	*ib.* 1681	10-6 Cuthel
1515	Cardani Opera Philoſophici ac Medici, 10 tom.	*Lugd.* 1663	16 — Wilcher
1516	Nichols on the Common Prayer, 2 vol.	1710	1-9 Wilcher
1517	Hiſtoria del Concilio di Trento, 2 tom.	*Rom.* 1656	5-6 Wilcher
1518	Morery Dictionaire Hiſtorique, *avec Supplement*, 4 tom.	*Utrecht* 1682	12-6 Elphinston
1519	Gruteri Inſcriptiones, 2 tom.	*Amſt.* 1707	1-15 — Heber
1520	Beverigii Pandectæ Apoſtolorum, 2 tom.	*Oxon.* 1672	11-6 Bond
1521	Balye Dictionaire Hiſtorique, 4 tom.	*Rotterd.* 1697	13 — ×
1522	Gale Rerum Anglicarum Scriptores, 2 tom.	*Oxon.* 1684	2-2 — Chapman
1523	Sully Memoires, 2 tom.	*Par.* 1664	4-3 ×
1524	Limborchi Theologia	*Amſt.* 1695	1-3 Fisher
1525	Burnet's Hiſtory of his Own Times, 2 vol.	1724	
1526	Alſtedii Encyclopœdia, 4 tom. in two	*Lugd.* 1649	2-9 Jee
1527	Plutarchi Opera, a Xylandre, tom. 2d	*Francof.* 1620	6-6 Sneddel; 3 — Priestly
1528	Corpus Juris Civilis	*Amſt. Elz.* 1663	2 — Priestly
1529	Coke's Inſtitutes, 2d Part	1669	
1530	Townſhend's Hiſtorical Collections	1680	6 — Chapman
1531	Lubienietſki Theatrum Cometicum, ~~2 tom.~~	*Lugd. Bat.* 1681	4-4 — Leigh
1532	*Motetti e Inni di Paleſtrina, Manuſcript Muſic*, 5 vol.		
1533	A Parcel of Muſic, Printed and Manuſcript		15-6 Leigh
1534	Blow's *Amphion Anglicus*	1700	5 — Kitchener
1535	Purcell's *Orpheus Britannicus*, 1ſt Part	1698	5-6 Birchal — 5.6
1536	Purcell's Orpheus Britannicus, *gilt leaves*, 2 Parts	1698, 1702	1-7 — Birchal — 1.7 —
1537	*Palermo Magnifico nel Trionfo di S. Roſalia*, con fig.	*Palermo* 1686	3-6 Leigh — 3
1538	Camdeni Annales Elizabethæ	*Lond.* 1615	4-3 Cuthel
1539	*Vega (De la) Hiſtoria General del Peru*	*Cordova.* 1617	
1540	Demoſthenis Orationes, Libanii Sophiſtæ in eas ipſas orationes argumenta. Vita Demoſthenes per Libanum. Ejuſdem Vita per Plutarchum, *Græcè*	*Venet. ap. Ald.* 1504	1-1 — Gosset
1541	Alexandri Aphrodiſienſis in Sophiſticcos Ariſtotelis Elenchos Commentaria, *Græcè*	*ib.* 1520	4-3 Delorychamp — 4.3 —
1542	Pontificalis Romani, *caret tit.*		

1543 Ciceronis

£96.10.9

(46) 96.. 10.. 9

1543 Ciceronis Epiſtolæ ad Atticum, Brutum et Quintum Fratum, *firſt leaf illuminated.* EDITIO PRINCEPS *Venet. ap. Nicolaum Jenſon* 1470 — 6 - 12 - 6 Alchorne

1544 Francifci Philelfi Satyrarum Hecatoſtichon Decades X. EDITIO PRINCEPS—*Midiolani* … *C*… *opherum Valdarpher*, 1476.—Francifci Philelp… Orationes cum aliis Opufcula — — *Venet.* 1496. — 1 - 11 - 6 Payne

1545 St. James's Chronicle from April 24th, 1764, to Dec. 29th, 1764, both incluſive — 3 - 6 Burney

1546 Senex's Modern Geography of all the known Countries in the World, *maps coloured* — 7 - 6

£ 105.. 13.. 9

FINIS.

First Day	22 : 14 : 9
Second Day	55.. 13.. 9
Third Day	35.. 5.. 9
Fourth Day	68.. 12.. 3
Fifth Day	36.. 15.. 6
Sixth Day	105.. 13.. 9
	£ 324.. 15.. 9

TITLES IN THIS SERIES

1. David Berman, ed., *George Berkeley: Eighteenth-Century Responses*, New York: Garland Publishing, Inc., 1988, in two volumes.

2. Stephen R. L. Clark, ed., *Money, Obedience, and Affection: Essays on Berkeley's Moral and Political Thought*, New York: Garland Publishing, Inc., 1988.

3. Willis Doney, ed., *Berkeley on Abstraction and Abstract Ideas*, New York: Garland Publishing, Inc., 1988.

4. R.C.S. Walker, ed. *The Real in the Ideal: Berkeley's Relation to Kant*, New York: Garland Publishing, Inc., 1988.

5. Thomas K. Abbott, *Sight and Touch: An Attempt to Disprove the Received (or Berkeleian) Theory of Vision*, London: Longman, Green, Longman, Roberts, and Green, 1864.

6. D. M. Armstrong, *Berkeley's Theory of Vision: A Critical Examination of Bishop Berkeley's "Essay Towards a New Theory of Vision,"* Melbourne University Press, 1960.

7. Samuel Bailey, *A Review of Berkeley's Theory of Vision, Designed to Show the Unsoundness of That Celebrated Speculation*, London: James Ridgway, Piccadilly, 1842.

James F. Ferrier, "Berkeley and Idealism," London: *Blackwood's Magazine* (June 1842).

John Stuart Mill, "Bailey on Berkeley's Theory of Vision," London: *Westminster Review*, 38 (1842).

Samuel Bailey, *A Letter to a Philosopher in Reply to Some Recent Attempts to Vindicate Berkeley's Theory of Vision, and in Further Elucidation of its Unsoundness*, London: James Ridgway, Piccadilly, 1843.

James F. Ferrier, "Mr. Bailey's Reply to an Article in Blackwood's Magazine," Edinburgh and London: *Blackwood's Magazine* (June 1843).

John Stuart Mill, "Rejoinder to Mr. Bailey's Reply," London: *Westminster Review*, 39 (1843).

8. George Berkeley, *Philosophical Commentaries, Transcribed from the Manuscript and Edited, with an Introduction and Index by George H. Thomas: Explanatory Notes by A. A. Luce*, printed by Mount Union College, 1976.

9. A. C. Crombie, *George Berkeley's Bicentenary, The British Journal for the Philosophy of Science*, 4 (May 1953). Edinburgh and London: Thomas Nelson and Sons Ltd.

10. Alexander Campbell Fraser, *Life and Letters of George Berkeley, Formerly Bishop of Cloyne, and an Account of His Philosophy. With Many Writings of Bishop Berkeley Hitherto Unpublished*, Oxford, At the Clarendon Press, 1871.

11. G. Dawes Hicks, *Berkeley*, New York: Russell & Russell, 1932.

12. G. A. Johnston, *The Development of Berkeley's Philosophy*, London: Macmillan and Co., 1923.

13. A. A. Luce, *Berkeley and Malebranche: A Study in the Origins of Berkeley's Thought*, Oxford, At the Clarendon Press, 1934.

14. C. B. Martin and D. M. Armstrong, eds., *Berkeley: A Collection of Critical Essays. The Articles from "Locke and Berkeley: A Collection of Critical Essays"*, Garden City, New York: Anchor Books, Doubleday & Company, Inc., 1968

15. I. C. Tipton, *Berkeley: The Philosophy of Immaterialism*, London: Methuen & Co. Ltd., 1974.